Christian Fiction

Genreflecting Advisory Series

Diana Tixier Herald, Series Editor

Genreflecting: A Guide to Reading Interests in Genre Fiction, 5th Edition
By Diana Tixier Herald

Teen Genreflecting
By Diana Tixier Herald

Romance Fiction: A Guide to the Genre
By Kristin Ramsdell

Fluent in Fantasy: A Guide to Reading Interests
By Diana Tixier Herald

Now Read This: A Guide to Mainstream Fiction, 1978–1998
By Nancy Pearl with assistance from Martha Knappe and Chris Higashi

Now Read This II: A Guide to Mainstream Fiction, 1990–2001
By Nancy Pearl

Hooked on Horror: A Guide to Reading Interests in Horror Fiction
By Anthony J. Fonseca and June Michele Pulliam

Junior Genreflecting: A Guide to Good Reads and Series Fiction for Children
By Bridget Dealy Volz, Lynda Blackburn Welborn, and Cheryl Perkins Scheer

Christian Fiction: A Guide to the Genre
By John Mort

Strictly Science Fiction: A Guide to Reading Interests
By Diana Tixier Herald and Bonnie Kunzel

Christian Fiction

A Guide to the Genre

John Mort

2002
Libraries Unlimited
A Division of Greenwood Publishing Group, Inc.
Greenwood Village, Colorado

Libraries Unlimited
A Division of Greenwood Publishing Group, Inc.
7730 East Belleview Avenue, Suite A200
Greenwood Village, CO 80111
1-800-225-5800
www.lu.com

Library of Congress Cataloging-in-Publication Data

Mort, John, 1947-
   Christian fiction : a guide to the genre / John Mort.
      p. cm. -- (Genreflecting advisory series)
   Includes bibliographical references (p.) and indexes.
   ISBN 1-56308-871-1
     1. Christian fiction--History and criticism. 2. Christian fiction--Stories, plots, etc. 3.
Christian fiction--Bibliography. I. Title. II. Series.

PN3448.C48 M67 2002
809.3'93823--dc21

                                         2001050840

Contents

103241

Acknowledgments

I wish to thank the staffs of River Bluffs Regional Library, MidContinent Library, Johnson County Public Library, and Kansas City Public Library for their forbearance and unfailing courtesy with my endless reserves and interlibrary loans.

My thanks to Bill Ott and *Booklist* for permission to use, in altered form, some of the reviews that first appeared in my column, "Christian Fiction."

My thanks to Bethany House for permission to quote from Robert Funderburk's novel, *The Fires of Autumn* (1996); to Writer's Digest Books, for permission to quote from Penelope Stokes's *The Complete Guide to Writing and Selling the Christian Novel* (1998); to Ohio State University Press, for permission to use a passage from the introduction to Royal Rhodes's *The Lion and the Cross: Early Christianity in Victorian Novels* (1995); and to Scribner, for permission to quote from Reed Arvin's *The Will* (2000).

My thanks also to all the publishers who helped, and special thanks to Jeanne Mikkelson, Carol Johnson, and David Horton at Bethany House; Lyda Hope at Harvest House; Beth Thornton at B & B Media; Rebecca Germany at Barbour Publishing; and Robby Nichols at Covenant Communications.

All Bible quotations are from the King James translation.

Libraries Unlimited is grateful to NoveList (of EBSCO Publishing) for their permission to adapt and use images from their program throughout the Genreflecting Advisory Series.

Introduction

This book aims to define the literary genre of Christian fiction for anyone who is in the business of answering questions about it: librarians, booksellers, home-school teachers, writers, and editors. The broad traditions of the field are explored, and where it stands today is described. Almost 2,000 titles, classic and contemporary, are covered and in most cases annotated.

Christian Fiction is also a self-help book for those readers who hate to ask anything of the librarian.

Christian Fiction is a collection development tool, enabling the librarian to search out gaps in her collection or even instructing her on how to build it from the ground up. Home-school and public high school teachers can use the chapter on young adults and the designation **YA** to extend their reading lists. Writers wanting to break into the field will find the descriptions of subgenres and the annotations instructive, as will booksellers and publishers who are puzzled by the library market or seek a snapshot of their industry. Finally, *Christian Fiction* provides instant bibliographies for church activity workers, teachers, and book group moderators.

Classics as diverse as *Pilgrim's Progress* and *Blood of the Martyrs* are placed historically and summarized. Classics are not always in print, but they remain available in many libraries, and are a vital portion of the lingua franca shared by the writers and readers of Christian fiction.

This book's emphasis, however, is on fiction from the mid-1990s through the beginning of 2002, including also the earlier entries of ongoing series and contemporary classics such as Frank Peretti's *This Present Darkness*. Titles are summarized, or series are summarized where they encompass many individual titles, as in the case of Gilbert Morris's House of Winslow series.

Some iconoclastic or at least controversial titles are included, with the full realization that the very mention of *The Last Temptation of Christ* causes some readers to see red. Others regard the novel as a profoundly reverent work, illustrating that what the majority wants is never the whole story, and that readers' advisors should always be prepared with an alternative.

Like other titles in the Genreflecting series, this book is organized according to genres, subgenres, and themes, enabling readers and those who work with them to easily identify read-alikes and groups of titles that will appeal to particular tastes. Beyond these groupings, readers' advisors should take note of the descriptions and designations within the annotations.

For example, **⬛🐟** indicates evangelical titles, that is to say, titles published by members of the Evangelical Christian Publishers Association (ECPA) and belonging to the Christian Booksellers Association (CBA). Such titles are assured of a certain theological stance, but the designation's practical application is that ECPA and CBA subscribe to a publishing code that excludes profanity or explicit sexuality. That there are many readers demanding such guarantees is not to be doubted. Consider this testimony from an anonymous amazon.com customer:

> I recently started reading Christian fiction as I am so sick of the filth in secular reading. This story made me smile and cry and praise the lord all at the same time. It was beautifully written and the characters all seemed alive to me. If more of our young people would read these kinds of books maybe the world wouldnt [sic] be going to hell the way it is!

The annotations will generally take note of the sexual content of the novels covered in this volume, whether they are evangelical or something other. Notwithstanding, there is no attempt to label those many titles that are clearly evangelical and "clean," but that were not published in the ECPA, or those evangelical titles with half a dozen mild swear words, such as James BeauSeigneur's Christ Clone trilogy. To do so seemed to the author akin to painting fig leaves on statuary. However, any discerning reader can figure out which publishers belong to ECPA. The ⬛✕ , therefore, is offered as a convenience for those who work with readers who insist upon "clean" fiction.

Beginning with the publication of Janette Oke's *Love Comes Softly* in 1979—with a nod to Catherine Marshall from a few years earlier—evangelical publishers have dominated Christian fiction. They invigorated—really, reinvented—a moribund genre. But Mormon fiction and Catholic fiction, each with contrasting traditions, are also surveyed here, as well as a number of what might almost whimsically be called ecumenical novels—Christian, but undoctrinaire and more tolerant of such evangelical taboos as profanity and sex.

Mainstream horror novels and thrillers often contain a Christian element—the power of Satan, or the international search for an ancient scroll—but unless they seem to have religious intent, they are excluded.

Privately published titles and Internet tomes are not included, although in a perfect world, some would be. Religion isn't like other subjects. Through history, people have felt strongly enough about it to die for it, and to kill for it. Thus, even a badly written exercise, an outright rant, can be arresting and original, and *Books in Print,* amazon.com, and barnesandnoble.com list hundreds of such treatises that amateurs felt so strongly about that they paid to have them printed and perhaps made an effort to promote. But no one reviews such books, and thus they lack that fundamental attribute librarians require: authority.

Nor will readers ask for them.

Readers *will* ask for "spiritual fiction," also excluded here. That is, Christian fiction is certainly spiritual, but readers may be looking for the likes of James Redfield's *The Celestine Prophecy* (1994, Warner, 246 pp. ISBN 0-446-51862-X) or Starhawk's *The Fifth Sacred Thing* (1993, Bantam, 486 pp. ISBN 0-553-37380-3). Though spiritual or New Age fiction often covers the same territory that Christian fiction does, and is often grouped with it as inspirational fiction, there remains a yawning gulf between the two. Evangelical readers are offended by Starhawk's Wiccan ways. Starhawk loyalists think evangelical is a synonym for right wing.

Spiritual fiction, in other words, is another book.

Jewish fiction is not included, although the question was pondered for some time. Jewish fiction is highly literary. Because of the Jewish diaspora, Jewish fiction is also highly international, with settings in Russia, Argentina, the United States, and, of course, Israel. These two factors alone take Jewish fiction so far from the world of Janette Oke and even Brock and Bodie Thoene that it seems incomparable.

Further, the horrors of history caused post-war Jewish writers to question the existence of God, or at least to elucidate His indifference, and for many of their successors, the Jewish legacy is less religious than historical. Judaism and Christianity share a great deal, and much Jewish fiction will appeal to Christian readers, but in the end this subject, too, seems to call for another book. Readers' Advisory librarians may want to consult Ray Keenoy's *Babel Guide to Jewish Fiction* (1998, Boulevard, paper, ISBN 1-899460-25-X).

A popular way to stock fiction is to buy the prize winners, and these are listed in the "Sources" chapter (2). They are also indicated in the text with these symbols:

  Gold Medallion

  Rita

🅒 Christy

The designation **YA** refers to adult titles that have particularly strong young adult interest, of which there are a great many, because Christian fiction often uses young people as protagonists, there's an emphasis on strong stories, and, of course, Christian fiction is "clean." Where adult titles have overwhelming young adult interest, the discussion will be found in the adult sections, and the citation repeated only in chapter 15, "Young Adult."

"See" and "see also" references are used liberally. For example, readers of apocalyptic fiction, treated in chapter 9, "Fantasy and Science Fiction," will probably also be interested in Catholic apocalypse, treated in chapter 12, "Catholic Fiction." Similarly, readers referring to the "Early Christianity" section of the chapter on biblical fiction, chapter 4, will find references to such titles as *Quo Vadis,* treated in chapter 3, "Christian Classics."

Titles with exceptional literary merit, that are strikingly original, or that have caused a stir beyond the ordinary are designated with a star ★.

Discussion indicates fiction that seems particularly well suited for book clubs and other discussion groups, often because of its treatment of women's issues, but sometimes also because it is controversial or because its characters are uncommonly appealing. In the author's experience with book groups, a character with great depth or vividness—let's say, Joe Christmas in William Faulkner's *Light in August*—can provide a surefire focus for initiating discussions.

[Historical] indicates a title where history has been carefully re-created.

The index will guide you by subject, title, and author.

Full citations are given in most cases. New Christian fiction stays in print from three to perhaps five years; thus, most items listed here are available.

Where no bindery designation is given, the title is in cloth.

Good reading to you!

Chapter 1

The Christian Alternative

DEFINITIONS AND BACKGROUND

When imaginary people, or characters, meet with conflict, the result is fiction. In Christian fiction, the conflict must have something to do with Christian principles. In romances, for example, frequently a conflict occurs between the young woman's attraction to a man who is a nonbeliever and her own salvation. In Janette Oke's *Beyond the Gathering Storm* (p. 122), Christine Delaney takes her first job in Edmonton and falls in love with the boss's son. But he refuses to convert, and Christine breaks off the engagement—the right thing to do, Oke suggests.

The conflict can be indirect, didactic, subtle, political, and multifaceted, but its Christian content is what turns Christian fiction into a genre. That is—at least in evangelical fiction—readers know the outcome to begin with; it is the details of the struggle that interest them. By contrast, in literary fiction the outcome is not always clear, and for some genre readers this is deeply unsatisfying.

The writer of evangelical fiction must operate under certain rules or constraints. These include accepting the infallible authority of the Bible, addressing life's dilemmas through faith in Jesus, and, particularly, believing that Jesus is divine, died, and rose again for the sins of humankind. He sits on the right hand of God, awaiting the proper moment for his return—this time as a warrior. Writers of Christian fiction can be most innovative in fleshing out these beliefs, but they don't usually trifle with their veracity.

This matters, because evangelical fiction so dominates contemporary Christian fiction that in the minds of many readers the two are synonymous, even as the terms *fundamentalist* and *evangelical* are nearly the same. The possibility exists for Unitarians to begin evangelizing, no doubt, but it seems remote.

Still, there are many fiction writers who don't fit the evangelical mold and yet are clearly Christian writers. To offer one example, since the 1950s, Frederick Buechner has written lyrically of suffering, exploratory Christians. Should evangelicals give him a try? Of course, but in any case, Buechner does not lack for readers, either "secular" or Christian.

At the extreme, one can find iconoclasts such as Michael Moorcock, the science fiction writer who in 1966 wrote what has become an underground classic, *Behold the Man* (p. 41). A time-traveler goes looking for Christ, finds a depraved Mary and her idiot son named Jesus, and proceeds himself to become the Jesus required of history. This is plainly too much for an evangelical reader, as is Gore Vidal's somewhat less imaginative, even more forthrightly blasphemous *Live from Golgotha* (1992).

Catholic fiction, with its grand literary tradition, is described in the longest chapter of this book. Mormon fiction also exists, although it is little known outside of Utah.

This book ranges widely; in other words, into Christian fiction that some might not consider Christian. But for many readers, what matters is a spiritual search that's made in Christian terms. For them, many evangelical novels will prove too rigid and unimaginative.

Nonetheless, when readers ask for Christian fiction, most of the time what they mean is evangelical fiction.

THE EVANGELICAL NOVEL

Through the 1950s the Christian novel was so well established in mainstream publishing that it wasn't necessary to think of it as a distinct category or to give it labels, such as *evangelical.* Novelists such as Lloyd C. Douglas, Agnes Sligh Turnbull, Taylor Caldwell, and Grace Livingston Hill sold extremely well, and indeed they still have a great deal of currency in public libraries. Catholic and Jewish writers, producing work of the highest literary merit, were also popular. The great C. S. Lewis himself published in the mainstream, rather than with religious publishers.

But in the 1960s American mainstream writers took a different turn. It was a tumultuous time. To the intellectual vanguard, organized religion seemed reactionary and, finally, irrelevant. With exceptions such as John Updike, Walker Percy, and the evangelical Catherine Marshall, our most influential writers saw no place for God in fiction. They wrote novels that questioned the existence of God—if He could allow a war like the Vietnam War, or the Holocaust, or the suppression of African Americans. They celebrated the meaninglessness of life.

It was a grand inquiry, but it began to lose its punch. The generation of writers following them—with their complex literary experiments, their high style, their celebrations of the drug culture and homosexuality, and their contempt for family values—lost contact with the reading public.

Mainstream fiction of this sort retreated to the academy, where it began its death throes.

Such a scenario is both an exaggeration and an oversimplification but nonetheless broadly outlines why the time was ripe for simple, straightforward fiction that celebrates the glories of America's past, romantic love, and the hope for redemption.

Such fiction arrived—or re-emerged—in 1979 with Bethany House's publication of Janette Oke's *Love Comes Softly,* a romance with a strong Christian message but that struck a genuine note among women in particular. Twenty years later, every new Oke novel has a first printing of 250,000 copies. Altogether, as the millennium began, her book sales totaled more than 19 million copies (Johnson 2000).

Though Oke owes a clear debt to Laura Ingalls Wilder, and perhaps even more to Beth Streeter Aldrich, she could still be said to have invented the prairie romance—a genre romance celebrating old-fashioned, pioneer virtues.

Largely because of Oke as well, the concept of the sequel quickly took hold among evangelical publishers. Sequels maximize profits, but they appeal to the same readers time after time, and they are seldom treated with critical seriousness. Thus, while Oke and others made the field a popular success, they also ensured its marginalization critically. In a word, evangelical fiction has preached to the converted, or to the 3 million to 10 million regular patrons of the Christian Bookstore Association's (CBA's) 2,500 bookstores. About 80 percent of evangelical fiction is sold there.

CBA and ECPA (Evangelical Christian Publishers Association) offer their members a guaranteed and attractive market. A Christian bookstore can thrive in a mall or small town where a Walden's bookstore would go out of business. However, these strong organizations are also quite insular. As Christian novelist James Calvin Shaap puts it, "A vast chasm separates evangelical Christian books from the mainline readership—something that threatens those writers who profess the Christian faith but who see a world much less sanitized than the one prescribed and enforced by CBA censors" (Schaap 1997).

Schaap speaks eloquently to the plight of Christian writers who would treat the world realistically, such as himself, Larry Woiwode, and Augusta Trobaugh. But literary fiction isn't nearly as popular in the mainstream as it used to be. Genres—mysteries and romances, in particular—are what readers want. Christian fiction is an alternative universe, but its readers are often fans of Danielle Steele, John Grisham, and Scott Turow. The problem they have with mainstream fiction is not its lack of literary quality but its lack of Christian content. From the point of view of a certain group of readers—readers who routinely drive up circulation figures in public libraries—the CBA "product" is perfect.

Sales of evangelical fiction rose steadily through the 1980s and were booming by the end of the 1990s. Oke's prairie romances were the first wave, but there have been four others (Johnson 2000), each strengthening the field as a whole and making it more sophisticated in its marketing strategies.

Frank Peretti's *This Present Darkness,* from Crossway in 1986, struck like a thunderbolt, spilling the concept of "spiritual warfare" even into the mainstream.

Almost simultaneously, though with less fanfare, Brock and Bodie Thoene's stories of Israel showed that Christian historicals could be carefully researched, and inspired a wave of imitations throughout the 1990s.

Jan Karon's Mitford series, launched without distinction in 1994 by the evangelical publisher Chariot Victor, crossed over to the mainstream publisher Penguin in 1996 and became a smash success, so much so that this mainstream series is one of the few to be stocked in CBA bookstores. Karon proved that a "gentle read" could also be literary, Christian, and universally appealing. In fact, although a number of genre labels fit Karon's series, including nostalgia, under which it is placed in this book, ultimately it transcends genres.

Finally, there is evangelical fiction's largest ever commercial success; Tim LaHaye and Jerry Jenkins's apocalyptic Left Behind series, beginning in 1996 and continuing into the new century, with almost 30 million copies sold. Tyndale's phenomenon clung atop the *New York Times* bestseller list for weeks through 1999, when apocalyptic musings and fears were at their height, doing battle with the likes of Stephen King and J. K. Rowling (Rabey 1999). Left Behind went on as strongly into 2002, spawning audios, an R-rated movie (for the violence), and a juvenile series itself responsible for more than 5 million in sales.

Yet there are growing pains. Despite its increased sophistication and quality, evangelical fiction is reviewed only by pre-publication media aimed at libraries and bookstores, and by Christian media. Newspapers and the literary establishment regard it as a sideshow, and routinely ignore it. In part, this continues a long-standing literary prejudice against religious fiction. It's also a feature of the culture wars, pitting left against right or, if you like, hip against square.

Huge sales for a handful of writers have attracted agents, causing writers to jump among evangelical publishing houses for the best advances. Some houses, such as Bethany, routinely pass on their profits to church work, and are unaccustomed to giving out large advances. Houses such as WaterBrook, a Doubleday imprint, operate exactly as other evangelical houses, except that books are their only business. Thus, they have more money to spend.

Moreover, the possibility for profits attracts mainstream publishers, and crossovers such as Brock and Bodie Thoene (to Viking) become more likely. Will evangelical publishers move more strongly into the secular chains and start shelling out huge advances? Is spiritual warfare between evangelical and mainstream houses on the horizon?

Time will tell. And in the end it may not matter to librarians or booksellers, whose job it is to give readers what they want, wherever it comes from.

Finally, the CBA code restricts the ways writers can express their faith. For example, take Reed Arvin, whose *The Wind in the Wheat* (p. 227) is one of the most lyrical and affecting evangelical novels ever written. Published by Thomas Nelson, *The Wind in the Wheat* is a coming-of-age story about a Kansas farm boy with a gift for music who won't let his Christian principles be corrupted by the recording industry. But *The Will* (p. 205), Arvin's second novel, was published by the mainstream publisher Scribner. Its protagonist, a lawyer and former seminary student in the midst of a profound spiritual search, makes this observation:

> It could never be like it had been, that he realized absolutely. It could never be the kind of faith that asked no questions and believed blindly. He could never take his requests to the God of his childhood, that imaginary beast, half ogre, half heavenly honey bear. He never knew whether to be terrified of that God or to beg Him for treats, like a puppy. That was gone forever. But a tremor of something else moved very quietly within, a vibration that he was tempted to quell before it developed pitch and voice. (Arvin 2000)

Such a nuanced expression of faith is hard to find in a novel from an ECPA publisher, and those readers to whom it appeals should look elsewhere.

THE READERS

One librarian described the typical Christian fiction reader this way: "I have a patron who wants to be with her husband at night. He's tired, and all he wants to do is watch sports. She hates sports, so she sits reading Christian romances. They don't take much concentration and they end happily."

Readers' Advisory in such a case is simple. This reader probably reads formula romances and Christian romances interchangeably. But it's important to acknowledge exactly what role Christian fiction plays for such readers: It is clean and inoffensive. Often, it is like a soap opera, much like the soap operas on the TV the woman sits before. Older notions of Readers' Advisory, in which reading is a bootstrap activity and patrons go from comic books to Proust in a six-week program, become absurd in such a context.

Maybe the patron is bone-weary, and the sweet lies of a romance, the pure dream of love, are all that remains of her youthful hopes. Possibly a light Christian romance is her fledgling attempt at a spiritual search. Yet she's akin to the woman identified by the industry, too. Here's how evangelical editor and fiction writer Penelope Stokes (1998) describes her in *The Complete Guide to Writing and Selling the Christian Novel*:

> Let's be honest here. Our customers are not, by and large, bright-eyed, eager, deeply spiritual intellectuals who want to be challenged, educated, and stretched. They are ordinary people—usually women and usually middle-aged—who want a good story with strong values, likable characters, a fast-moving plot and a satisfying ending.

Stokes's description of what Christian fiction readers want applies to her own novel, *The Blue Bottle Club* (Word, 1999, ISBN 0-8499-1573-2), worth considering in some detail because it describes the heart of Christian fiction, which is not apocalyptic, not didactic, not even particularly evangelical, but simply female.

The Blue Bottle Club was formed more than 70 years ago at the tail end of the prosperous 1920s. Four giddy young girls challenged each other to write down what they wanted to be in life, and they hid their secret ambitions in a blue bottle. Then, of course, the Depression hit.

When the house where the club met is finally razed, the blue bottle comes into the hands of Brendan Delaney, a TV reporter disillusioned with the singles life and with her unsatisfying career. But she senses a good story and tracks down the four women of the club.

There is one survivor, and she tells the sad but quietly triumphant stories of each of the club's members: a social worker, an actress, a loyal wife, and an artist. Stokes's structure is almost monotonously precise, but she escapes a mere mechanical exercise by making each of the four lives a fine and ennobling instruction in faith for the jaded Brendan. In contrast to Grace Livingston Hill's stories, no rich man arrives to rescue the women from poverty. Stokes's novel is driven by character, rather than plot—one mark of superior fiction.

Although it's a fine example of an evangelical novel, *The Blue Bottle Club* is capable fiction in any context: The characters are engaging, and their fates matter to us; suspense is generated as we move from one story to the next and wonder what effect there will be on Brendan's life (essentially the back story); and we come to care about Brendan. The focus is on women, important because the readers will be female. Moreover, bearing in mind the audience that Stokes has described, Brendan is the right kind of woman: a professional, but not entirely satisfied with her work; a bit lonely and unlucky in love; and a little sinful and doubting, so that she's in need of a Christian lesson. Importantly, the novel is not merely about religion; it's also about loneliness, an unmarried woman's difficult course through life, and what the past has to teach us. But in the end, without being preachy or sanctimonious, the novel does indeed turn its readers toward the religious life.

BEYOND ROMANCE

Stokes's novel is a "gentle read," a term describing perhaps two-thirds of what's thought of as Christian fiction. But although Stokes's description fits her own work and the work of dozens of others, including Janette Oke, it passes over literary Christian fiction (Frederick Buechner), novels classic to the field (Lloyd C. Douglas), apocalyptic fiction (evangelical fiction's sassiest subgenre), Mormon fiction (all but antievangelical, or at least most evangelicals think so), and Catholic and Jewish fiction (with their long literary traditions), all of which attract readerships, too. Her description does not account for the superb C. S. Lewis, whose many readers hunger for—and never find—a fantasy writer to match him.

Stokes's description also leaves out men. Of course, men don't read fiction of any sort in the numbers that women do. A 1997 *Publishers Weekly* survey (Baker 1997) showed that the general fiction market is 55 percent female, and any circulation librarian can tell you that the percentage of men reading romances is almost too small to measure. As for evangelical fiction, 90 percent of purchasers are female, and the average age is 42 (Duffy and Sachs 1995).

Even so, there are genres other than romance in Christian fiction that appeal more to men: westerns, science fiction, and apocalypse. Christian westerns, for example, can do a great deal to invigorate out-of-date western shelves and are generally popular with men who read westerns.

Stokes's characterization omits apocalypse. Evangelical readers are convinced that the return of Christ is imminent. They see a society in grave moral disarray. Apocalyptic novels (see chapter 9, "Fantasy and Science Fiction"), as well as novels portraying an America sold down the river by its godless, decadent ruler elite (see chapter 11, the section titled "Morality Tales"), can have a profound appeal. Then there are the time-honored wages-of-sin stories, biographical novels of historic church figures, and biblical fiction, where writers, on holy ground, put forth the field's most conscientious efforts.

Stokes's description leaves out both the women and men who are literary readers—English teachers, writers, and English majors who have made their way in the business world but harbor a secret love for literature. They, too, may be looking for an alternative to the bleak mainstream landscape, but they won't respond to soap opera. Try them with Augusta Trobaugh, Jane Kilpatrick, and Sigmund Brouwer.

Stokes's description seems to assume that romances represent the entire field. They dominate, but once the Christian theme has been established, Christian fiction—whether evangelical or ecumenical—divides into the genres of mainstream publishing: romance, historical, science fiction and fantasy, mystery, western, young adult, children's, and, if it can be thought of as a genre, literary. And it observes the conventions of these subgenres: the down-on-his-luck detective, recovering from alcoholism and divorce; the independent young woman, disappointed in love and looking for Mr. Right; and the lone rider, used hard by the corrupt men of encroaching civilization, brought at last into the fold by the love of a good woman.

Now let's take a look at the underpinnings of the field, and the books themselves.

Chapter 2

Readers' Advisory Sources

Only a few years ago, there was hardly any way for Readers' Advisory librarians to isolate, much less evaluate, Christian fiction. The author's column in *Booklist* began for that reason: Librarians kept calling the magazine asking for guidance. A column in *Library Journal* began almost simultaneously. Now, books and Web sites proliferate.

BOOKS

Readers' Advisory

Adamson, Lynda G. *American Historical Fiction: An Annotated Guide to Novels for Adults and Young Adults.* 1999. Oryx Press. 405 pp. ISBN 1-57356-067-7.
   A detailed genre index guides readers to Christian titles.

Aue, Pamela Willwerth, and Henry L. Carrigan, Jr. *What Inspirational Literature Do I Read Next?* 2000. Gale. 479 pp. ISBN 0-7876-3942-7.
   Wide-ranging source with 200 pages devoted to nonfiction, 100 to fiction. The fiction section covers 336 titles, of which about 85 percent are Christian titles. The Christian titles include a handful of classics and a selection through the twentieth century. Aue and Carrigan number their titles sequentially. They provide indexes for title, author, character description, character name, subject, category, and time period.

DeLong, Janice, and Rachel Schwedt. *Contemporary Christian Authors: Lives and Works.* 2000. Scarecrow. 383 pp. ISBN 0-8108-3688-2.
   Information about Christian fiction writers is somewhat hard to find, and the authors profile 68 of them, listing major works, discussing representative works, and, though every profile is positive, suggesting their subjects' relative popularity. The most intriguing feature is the interviews, which are uniformly frank and revealing, and, because they are often long, give the book a certain authentic feel. The authors leave out Catholic writers, mainstream figures such as Frederick Buechner and Larry Woiwode, and quite a few ECPA writers as well, such as Francine Rivers and Walter Wangerin.

Walker, Barbara J. *Developing Christian Fiction Collections for Children and Adults: Selection Criteria and a Core Collection.* 1998. Neal-Schuman. 224 pp. ISBN 1-55570-292-9.

> Covers adult, children's, and young adult books as well as videos and contains a chapter on Christian fiction promotional activities and a chapter of author profiles.

Writers' Guides

Stocking writers' guides to Christian fiction serves two Readers' Advisory purposes: It identifies subgenres and good examples of the genre, and it addresses the needs of Christian fiction readers who want to write for the field, as well as mainstream writers who want to cross over. In the author's experience, budding or established talents tend to be female and interested in writing romances.

Herr, Ethel. *An Introduction to Christian Writing.* 1999. ACW Press, paper. 308 pp. ISBN 1-892525-16-X.

> A basic writers' guide, including exercises, by the author of the Seekers historical series.

Morris, Gilbert. *How to Write and Sell a Christian Novel.* 2000. ACW Press, paper. 186 pp. ISBN 1-892525-17-8.

> Morris's pragmatic guide has been through a number of editions and is probably the best for entrants into the field.

Stokes, Penelope. *Complete Guide to Writing and Selling the Christian Novel.* 1998. Writer's Digest Books, paper. 256 pp. ISBN 0-89879-810-8.

> Editor and fiction writer Stokes offers her editorial and religious philosophy, tempered with talk of markets, manuscripts, and publishers.

Stuart, Sally E. *Christian Writers' Market Guide: 2002.* 2002. WaterBrook, paper. 629 pp. ISBN 0-87788-190-1.

> Laid out methodically much like *Writer's Market,* this is the best single source for the beginning Christian writer. Its only drawback is that it does not cover small press or literary publishers that sometimes publish Christian fiction, such as Hampton Roads (discussed later in this chapter). Stuart is particularly comprehensive on the magazine market for Christian fiction—a vital, if poorly paid, starting point—and offers listings of conferences, agents, and writers' support organizations.

JOURNALS

Booklist. This publication offers a regular column by the author, reviews of mainstream titles in the fiction pages, and reviews of major titles in the "Upfront" section.

Bookstore Journal. This journal is the official publication of the Christian Booksellers Association and offers uncritical reviews of Evangelical Christian Publishers Association titles.

Catholic Library World. Under "Literature," *Catholic Library World* publishes some highly critical reviews of Catholic and evangelical fiction.

Christian Library Journal. Published quarterly, *Christian Library Journal* is one of the best sources for reviews of Christian fiction, running 15 to 30 young adult reviews and 15 to 30 adult reviews in each issue. Some of the young adult titles are from the mainstream press; all of the adult titles are evangelical. Christian romances predominate.

Christianity and the Arts. This publication often runs articles on Christian fiction.

Library Journal. This journal offers a regular column and some coverage in fiction and advance pages.

Library Materials Guide. A semiannual guide, *Library Materials Guide* is published by Christian Schools International.

Publishers Weekly. A periodical that publishes evangelical Christian bestsellers' lists and individual reviews and periodically runs articles on the industry in its Spring and Fall roundup sections.

Romantic Times. This publication reviews new Christian fiction under the section "Inspirational Fiction."

VOYA (Voice of Youth Advocates). This publication doesn't target Christian novels specifically, but it covers several per issue, all aimed at young adults.

WEB SITES

Note: All Web sites were accessed December 2001.

Bethany House—www.bethanyhouse.com
> Bethany maintains a site particularly useful for Readers' Advisory work, listing all entries in Bethany's series, both adult and juvenile. The majority of Christian novels that public library patrons ask for are in these series, and they will want to know the order.

BookBrowser—www.BookBrowser.com
> BookBrowser is the effort of two librarians, Janet Lawson and Cindy Orr. They maintain a variety of genre lists. Most of the Christian fiction covered is evangelical, and coverage is far from exhaustive, but this is a dynamic site that keeps growing. The site lists evangelical series, but perhaps the most useful feature is the listing of new titles by month of publication. Some reviews can be found here as well.

Christian Bookstore Association—www.cbaonline.org
> The CBA site offers bestsellers and the bestselling backlist.

Christian Classics Ethereal Library—www.ccel.org
> The site provides online classics.

Christian Library Journal—www.christianlibraryj.org
> This site offers the electronic version of the magazine.

Christianity and the Arts—www.christianarts.net
> The site is the Web site for the magazine.

Evangelical Christian Publishers Association—www.ecpa.org/
> The site provides links to publishers and new books.

Fiction_L—www.webrary.org
> Fiction_L is the pride and joy of the Morton Grove Public Library, in Morton Grove, Illinois. If you sign up on the Fiction_L listserv, you can ask questions about obscure titles and someone will almost always answer you. This can be particularly useful in Readers' Advisory work, when a patron remembers that the desired novel is "about

a little girl who went to a magic kingdom where there were all these animals, and there was a famous author in it, too." Fiction_L also maintains many genre lists, which are varied in terms of quality and slant of the compiler, but provide a useful starting point in collection building.

Genreflecting.com—genreflecting.com
Libraries Unlimited's Web site for the Genreflecting Advisory series offers author and title lists for each genre, descriptions of new mainstream and genre favorites, expert advice on genre fiction and Readers' Advisory, Readers' Advisory news, and more.

Inspirational Book Distributors (IBD)—http://www.ibd-read.com
Originating from a small chain of bookstores in Ohio, Inspirational Book Distributors is the chief one-stop distributor of evangelical Christian books. Their discount is smaller than the bigger jobbers, but their service is more personalized, and for the librarian in a hurry without much knowledge of Christian fiction, IBD can be the answer. For Readers' Advisory librarians, the IBD site is a professional one, where a search for almost any contemporary, evangelical fiction title will be rewarded with a reproduction of the book jacket and an annotation from jacket copy. IBD is also a good site for staying informed about forthcoming titles. Contact ISP, 7518 Sylvania Ave., Sylvania, Ohio 43560, 419-843-9442.

Omnilist of Christian Links—http://members.aol.com/clinksgold/
This site provides links to all things Christian, including books and music.

Overbooked—www.overbooked.org/index.html
This site lists links to publishers and a list of titles in series.

Romantic Times—www.romantictimes.com
This site is the highly commercial site of the magazine.

DATABASES

No database is good enough to substitute for informed librarians who read reviews and fiction regularly, but, on the other hand, no individual can be equally well informed in all areas.

NoveList, which had its origins in library work and the classic Readers' Advisory guide Genreflecting, is based on greatly expanded subject headings for fiction. It is increasingly available in midsized to large public libraries. It is a commercial database, but, for an electronic source, a relatively cheap one. It makes finding Christian fiction easy and often offers reviews from *Booklist* and other media. It is a constantly evolving database, and developments late in 2001 made its keyword searching feature comprehensive, not merely in titles and subject headings but in reviews and features as well. The author's own articles appear there.

As one might expect, Gale's database What Do I Read Next? draws from its print series with the same title for recommendations and plot summaries. The print series, of course, is a direct competitor to Libraries Unlimited's Genreflecting series, whereas its electronic expression is a direct competitor to NoveList; however, it is still playing catch-up to NoveList and works with a smaller body of knowledge. It contains no reviews, one of NoveList's chief virtues, nor does it do a percentage ranking of matches, another popular NoveList feature. There are no articles or tips on book talks. Effectively, it may be cheaper than NoveList in states where libraries access it through consortia. Many Christian titles are contained in the database, though evangelical users may be mildly annoyed when their searches bring up quantities of New Age titles as well. What Do I Read Next? operates efficiently and is perhaps more intuitive than NoveList.

The Web sites of Amazon.com and Barnes & Noble (www.bn.com) contain most Christian novels, sometimes with reviews. The sales rankings both sites offer is an interesting feature, giving at least one guide to popularity. Both sites also contain a suggested further reading feature as well as customer comments and occasional comments from authors. These can be useful, but lack the rigor of NoveList. The customer comments, in fact, are often crude and, to be kind, anti-intellectual, and must make authors cringe. Even so, they are an unavoidable reference point for Readers' Advisory librarians and booksellers.

Books in Print has moved aggressively to incorporate the best innovations of these other sources into its Web product. It contains the most exhaustive listing of Christian fiction titles, offers prepublication reviews, and, like NoveList, uses subject headings for a Readers' Advisory feature. Though laid out clearly and with many search options, *Books in Print* tends to operate more slowly than Amazon.com.

CHRISTIAN FICTION PUBLISHERS

The following are the most active publishers of Christian fiction, from most active to least. Most are members of the Evangelical Christian Publishers Association. Catholic, Mormon, and Amish/Mennonite publishers are treated in the chapters pertaining to their fiction.

The list is not exhaustive because Christian novels are sometimes published under mainstream imprints and aren't marketed as such. Small press literary publishers publish Christian novels, as in the case with MidList Press's 1996 novel *The Latest Epistle of Jim,* by Roy Shepard. (See chapter 11, the subheading "Pastors.") There is no methodical way to track such novels other than through reviews and word of mouth, though they can be excellent purchases.

BETHANY HOUSE PUBLISHERS
11400 Hampshire Avenue South
Minneapolis, MN 55438
612-829-2500
www.bethanyhouse.com

Bethany is the largest and most significant publisher of Christian fiction. Its profits support Bethany College for Missions and Bethany Fellowship International, an interdenominational organization sending evangelical missionaries around the world. Bethany prints most of its own books in a modern facility near the editorial offices and often prints the overflow work from other ECPA companies such as Multnomah and Tyndale.

Bethany's flagship author is, of course, minister's wife Janette Oke, who essentially made the company. Beverly Lewis's series of Amish novels has also been highly successful, as well as many of Bethany's juvenile series, most notably Robin Jones Gunn's Christy Miller series. Bethany has been the leader in evangelical fiction publishing, laying down the series model and the romance model for their ECPA colleagues.

Most of Bethany's output is romances and romantic historicals, although it also publishes some fine mysteries and occasionally publishes westerns. Sometimes a literary novel surfaces, but Bethany's emphasis is on strong stories with believable characters, somewhat on the sentimental side. All of Bethany's fiction is edited to a high standard, and, as their writers' guidelines suggest, without being either "preachy" or too obscure. For both adult and juvenile Christian titles, Bethany is a public librarian's best friend.

BARBOUR PUBLISHING, INC.
P.O. Box 719
Uhrichsville, OH 44683
740-922-6045
www.barbourbooks.com

Barbour publishes at least as many titles as Bethany, including romances and romantic historicals edited with extreme conservatism regarding language and sex. In part because

Barbour markets aggressively through its own book club and also because Barbour's novels are infrequently reviewed, their books are not commonly found in libraries. Also, their authors are often first-timers and unknowns, and some do not reappear.

Barbour's Heartsong imprint began in 1992 and in 1999 was up to 52 titles per year; half contemporary romances, half historical. These are mass market paperbacks that look much like Harlequins and are a great buy for paperback racks. Barbour also publishes an attractive trade paperback series of novellas—four novellas in each—themed around such topics as frontiers, the Northwest, Greece, prairie brides, and friendship, all priced a bit under their equivalents with other Christian publishers.

HARLEQUIN/STEEPLE HILL (Love Inspired)
300 E. 42nd St., Sixth Floor
New York, NY 10017
212-682-6080
www.steeplehill.com

Harlequin's Love Inspired line, an interloper in the ECPA world, has published three Christian romances a month since mid-1997. These are mass markets and are more often to be seen in libraries than Barbour titles. They are also somewhat less stringently edited for innuendo, but are otherwise similar to Barbour titles. Many of Steeple Hill's writers also publish with ECPA members, so the writers will be more familiar to veteran readers than Barbour's authors. The romances themselves tend to feature strong heroines maintaining their faith against all odds; the reward for their faith is a good man, a baby, or a sharp upturn in fortunes. Harlequins are perishable, thus only representative titles are covered in this book.

MULTNOMAH PUBLISHERS
P.O. Box 1720
Sisters, OR 97759
541-549-1144
http://www.multnomahbooks.com

Multnomah began in 1987 as Questar (still retained as a Multnomah imprint) and changed its name to Multnomah Publishers with its merger in 1992 with Multnomah Press of Multnomah Bible College and Bible Seminary. Multnomah published 31 fiction titles in 1999 "that tell the truth about living as a Christian in a fallen world." Its Palisades line features the strongest stand-alone romances among ECPA publishers, with unformulaic stories from familiar writers Lisa Tawn Bergren, Linda Chaikin, Annie Jones, Lorena McCourtney, and Diane Noble. Multnomah has also experimented with humor in its romances, particularly from Jones and McCourtney. Multnnomah Publishers is a hard charger in the world of evangelical fiction and threatens to overtake Bethany.

TYNDALE HOUSE PUBLISHERS
P.O. Box 80
Wheaton, IL 60189-0080
630-668-8300 ext. 260
www.tyndale.com

Tyndale began in the 1950s as a Bible publisher and has never displayed the sagacity toward fiction typical of Bethany, Nelson, or Multnomah. Nonetheless, Tyndale publishes one of the best writers in the business, Francine Rivers, and has vaulted onto center stage with LaHaye and Jenkins's Left Behind series, the biggest thing ever to hit Christian fiction.

ZONDERVAN PUBLISHING HOUSE
5300 Patterson Ave., S. E.
Grand Rapids, MI 49530
616-698-6900
www.zondervan.com

Zondervan, a Bible house linked corporately with HarperCollins West (meaning that the same vast entity publishes Walter Wangerin's *Book of God* and various New Age treatises), averages 20 fiction titles a year. These include some of the best-known writers, such as Terri Blackstock, Stephen Lawhead, Patricia Sprinkle, and Bill Myers. The house is particularly strong in its mystery line, and, perhaps because of its association with HarperCollins, draws a number of crossover talents, such as Blackstock and Sprinkle. Zondervan has won more Gold Medallions, mostly in nonfiction, than any other house.

WATERBROOK PRESS
5446 N. Academy Blvd., Suite 200
Colorado Springs, CO 80918
719-590-4999
www.randomhouse.com/waterbrook

WaterBrook is not an independent press but an imprint of Doubleday. Doubleday had a long history of publishing Christian fiction before ECPA or CBA were established, but Doubleday is itself an imprint of Random House, so it's hard to predict WaterBrook's future. The imprint published 15 fiction titles in 1999, and some of Christian fiction's finest, including T. Davis Bunn and Jane Kirkpatrick, have moved to it, at least temporarily.

CROSSWAY BOOKS
1300 Crescent St.
Wheaton, IL 60187
630-682-4300
www.gospelcom.net/goodnews

Crossway had the distinction of publishing Frank Peretti's groundbreaking *This Present Darkness* (p. 304). Publication of Stephen Lawhead's mass market success, the Pendragon Cycle series, began at Crossway. The company's romances and mysteries are well edited and tend to be less preachy than some of their competitors' books. One of their most popular current authors is W. E. ("Wally") Davis, author of a private-eye series, Gil Beckman, and several westerns.

BROADMAN and HOLMAN PUBLISHERS
127 Ninth Ave., North
Nashville, TN 37234-0198
615-251-2000
www.broadmanholman.com

Broadman and Holman, representing the Southern Baptist Convention, is a Bible house that traces its origins to 1743. In 1999 the house published 13 fiction titles, including historical romances from Bonnie Leon and Kay Rizzo and some superior legal thrillers from James Scott Bell. A significant editorial change was announced in the fall of 2000. "We're getting out of the Christian birdhouses and watering cans business," said David Shepherd, senior vice president. By early 2002, this sentiment seemed to have had little effect on Broadman and Holman's fiction.

THOMAS NELSON, INC.
501 Nelson Place
P.O. Box 141000
Nashville, TN 37214-1000
615-902-1141
www.thomasnelson.com

Thomas Nelson started his publishing company in 1798 in Scotland. It is a large company. Although primarily a nonfiction and Bible publisher, Nelson has in recent years published many evangelical fiction titles, always to a high literary standard, such as the mysteries of Gary Parker and the fantasies and realistic novels of Joseph Bentz. Nelson owns W Publishing Group.

W PUBLISHING GROUP
545 Marriott Dr., Suite 750
P.O. Box 141000
Nashville, TN 37214
615-902-3400
www.wpublishinggroup.com

W Publishing, formerly called Word Publishing, has been owned by Thomas Nelson since 1992. Although it does not publish the quantity of fiction of Zondervan, its titles also are often blockbusters, such as Sigmund Brouwer's *Blood Ties* (p. 197) and Frank Peretti's *The Visitation* (p. 182). W Publishing, in fact, is a good source for Christian thrillers, often with a biting political edge.

HARVEST HOUSE PUBLISHERS
1075 Arrowsmith
Eugene, OR 97402
541-343-0123
www.harvesthousepubl.com

Though a smaller operation than Bethany or Multnomah, Harvest House titles, primarily romances, are similar. One of the most popular of all Christian writers, Lori Wick, publishes with Harvest House.

BAKER BOOK HOUSE/REVELL
P.O. Box 6287
Grand Rapids, MI 49516
616-676-9186
www.bakerbooks.com

Both Baker, which owns Revell, and Revell are long-established companies. Though their output is smaller than Bethany's or Multnomah, they publish many of the same authors. They also publish novels of exceptional literary quality, such as Augusta Trobaugh's *Praise Jerusalem!* (p. 223) and James Calvin Schaap's *The Secrets of Barneveld Calvary* (p. 223).

HAMPTON ROADS
134 Burgess Lane
Charlottesville, VA 22902
804-296-2772
http://www.hrpub.com

Not really a Christian publisher per se, Hampton Roads is nonetheless the home of two beautifully written novels about the Crucifixion by D. S. Lliteras (p. 43). What Christian fiction the house does publish, at the rate of three or four per year, is among the best in the field. The house also publishes intriguing explorations of Native American religions and fiction that mix New Age and Christian sensibilities. The best thing about Hampton Roads is that it brings forth fresh, exploratory voices that are free of cant.

MOODY PRESS
820 N. LaSalle Blvd.
Chicago, IL 60610
312-329-2101
www.moody.edu

Moody is a major publisher that has been active with adult fiction in the past but in recent years has seemed to focus on juvenile fiction.

The following publishers release significant work, but their fiction outputs are small.

**CHARIOT—VICTOR
PUBLISHING/SCRIPTURE PRESS**
4050 Lee Vance View
Colorado Springs, CO 80918
719-536-3295
www.cookministries.com

CHRISTIAN PUBLICATIONS
3825 Hartzdale Dr.
Camp Hill, PA 17011
717-761-7044
www.cpi-horizon.com

HONOR BOOKS
P.O. Box 55388
Tulsa, OK 74155
918-496-9007
www.honorbooks.com

EERDMAN'S
255 Jefferson Ave., SE
Grand Rapids, MI 49503-4554
616-459-4591
www.eerdmans.com

PACIFIC PRESS
P.O. Box 5353
Nampa, ID 83653-5353
208-465-2500
www.pacificpress.com

PARACLETE PRESS
P.O. Box 1568
Orleans, MA 02653
508-255-4685
www.paracletepress.com

PREP PUBLISHING
P.O. Box 66
Fayetteville, NC 28302
910-483-6611
http://www.prep-pub.com

WINEPRESS PUBLISHING
P.O. Box 428
Enumclaw, WA 98022-0428
360-802-9758
www.winepresspub.com

KREGEL PUBLICATIONS
P.O. Box 2607
Grand Rapids, MI 49501-2607
616-451-4775
www.gospelcom.net/kregel

AWARDS

Christy Awards

The Christy Awards for excellent Christian fiction were established in 2000. Titles that somehow express the spirit of Catherine Marshall's *Christy* (p. 234) are chosen in several categories by industry insiders, including editors, reviewers, bookstore owners, and book buyers.

Contemporary/General Fiction

2001: Tie between *Home to Harmony,* by Philip Gulley (Multnomah), and *The Trial,* by Robert Whitlow (W Publishing Group)

2000: *A New Song,* by Jan Karon (Viking)

Futuristic Fiction

2001: *Trangression,* by Randall Ingermanson (Harvest House)

2000: *By Dawn's Early Light,* by Grant R. Jeffrey and Angela Hunt (W Publishing Group)

International Historical Fiction

2001: *Unashamed,* by Francine Rivers (Tyndale)

2000: *Out of the Red Shadow,* by Anne DeGraaf (Bethany)

North American Historical

2001: *Reaping the Whirlwind,* by Rosey Dow (Winepress)

2000: *The Meeting Place,* by Janette Oke and T. Davis Bunn (Bethany)

Romance Fiction

2001: *A Touch of Betrayal,* by Catherine Palmer (Tyndale)

2000: *Whispers from Yesterday,* by Robin Lee Hatcher (WaterBrook)

Suspense

2001 *The Great Divide,* by T. Davis Bunn (WaterBrook)

2000 *Final Witness,* by James Scott Bell (Broadman and Holman)

First Novel

2001 *Passing by Samaria,* by Sharon Ewell Foster (Multnomah)

Gold Medallion

The evangelical Gold Medallion, the most well-known award for Christian fiction, was established in 1978 by the Christian Booksellers Association. CBA retailers are the judges, and, perhaps because of that, winners tend to be bestsellers.

2001: *Paul,* by Walter Wangerin, Jr.

2000: *The Indwelling,* by Tim LaHaye and Jerry B. Jenkins

1999: *The Last Sin Eater,* by Francine Rivers

1998: *Only the River Runs Free,* by Bodie and Brock Thoene

1997: *The Book of God,* by Walter Wangerin, Jr.

1996: *The Oath,* by Frank Peretti

1995: *Twilight of Courage,* by Bodie and Brock Thoene

1994: *Say To This Mountain,* by Bodie Thoene

1993: *In My Father's House,* by Bodie Thoene

1992: *Warsaw Requiem,* by Bodie Thoene

1991: *Munich Signature,* by Bodie Thoene

1990: *Piercing the Darkness,* by Frank E. Peretti

1989: *The Key to Zion,* by Bodie Thoene

1988: *Taliesin,* by Stephen R. Lawhead

1987: *The Gates of Zion,* by Bodie Thoene

1986: *More Than Seven Watchmen,* by Helen Norris

1985: *Johnny Come Home,* by R. C. Sproul

1984: *MacIntosh Mountain,* by Victor J. Kelly

1983: *Love's Long Journey,* by Janette Oke

1982: *The Iron Sceptre,* by John White

1981: *Alpha Centuri,* by Robert Siegel

1980: *Caught in the Crossfire,* by Levi Keidel

1979: *The Kiowa,* by Elgin Groseclose

1978: *I Came To Love You Late,* by Joyce Landorf

Rita (Romance Writers of America, Inspirational Category)

Ritas are chosen by member romance writers.

2001: *The Sheperd's Voice,* by Robin Lee Hatcher

2000: *Danger in the Shadows,* by Dee Henderson

1999: *Patterns of Love,* by Robin Lee Hatcher

1998: *Homeward,* by Melody Carlson

1997: *The Scarlet Thread,* by Francine Rivers

1996: *As Sure As the Dawn,* by Francine Rivers

1995: *An Echo in the Darkness,* by Francine Rivers

[category suspended, 1987–1994]

1986: *From This Day Forward,* by Kathleen Karr

1985: *For the Love of Mike,* by Charlotte Nichols

Chapter 3

Christian Classics

The chief antecedent of Christian fiction is, of course, the Bible. Accounts of settlers moving West seem always to mention it—along with Shakespeare and perhaps a *Webster's* dictionary—among the books they took along, and that their children grew up on. It is hard to write English without making reference either to Shakespeare or the King James Bible; our figures of speech, the way we shape sentences, remain dependent on them, even if we don't realize it.

The Book of Ruth, whatever its historical or spiritual truth, is a compressed but highly sophisticated short story about a Hebrew woman, Naomi, and the Moab wife of one of her sons, Ruth. When her husband and sons die, Naomi must return in poverty to Bethlehem. She encourages her two daughters-in-law to return to their native land, but Ruth, in a beautiful statement of loyalty, refuses:

> whither thou goest, I will go; and where thou lodgest, I will lodge;
> thy people shall be my people, and thy God my God.

Ruth's statement is a standard for marriage vows. Her loyalty, her humility, and her ingenuity—in finding a way to feed herself and Naomi, and in finding another husband, Boaz—are rewarded, and thus, among other things, her story becomes an archetype for romance fiction.

The less joyous and ultimately puzzling story of Job also continues to instruct fiction writers. The Devil makes a deal with God to send plagues upon Job, his most faithful servant, to see if Job will deny his Master. Job never does, despite his complete ruin, and thus the ages are given a model for suffering and service. However, scholars quarrel over what this joke that God plays on even his most faithful means. Although evangelical writers avoid the idea of a Jehovah who could seem capricious or malevolent, Jewish fiction writers find the tale endlessly evocative, of a God not so much capricious as inscrutable. Secular writers see Job as an existential parable.

Other biblical stories don't have the made-to-order fictional coherence of these two but are still wonderfully archetypal: Samson and Delilah; the prophet Nathan standing up to the lascivious deceits of David; the wisdom of Solomon; Adam and Eve; the tower of Babel; Daniel in the lion's den; and the stunningly rich, panoramic tale, often retold by Christian writers, of the flight from Egypt. The Old Testament is a treasure trove for fiction writers.

And so is the New Testament. The Crucifixion has been rendered in fiction dozens of times, both reverentially and with blasphemy, and Revelation is the backbone of a host of contemporary apocalyptic novels.

BRITISH CLASSICS

The first example of Christian fiction more or less resembling modern fiction is probably John Bunyan's *Pilgrim's Progress.* Bunyan was a persecuted nonconformist preacher who did most of his writing in jail. His masterpiece first appeared in 1678 and became immensely popular, though it did little to relieve his poverty.

Bunyan's work is an allegory; thus, he named characters after virtues or vices, and places after the trials and temptations one encounters in life on the journey to the Promised Land. Many of Bunyan's most clever conceits, such as the *slough of despond* and *vanity fair,* have entered the language. *Pilgrim's Progress* is another of those works the pioneers carried West, because the trials the pilgrim Christian undergoes seemed to speak to their own perils, and Christian writers still write allegories, all of them paying homage, whether or not they are aware of it, to Bunyan. Hannah Hurnard's contemporary classic *Hinds' Feet in High Places* (p. 160) is a sort of rewrite of Bunyan's work.

Fielding, Richardson, and Sterne duly noted, it was really not until the nineteenth century that British fiction came into its own, beginning at last to cast off the notion, always with us to an extent, that fiction is no more than frivolous entertainment. A notable exception was Oliver Goldsmith's *The Vicar of Wakefield,* first published in 1766.

As recently as a generation ago, Goldsmith's classic was still taught in public schools, and it's easy to see why: Goldsmith's smooth style is entirely readable, more so than that of many writers a century later. A distant ancestor of Father Tim of Jan Karon's Mitford novels, Goldsmith's vicar, Dr. Primrose, is a bumbler, and it is partly through his trusting incompetence that the family he is so proud of loses its fortune, his daughter is seduced, his house is burned down, and he is thrown in jail. Tempering all the melodrama, however, is Dr. Primrose's ironic humor—for instance, he considers that the six children he's fathered are a great service to humankind, and that the state, even as it proceeds to incarcerate him, is in his debt.

The Romantic Movement was in full flowering when Lord Edward Bulwer-Lytton, of "It was a dark and stormy night" fame, gave the world *The Last Days of Pompeii* (1834). Bulwer-Lytton's ornate style is tough for today's readers to wade through, and was criticized even in his own time. Nonetheless, his melodramatic tale, set in A.D. 79, is beautifully researched and compellingly lays down the conceits of the contemporary apocalyptic novel, with effete Pompeiian society sounding rather like Victorian England; a delicate, sightless Christian girl taking on the role of prophet; and the wrath of God spewing from Mt. Vesuvius.

There were many such novels, most of them deservedly forgotten. According to Royal Rhodes, author of *The Lion and the Cross: Early Christianity in Victorian Novels:*

> religious-historical novels produced during the Victorian era . . .
> share concerns found in secular or nonconfessional examples of
> historical fiction: criticism of contemporary culture and society, a
> sense of historical nostalgia, a deep sense of nationhood, various
> Romantic literary devices, and a proclivity toward sensationalism.
> (Rhodes 1995)

This description captures many contemporary Christian historicals. Except for its modern style, Francine Rivers's Mark of the Lion series (p. 48) could fit comfortably into the Victorian mold.

Much fiction was written in explication of the Oxford Movement, a call for purity that passed through the Anglican Church in the 1830s and 1840s. The essence of the Oxford Movement was that the Anglican Church had grown too political and too beholden to the state. It needed to throw off its "liberalism" and empty rituals and return to the simplicity of Paul's fiery gospel—and of the early Catholic Church (Fairweather 1964).

The schism was aggravated by virulently anti-Catholic writers, notably the Anglican prelate Charles Kingsley, with his fifth century tale *Hypatia* (1853) and especially with his vivid account of Elizabethan adventures at sea, *Westward Ho!* (1855).

Cardinal John Henry Newman, originally the leader of the Oxford Movement, later to shock the Anglican Church by converting to Catholicism, was intellectually much at odds with Kingsley. In some ways, his 1855 novel *Callista* (2001, University of Notre Dame, 416 pp., ISBN 0-268-02260-7), the tale of a third century Greek girl who converts to Christianity, is a rebuttal to Kingsley. *Callista* is highly romantic but has no love story, unless Callista's passionate union with Christ could be called a love story. (For a further discussion of Newman and the Catholic literary revival, see chapter 12, "Catholic Fiction," the "Classics" section.)

The Romantic Movement was already dying by the time George Eliot published her first novel, *Scenes of Clerical Life,* in 1858, set in a sharply etched rural England and featuring three realistically drawn ministers. Actually, the novel is three novellas: "The Sad Fortunes of the Reverend Amos Barton," "Mr. Gilfil's Love Story," and "Janet's Repentance." Each is noteworthy for its modern psychological insights, and it's no accident Eliot is often thought of as an early feminist. Eliot's believable characters include not only her ministers, who are variously awkward, lovelorn, and admirable, but also the women in their lives, particularly Janet Dempster, driven to alcoholism by an abusive husband.

The late Victorian passion to substitute science—or at least rationalism—for religion is reflected in Samuel Butler's *The Way of All Flesh,* published in 1903, a year after his death. Its anti-hero, Ernest Pontifex, a thinly disguised version of Butler himself, anticipates twentieth century ironic realism in every way as Butler skewers Ernest's (and his own) proud Victorian family for its repression, materialism, shallow spirituality, class consciousness, and even dishonesty. Young Ernest is forced into the clergy. His ignorance, lack of belief, and repressed sexuality bring him to ruin when he naively confuses a decent woman with a prostitute and grows violent with her. He's disgraced and sent to jail. In the end, he manages a modest comeback, but not before he has rejected every facet of his upbringing. For its time, Butler's novel was pure sabotage—a grenade thrown into the sacristy.

George MacDonald

The most significant figure of Victorian fiction as far as contemporary evangelical fiction is concerned is the Scottish novelist, poet, essayist, and children's author George MacDonald, who lived from 1824 to 1905.

Queen Victoria died in 1901, perfectly symbolizing the end of the era named for her and the birth of a most unromantic century. The popularity of MacDonald, whose realistic novels were romantic by twentieth century standards, was eclipsed by the new century as well. Religion had lost favor to science (Phillips 1987).

Among a select group of writers, however, notably C. S. Lewis, MacDonald's influence lived on. And his popularity was actually growing again by the end of the twentieth century, in considerable measure because of the efforts of evangelical novelist Michael Phillips.

In the 1980s, working for Bethany House, Phillips went to great lengths to dust off MacDonald's romances, re-titling them (sometimes pointlessly), condensing them (by as much as half), and modernizing their language for impatient modern readers. No writer could be comfortable with such treatment, but Phillips would have been the first to recommend the originals over his modernizations: He was simply trying to reintroduce a forgotten master. He even wrote a biography (*George MacDonald: Scotland's Beloved Storyteller,* 1987, Bethany, 400 pp., ISBN 0-87123-944-2).

Other reprints and rewrites came from Harper & Row and Chariot Victor. MacDonald's perennially popular children's fantasies—clearly an inspiration for C. S. Lewis's Narnia series, and perhaps an influence on Tolkien as well—have generally remained in print.

MacDonald was an intriguing writer in several genres: realistic, historical, romantic, and fantastic. He wrote about 50 books, 31 of them adult novels. All contain religious inquiries, ranging from astounding fantasies of Heaven to speculations on the afterlife of animals.

MacDonald was a virtuous and generous man, and his devotion, not unlike Tolstoy's, to leading a life modeled on Christ's attracted C. S. Lewis, whose reading of *The Phantastes* set him on the road to conversion. Lewis was struck by the extraordinary intricacy and dreamlike quality of MacDonald's fantasies and took away the lesson that a novelist could write about good people, and goodness, without being boring. MacDonald, a true Christian mystic, was also an original. The sheer wild invention of his fantasies and fairy tales, in particular, grabbed hold of readers and wouldn't release them. They still do.

Libraries without any of MacDonald's titles might begin with the following books, representing what Lewis and others have thought to be his best work.

The Complete Fairy Tales. 1999. Penguin Classics, paper. 352 pp. ISBN 0-14-043737-1.
Collects MacDonald's eleven short fairy tales, including "The Light Princess" and "The Golden Key," which have also been published as stand-alone children's stories.

The Maiden's Bequest, the Minister's Restoration, the Laird's Inheritance: Three Novels in One Volume.
Michael Phillips, ed. 1998. Bethany. 640 pp. ISBN 0-7642-2148-5.
Many of MacDonald's novels inspired sequels, but these three are stand-alone, realistic novels set in Scotland, and among his best. For good or ill, Phillips edited out MacDonald's difficult Scottish dialect. Respectively, the three were originally titled *Alec Forbes of Howglen* (1865), *Salted with Fire* (1897), and *Warlock O'Glenwarlock* (1882).

Lilith. 1981. Eerdman's, paper. 252 pp. ISBN 0-8028-6061-3.
The solitary and loveless Mr. Vane returns to his ancestral home, and in the pursuit of quiet scholarship finds himself slipping into the spirit world. His magic house makes the journey five times, encountering, among myriad others, Adam and Eve, who give the impetus to Mr. Vane's ever-deepening understanding of good, evil, and redemption. Beasts, angels, and fairy-like women greet him at every interval and draw him through paradoxical adventures. He falls in love, but only to find himself once more in his odd house, unsure if he is awake, asleep, or dead.

Phantastes: A Faerie Romance. 1981. Eerdmans, paper. 185 pp. ISBN 0-8028-6060-5.
MacDonald's first novel, one of the most arresting and difficult fantasies ever written, chronicles the adventures of its narrator, Anodos, in fairyland, or the spiritual kingdom beyond death. Allegorical in the tradition of Bunyan, and hopeful, it is also darkly psychological, like the musings of Edgar Allan Poe, and dreamlike. It is in fact MacDonald's profound understanding of dream logic that make the *Phastastes* so believably bizarre; he anticipates not Kafka, but Jung.

At the Back of the North Wind. 1998. Tor, paper. 305 pp. ISBN 0-812-56712-9.

The Princess and Curdie. 1994. (Originally published in 1882.) Penguin (Puffin Classics), paper. 256 pp. ISBN 0-14-036762-4.

The Princess and the Goblin. 1996. (Originally published in 1872.) Penguin (Puffin Classics), paper. 241 pp. ISBN 0-14-036746-2.

The Inklings

The Inklings were a small group of Oxford Christians organized by C. S. Lewis in the 1930s, consisting of Lewis, J.R.R. Tolkien, and Charles Williams, to name only the most influential among them. They met in Lewis's home or at a local pub called the Eagle and Child. Both Williams and Tolkien were great friends of Lewis, and their influence clearly shows in his work, in turn the most

influential on the Christian fantasy to follow. But Williams and Tolkien, though not enemies, were far apart aesthetically and in their religious views and were never on intimate
terms (Carpenter 1978).

All of the Inklings much admired George MacDonald's work, particularly his fantasies, as well as the works of Catholic writer G. K. Chesterton, almost their contemporary,
for his Father Brown mysteries and for his extraordinary metaphysical mystery *The Man
Who Was Thursday*. (See chapter 12, "Catholic Fiction," the "Classics" section.)

C. S. Lewis

Often given such labels as "Christian Apologist" and "Defender of the Faith," C. S.
Lewis is one of a handful of Christian fiction writers who are universally respected. Among
evangelical writers he is revered and proudly acknowledged as an influence.

Lewis's interesting life—his unfashionable championing of faith, his late-life,
tragic romance with and marriage to Joy Davidman—is well documented in films, biographies,
and Lewis's own writings.

Much of what Lewis had to say is nonfiction. And in the end, Lewis's most valuable,
and certainly his most accessible, title may be *Mere Christianity* (1952), which sets out with his
customary wit, firmness, and clarity the case for Christianity in a scientific century. It is the
traditional case, in particular for marriage, causing some to label him a misogynist for proclaiming the necessary subjectivity of women. *Surprised by Joy* (1955), Lewis's autobiography,
also remains popular, but *A Grief Observed* (1963), a sort of sequel, is less well-known. It's
a beautiful though heartbreaking book in which Lewis attempts to analyze his own grief
over the death of Joy Davidman and to make sense of it in Christian terms. Some feel he
failed and feel that the book, published under the pseudonym of N. W. Clerk, amounts to a
repudiation of faith. The remainder of this section describes some of Lewis's fiction.

The Complete Chronicles of Narnia. 2000. HarperCollins. 528pp. ISBN 0-06-028137-5.
The children's novels that make up the complete chronicles are available individu-
ally in a number of editions and are often purchased that way for children's collec-
tions: *The Lion, the Witch, and the Wardrobe* (1950); *Prince Caspian* (1951); *The
Voyage of the Dawn Trader* (1952); *The Horse and His Boy* (1954); *The Magician's
Nephew* (1955); and *The Last Battle* (1956).

Lewis placed ordinary, though somewhat spoiled and not always admirable,
English children into the rather scary world of Narnia in the first story, and he never
expected to write a sequel; the story's popularity called for it. Though splendidly entertaining for children as adventure stories full of delightful creatures, each story also
had an element of menace about it, and each demonstrates the differences between
wrong and right.

There is a nether region in Narnia, the Shadowlands, and a Christ-like figure,
the lion Aslan, who becomes the great hero of the series. Though always conscious of
his juvenile audience, Lewis interwove a subtext of Christian thought throughout the
series, as well as references to Greek mythology and the works of George MacDonald
and H. Ryder Haggard, which may well account for the appeal of the series to adults.

The concluding tale, with its anti-Christ figure, scheme of death and resurrection, and powerful portrait of the sparkling shores of the New Narnia, will remind
readers of J.R.R. Tolkien's *The Return of the King* (discussed later). The series
would also seem to be a clear antecedent not only for Madeleine L'Engle's time
travel tales (p. 302) but also for J. K. Rowling's Harry Potter stories, though some
evangelical groups have raised objections to the latter.

The Great Divorce. 2000. (Originally published in 1945.) Broadman and Holman, paper. 128 pp. ISBN
0-8054-2048-7.

> Lewis's modernized *Divine Comedy* begins with Lewis as a character, walking the fearful
> and depressing streets of Hell. Ghosts accompany him and others to the outskirts of Heaven,
> where appropriate guides offer a tour and invitation to remain. Lewis's guide is his literary
> mentor George MacDonald, who gently answers a number of vexing questions. A more pro-
> found and ambitious work than *Screwtape* (below), *The Great Divorce* never attained similar
> popularity, though Michael Phillips imitates it in *The Garden at the Edge of Beyond* (p. 162).

The Screwtape Letters. 1938. (Many editions.)

> Outside the Narnia tales, *The Screwtape Letters* is Lewis's most popular book and a great favorite
> among evangelical writers. It's a series of letters between the clever Screwtape, an administra-
> tive assistant in Hell, and his novice field worker, Wormwood, who has been assigned to
> corrupt an ordinary young man. The wit of Lewis's inversion (telling the tale from the point
> of view of Hell) comes partly from Wormword's almost saintly desire to please his supervisor,
> and succeed in Hell, and from Lewis's uncanny appreciation for the subtleties and rationali-
> zations of sin.

RANSOM (SCIENCE FICTION) SERIES

Out of the Silent Planet. 1938. (Many editions.)

> Brave philologist Dr. Elwin Ransom, said to be modeled on J.R.R. Tolkien, is abducted by a
> mad scientist, Dr. Weston, and his henchman to the planet Malacandra (Mars). He escapes to
> make a Lilliputian sort of tour among several intelligent races, allowing Lewis to satirize terres-
> trial society, which at the time is about to plunge into World War II.
>
> Ransom, a good or "unbent" man, eventually comes before Oyarsa, ruler of the world
> but himself a servant of Maleldil, or God. Unwittingly, Dr. Ransom has brought news from
> the silent planet setting cosmic events in motion. Maleldil hints that Ransom has not been sent
> to Malacandra by accident; great events are mounting in the heavens, and a battle with the evil
> one, who rules the silent planet Thulcandra, or Earth, is imminent.

Perelandra. 1944. (Many editions.)

> Commanded by Maleldil but unaware of his mission, Dr. Ransom journeys to Perelandra, or
> Venus, to save it from malevolent powers represented by Dr. Weston, the emissary of the
> "bent" Oyarsa of Earth, or Satan. Lewis's Venus is a highly fanciful island kingdom, full of
> dragons and sentient seahorses, and with bizarre gravitational effects. It is a world without
> sin, and no one, including Ransom, wears clothes. Ransom encounters a green goddess, the
> "Lady," who rules her strange kingdom with innocence and naiveté, like Eve in her garden.
> Weston-as-Demon tempts her, appealing to her vanity first. It is Ransom's task to guide her
> toward the light, in a spiritual experiment to determine whether Venus must perforce follow
> the same history as Earth. With *Till We Have Faces,* Lewis thought *Perelandra* his most suc-
> cessful fiction; it seems much influenced by the novels of Charles Williams (discussed later).

That Hideous Strength. 1945. (Many editions.)

> With a tale anticipating apocalyptic novels 50-odd years in the future, Lewis manipulates the
> dark and light forces of his first two novels in a battle for Earth. The powers of darkness are
> symbolized by the governmental agency N.I.C.E. (the National Institute of Coordinated Exper-
> iments), an Orwellian conceit, and the lip-service N.I.C.E. gives to progressivism and rationalism
> while undertaking heinous evil links Lewis almost directly to the spiritual warfare novels of
> the 1990s. (See chapter 9, "Fantasy and Science Fiction," the "Spiritual Warfare" section.)
> Dr. Ransom counters N.I.C.E. with the Logres, a group seemingly too weak and eccentric to

battle absolute evil, again anticipating novels such as *This Present Darkness* (p. 304). In his most vivid scenes Lewis revives the wizard Merlin, a magnificent, primitive, but crafty soul who takes on godlike qualities and who crowds out Ransom as the novel's hero.

Till We Have Faces: A Myth Retold. 1985. (Originally published in 1956.) Harcourt, paper. 313 pp. ISBN 0-15-690436-5.

Although Lewis considered *Till We Have Faces* to be his masterpiece, like *Lilith,* the great fantasy of his mentor George MacDonald, it is difficult to read and has never attracted the vast readerships of his science fiction and children's stories. A retelling of the Greek myth of Cupid and Psyche, what Christian mythology can be found in it is too obscure for most readers. It is a joyous work, however, exploring the facets of romantic love and friendship, with one character, Orual, in part based on the love of Lewis's life, Joy Davidman.

J.R.R. Tolkien

The most eminent of the Inklings is J.R.R. Tolkien, a philology professor at Oxford who was heavily influential in C. S. Lewis's development as a Christian, not to mention in his development as a writer, most notably in the Narnia series. Tolkien was a Catholic and was somewhat disappointed in Lewis's Protestantism. An extremely private man, he avoided public pronouncements and concentrated on his writing.

Tolkien invented Middle Earth, an ancient land peopled with hobbits—about half the size of humans but much like them. Middle Earth also contains elves, dwarves, and orcs, not to mention dragons, sentient trees, and other fanciful creatures.

Tolkien is less influential on Christian fiction than on fantasy writing as a whole. Frodo Baggins is arguably a Christ-figure, and the lines between good and evil are clear. But Tolkien is such a subtle and referential writer, his mythology of Middle Earth so full, that some readers are not consciously aware of his Christian intent.

Still, every hobbit's—or every man's—prime task in life is to determine the right way to live. This requires courage, humility, purity of heart, and a willingness to sacrifice one's own time and energy for the good of the community. These may be universal virtues, but they are also Christian. And the passing of Middle Earth and the innocent goodness of the hobbits is like the fall of man in Eden. Men, intrinsically neither good nor evil, fight among themselves and neglect the true evils before them. Hobbits knew better.

The Hobbit. (Many editions.)

First published in 1937, *The Hobbit* was so popular in England that a sequel was imperative, much as has been the case for J.K. Rowling's tales of wizardry on the contemporary scene.

Not unlike Tolkien himself, the hobbit, or Bilbo Baggins, is a peaceful, retiring, decidedly middle-class creature. On the recommendation of Gandalf, perhaps the greatest fictional wizard ever created, he is hired by a group of dwarves to aid them in their quest for family treasure, which is guarded by the fierce dragon Smaug in the Lonely Mountain in the East. Their quest is comic and yet quite serious. Naturally, they are beset with all manner of perils during their quest: wolves, orcs, and horrid spiders. Often, Gandalf must rescue them, but Bilbo becomes vital to the quest as well, because of his cleverness and because of the power of the magic ring that he takes from a strange creature named Gollum, who will also appear in the Lord of the Rings trilogy. That ring was originally the property of the Dark Lord Suaron, and if he can secure it once more, he will have the power to destroy Middle Earth, and rule absolutely.

Though *The Hobbit* is perhaps more of a precursor than a prequel, it's the best introduction to the Lord of the Rings trilogy and a brilliant epic on its own.

LORD OF THE RINGS (many editions)

The Fellowship of the Ring. 1954.

Reluctant hero Frodo Baggins none too eagerly accepts the One Ring as his inheritance from Bilbo Baggins, his uncle. The ring can control the world, but once its powers are invoked, it also controls its bearer. One of the extraordinary qualities of Tolkien's masterpiece is that the reader is never completely convinced that Frodo will win his struggle. He is determined not to use the ring, but he is an every man, even the weakling Christ, and he is sorely tempted. The ongoing moral is clear: You cannot attain goodness by evil means.

A great council of the good peoples decides that the ring must be destroyed, but that can only be done by casting it into the fire from which it came. The fire rages in Mordor, where the enemy, Sauron, and his Black Riders dwell. Thus, the long and difficult journey begins.

The Two Towers. 1954.

Frodo's dauntless companions are caught in Sauron's endless treacheries, and Frodo, now considerably toughened, soldiers on with his servant, Sam Gamgee, at his side. As the novel closes, a great darkness falls over Middle Earth, and the War of the Rings begins.

The Return of the King. 1955.

Frodo enters the haunted landscape of Mordor and is at last able to destroy the ring, but his every step is beset with temptation, and the ring's terrible power draws him down both physically and spiritually. In the end, even the great Gandalf cannot help him. He must prevail over ghastly, palpable evil with his own free will.

Meanwhile, in the War of the Rings itself, Sauron is at last defeated. And yet there is a note of sadness to the triumph, for the Third Age of Middle Earth has come to an end. The fate of the world will henceforth be in the hands of humans.

The first installment of director Peter Jackson's faithful adaptation of the Lord of the Rings trilogy, *The Fellowship of the Ring*, was released at Christmas time 2001. The remaining two installments will be released at Christmas time 2002 and 2003. The film stars Elijah Wood as Frodo and Sir Ian McKellen as Gandalf.

The Silmarillion. 2001. (Originally published in 1974.) Mariner Books, paper. 384 pp. ISBN 0-618-12698-8.

Christopher Tolkien edited his father's lifelong work for publication after his death, at 81, in 1973. It lays out the deep mythology of Middle Earth in the First Age, setting up *The Hobbit* and the Lord of the Rings series. Though majestic, it is also dense, and not as compulsively readable as the better-known novels. It tells of the Dark Lord Morgoth's quest for Silmarils, magic jewels invested with great power. He is at last defeated in the War of Wrath, but then Sauron begins his own consolidation of evil and rise to power.

Charles Williams

Charles Williams was an Anglican, an editor at Oxford University Press, and a charter member of the Inklings. A highly influential fantasy writer, his novels have nonetheless fallen into obscurity, though several are available from Eerdman's. Most academic libraries, and most midsize and large public libraries, retain Williams's novels, and there is a vigorous appreciation of him on the Internet.

T. S. Eliot said of Williams that "to him the supernatural was perfectly natural, and the natural was also supernatural" (Eliot 1948). This led him down trails bordering on the occult, and evangelical readers, by and large, would not be comfortable reading his novels.

Others will find him difficult and obscure, particularly in his later novels, such as *Descent into Hell.* Nothing is as it seems in a Williams novel. The spiritual world, which Williams portrays by drawing not only from Christian teachings but also from Greek mythology, freely intermingles with the observable world. This can seem baffling to the uninitiated reader, but once he or she understands what Williams is up to, the novels become a rare delight. A good novel to start with is *The Place of the Lion.*

All Hallows' Eve. 1948. (Out of print.)

Lester Furnival, who has died, finds herself in a peculiar London where the past, present, and future exist simultaneously. Is she in Heaven? Not exactly: It's Williams's version of Purgatory, and Lester must regress in time to sort out the flaws in her soul before she can progress toward selfhood. Another character, Simon LeClerc, uses sorcery to manipulate spiritual life and also regresses, but to evil effect.

Descent into Hell. 1999. (Originally published in 1937.) Eerdman's, paper. 222 pp. ISBN 0-8028-1220-1.

Hell may be around us always: a bleakness or dying of the spirit where a man can commit suicide but still "live" on in agony. Hell on Earth is a world so obsessed with self that love for others is no longer possible. But obsessed Lawrence-Wentworth, determined to break down the barrier between the phenomenological world and the spirit world, does descend into Hell in Williams's darkest meditation and perhaps greatest novel.

The Greater Trumps. 1932. (Out of print.)

The Greater Trumps is the story of widower Lothair Coningsby, who is willed a deck of ancient Tarot cards that he is supposed to turn over to the British Museum. When he doesn't, evil forces are unleashed as various characters hold the cards and put in motion their prophecy.

Many Dimensions. 1993. (Originally published in 1931.) Eerdman's, paper. 269 pp. ISBN 0-8028-1221-X.

The object of the quest in this novel is a precious stone that once adorned King Solomon's crown. An upright man, Lord Arglay, and an amoral or perhaps Satanic figure, Sir Giles, seek out its miraculous powers, which, even when divided, are still retained. But the stone is hard to control. For instance, one man tries to go back in time. But he can only return to one particular time and must live out his life exactly as he did before.

The Place of the Lion. 1933. (Out of print.)

Damaris Tighe, a young philosopher, is trying to write about ancient Greek archetypes. The vaguely occultist group of intellectuals to which she belongs imagines these archetypes into the real world, and with horrid effects. Individual attitudes and psychic imperfections are projected into the archetypes so that a righteous eagle in one person's imagination becomes an evil pterodactyl in that of Damaris. Anthony Durrant, the other major character, is at last able to put the world right by becoming a sort of Adam, naming the beasts and describing their correct roles.

Shadows of Ecstasy. 1933. (Out of print.)

Roger Ingram, an English teacher who has a theory that poetry, religion, and other psychic expressions are "shadows" of a deep ecstasy that humankind is not in touch with, finds himself drawn to an activist of his theory, Nigel Considine. After much anthropological work in Africa, Considine has learned how to draw upon the great, dark forces of ecstasy—for instance, he has lived for 200 years. Roger is swept up by the power and inescapable logic of Considine, who mounts a small invasion with his African forces on England. As his power spreads across Europe, it becomes clear that Considine is the Antichrist, but a most curious one: tolerant of Christianity as interesting but inferior to his own philosophy, and the bearer of dark tidings that may be inevitable.

War in Heaven. 1999. (Originally published in 1937.) Eerdman's, paper. 256 pp. ISBN 0-8028-1219-8. Williams sets a search for the Holy Grail in contemporary (pre-War) England, pitting various personalities—Archdeacon Davenant, a Father Brown sort of figure who unravels the true nature of the Grail, and the evil though sometimes agreeable anthropologist Sir Giles of *Many Dimensions*—in competition and at odds. Though dark forces are at work, Williams makes a romp out of things, including a wild car chase across the English countryside very much reminiscent of Chesterton's *The Man Who Was Thursday.*

AMERICAN CLASSICS

Although the earliest American literature is deeply Christian—the sermons of Cotton Mather and Jonathan Edwards, for example—there is little fiction of note until the mid-nineteenth century, when Edgar Allan Poe and Nathaniel Hawthorne appeared almost simultaneously. Poe, of course, wrote short stories and is variously tagged as the father of the short story, the macabre short story, and the detective story.

Hawthorne wrote the first great American novel, *The Scarlet Letter,* in 1850, and it is also the first American Christian novel of any consequence. One measure of its continued power is Frank Peretti's *The Oath* (p. 182), in which the stain of sin physically manifests itself on the protagonist Steve Benson's flesh, a device that alludes, consciously or not, to Hester Prynne's famous letter and to her lover Arthur Dimmesdale's physical weight of sin as well.

The Scarlet Letter is actually a historical novel set in the 1600s in the Massachusetts Bay Colony. Ever ambivalent and suggestive, Hawthorne called it a story of "human frailty." The reader certainly sees frailty's results: sexual repression, guilt, and endless punishment following the apparent but secret affair between Hester Prynne and the tormented, hypocritical Reverend Arthur Dimmesdale. And, of course, there's Hester's love child, Pearl, a wild, elfin-like creature, the embodiment of the freedom poor Dimmesdale can never embrace and that Puritanism tries relentlessly to suppress.

Over the fate of all looms the dour, *chilling* Roger Chillingsworth, Hester's husband, a scourge representing legalistic, unforgiving Puritanism. The genius of Hawthorne's complicated masterpiece is that it is not merely a wages-of-sin tale, full of evangelical fervor, but also a profound psychological portrait of the Puritan consciousness—and of a split American consciousness that is with us still.

Hester does not regard herself as a fallen woman, and eventually the scarlet letter she wears becomes a badge of honor. She becomes, in contemporary terms, a feminist heroine, even a kind of Madonna. Dimmesdale, however, is crushed beneath the weight of his sins, and falls to ruin. The real effects of sin take up residence in the psyche of Hawthorne's enigmatic characters, victims not only of an uncompromising moral code but also of their own free wills.

Three years later a much different sort of classic was published; Harriet Beecher Stowe's *Uncle Tom's Cabin*. The novel is a classic slave narrative—the story of the faithful, cruelly used Tom—juxtaposed with a freedom narrative, the story of Eliza and Harry, slaves who escape from Kentucky and make their way through the Quaker-run Underground Railroad to Canada, where they plan to found a new nation in Africa.

Beyond its importance historically, *Uncle Tom's Cabin* is a rip-roaring yarn, and Stowe, a fervent Christian and early feminist, took pains to portray her black characters with depth—in fact, it's her white characters who are one-dimensional. And Uncle Tom, who has survived in popular consciousness mainly as a stereotype of the browbeaten Negro, is not that at all. Rather, he's Christ: humble, kind, and doomed to suffer.

For the record, what Abraham Lincoln actually said to Stowe was, "So you're the little woman who wrote the book that started this great war" (Hedrick 1994). Although the Civil War cannot really be blamed on Stowe, her novel's mix of sentimental wailing and brutal portraits of slavery certainly moved a great many people to oppose slavery, and inflamed others who had a vested interest in it.

Perhaps the most famous novel of all about Jesus, Lew Wallace's *Ben-Hur: A Tale of the Christ,* appeared in 1880 and slowly climbed the bestseller list. It's about a young Jewish nobleman, Judah Ben-Hur, who, through treachery, is deprived of his status and sold into slavery. Later, he seeks revenge and eventually becomes a Christian. The novel breaks the ground for the much better biblical novels to appear later, such as Lloyd C. Douglas's *The Robe* (p. 47). The subject caught the public's fancy. But Wallace's turgid prose, wooden dialogue, and painful slowness in cutting to the chase—or chariot race—make his classic tough sledding for contemporary readers. That this almost unreadable novel remains in print is because of Charlton Heston and his virile, electric performance in William Wyler's 1958 film *Ben Hur.*

Though one of the most important books ever published, Charles Sheldon's *In His Steps* (1896) doesn't show up in literary guides. Its influence was social and religious, rather than literary. Sheldon's novel is almost the sole survivor of scores of novels, or evolved tracts masking as novels, reflecting the social gospel movement of the late nineteenth and early twentieth centuries (Ferré 1988).

The liberation theologians of their day, social gospel advocates held that the terrible waste of human beings found in rapidly industrializing English and American cities could be addressed if only business were to be conducted according to Christian principles. These theologians were activists among the poor: The Salvation Army, founded in England in 1865, is a real-world expression of social gospel.

Sheldon was the pastor of Central Congregational Church in Topeka, where one day he preached a sermon about a young printer, in desperate straits, who comes to a town very much like Topeka and appeals for help to a busy minister. With regret, the minister turns him away. Later, the young man collapses dead in his church, but not before crying out, "Is that what you mean by following in his steps?" The minister, deeply moved, then exhorts his congregation to ask themselves, before every meaningful action, "What would Jesus do?" and to follow in his steps. From this simple message a mighty revival sweeps across the country.

Sheldon worked hard among the poor and to instill the "What would Jesus do?" attitude among businessmen, but he saw little profit from his book. He published it in installments with an uncopyrighted religious magazine, which book publishers raided as Sheldon's movement grew. Even today, the novel has more than one publisher.

The WWJD (What Would Jesus Do?) youth movement of the 1990s is evidence of how relevant Sheldon's classic remains, although more as a model for personal conduct than for social change. Still, from Grace Livingston Hill's novels of the 1920s and 1930s to Catherine Marshall's *Julie* (1984) to Ann Tatlock's *A Room of My Own* (1997), it's clear that we will always have with us fiction advocating Christian activism among the poor. (See chapter 11, the section "Pastors.")

Harold Bell Wright's *The Shepherd of the Hills* (1904) was a hybrid of the social gospel novel and the western. It's about a sad old easterner, Daniel Howitt, who comes to the Missouri Ozarks in the late nineteenth century to take up the simple life of a shepherd. Slowly, the reader learns he's on a mission, to heal a wrong he committed long before. In the process, he puts things right in other respects as well, dispensing his Christ-like wisdom in moralistic speeches and selfless good deeds. The novel remains popular because of its continued celebration in a Branson theme park and has been filmed several times, most enduringly in 1941. John Wayne starred as Young Matt, the strapping lad that old Dan befriends; the director was Henry Hathaway.

Wright's influence is small, however, compared to that of Grace Livingston Hill, an important pioneer who might be said to have invented the Christian romance. In the years before Janette Oke made her mark, Christian romance readers lamented that there was nothing to read but Grace Livingston Hill, and they were nearly right. There were Pearl Buck and Beth Streeter Aldrich perhaps, whose works were uplifting and about women, but only Hill combined love stories with an overtly Christian message.

Although it is true that all of Grace Livingston Hill's novels have a clear gospel message, it is not true, as some readers say, that they all read the same. Early in her long career—from the turn of the twentieth century through much of 1946—she drew from family stories and on occasion used men as her protagonists (as in her spy novel, *The Best Man,* published in 1914).

But she is best known as a writer of Horatio Alger, Jr. types of tales for women. A young woman, usually poor, marries a rich young man who is a little in need of reforming; as if instinctively, the young man responds to the heroine's modesty and spiritual beauty. The plot does not take long to reveal itself. In the very first scene of *White Orchids* (1935), Camilla Chrystie's beat-up little car is wrecked by a veering truck. Luckily, handsome, rich Jeffrey Wainwright is passing in his fancy automobile and carries away poor Camilla to the bedside of her dying mother, to whom Camilla was carrying medicine.

Alternatively, there's *The Prodigal Girl* (1929), in which a spoiled rich girl embraces the wicked world (Hill hated the flappers of the 1920s, with their heavy makeup, short skirts, and dubious morality) and descends into ruin both financially and spiritually. She crawls home, where, exactly as in the New Testament parable, her family receives her with joy.

Appropriately for such fare, the style is breathless, drawing from Hill's inexhaustible store of adjectives and exclamation points. But it's worth noting that she was something of a rags-to-riches tale herself. The daughter of a Presbyterian minister, she married a Presbyterian minister and settled into the role of pastor's wife in Germantown, Pennsylvania. Then her husband died of appendicitis, leaving Hill with two young girls to raise, and the necessity to make a living. A hard-working, courageous woman, Hill literally wrote herself out of poverty.

Almost 20 years later, when she was a financial success and deeply involved both in her writing and church work, she married again. The marriage was a quick failure, resulting in a lifelong separation because Hill did not believe in divorce. Ironically, the woman who held out the Holy Grail of marriage for so many young women herself had no luck with it, and effectively became a spinster (Karr 1948).

Altogether, she wrote 117 novels, and the formulas she laid down in the 1920s and 1930s, when she did her best-known work and was at her most prolific, are still used by today's evangelical writers. If only for her quaintness, she is still worth reading, though in small and infrequent doses.

Barbour Publications, which directs its publications to an audience of older, conservative women, issues Hill romances periodically. Otherwise, they are out of print.

One would be remiss not to mention Sinclair Lewis's *Elmer Gantry,* first published in 1927. "Elmer Gantry was drunk," begins Lewis's satire of a traveling evangelist who will be a Methodist or a Baptist, depending on the money and the sex. Lots of small-town hypocrites—Lewis's specialty—also come in for a drubbing in this classic that rings as true as ever. The novel caused an uproar, and other major novelists put forth their own versions; for example, Erskine Caldwell with *Journeyman* (1938). Burt Lancaster played Elmer in the 1960 film, and Jean Simmons played Sister Sharon Falconer, the passionate evangelist he corrupts.

WORLD CLASSICS

The following are merely those best-known novels that Christian fiction readers—and, indeed, general readers—remain interested in.

Dostoevsky, Fyodor. *The Brothers Karamazov.* 1880. (Many editions.)

There's a murder at the heart of Dostoevsky's greatest novel, and a courtroom drama, both prefiguring, as does *Crime and Punishment* in a more direct way, the contemporary crime novel. But long before the murder of old Karamazov, a figure of almost pure lust who clearly deserves murdering, we meet the brothers. There's Alyosha, the saintly one and the embodiment of all that Dostoevsky tried to believe in; Dmitri, the romantic one, hot tempered, reckless, desperate, even mad; Ivan, the cool intellectual whose logic cannot save him; and Smerdyakov, the epileptic, nihilistic, weak result of old Karamazov's rape of an idiot servant girl. Together, they represent philosophical stances, which Dostoevesky works out on many planes through the interactions of serfs, tradespeople, and courtesans; even the Devil, a drab, modest, but clever middle-age man, rather down on his luck, makes an appearance in one of Dostoevsky's rare humorous asides. A masterpiece on the order of *Moby Dick, The Brothers Karamazov* is not easy reading. It's best reserved for a long trip or a series of frigid winter nights. Slowly, it grabs you and won't let you go.

The Idiot. 1869. (Many editions.)

Dostoevsky's profound and difficult novel, his personal favorite, is steeped deeply in the Russian Orthodox faith to which Dostoevsky himself turned during his years in prison. It's the story of an entirely good man, a hero, the Christlike Prince Myshkin. Like Jesus, he is loved by mortal women, the extraordinary Nastasya, consumed with love (for Myshkin's perfection) and hate (that she cannot corrupt him) and the not necessarily simpler, but devoted Aglaia. Myshkin marries neither; he is not of the flesh. In fact, he is too good for the world. His suffering and humility, his goodness of heart, prove inadequate weapons before evil, and he descends into a divine idiocy.

Sienkiewicz, Henryk. *Quo Vadis.* 1895. (Many editions.)

Sienkiewicz's scenes of the martyrdom of Christians in the Coliseum are graphic even by contemporary standards. They viscerally drive home Sienkiewicz's portrait of the rapacious Romans as ruled by Nero, and of the passive Christians who win by not fighting. (They also play out an allegory of the Russian persecution of Poles in Sienkiewicz's time.) But the principal story is of Lygia, a Christian, and Marcus Vinicius, a soldier. Lygia loves Vinicius but loves Christ more, whereas Vinicius, a young, impetuous noble, is gentled by Lygia and her faith. Both characters are touching and believable, but the vain and fickle Nero, who sets Rome afire as a sort of performance piece (and then blames it on the Christians), is brilliantly rendered; and Nero's clever nemesis, Petronius, is as refined, cynical, debauched, and ultimately noble a character as any ever conceived. *Quo Vadis* means "Where are you going?" and indeed Sienkiewicz does examine where we go in life, and where our choices lead us, in a profound and timeless manner.

The novel has been filmed many times; the best-known version was released in 1951 and stars Robert Tayler as Marcus Vinicius, Deborah Kerr as Lygia, and Peter Ustinov as the unctuous, dangerous Nero. The director was Mervyn LeRoy.

Stendhal (pseudonym of Marie Henri Beyle). *The Red and the Black.* 1830. (Many editions.)

Julien Sorel, a carpenter's son, has ambitions to power. But in the post-Napoleonic France of the 1830s, men rise to power in the State (the Black) through the accident of their birth or through the Church (the Red). Thus, Julien becomes a priest and seemingly a smart, devout one. Actually, he is a hypocrite, using the Church to meet wellborn women, with whom he sleeps, in hopes of advancing in society. His plan works but with dire consequences, giving occasion for Stendhal's scathing critique of French society, and giving impetus to the stark realism that was to come later from writers such as Flaubert and Zola.

Chapter 4

Biblical Fiction

For most of the twentieth century, biblical fiction was what was meant by "Christian fiction." *The Robe,* for example, and *Dear and Glorious Physician,* became bestsellers as well as widely popular films, and were part of the mainstream culture.

Biblical fiction remains vital, and some of the field's best, most deeply felt writing can be found here. Perhaps because writers are working with the essence of their faith, they write closest to the heart, and are less inclined to lean on formulas. Even so, biblical fiction is now a clear subgenre of Christian fiction, and its sales are dwarfed by Christian romances, which dominate the field.

Many mainstream writers, from Robert Graves to Taylor Caldwell, have retold Bible stories. Evangelical writers, such as Angela Elwell Hunt and Francine Rivers, carry on their tradition, but interesting mainstream contributions still appear: for example, Norman Mailer's *The Gospel According to the Son* and Anita Diamant's *The Red Tent* (both discussed in this chapter).

At the least, biblical fiction is an entertaining way to better acquaint oneself with the Bible because writers of biblical fiction are generally careful with their scholarship.

OLD TESTAMENT

AUSTIN, LYNN M.

✒ *CHRONICLES OF THE KINGS*
Set about 700 years before the birth of Christ, Austin's account of Jews as a people in bondage to the Assyrians, featuring the rise of King Hezekiah, is full of clever characterizations and court intrigue.

YA *The Lord Is My Strength.* 1995. Beacon Hill, paper. 206 pp. ISBN 0-8341-1538-7.
The weak King Ahaz plots to sacrifice his son, Hezekiah, while Hezekiah's mother, Abijah, fights for his life.

The Lord Is My Song. 1996. Beacon Hill, paper. 304 pp. ISBN 0-8341-1602-2.
Hezekiah becomes king of Judah and sings God's praises, but not everyone is happy with his brand of piety in the sequel to *The Lord Is My Strength.*

The Lord Is My Salvation. 1996. Beacon Hill, paper. 272 pp. ISBN 0-8341-1603-0.
Hezekiah faces crises of the state and in his household in the third entry of Chronicles of the Kings. His wife, confronting infertility, embarks on ungodly measures, and gets everyone in trouble.

YA **My Father's God.** 1997. Beacon Hill, paper. 283 pp. ISBN 0-8341-1675-8.
Hezekiah's son, Manasseh, grows up with Joshua, son of a prominent man of court. But the friends fall apart when Manasseh departs from the true faith and persecutes Joshua's family in the fourth entry of Chronicles of the Kings.

Among the Gods. 1998. Beacon Hill, paper. 300 pp. ISBN 0-83411733-9.
In the last volume of Chronicles of the Kings, Joshua makes a home for himself in Egypt, leading his exiled people, the Levites. King Manasseh descends further into corruption, until finally the Kingdom of Judah is overwhelmed from without, and Manasseh is imprisoned.

★ **BUECHNER, FREDERICK.** *Son of Laughter.* **1993. HarperCollins. 274 pp. ISBN 0-06-250116-X.**
An exquisite stylist, Buechner evokes the earthy, semi-nomadic, nearly pagan lifestyle of the Israelites in this poetic rendering of Jacob, son of Isaac (whose name means laughter). Although Buechner follows the biblical account, he brings it to life with sensory imagery so vivid that his setting seems like another planet. Still, Jacob is very much a character, mourning for Joseph who is sold into slavery, giving his version of the bully Esau's bargaining over porridge.

CARD, ORSON SCOTT

WOMEN OF GENESIS

★ **Sarah.** 2000. Deseret (Shadow Mountain). 400 pp. ISBN 1-57008-994-9.
Sarah comes intimately to life as the sacrificing, tough, wise wife of Abraham and mother of Isaac in Card's skillful rendering. He gives Sarah an older sister, the vain and materialist Qira, nearly Sarah's opposite. Qira becomes Lot's wife and is almost as prominent as Sarah in the narrative. Sarah is Abraham's unswervingly loyal wife even when he dallies with Hagar, but that doesn't keep her from stating her point of view. In essence, she has the faith of Abraham, even though the Lord's blessings are few. In an afterword, Card discusses some of the liberties he took with the tantalizing but often puzzling Genesis account, and why. He also gives one of his sources as the Mormon scripture, *The Pearl of Great Price,* which may distress some evangelical readers. The second novel in the series will be about Rebecca, wife of Isaac. **Discussion**

CARDWELL, BROWN. *Jericho.* 2001. Panda. 344pp. ISBN 0-75960-711-7.
From biblical, Jewish, and archeological accounts, Cardwell admirably fashions life in ancient Jericho a little before the walls come tumbling down. For the most part, she tells the story of Rahab, not a prostitute in this rendering but a feminist heroine, striving to maintain her independence and dignity as a weaver and dye maker in a bazaar dominated by a guild of males. Joshua's two spies, Jochtar and Eberon, visit Jericho, and Rahab falls in love with Jochtar after he saves her life. A rebel about to be turned into an outcast by the political machinations of the guild, Rahab aids the enemy she loves.

★ **COELHO, PAULO.** *The Fifth Mountain.* **1998. Tr. by Clifford E. Landers. 1998. HarperFlamingo. 244 pp. ISBN 0-06-017544-3.**

When Queen Jezebel declares that all Israelites must worship Baal and that every prophet of the One God must be killed, the young prophet Elijah concludes that his days are numbered. But an angel appears to him and sends him on a long journey into the Phoenician homeland of Jezebel, where, on the fifth mountain, Baal supposedly dwells. Elijah's lonely journey into the land of the enemy becomes a great spiritual quest, full of miracles, fear, and wisdom, with Israel's fate in the balance.

★ **DIAMANT, ANITA.** *The Red Tent.* **1997. St. Martin's. 271pp. ISBN 0-312-16978-7.**

According to the brief account in Genesis, Diamant's heroine Dinah was the only daughter of Jacob. Through trickery, her brothers cornered the Canaanites and murdered them in revenge for Dinah's rape. In Diamont's version there is no rape. Diamont's Dinah is in love with a handsome Canaanite; by killing him, her brothers betray her. She flees to Egypt, where eventually she establishes herself as a midwife. As Dinah relates her story, she also brings to life Rachel, Leah, Jacob, and Esau. Her story—and every woman's story—is told in the red tent, where women sequester themselves during menstruation and childbirth. In their frankness and attitude toward men, Diamant's biblical women seem contemporary, and, possibly because of that, *The Red Tent* has been enormously popular with women. It is often used in book discussion groups. **▪Discussion▪**

RIVERS, FRANCINE

◆X *LINEAGE OF GRACE* **▪Discussion▪**

A departure for the highly regarded Rivers, these novellas tell of strong biblical women, each in the lineage of Christ, each illustrating some concept of courageous faith—and each followed by lengthy study guides for discussion groups.

Unveiled. 2000. Tyndale. 167 pp. ISBN 0-8423-1947-6.

Tamar, the heroine of *Unveiled,* was the Canaanite woman given in marriage to the house of Judah whose heart slowly turned to the God of the Hebrews. Judah, in particular, is well drawn as the weak patriarch plagued with guilt over the fate of his brother, Joseph. Er and Onan, Tamar's husbands who die from the Lord's wrath before she can conceive, are simply monsters, and Rivers has little patience with them. In Rivers's hands, the story is compelling enough, though the story is a quaint one and hard to draw much from in the way of moral instruction.

 Unashamed. 2000. Tyndale. 165 pp. ISBN 0-8423-3596-X.

Unashamed tells the story of Rahab, a prostitute from the book of Joshua who gave shelter to Israelite spies for the promise that she'd be spared. When Jericho fell, she went to live among the enemy. Though it departs from biblical clues, Cardwell's *Jericho* (discussed previously) is a more entertaining version of this story.

Unshaken. 2001. Tyndale. 175 pp. ISBN 0-8423-3597-8.

The beautiful, simple story of Ruth, faithful to God and duty despite privation, is told in *Unshaken.* Rivers makes a bit more of this Moabite's devotion to the Israelite god than the Book of Ruth actually suggests, and a bit more of the love between Ruth and Boaz because Boaz, too, was motivated by duty. In any case, Rivers's fleshing out of Ruth's relationship to her mother, to her mother-in-law (Naomi), and of course to Boaz, are entertaining and vivid.

Unspoken. 2001. Tyndale. 165 pp. ISBN 0-8423-3598-6.
Rivers turns in an undistinguished version of Bathsheba's oft-told story, marrying the trappings of a genre romance with a sanctimonious tone as her heroine courses through adultery and betrayal and yet finds grace through repentance. On the other hand—and as usual—Rivers's style is agreeably unadorned, and her passion shines through. Readers should try Louis DeWohl's *David of Jerusalem* (p. 37) for an interesting variation on Rivers's effort.

Unafraid. 2001. Tyndale. 165 pp. ISBN 0-8423-3599-4.
In the final entry of her Lineage of Grace series, Rivers takes on the most revered of biblical women: Mary, the mother of Jesus. Because the New Testament says nothing on the boyhood of Jesus, some readers may be offended by Rivers's fabrications of Mary's young motherhood and Jesus's precocious ways. Rivers's insistence that Mary was an ordinary—in fact, a willful and not entirely likable—person may prove offensive to Catholics. Rivers is trying hard here, however, to create a memorable portrait. Does she succeed? Not entirely, and readers may find more sustenance in Marjorie Holmes's *Two from Galilee* (p. 39), on the whole a more tender story, and with a more intuitive feel for Mary's relationship with Joseph.

SLAUGHTER, FRANK. *The Song of Ruth.* **1954. Doubleday. (Out of print.)**
Slaughter's popular rendering of Ruth, the "steadfast one," is a smooth alternative to Rivers's more pious *Unshaken* (discussed previously).

✦ ★ TRAYLOR, ELLEN GUNDERSON. *Jerusalem—The City of God.* **1995. Harvest House, paper. 450 pp. ISBN 1-56507-985-8.**
Jerusalem is a massive historical treatment of Jerusalem from prehistoric geology through the struggles of refugees in contemporary Israel. It's too much history to try to cover, perhaps, but much of it is compelling, particularly the novella within the novel that retells the oft-told story of David and Bathsheba. In Traylor's rendering, David is mired in an unhappy marriage, and Bathsheba conspires with her maid for the king to witness her infamous rooftop bath.

✦ ★ TRAYLOR, ELLEN GUNDERSON. *Melchizedek.* **1997. Harvest, paper. 224 pp. ISBN 1-56507-528-5.**
Not much is known about the priest and king of ancient Salem, precursor to Jerusalem. In Traylor's hands he's a mysterious, incalculably old figure who rhapsodizes on mythic beings and primitive religions to his rapt young listener, Avi. There's Melchizedek's superb retelling of the story of Nimrod and his Tower of Babel, accurate as it can be but also fanciful, a fairy tale. Throughout, Traylor's strong writing and sense of myth keep readers as spellbound as Avi.

✦ ★ WANGERIN, WALTER. *The Book of God: The Bible As Novel.* **1996. Zondervan. 864pp. ISBN 0-310-20005-9.**

Wangerin's widely admired talents shine brightest in his 300-page synthesis of the Gospels. He poetically captures the courtship of a small-town couple named Mary and Joseph, the birth of their son, and the rise, political repression, and crucifixion of a Messiah. Fictionalizing the entire Old Testament proves daunting even for Wangerin, but his version of Abraham and

Sarah's story is evocative and even rather amusing as he conjures up the dialogue between this old married couple concerning Abraham's potential assignation with Hagar. **Discussion**

David

DE WOHL, LOUIS. *David of Jerusalem*. 1965. Doubleday. (Out of print.)

De Wohl emphasizes the overwhelming power of David: not quite brutal but not to be denied. His Bathsheba is young, innocent, and compliant rather than complicit.

HAWKINS, KATHY

◀❯ *HEART OF ZION*

> ***Heart of a Stranger.*** 1996. Kregel, paper. 301 pp. ISBN 0-8254-2867-X.
> Hawkins portrays the court of David when he was about 50 years old, and when Bathsheba was around 20, but their famous affair is merely the backdrop for the story of his *Gibborim,* or those soldiers closest to him, almost body-guards. The *Gibborim* include not only Bathsheba's unfortunate husband, Uriah, but also a number of extra-biblical characters, with a focus on Ailea and Jonathan. Ailea is a young Aramean woman, the tomboy daughter of a general who becomes the captive bride of Jonathan, one of the *Gibborim.*

> ***The Desires of the Heart.*** 1998. Kregel, paper. 276 pp. ISBN 0-8254-2871-8.
> Ailea and Jonathan live through their troubled but eventually happy marriage as the sometimes violent intrigues of David's kingdom play out in the background.

> ***The Heart of a Lion.*** 1998. Kregel, paper. 336 pp. ISBN 0-8254-2872-6.
> Jonathan and Ailea's children gather with their parents when Jonathan's father, the "Rab" or wise man, dies; the Rab calls forth Micah, Jonathan and Ailea's son, to throw off his vow against violence and undertake an important mission for the Hebrews, something he finds difficult to do.

SLAUGHTER, FRANK, G. *David*. 1962. (Out of print.)

A bestseller in its day, Slaughter's *David* is faithful to the biblical account, chronicling David's life from shepherding days through his consolidation of kingly power. Long passages never rise above flat explication, but others are immensely entertaining, in particular the dramatic rendering of David's battle with Goliath.

Egyptian Captivity

CARD, ORSON SCOTT. *Stone Tables*. 1998. Deseret. 432 pp. ISBN 1-57345-115-0.

While serving as a missionary in Brazil, science fiction writer Card wrote a play based on the Egyptian flight from Egypt. Many years later, he wrote this novel telling the same story. He draws out the military side of Moses, emphasizing that he was an Egyptian general as well as the leader of his persecuted people. Some of his Mormon theology may put off evangelicals, but he makes flesh and blood of Moses. His minor characters, such as Zeporah, his devout betrothed; Aaron, his ambitious brother; and the shrewd Hapshepsut, his adopted mother, are also ably drawn.

HUNT, ANGELA ELWELL

◆✖★ *ALONG THE ANCIENT RIVER SERIES*

Dreamers. 1996. Bethany, paper. 400 pp. ISBN 1-55661-607-4.
Hunt chronicles the early history of God's chosen people in this popular trilogy, offering, in the first volume, the Egyptian point of view through the eyes of Tuya, a slave and companion to a princess who falls in love with Joseph.

Brothers. 1997. Bethany, paper. 368 pp. ISBN 1-55661-608-2.
In the sequel to *Dreamers,* set about 22 years later, Joseph has become the powerful and prosperous leader of his people. He turns the tables on the brothers who sold him into slavery when, stricken by famine, they come to him. Romance arises when Joseph confines the brash Simeon to teach him some manners; his restless spirit appeals to Mandisa, a widow assigned to serve him.

Journey. 1997. Bethany, paper. 384 pp. ISBN 1-55661-609-0.
The patriarch Jacob gives his blessing to Ephraim rather than Manasseh in the last volume of Hunt's trilogy, igniting a rivalry that divides the tribe of Israel far into the future.

◆✖ ★ **LANDORF, JOYCE.** *Joseph.* **1980. (Out of print.)**
Landorf follows the familiar story of Joseph, but her manner of telling is unusually engaging. She takes the points of view of women who loved Joseph: his mother, Rachel; his stepmother, Leah; his sister-in-law, Sherah; his wife, Asenath; and the jealous Khnumet, wife of an eminent Egyptian official who attempts to seduce Joseph and who brings him grief when he refuses her. Landorf's ancient Egyptian setting is well realized, and her women are convincing, not merely as biblical stick figures but also as real, imperfect people.

RAY, BRENDA. *The Midwife's Song.* **2000. Karmichael, paper. 256 pp. ISBN 0-9653966-8-1.**
Puah, an ancient Hebrew midwife, recalls her youth when she saved the infant Moses, even though Pharoah's decree against protecting newborn Hebrew males carried the penalty of death. In her old age, Puah understands that her bravery was the vital first step in her people's long march to freedom.

WHITTEN, LESLIE H., JR. *Moses: The Lost Book of the Bible.* **1999. New Millennium. 270 pp. ISBN 1-893224-03-1.**
Though his style lacks the pungency of Frederick Buechner's *Son of Laughter* (discussed previously) or the passion of Orson Scott Card's version of the same story, *Stone Tables* (discussed previously), Whitten does manufacture a convincing historical air—as if, indeed, his story were the lost book of the Bible it purports to be—in his tale of Moses as told by Zetes, a wandering merchant who, almost by mistake, saves Moses's life.

NEW TESTAMENT

Life of Jesus

ASHCROFT, MARY ELLEN. *The Magdalene Gospel.* **1995. Doubleday. 128 pp. ISBN 0-385-47855-0.**
A fine source for study groups, *The Magdalene Gospel* gives voice to the women of the Gospels—Salome, Joanna, Martha, Lydia, and particularly, Mary Magdalene. Together, they evoke the

desperate sadness of the Crucifixion and the subsequent triumph of the Resurrection. Though never pedantic, Ashcroft intersperses scriptural references to show the basis of her careful but passionate scenes. **⬛Discussion**

CALDWELL, TAYLOR. *I, Judas.* 1977. (Out of print.)

Caldwell tells the life story of Judas in his own words in this diverting exercise, imagining his life before he knew Jesus, departing somewhat from Gospel accounts afterward. Judas follows Jesus because he was a Zealot opposing the rule of Rome; he is never sure if Jesus is the Messiah but begins to wonder. He is not quite the villain of popular myth, but neither is he a pleasant man: He is arrogant, impetuous, lascivious, and corruptible.

CARSE, JAMES P. *The Gospel of the Beloved Disciple.* 1997. HarperSanFrancisco. 144 pp. ISBN 0-06-061576-1.

Carse offers an alternative gospel, full of parables and spare wisdom, retelling Jesus' birth, ministry, trial, and Crucifixion from a woman's point of view—a Samaritan woman and, according to her, Jesus' most important influence. **⬛Discussion**

CRACE, JIM. *Quarantine.* 1997. Farrar. 243 pp. ISBN 0-374-23962-2.

Jesus does not survive his 40-day trial in the wilderness in this gospel variant, nor is he necessarily the Messiah. He is beset with various temptations, devilish enough, but altogether terrestrial. At last, he sinks into a final madness born of his hunger, though Crace, perhaps overly impressed that no human being could survive 40 days of fasting in combination with physical trial, does not quite dismiss the possibility of resurrection.

FORTNEY, STEVEN. *The Thomas Jesus.* 2000. Waubesa. 232 pp. ISBN 1878569-65-1.

Fortney, an American Buddhist, was much under the influence of the Jesus Seminar in this first novel. The Jesus Seminar (http://religion.rutgers.edu/jseminar), loosely associated with the religion department at Rutgers University, has devoted its efforts to finding consensus on what can be verified historically about Jesus. Fortney's portrait, seen through the eyes of the apostle Thomas, will not please evangelical readers; Jesus is overtly heterosexual, and he's something of a madman. Even so, doubting Thomas does not doubt that Jesus is divine.

GRAVES, ROBERT. *King Jesus.* 1946. Farrar, paper. 424 pp. ISBN 0-374-51664-2.

Some may see Graves as a better libertine than Christian, and his novel should be a New Age classic for its sharp scrutiny of Judeo–Christian patriarchy and Graves's celebration of his own version of goddess theology. But after he's flexed his scholarly muscles and weighed in splendidly on the politics of King Herod's court, he writes a most respectful gospel, ostensibly from the point of view of Greek historian Agabus the Decapolitan, gathering his objective thoughts some 50 years after the Crucifixion.

HOLMES, MARJORIE

◆✗ *Two from Galilee.* 1972. (Out of print.)

Nonfiction inspirational writer Holmes wrote this bestselling trilogy reverentially, but with the intention of revealing the ordinary, human side of Jesus and those close to him. Indeed, Jesus, his parents, and his followers seem contemporary, though Holmes's novels are well researched and she is faithful to New Testament accounts, such as they are, in dealing with the love between Mary and Joseph, the "two from Galilee."

◀️✝★ *Three from Galilee: The Young Man from Nazareth.* 1985. (Out of print.)
In the sequel to *Two from Galilee*, Holmes imagines the boyhood and young manhood of Jesus, which goes all but unmentioned in the Gospels and has rarely been treated in fiction.

◀️✝ *The Messiah.* 1987. (Out of print.)
The conclusion to Holmes's trilogy resembles other conservative accounts of the ministry and Crucifixion of Jesus, such as Frank Slaughter's *The Crown and the Cross* (discussed later). But although she adheres closely to Gospel accounts, she tells her story from the point of view of Jesus, once again using her uniquely intimate approach.

JOHNSON, SKIP. *The Gospel of Yeshua.* 2001. Corinthian. 224 pp. ISBN 1-0929175-03-5.
Relying on scholarship to sort out the contradictions between John and the Synoptic Gospels, and making some educated guesses to fill gaps, Johnson tells in simple but affecting prose the straightforward story of Jesus the great teacher. His effort is reminiscent of other efforts to tell the gospel story with scholarly precision: Fulton Oursler's *The Greatest Story Ever Told* and Walter Wangerin's *Book of God* (both discussed later).

★ KAZANTZAKIS, NIKOS. *The Last Temptation of Christ.* 1960. Tr. by P. A. Bien. Simon & Schuster/Touchstone, paper. 506 pp. ISBN 0-671-67257-6.
The battle within every human between the spirit and the flesh fascinated Kazantkakis, the Greek philosopher/novelist whose friends included Henri Bergson and Albert Schweitzer. The supposed heresy of his tale of Jesus, which in large measure follows the gospel accounts, comes, in a minor way, from his fascinating portrait of Judas, who is Jesus' most intimate confidant, and betrays his master only because it is a necessary part of the Crucifixion—and from his rendering of the resurrection of Lazerus, who is restored to life but not to good health.

In larger measure, objections rose because of Jesus' refusal to be crucified. He marries Mary Magdalene instead, and leads a pleasant pastoral life. This alternative history turns out to be a fantasy that Jesus entertains while dying on the cross, a last sweet temptation of Satan's, which Jesus, in reverie, rejects. To become divine, in Kazantkakis's view, Jesus had to overcome the temptations of power, family, and love. Sometimes, in overcoming temptation, he had to succumb.

Martin Scorcese's 1988 film of the novel, starring Willem Dafoe as Jesus, Harvey Keitel as Judas, and Barbara Hershey as Mary Magdalene, was faithful to Kazantkakis's subtle intent. Nonetheless, particularly because of the love scenes between Jesus and Mary, some evangelicals were outraged and mounted a national campaign to ban or boycott the film.   ■Discussion■

◀️✝ ★ LANDORF, JOYCE. *I Came to Love You Late.* 1977. Revell. (Out of print.)
Landorf's beautiful title comes from a line of St. Augustine's poetry: "Late have I loved thee." It summarizes Martha, a pragmatic woman so caught up in care for her ailing brother, Lazerus, that she nearly misses the growing importance of her frequent houseguest, Jesus. Jesus is a likable, even wise, man, but it is not until Lazerus is raised from the dead, and the final days of Jesus' life come upon her in a rush, that Martha's innate decency and tragically latent faith become one.

LAWRENCE, D. H. *The Man Who Died.* 1929. Ecco. 101 pp. ISBN 0-88001-353-2.
Lawrence's last novel is a strange parable of Jesus after his crucifixion, when he entertains doubts about his mission on Earth and begins an affair with a priestess of Isis.

LUND, GERALD N.

THE KINGDOM AND THE CROWN

Leaning somewhat on the plots of *Ben Hur* and *The Robe,* Lund begins his ambitious epic with the story of David ben Joseph, a merchant who, unlike others, is looking for signs of the Messiah, and quickly recognizes Jesus for what he is. Lund also treats the Roman authority in depth, and Jesus himself. Sequels will cover the ministry of Jesus and the adventures of the apostles.

> *Fishers of Men.* Deseret (Shadow Mountain). 640 pp. ISBN 1-57345-820-1.

> *Come Unto Me.* Deseret (Shadow Mountain). 640 pp. ISBN 1-57008-714-8.

★ **MAILER, NORMAN.** *The Gospel According to the Son.* **1997. Random. 242 pp. ISBN 0-679-45783-6.**

Assuming the voice of Jesus might seem to be another example of Mailer's audaciousness, but he turns in a bravura performance. Synthesizing historical accounts and the gospel according to John, he strives mightily to rectify errors and embellishments in accounts of Jesus, offering a Jesus sitting on the right hand of God, humble and loving, grieving over the monstrous evil that dominated the 2,000 years following his death, but hopeful that good may still triumph.

MEYER, GABRIEL. *The Gospel of Joseph.* **1994. Crossroad. 201 pp. ISBN 0-8245-1406-8.**

Though Meyer's attempts to interject suspense into the discovery of Joseph's epistles on his holy son's childhood wear thin, his scholarship and mock scholarship form a clever, insightful portrait of the young Jesus as a middle-class prodigy, already an inventor of revolutionary parables.

MOORCOCK, MICHAEL. *Behold the Man.* **1966. MoJo Press, paper. 130 pp. ISBN 1-885418-05-1.**

See discussion in chapter 9, "Fantasy and Science Fiction."

OURSLER, FULTON. *The Greatest Story Ever Told.* **1989. (Originally published in 1949.) Image Books, paper. 299 pp. ISBN 0-385-08028-X.**

Oursler's novel, or New Testament stories in plain English and in sequence, is derived from ABC radio broadcasts in the early 1940s. Oursler reconciles the chronological conflicts of the Gospels and synthesizes differing versions of the major events in Jesus' life, scrupulously avoiding any interpretation other than his assumption that the Gospels are divinely inspired.

PARK, PAUL. *The Gospel of Corax.* **1996. Soho. 297 pp. ISBN 1-56947-061-8.**

Corax, a runaway slave and possibly a murderer, meets Jesus and the two go adventuring into the Himalayas, where Corax's father is from, in this highly fanciful, sometimes profane, rendering of the story of Jesus.

PEVEHOUSE, DOLORES. *I, the Christ.* **2000. Hampton Roads, paper. 320 pp. ISBN 1-57174-177-1.**

>   Like Candide or Gulliver, young Jesus is a wanderer in Pevehouse's episodic novel, except that his encounters in Tibet, Egypt, India, and Israel are entirely philosophical, introducing Jesus to Buddhism and Zoroastrianism but never establishing him as a flesh-and-blood character. The tale's most dramatic moments come when Jesus raises himself from the dead and when Jewish priests recognize him as the Christ. But his intention to reveal to the masses the immediacy and universality of God alienates him from established Judaism, and he becomes a doomed prophet.

★ **SARAMAGO, JOSE.** *The Gospel According to Jesus Christ.* **1994. Tr. by Giovanni Pontiero. Harcourt. 377 pp. ISBN 0-15-136700-0.**

>   Jesus' awful destiny is filtered through Saramago's view of a vengeful and mocking God, most clearly manifest in the extraordinary dialogues between God, Satan, and Jesus during Jesus' sojourn in the desert. Reading, at least in translation, much like Faulkner, with his long paragraphs and multilayered sentences, Saramago's best-known work is a sly, mystical masterpiece of magical realism. It's full of the smells of men, women, and animals in an ancient land; days of work to the point of exhaustion; and superstitions that can turn on the innocent without warning, dooming them. Jesus is a sweet, naive young man, who embarks on the puzzling path toward wisdom, and yet his destiny is not in his own hands; he is a lamb bound for slaughter. He is also a normal young man curious about women, and in scenes of great sensuality but also of innocence and beauty, finds love in the arms of Mary Magdalene. He is profoundly changed, perhaps even redeemed. Saramago, winner of the Nobel Prize in 1998, has written a dark masterpiece that seems to have escaped the wrath of book banners in the United States, perhaps because his style is so difficult, hardly designed to inflame masses.

SLAUGHTER, FRANK G. *The Crown and the Cross: The Life of Christ.* **1959. (Out of print.)**

>   Slaughter uses the lowly servant of a Pharisee, Jonas, as a point-of-view character. Contriving for him to appear in the vicinity of every major setting—including both the Nativity and the Crucifixion—can prove awkward. But this is a quibble, for on balance Slaughter is slavishly attentive to New Testament accounts. If a reader seeks a completely orthodox fictionalization of the Gospels, this is the one.

VIDAL, GORE. *Live from Golgotha.* **1992. Random.**

>   See discussion in chapter 9, "Fantasy and Science Fiction."

WALLACE, LEW. *Ben-Hur: A Tale of the Christ.* **1880.**

>   See discussion in chapter 3, "Christian Classics."

WATTS, MURRAY. *The Miracle Maker.* **2000. Hodder & Stoughton, dist. by Trafalgar Square, paper. 299 pp. ISBN 0-340-73563-5.**

>   Watts novelizes the animated film of the same title, telling the story of Jesus from the point of view of a young girl, Tamar.

Crucifixion

AURELIO, JOHN R. *Earth Stories: Signs of God's Love and Mystery.* 1997. Continuum. 132 pp. ISBN 0-8264-0949-0.

Aurelio's subtle collection of parables and fables is as much about the mystery of God as His love. In his fable of a man who dreams he has killed a rare butterfly for the sake of science, then encounters the actual butterfly, the moral turns out to be, "What is sometimes deemed virtue may just be the absence of temptation." His long parable, "The Leper," tells the ironic, extra-biblical tale of a man whose strange birthmark allows a rival to force him into a leper's exile. When Jesus heals actual lepers, the man's birthmark also disappears, and he is free to pursue revenge upon his rival. Instead, moved by the Crucifixion, he forgives his enemy. **Discussion**

BLYTHE, LEGETTE. *Bold Galilean.* 1948. (Out of print.)

Blythe tells the story of Christ from his final weeks through his Resurrection from the points of view of two Romans: the centurion Gaius, who respects the traditions of Jewish law, but respects the might of the sword even more; and his rich friend Marcus, who feels anything can be bought with money, even, or perhaps especially, love. Both are proven wrong through the preaching and example of Jesus, and become Christians. Blythe constructs some provocative subplots: Judas makes his famous bargain with Caiaphas, the Jewish high priest, and Marcus falls in love with Mary Magdalene.

H. D. *Pilate's Wife.* 2000. New Directions, paper. 135 pp. ISBN 0-8112-1433-8.

Somewhat in the spirit of D. H. Lawrence's *The Man Who Died,* the famous poet (Hilda Doolittle) wrote this gospel variant throughout her lifetime, but was never able to publish it. Matthew 27:19 speaks of Pilate's wife and her plea of mercifulness as Jesus is brought to trial. H. D. builds her novella around the passage, devising, out of Veronica's patrician boredom, a scheme for Jesus to escape crucifixion.

★ **LLITERAS, D. S.** *Judas the Gentile.* 1999. Hampton Roads. 240 pp. ISBN 1-57174-144-5.

Lliteras portrays with almost unbearable intimacy the agony of Judas, who must at last confront the lies he has told himself. He believed that Jesus should have been a political revolutionary, actively fighting against Roman tyranny. In the end, his turmoil is all the worse because he at last understands that he has aided in slaying the Son of God. Lliteras is a subtle stylist, writing in compact sentences and with punchy, realistic dialogue reminiscent of Ernest Hemingway. The powerful result is in no way a gospel variant, but it's raw, understated, and full of Judas's rationalizations. It is so honest and elemental that it seems like the truth. **Discussion**

★ **LLITERAS, D. S.** *The Thieves of Golgotha.* 1998. Hampton Roads. 182 pp. ISBN 1-57174-085-6.

Lliteras uses plain, deceptively simple prose and frank dialogue to flesh out the anguished stories of the two thieves who died with Christ on Golgotha. Despite their depravity, the reader is drawn to the two men, hoping for their redemption from the cruel Roman prison and the meanest of deaths. A tough, vivid, extraordinary novel.

MANDINO, OG. *The Christ Commission*. 1981. (Out of print.)

> A writer modeled on Mandino himself, Matt Lawrence makes an appearance on *The Tonight Show* where he announces that he has stopped working on a book about Jesus because he's become convinced that Jesus didn't rise from the dead. Later, in a hotel bar, a customer slugs him for his irreverence, and he passes out. When he awakens, he's in Israel in A.D. 36.

★ **MONHOLLON, MICHAEL L.** *Divine Invasion*. 1997. Reflection. 340 pp. ISBN 0-9657561-0-6.

> Monhollon's Jesus is a thoughtful man, witty and wise, conscious of his terrible destiny, in many ways similar to the Jesus of *The Last Temptation of Christ*. John the Baptizer is also drawn fully, as a fire-breathing revolutionary, and Herod and his wife come across as a real married couple, playful and flippantly lascivious. In fact, all of Monhollon's characters are wonderfully rendered.

◄✗ **SWINDOLL, CHARLES R.** *Suddenly One Morning: The Shopkeeper's Story*. 1998. Word. 96 pp. ISBN 0-8499-1356-X.

> A Jewish shopkeeper witnesses the events leading up to the Crucifixion.

Barabbas

Like Simon of Cyrene (discussed later), little is known of Barabbas, who may have been a robber, a murderer, an insurrectionist, or all of these. Following a Passover custom allowing for release of one prisoner, Pontius Pilate must free Barabbas instead of the blameless, but politicized, Jesus.

CORELLI, MARIE. *Barabbas: A Dream of the World's Tragedy*. 1942. Kessinger. 320 pp. ISBN 0-7661-0142-8.

> Corelli was a British romance writer at the turn of the twentieth century, and her version of the story of the prisoner released instead of Jesus, first published in 1893, is more emotional than Lagerkvist's better-known one (discussed later). But it reads as well today as ever, and some readers may prefer it.

◄✗ **JOHNSON, GRACE.** *The Rebel*. 1996. Tyndale, paper. 426 pp. ISBN 0-8423-5301-1.

> Whereas Corelli and Lagerkvist both begin with the release of Barabbas, Johnson's highly sympathetic portrait concentrates on Barabbas's young manhood, during which he hides in the hills and plots a rebellion against Rome. Gospel figures such as John the Disciple and Martha make an appearance in events leading up to the Crucifixion. Barabbas is a fierce young man whom Martha loves, and Barabbas, when belief in Jesus mellows him, returns her love.

★ **LAGERKVIST, PAR.** *Barabbas*. 1953. Tr. by Alan Blair. Random (Vintage International), paper. 144 pp. ISBN 0-67972544-X.

> The story of the murderer pardoned instead of Jesus is made a subtle inquiry into the nature of salvation by the Swedish Nobel Laureate Lagerkvist. Despite his crimes, Barabbas is more sinned against than sinning, and lives out a doomed, tragic life in puzzlement over the significance of Christ, until at last he, too, believes. Lagerkvist's novel became a movie in 1953 and

again in 1962 in the version best known in the United States, starring Anthony Quinn in a tender and vital performance, directed by Richard Fleischer.

Simon of Cyrene

Though he makes for a marvelous story, little is actually known of Simon (or Simeon) of Cyrene, the traveler impressed by Roman executioners to carry the cross of Jesus up to Golgotha. Verses referring to him, Mark 15:21 and Romans 16:23, suggest that he later became a Christian and that he may have been a black man.

◢◣ BROUWER, SIGMUND. *The Weeping Chamber*. 1998. Word, paper. 312 pp. ISBN 0-8499-3703-5.

Brouwer's seeming reluctance to enter the point of view of Jesus makes of him a remote and stilted figure. His Simeon is a complex study, however. A rich merchant who has come to Jerusalem to do business with an old friend, Simeon is a sorrowful man, estranged from his wife and family. His conversion is painful, springing as it does out of Jesus' suffering, but it is also full of poetry and the richness of tradition.

CHRISTIAN, JOHAN. *The Miracle of the Sacred Scroll*. 1997. Starburst. 108pp. ISBN 0-914984-73-X.

"No good deed goes unpunished" describes poor Simon's lot in life. He saves a child from fire but is disfigured and loses his confidence as a trader. He falls into poverty and, to break his cycle of bad luck, journeys to Jerusalem to participate in a great race. The prize is a rich man's fortune, but he's diverted from his goal so he can perform yet another good deed—bearing the cross of Jesus up Golgotha. Then at last Simon receives his earthly reward: custodianship of the Divine Covenant.

Mary Magdalene

FREDRIKSSON, MARIANNE. *According to Mary Magdalene*. 1999. Tr. by Joan Tate. Hampton Roads. 233 pp. ISBN 1-57174-120-8.

A bestseller in Europe, Swedish writer Fredriksson's account of Jesus through the eyes of the prostitute Mary Magdalene has made small impact in the United States, perhaps because it postulates a sexual relationship between Jesus and Mary. Fredriksson's Mary is an orphan raised in a brothel under the protection of a homosexual Greek soldier, and she receives a fine education in Latin and Greek. Long after Jesus' death, Paul and Simon Peter come to her for her account of events, and they are not entirely pleased with what they hear. Mary's view is that they have already, if unwittingly, begun to distort the true, simple, yet somewhat enigmatic gospel that Jesus taught.

SLAUGHTER, FRANK G. *The Galileans*. 1953. Doubleday. (Out of print.)

It's love at first sight for the physician Joseph of Galilee when he first sees Mary Magdalene dancing in the market. Unfortunately, a young Roman official also sees her and proceeds to seduce and rape her, setting the stage for Mary's fall from honor and deep rage. Joseph remains her friend, but only Jesus can save her tortured soul.

See also Brock and Bodie Thoene's *The Jerusalem Scrolls,* p. 79.

Early Christianity

ASCH, SHOLEM

★ *ROMAN TRILOGY*

Asch was a much-traveled, Russian-Polish Jew who emigrated to the United States before World War II and produced much of his work there. The Roman Trilogy made him the first Yiddish writer to enjoy international success. Though his emphasis was on the Jewish heritage of the founders of Christianity, he respected Christianity and he respected Jesus as a great Jewish prophet. Thus, he addressed the gap between Christianity and Judaism.

The Nazarene was greeted with extraordinary praise in the English-language press, but not so in the Yiddish, where Asch was at best a controversial figure. In part because the novel appeared in 1939 when the fate of European Jews was already clear, Asch's novel was for some a kind of betrayal.

In retrospect, now that the controversy has receded into literary history, Asch's novels seem among the most thoughtful ever to retell the gospel story.

> **The Nazarene.** Tr. by Maurice Samuel. 1939. Putnam's. (Out of print.)
> Asch chronicles the life of Jesus from three points of view: Cornelius, the governor of Jerusalem; Judas Iscariot; and a student of Nicodemus's named Joseph. The narrative is dramatic, but Asch emphasizes the actual preaching of Jesus and is more concerned with early Christian thought than with the contrivances of plot.

> **The Apostle.** Tr. by Maurice Samuel. 1943. Putnam's. (Out of print.)
> The almost immediate sequel to *The Nazarene* finds Saul of Tarsus dealing incredulously with the story of the Resurrection, but then he is converted and fights the good fight of his evangelizing all the way to Rome. (See also section titled "Paul" later in this chapter.)

> **Mary.** Tr. by Maurice Samuel. 1949. Putnam's. (Out of print.)
> The concluding volume of Asch's trilogy actually steps back some years to the young marriage of Mary and Joseph, where Mary is revealed to be a devout Jewish woman, struggling with the significance of her unusual son.

⬛ ★ BUNN, T. DAVIS. *To the Ends of the Earth.* 1996. Nelson. 400 pp. ISBN 0-7852-7898-2.

The versatile Bunn is at his best in this atypical historical set in A.D. 300, when the Byzantine Empire has lapsed into corruption. A North African merchant sends his son, Travis, to Constantinople to negotiate new terms for his estate because the plundering of his ships by pirates and high taxes have brought him nearly to ruin. Young Travis learns leadership on his journey and turns to Christianity in part because of his love for a Christian woman, Lydia.

COSTAIN, THOMAS B. *The Silver Chalice.* 1952. (Many editions.)

Costain's perennially popular tale, a lesser version of *The Robe,* features a sensitive Greek artisan, Basil, who is commissioned to design the case holding the cup used at the Last Supper. Then he must find the cup (the Holy Grail). There are scenes in Greece, Jerusalem, and Rome among the early Christians; Basil meets several followers of Jesus, including Luke and Peter. Paul Newman's first movie role, rather thin stuff, was as Basil. The film is watchable because of Jack Palance's bizarre performance as a sort of Antichrist, Simon the Magician. It was directed by Victor Saville in 1954.

DE CARVALHO, MARIO. *A God Strolling in the Cool of the Evening.* **1997. Tr. by Gregory Rabassa. Louisiana State. 265 pp. ISBN 0-8071-2235-1.**

Lucius Valerius Quintius is magistrate of what will one day be Portugal in the second century A.D., when Marcus Aurelius was emperor. Lucius is a just and moral man surrounded by corruption and ruling a populace who would rather go to the games and watch the persecution of a rapidly growing cult, the Christians, than attend to the growing threat of Moor invasion. Matters grow still more complicated when Lucius finds himself falling in love with Iunia Cantaber, an aristocrat who has converted to Christianity. She runs afoul of Roman law and places Lucius in the terrible dilemma of judging her. Winner of the Pegasus Prize for 1996.

DE WOHL, LOUIS

The Spear. 1955. Lippincott. (Out of print.)
Readers of *The Robe* (discussed later) will also enjoy *The Spear,* which focuses heavily on political squabbling among the Jews and Roman administrators but features Cassius Longinus, the soldier who impales Jesus to ensure absolutely his death.

The Glorious Folly. 1957. Lippincott. (Out of print.)
Cassius Longinus, now a fervent Christian, intermittently appears in this loose sequel to *The Spear,* but the novel is really about Paul and the quick spread of Christianity. (See also subsection "Paul" later in this chapter.)

★ **DOUGLAS, LLOYD C.** *The Robe.* **1942. (Many editions.)**
Douglas held his melodramatic tendencies in check for this deeply moving tale of Marcellus Gallio, the son of a Roman senator who has been banished to the backwater garrison in Judea. He and his Greek slave Demetrius, a man both subtle and fierce and nearly as compelling as Marcellus, make the best of things until Marcellus must put to death a crucified Jewish rebel named Jesus. Repelled by the act, Marcellus drinks himself to oblivion, but not before he gambles for Jesus' robe, and wins. The robe and the enormity of what he has done drive Marcellus insane. When at last his senses return to him, he, like Demetrius, pursues the new faith that has already spread to Rome. The film (1953), directed by Henry Koster, features a marvelous cast (Richard Burton as Marcellus, Victor Mature as Demetrius, Richard Boone as Pilate, and Jean Simmons as Marcellus's noble sweetheart, Diana) but is somehow passionless compared to the novel.   ▮Discussion▮

DOUGLAS, LLOYD C. *The Big Fisherman.* **1948. (Many editions.)**
Loosely related to *The Robe* though not a true sequel, *The Big Fisherman* is a parallel story of how rough Simon Peter came to follow Christ. Douglas also conjures the tale of a young misfit named Fara, the daughter of Herod and a Jewish woman. Peter and Fara dislike each other instantly but become close friends in their service of the new religion. The 1959 film starred Howard Keel and was directed by Frank Borzage.

HAGEE, JOHN. *Devil's Island.* **2001. Nelson.320 pp. ISBN: 0785267875.**
This opener to the projected series, Apocalypse Diaries, features John in his latter days, wrestling with the authority of Rome, barbarous acts against Christians, and most important, his divine revelations. Hagee is the author of several nonfiction treatises on apocalyptic themes.

LEMMONS, THOM

⮞✝ DAUGHTERS OF FAITH

> ★ *Daughter of Jerusalem.* 1999. Multnomah, paper. 325 pp. ISBN 1-57673-477-3.
> Though other characters appear in Lemmons's sensitive evocation of the hours and days surrounding the Crucifixion, the prime consciousness is that of Mary Magdalene. She's giddy with her new faith and its bold early days, and then she's devastated by her Lord's brutal death. Perhaps Lemmons's finest scenes are between Mary and the newly risen, incorporeal Christ, whom Mary, overwhelmed with love, tries to touch.   **▮Discussion▮**

> *Woman of Means.* 2000. Multnomah, paper. 320 pp. ISBN 1-57673-612-1.
> The second in Lemmons's series grafts a contemporary sensibility onto the characterization of Lydia, Paul's first convert. Almost nothing is known of Lydia, but in Lemmons's rendering she's a middle-class Greek girl, a tomboy who grows up worshipping Apollo and marrying her childhood sweetheart. Misfortunes strike. Widowed, destitute, and with children, Lydia makes her way to Philippi in A.D. 28, where her path crosses Paul's.

> *Mother of Faith.* 2001. Multnomah, paper. 320 pp. ISBN 1-57673-794-2.
> The third in the Daughters of Faith series features an extra-biblical character, Amanis of Ephesus, a kind, maternal young Ethiopian slave woman forced to flee her master's house when she saves an infant destined by the gods for slaughter. She joins a dancing troupe and becomes a performer herself, in her travels meeting the apostle John.

MITCHISON, NAOMI. *Blood of the Martyrs.* 1939. (Out of print.)

Though not with the same subtlety or grand sense of history, the Scottish Mitchison covers much the same ground as *Quo Vadis*: the wise Seneca makes an appearance, plotting against Nero; mad Nero persecutes Christians, and blames his big fire on them; and there is a full portrait of Paul. Somewhat in contrast to Sienkiewicz, Mitchison portrays the rise of Christianity among slaves in two Roman households, that of Flavius Crispus, who wishes slavery could be abolished, and that of Aelius Balbus, who sees it as inevitable. Beric, the adopted son of Crispus, bridges the Roman and slave worlds by himself becoming a Christian.

RIVERS, FRANCINE

★ MARK OF THE LION   **▮Discussion▮**
This passionate trilogy is set during the period of Christian persecution following the Crucifixion.

> *A Voice in the Wind.* 1993. Tyndale, paper. 442 pp. ISBN 0-8423-7750-6.
> The first and perhaps the best entry in Rivers's trilogy features the ordeals of Hadassah, the gentle Christian woman whom we meet during the Emperor Titus's sacking of Jerusalem. In its emotionally charged, naturalistic passages it bears comparison with epics such as *Quo Vadis* and the nineteenth-century English classic Hugh Farrie's *Acte*. The scenes aboard a slave ship and Rivers's brutal portrait of the Roman games are particularly harrowing. At the least, *A Voice in the Wind* is the most arresting biblical novel to appear in the 1990s.

> *Echo in the Darkness.* 1994. Tyndale, paper. 442 pp. ISBN 0-8423-1307-9.
> The somewhat disappointing sequel to *A Voice in the Wind* resolves Hadassah's story with a tortured, repressed romance with Marcus Valerian, a Roman noble who converts to Christianity.

As Sure As the Dawn. 1995. Tyndale, paper. 448 pp. ISBN 0-8423-3976-0.
The loose sequel to *A Voice in the Wind* and *Echo in the Darkness* tells the story of an enemy of Rome, the German gladiator Atretes briefly encountered in the first novel. Sex isn't far beneath the surface when Rivers pits the fierce, menacing Atretes against the widowed, passionate Risdah, nor is violence, but eventually the animosity between the two becomes attraction, and Atretes's hard but wounded heart melts into love for his new wife and for God.

SIENKIEWICZ, HENRYK. *Quo Vadis.* **1895.**
See discussion in chapter 3, "Christian Classics," p. 19.

SLAUGHTER, FRANK G. *The Sins of Herod.* **1968. Doubleday. (Out of print.)**
The declining fortunes of Herod Antipas—who ordered the beheading of John the Baptist and presided, at least remotely, over the Crucifixion—and the rise in status of Herod Agrippa are chronicled from the point of view of Prochorus, a Roman citizen of Judea. Though in the service of both Herods, Prochorus becomes a Christian and secretly aids them.

SLAUGHTER, FRANK G. *Upon this Rock.* **1963. Coward-McCann. (Out of print.)**
Slaughter's version of Simon Peter is not the crude fellow he is sometimes pictured to be but the bold leader of the disciples, a pivotal organizing figure for the early church, and deferential to the even greater ministry of Paul.

SNYDER, JAMES D. *All God's Children.* **2000. Pharos Books, paper. 680 pp. ISBN 0-9675200-0-2.**
Snyder offers a minimally fictionalized account of Rome and the rise of Christianity after the Crucifixion, or from A.D. 31 to A.D. 71. He uses an ex-slave become bookseller, Attalos, for a narrator, at times achieving the ironic power of Robert Graves's *I, Claudius.*

WILE, MARY LEE. *Ancient Rage.* **1995. Larson. 144 pp. ISBN 0-943914-70-1.**
Ancient Rage is a feminist meditation on loss, motherhood, and the harsh patriarchy of the Bible that constructs a grieving dialogue between the mothers of two martyrs: Mary, mother of Jesus, and Elizabeth, mother of John the Baptist. The two share their losses through a long night, and John, in particular, comes to life. When the night is done, the women part, their faith reaffirmed. **◼ Discussion**

Luke

CALDWELL, TAYLOR. *Dear and Glorious Physician.* **1959. Doubleday. (Out of print.)**
In what amounts to a prequel to the Gospel According to Luke, Caldwell draws from Catholic traditions and her own imagination to portray the brash, adventurous, but chaste young manhood of the young Greek Lucanus, or Luke. He is the only non-Jewish disciple, and he never meets Christ. After becoming a physician, he wanders in Rome and Syria and at last meets Mary, the mother of Jesus, and it is mostly through her tutelage that he becomes a Christian.

SLAUGHTER, FRANK G. *The Road to Bithynia.* **1951. (Out of print.)**

Bithynia is heaven on Earth—the peace one finds through Jesus. The Greek physician Luke follows the road thoughtfully, meeting Peter and then Paul, whom he accompanies on his evangelical campaigns. Slaughter also develops a love story between Luke and Thecia, a follower of Paul.

Paul

★ **CALDWELL, TAYLOR.** *Great Lion of God.* **1970. Doubleday. (Out of print.)**

In her most scholarly and dignified biblical novel, Caldwell portrays Paul from his childhood as a Hellenistic, privileged Jew, a principled but ruthless opponent of what he regards as the blasphemy of Christianity. With the high priest Caiaphas he tries to make a public example of Stephen's conversion and evangelizing, even though Stephen is a friend of the family. But when he witnesses Stephen's stoning, Paul's resolve breaks, and, in modern terms, he comes near to breaking down. Then, on the road to Damascus, he does break down, and understands the truth at last. Caldwell's marvelous scenes of his conversion occur three-quarters through the novel; thus Paul's missionary work gets shorter shrift than in Walter Wangerin's *Paul* (discussed later).

◄ **EDWARDS, GENE.** *The Silas Diary.* **1998. Tyndale, paper. 238 pp. ISBN 0-8423-5912-5.**

Paul's adventures in Galatia are recalled by Silas sometime after the death of Paul and Barnabas. Silas, who is mentioned mostly in Acts, is Paul's traveling companion, and together they endure shipwrecks, wintry blasts, and privation on the first of Paul's many evangelical campaigns.

◄ **ELWOOD, ROGER.** *Stephen the Martyr.* **1998. Servant, paper. 319 pp. ISBN 0-89283-984-8.**

Stephen is converted and becomes a great evangelist in Elwood's account, which also chronicles the Crucifixion, portrays the Roman hierarchy including Pontius Pilate, and teases out the plot against Christians led by the Sanhedrin Caiaphas. Ironically, Caiaphas is allied with Saul, who becomes Paul and takes Stephen's place on the road to martyrdom.

SLAUGHTER, FRANK G. *God's Warrior.* **1967. Doubleday. (Out of print.)**

Paul is relentless and fierce in Slaughter's account, bold in his proclamation of the gospel unto the moment of his beheading, which he faces without a blindfold, looking up to Heaven.

◄ **WANGERIN, WALTER.** *Paul.* **2000. Zondervan. 512 pp. ISBN 0-310-21892-6.**

A quiet, scholarly work and companion to Wangerin's extraordinary *The Book of God, Paul* is more about the spread of Christianity than an imaginative re-creation of Paul of Tarsus. Paul's earthy and amusing companion, Barnabas, relates how Paul's fiery style often preceded his being run out of town, and, alternatively, how in some towns the two were received as gods. However, Paul appears in his own words only in Wangerin's translations of those New Testament books clearly attributed to him, such as Galatians and Corinthians. Otherwise, he is presented through the accounts of Barnabas, Timothy, Prisca, Luke, James the brother of Christ, and several others.

See also Asch, Sholem in "Early Christianity" earlier in this chapter.

Pontius Pilate

 BELWOOD, ROGER. *The Road to Masada*. 1994. Moody, paper. 154 pp. ISBN 0-8024-7938-3.

Elwood gives voice to Pontius Pilate, his wife, and the legionnaires attending Christ's crucifixion in this well-researched novel. Most striking is Decimus Paetus, whose life is profoundly changed by the task assigned to him: ascertaining Christ's death. He converts and eventually finds himself leading the last stand, and mass martyrdom, when the Jews rebel against Rome at Masada.

 ★ MILLS, JAMES R. *The Memoirs of Pontius Pilate*. 2000. Baker, paper. 176 pp. ISBN 0-8007-1773-2.

In retirement—or exile—30 years after the death of Jesus, Pontius Pilate reflects on the most controversial decision of his career: ordering the Crucifixion. The strength of his scholarly and vastly entertaining "memoir" is that he was an outsider to the internecine struggles of Jewish high officials and religious authorities, and can pretend to be objective: He was merely trying to govern an unruly—and relatively unimportant—Roman province. In the end, his decision having caused him untold turmoil, and he extends his grudging admiration for the stubborn new religion and its most famous prophet. **Discussion**

Chapter 5

Historical Christian Fiction

The most common Christian historicals are light entertainments spun around strong female protagonists who are placed in a finite number of settings, with the American West the most popular, World War II and the Civil War not far behind. A nebulous, nostalgic period between the turn of the twentieth century and the 1960s, thought to be a golden period when families were strong and patriotism was universal, is also popular.

Not many Christian efforts can be ranked with Michael Shaara's *Killer Angels* (1974), the novel of Gettysburg that so carefully and insightfully re-creates the battle that in the end our collective view of an era is changed. In fact, Christian historicals generally seem to come from an assembly line, but superior novels and series do sometimes emerge, such as Mark Ammerman's Cross and the Tomahawk (p. 59) and the Thoenes' Galway Chronicles.

Christian historicals broadly resemble the mainstream novels of James Michener and John Jakes, respectively, with the award-winning husband-and-wife team of Brock and Bodie Thoene coming nearest to Michener's blend of readability and plausible history. The Thoenes, particularly with their three Zion series that re-create the history of Israel, dominate the field, and rightfully so, though fans of the Thoenes may want to follow the fortunes of Jim and Terri Kraus, an up-and-coming team also distinguished by their careful research and smooth style.

The myriad sequel model laid down by Jakes and others—and in the Christian field by Janette Oke—can most readily be found with Gilbert Morris, whose long-running House of Winslow series (see chapter 6, "Sagas") boasts almost 30 sequels. Morris is the clear champion in numbers of series as well, not to mention numbers of collaborators who include his son, Alan, and his daughter, Lynn. Christian fiction is a close-knit world.

The myriad sequel model dominates Christian historicals even within distinct subgenres, though there are plenty of exceptions. For example, Crossroad publishes biographical novels about famous religious figures. Mennonite and Amish presses are known for moving stories about conscientious objectors (see chapter 13).

This chapter chronologically orders summaries of novels that are also tagged geographically.

Biblical fiction, westerns, and sagas, each distinct expressions of historical fiction, are treated in separate chapters.

The difference between a historical romance and a romantic historical is a subjective judgment: There is more history in the first, more romance in the second. The two are mixed below, but the designation *[Historical]* indicates a title in which the history has been rendered with particular sensitivity. For the soft historical category of nostalgia, see chapter 11, "The Christian Life."

FIFTH CENTURY

British Isles

WINDSOR, LINDA

◖ᴇ◗ FIRES OF GLEANNMARA

> *Maire.* 2000. Multnomah, paper. 400 pp. ISBN 1-57673-625-3.
> Maire is a young Celtic queen who goes to conquer a peaceful village full of Christian fishermen in this entertaining, sometimes amusing series opener. The Christians are defended by Rowan, a former mercenary who can no longer bring himself to kill. Maire and he engage in swordplay and high-spirited banter and in the end, to avoid bloodshed, Rowan gives himself to her as a hostage and husband. Maire needs a husband to fend off the conquering intentions of a rival druidic band and its brutal leader, but she's disappointed in Rowan's apparent gentility. Gradually, she learns that there are other ways to defeat enemies than by headlong violence.

> *Riona.* 2001. Multnomah, paper. 368 pp. ISBN 1-57673-752-7.
> The heroine of the second installment of Windsor's Fires of Gleannmara series is Riona, a pious gentlewoman who cares for orphans and toys with the idea of becoming a nun. Wooing her is Maire's great-grandson, Kieran, who swore to protect Riona as her brother lay dying. Riona has troubles but she doesn't want the protection of Kieran, a fugitive with no use for Riona's capricious God.

> *Deirdre.* 2002. Multnomah, paper. 350 pp. ISBN 1-57673-891-4.
> In a gender-switched version of the first entry in the series, *Maire*, Windsor's feisty heroine Deirdre is taken captive by a pirate who has no use for the godly. Under Deirdre's spell, he changes his tune.

ELEVENTH CENTURY

Turkey

CHAIKIN, LINDA

◖ᴇ◗ ROYAL PAVILIONS
> Set during the First Crusade when Christian knights invaded the Holy Land to free Christian shrines from the Seljuk Turks, Chaikin's series is a Dumas-like romantic adventure featuring Tancred Redwan, a half-Moorish, half-Norman knight with an almost magical feel for the mastery of animals.

Swords and Scimitars. 1996. Bethany, paper. 286 pp. ISBN 1-55661-881-6.
Tancred is falsely imprisoned in Italy but fights his way free to set upon two
missions: to avenge his half-brother's death by his cousin, Mosul, and, at his
dying great-uncle's behest, carry a sacred relic to Jerusalem. En route, he rescues Helena of the Nobility from barbarians; she's a noblewoman due for a
great inheritance if she can find a proper husband.

Golden Palaces. 1996. Bethany, paper. 349 pp. ISBN 1-55661-865-4.
The Crusade proceeds as Helena's scheming aunt, Lady Irene, tries to marry
her off to a Muslim prince, and once more Tancred comes to her aid.

Behind the Veil. 1998. Bethany, paper. 256 pp. ISBN 1-55661-513-2.
The plot is more or less repeated in the concluding volume of the series. The
knights fight on, Tancred continues to search for his treacherous cousin, and
Helena requires saving all over again.

TWELFTH CENTURY

Germany

OHANNESON, JOAN. *Scarlet Music: A Life of Hildegard of Bingen.* **1997. Crossroad, paper. 265 pp. ISBN 0-8425-1646-X.** *[Historical]*

Ohanneson explores the painful and exemplary life of the German nun and feminist
icon, Hildegard, with her difficult childhood and visions bordering on insanity.
Hildegard confronts popes and makes prophecies and, most of all, writes her music,
which, particularly in Europe, is sometimes still performed.

Ireland

HUNT, ANGELA ELWELL

◀▣✖ *THEYN CHRONICLES*
Hunt's first series mixes quest fantasies and romance to dramatize the plight of
Christians in barbarous medieval England and Ireland.

Afton of Margate Castle. 1993. Tyndale, paper. 490 pp. ISBN 0-84231-222-6.
Afton, a peasant girl, is raised like nobility in the castle. She takes on the ways
of the court but learns that she's mere chattel when she's given in marriage
against her will.

The Troubadour's Quest. 1994. Tyndale, paper. 383 pp. ISBN 0-84231-287-0.
In the loose sequel to *Afton of Margate Castle,* the troubadour Gislebert sets
off through England and France to find his lost love, Nadine.

Ingram of the Irish. 1994. Tyndale, paper. 419 pp. ISBN 0-84231-623-X.
In the conclusion of Hunt's trilogy, a young knight, Ingram, undertakes a long
journey to discover his Irish roots.

★ **LAWHEAD, STEPHEN R.**

◧✗★ *THE CELTIC CRUSADES [Historical]*

The Iron Lance. 1998. HarperPrism/Zondervan. 512 pp. ISBN 0-06-105032-6.
Murdo, the youngest son of his clan, is left behind when his father embarks for the Crusades, and schemers in the church, in league with a corrupt government, soon dispossess him. Ruined, Murdo leaves his true love behind and sets off himself for the Holy Land, in a personal crusade to turn wrong into right.

The Black Rood. 2000. HarperCollins. 512 pp. ISBN 0-06105-034-2.
Young Duncan, Murdo's son, itches to leave behind his mundane life when a crusader arrives at his father's door and tells of the loss of the Black Rood—a piece of the "True Cross" that Christ was nailed to. When his wife dies in childbirth, Murdo has his wish and follows his father's adventurous trail through Byzantium, accompanied by a sharp-tongued monk and his loyal, if not very respectful, servant. He must eventually reckon with the fearsome Knights Templar and the infidel Saracens.

The Mystic Rose. 2001. Ecco Press. 432 pp. ISBN 0-06-105031-8.
The concluding volume of Lawhead's vivid epic features a female protagonist, Lady Caitriona, who vows to avenge her father's death when he's stabbed to death while visiting the Holy Land. The ensuing journey is fraught with perils, of course, not to mention over-wrought romance. Caitriona's thirst for revenge is at last slaked by a higher purpose: she seeks the Mystic Rose—another name for the Holy Grail. In the bargain, she entertains an extraordinary vision graced by the appearance of Yeshua.

THIRTEENTH CENTURY

England

SAMSON, LISA
Samson gives her medieval romances a kind of fairy-tale quality.

Conquered Heart. 1996. Harvest House, paper. 391 pp. ISBN 1-56507-448-3.
A lonely weaver woman, Lilla, nurses a wounded monk back to health. But it seems he's not really a monk.

Love's Ransom. 1997. Harvest House, paper. 328 pp. ISBN 1-56507-529-3.
Jane Lightfoot is a cook for a high-born family, struggling to raise her son, Nicholas, by herself. Then the lord of the castle takes Nicholas away to rear him as a noble, and Jane's modest life grows complicated.

The Warrior's Bride. 1997. Harvest House, paper. 360 pp. ISBN 1-56507-636-2.
In a tale with overtones of *Beauty and the Beast,* a noblewoman, Lady Johanna Durwin, loses her heart to a poetic knight whom she isn't allowed to see.

FOURTEENTH CENTURY

England

BROUWER, SIGMUND

⬛✗ *MAGNUS*

Brouwer pulls out all the stops in his quest fantasy set in Magnus, a mythical but plausible British kingdom ruled by a thuggish band who practice Druidism. Brouwer ventures into the lore of Merlin and the Holy Grail and, like Sir Walter Scott in *Ivanhoe*, includes Robin Hood as a character.

> *Magnus.* 1994. Chariot Victor, paper. 500 pp. ISBN 1-56476-296-3.

> *Wings of Dawn.* 1995. Chariot Victor, paper. 432 pp. ISBN 1-56476-756-6.

CAVANAUGH, JACK

⬛✗ *BOOK OF BOOKS [Historical]*

> *Glimpses of Truth.* 1999. Zondervan, paper. 320 pp. ISBN 0-310-21574-9.
> Young Thomas Torr, son of peasants, is chosen by John Wycliffe to help translate the Bible into English from the Latin Vulgate. In the past, Rome has threatened death for anyone promulgating an English-language Bible, but now the Church seems to have relaxed its stand and invites the naive Thomas to Rome. Treachery ensues in this first of a projected series dramatizing various classic translations of the Bible.

SIXTEENTH CENTURY

Germany

⬛✗ GRANT, REG. *Storm.* 2001. WaterBrook, paper. 384 pp. ISBN 1-57856-189-2.

Grant's talky but engaging re-creation of Protestantism's great hero, Martin Luther, celebrates his achievements without ignoring his faults, such as anti-Semitism. Grant begins dramatically: In a great storm, young Martin nearly perishes, and swears to St. Anne that he'll become a monk. Luther's mission, to cast off the bonds of corrupt Catholicism, is made clear, and Luther himself emerges interestingly as outgoing, irritable, and profane. His "romance" with Katarina of Bora (see also the next entry) is less than ideal.

SCHEIB, ASTA. *Children of Disobedience.* 2000. Crossroad. 240pp. ISBN 0-8245-1695-8.

Set in 1523, Scheib's story gives life to the love affair of Martin Luther and the nun Katarina of Bora. Scheib follows Katarina through her escape from her convent, when, like other novices, she becomes drunk with the heady promises of Luther's Reformation. But without a husband or the safety of the convent, Katarina has no true role. She's an attractive woman and soon finds herself engaged to Hieronymus Baumgartner, but the young man's father nixes the match, calling Katarina a "cloister whore." She sets out to win over the aloof Luther, which she does after faithfully tending him when he's ill.

Holland

HERR, ETHEL

◄Ɛ✕★ *THE SEEKERS [Historical]*

Both politics and religion separate two childhood friends and would-be lovers, Aletta Engelshofen and Pieter-Lucas van den Garde, in Herr's tale of Protestantism's birth pangs in Holland. Aletta and Pieter are both Catholics, but Pieter's father has joined the Beggars, a radical, violent sect of Calvinists who commit acts of terrorism, such as kidnapping and church desecration. Aletta's father, a bookseller, bans Pieter from seeing his daughter because of his father's associations, but soon all principals are swept up in the service of William of Orange against King Philip II, the fanatic Spanish papist intent on ridding this new breed of infidels from the Low Countries. Young Pieter, a promising artist anointed for service in the church, must set aside his true callings to become a messenger for William of Orange, while Aletta becomes a nurse tending the Dutch wounded. Herr blends careful research with a triumphant love story, all the more affecting because of its persecuted quality; though published as a trilogy, the individual novels fit like one long novel.

> *The Dove and the Rose.* 1996. Bethany, paper. 331 pp. ISBN 1-55661-746-1.

> *The Maiden's Sword.* 1997. Bethany, paper. 320 pp. ISBN 1-55661-747-X.

> *The Citadel and the Lamb.* 1998. Bethany, paper. 311 pp. ISBN 1-55661-748-8.

SEVENTEENTH CENTURY

Caribbean

CHAIKIN, LINDA

◄Ɛ✕ *TRADE WINDS*

In this trilogy, Lady Devora Ashby is held for ransom by a French pirate in the days when the Spanish and English vied for control of the Caribbean.

> *Captive Heart.* 1998. Harvest, paper. 221 pp. ISBN 0-7369-7755-5.

> *Silver Dreams.* 1998. Harvest, paper. 215 pp. ISBN 0-7369-7755-5.

> *Island Bride.* 1999. Harvest, paper. 260 pp. ISBN 0-7369-0004-7.

KRAUS, JIM, AND TERRI KRAUS

★ *TREASURES OF THE CARIBBEAN [Historical]*

> *Pirates of the Heart.* 1996. Tyndale, paper. 501 pp. ISBN 0-8423-0381-2.
> The Krauses romanticize Britain's colonization of Barbados in the period 1627 through 1644. The series begins in Devonshire with the desperation and class resentment of a gamekeeper named William Hawkes. Will jumps at the chance to escape his impoverished, circumscribed life and ships for the Caribbean, where, briefly, he is a rather unconvincing

pirate. Raiding an English ship, he meets and rescues the devout Kathryne Spenser, on her way to join her father, the governor of Barbados.

Passages of Gold. 1997. Tyndale, paper. 500 pp. ISBN 0-8423-03.
Kathryne rather annoyingly illustrates William's prejudices against the upper classes in the sequel to *Pirates of the Heart,* but by the end they are married and cloyingly domestic.

Journey to the Crimson Sea. 1997. Tyndale, paper. 384 pp. ISBN 0-8423-0383-9.
Kathryne and William also appear in this concluding volume of the trilogy, but its principal character is the woebegone Thomas Mayhew, swept overboard and presumed dead on his journey to head a church in Barbados. Instead, he takes over a smaller congregation at the fort Will commands. There he becomes the subject of heavy gossip because of his romance with Eileen Palmerston, a high-born lady who fell into prostitution before being saved.

Colonial America

AMMERMAN, MARK

◆E✕★ *CROSS AND THE TOMAHAWK [Historical]*   `Discussion`
Splendidly researched, passionate, and amusing, this little-known series is set among the Narragansett Indians at the time of King Philip's War in 1676.

The Rain from God. 1997. Horizon, paper. 320 pp. ISBN 0-88965-134-5.
Ammerman takes great care in creating Katanaquat, a fierce warrior with a poetic soul who converts to Christianity under the influence of the preacher Roger Williams. Ammerman's research of Williams, his ancestor, inspired him to write the series.

The Ransom. 1997. Horizon, paper. 392 pp. ISBN 0-88965-135-3.
Katanaquat, now known as Jacob, returns in this heartfelt sequel. Ammerman emphasizes that the English brought not only Christianity but also guns and steel. Katanaquat is torn between the changes he sees overcoming Narragansett ways and his love of Jesus: Both impulses send him into battle, but the real battle is within his soul.

Longshot. 2000. Horizon, paper. 301 pp. ISBN 0-88965-165-5.
The third entry in Ammerman's series concerns Christopher Gist, a lay Anglican minister commissioned by the Ohio Company to establish a settlement deep in the wilderness. Christopher takes along his wily Narragansett friend, the great horseman and possible witch doctor Caleb Hobomucko, and the young men share adventures and Indian lore a la Fenimore Cooper.

HAWTHORNE, NATHANIEL. *The Scarlet Letter.* 1850.
See discussion in chapter 3, "Christian Classics," p. 28.

HUNT, ANGELA ELWELL

◆E✕ *KEEPERS OF THE RING [Historical]*

Roanoke: The Lost Colony. 1996. Tyndale, paper. 512 pp. ISBN 0-84232-012-1.

Hunt bases the first entry of her series on a historical mystery from 1587, when one of a fleet of English ships was lost in a storm, which may have led to the formation of the "lost" Roanoke colony. Her story centers on the tribulations of Jocelyn Colman, who reluctantly follows a new husband into the new, puritanical world with all its privations of hunger and spirit.

Jamestown. 1996. Tyndale, paper. 432 pp. ISBN 0-84232-013-X.
The sequel to *Roanoke* begins after the colony has been wiped out in an Indian massacre and features several survivors, most notably young Fallon Bailie. He flees with his sister to Jamestown and eventually marries another survivor, Gilda, but not before some adventures in England. Meanwhile, Gilda finds refuge with her cousin, Pocahontas. Other historical personages also make an appearance.

Hartford. 1996. Tyndale, paper. 350 pp. ISBN 0-84232-014-8.
The third entry in Hunt's popular series may be the most intrinsically interesting. It draws closely from historical sources to describe the Puritan massacre of Pequots in 1636, and it links to previous novels by featuring Daniel Bailie, Gilda and Fallon's rebellious son.

Rehoboth. 1997. Tyndale, paper. 356 pp. ISBN 0-84232-015-6.
Daniel Bailie, introduced in *Hartford,* becomes a missionary to the Indians at the time of King Philip's War (1675). But the romance of the story focuses on his daughter, Aiyana, who looks like her Indian ancestors and learns Indian ways, but marries a white man.

Charles Towne. 1998. Tyndale, paper. 432 pp. ISBN 0-84232-016-4.
The final and least compelling entry in Hunt's series features Rachelle Bailie, who, seeking her lost father Mojag (Aiyana's brother), is abducted by pirates and could well become a slave on one of the rice plantations of South Carolina.

EIGHTEENTH CENTURY

Canada

OKE, JANETTE, AND T. DAVIS BUNN

◄✕ *SONG OF ACADIA*
In this most realized of their several collaborations, Oke and Bunn dramatize the conflict between the French and English in eighteenth-century Acadia, or Nova Scotia.

The Meeting Place. 1999. Bethany, paper. 282 pp. ISBN 0-7642-2177-9.
Louise Robichaud, who is French, and the young Englishwoman Catherine Harrow, both of whom are about to be married, form a friendship across cultural and political divides even as surrogates of their faraway nations fight for dominance of the Maritimes.

The Sacred Shore. 2000. Bethany, paper. 256 pp. ISBN 0-7642-2247-3.
Set a generation later, the sequel to *The Meeting Places* chronicles the fate of the French, exiled to kinder American shores—sacred shores because they symbolize not only political freedom but also religious freedom. As is often the case in collaborations between this well-known pair, the story relies on coincidences and switched identities. Louise and her husband, Henri, settle in Louisiana, where fate has conspired for them to raise the English daughter of Catherine and Andrew, whom they call Nicole. When Earl Charles Harrow, Andrew's older brother, sails from England seeking an heir, he comes first to Acadia, then journeys to Louisiana in search of Nicole—really Elspeth.

The Birthright. 2001. Bethany, paper. 288 pp. ISBN 0-7642-2229-5.
Nicole journeys to England, perhaps to claim her inheritance. Anne, adopted daughter of Catherine and Andrew, follows when her husband dies, bringing her baby and, unknown to her, a birthright.

The Distant Beacon. 2002. Bethany, paper. 288 pp. ISBN 0-7642-2600-2.
The adventures of Anne and Nicole continue. Anne's roots in Great Britain and her new marriage renew her interest in life. Nicole still must seek her destiny, and considers returning to her childhood home in Louisiana. Then, as the American colonies burst into revolt against England, Anne's Uncle Charles asks her to sail to Massachusetts to look after his land there. En route, Anne meets a handsome ship's captain.

Colonial America

CRAWFORD, DIANNA

◆ *REARDON BROTHERS*

Freedom's Promise. 2000. Tyndale, paper. 310 pp. ISBN 0-8423-1916-6.
Beginning with her stern father, who indentured her into hard labor to a neighbor, young Annie McGregor hasn't much use for men, and when she learns of land at 50 cents an acre in unsettled Tennessee, she tries to join the caravan. She hopes to buy 10 acres and sell cheese and honey. No one wants a young woman without a man or a dowry, however, and Annie steals ahead on the trail, thinking to prove herself and buy land, which she does. After fighting off a number of unsavory men, her heart softens for a good one, Isaac Reardon, in this pleasant story filled with convincing details of pioneer farm life.

Freedom's Hope. 2000. Tyndale, paper. 335 pp. ISBN 0-8423-1917-4.
Noah Reardon, like his brother, Ike, of *Freedom's Promise,* has been jilted by a woman wanting no part of frontier life. He meets a backwoods lass, Jessica Whitman, and sparks fly, but Jessica isn't a Christian.

Freedom's Bell. 2001. Tyndale, paper. 316 pp. ISBN 0-8423-1918-2.
Drew Reardon is looking for a woman who will brave the wilderness with him, but he falls for schoolmarm Crystabelle Amherst, an educated and refined young woman who doesn't share his views.

LAITY, SALLY, AND DIANA CRAWFORD

◆ *FREEDOM'S HOLY LIGHT*
This series includes six romances set during the Revolutionary War.

The Gathering Dawn. 1994. Tyndale, paper. 357 pp. ISBN 0-8423-1303-6.

The Kindred Flame. 1994. Tyndale, paper. 320 pp. ISBN 0-8423-1336-2.

The Tempering Blaze. 1995. Tyndale, paper. 392 pp. ISBN 0-8423-6902-3.

The Fires of Freedom. 1996. Tyndale, paper. 449 pp. ISBN 0-8423-1353-2.

The Embers of Hope. 1996. Tyndale, paper. 350 pp. ISBN 0-8423-1362-1.

The Torch of Triumph. 1997. Tyndale, paper. 421 pp. ISBN 0-8423-1417-2.

MORRIS, GILBERT

⬛✖ *LIBERTY BELL*
The first installment of the Liberty Bell series starts in England with a hapless brother and sister, Daniel and Lyna Bradford, who come to America as desperate indentured servants. In Virginia, Daniel works his way to freedom, his wife dies, and eventually he marries his old master's wife (the master too has died). The story then hurtles through skirmishes at Lexington and Concord.

> *Sound the Trumpet.* 1995. Bethany, paper. 316 pp. ISBN 1-55661-565-5.
>
> *Song in a Strange Land.* 1996. Bethany, paper. 316 pp. ISBN 1-55661-566-3.
>
> *Tread Upon the Lion.* 1996. Bethany, paper. 302 pp. ISBN 1-55661-567-1.
>
> *Arrow of the Almighty.* 1997. Bethany, paper. 320 pp. ISBN 1-55661-568-X.
>
> *Wind from the Wilderness.* 1998. Bethany, paper. 320 pp. ISBN 1-55661-569-8.
>
> *The Right Hand of God.* 1999. Bethany, paper. 320 pp. ISBN 1-55661-570-1.
>
> *Command the Sun.* 2000. Bethany, paper. 286 pp. ISBN 1-55661-571-X.

MORRIS, GILBERT, AND AARON MCCARVER

⬛✖ *SPIRIT OF APPALACHIA [Historical]*
The series begins in the late 1700s with the bad luck of a Tennessee pioneer, "Hawk" Spencer, who heads into the wilderness after his young wife's death in childbirth. Hawk is embittered that God could bring such sorrow upon him, but his loss of faith is countered in love by another pioneer, Elizabeth McNeal. Subsequent volumes feature new characters and familiar ones as the Revolutionary War makes its impact; there are so many characters, in fact, and so many subplots, that readers will be lost unless they begin at the beginning.

> *Over the Misty Mountains.* 1997. Bethany, paper. 334 pp. ISBN 1-55661-885-9.
>
> *Beyond the Quiet Hills.* 1998. Bethany, paper. 320 pp. ISBN 1-55661-886-7.
>
> *Among the King's Soldiers.* 1998. Bethany, paper. 336 pp. ISBN 1-55661-887-5.
>
> *Beneath the Mockingbird's Wings.* 2000. Bethany, paper. 320 pp. ISBN 1-55661-888-3.

SCHALESKY, MARLO M.

⬛✖ *WINDS OF FREEDOM*

> *Cry Freedom.* 2000. Crossway, paper. 368 pp. ISBN 1-58254-169-5.
> In 1743, as once more the British and French battle for supremacy in North America, a young Englishman, Jonathan Grant, responds to the evangelical fervor known as the "Great Awakening." He leaves his sheltered life to preach the gospel on the Pennsylvania frontier, where the native people have allied with the French against the British settlers. There he falls in love with a desperate half-breed woman, Kwelik.
>
> *Freedom's Shadow.* 2001. Crossway, paper. 380 pp. ISBN 1-558134-266-7.
> Pontiac and George Washington make unconvincing appearances in this sequel to *Cry Freedom.* The first is the fierce companion of White Wolf, a battle-weary brave who has lost his entire tribe to the war; Colonel Washington gives Christian counsel to young Annie Hill, who also has lost everything to war. White Wolf and Annie find each other,

God, and freedom. Meanwhile, Jonathan Grant and his wife, Kwelik, principal characters of *Cry Freedom,* journey to England on an urgent mission.

England

CROW, DONNA FLETCHER

✖ *CAMBRIDGE CHRONICLES [Historical]*
This series of biographical novels was first published in the 1980s. It uses love stories and the stories of new converts to frame the history of Methodism and Protestantism generally in eighteenth century England. See also *Where Love Calls,* p. 66.

> *A Gentle Calling.* 1995. Crossway, paper. 222 pp. ISBN 0-89107-806-1.
> The story of John Wesley and the birth of Methodism.

> *Treasures of the Heart.* 1994. Crossway, paper. 224 pp. ISBN 0-89107-807-X.
> Evangelist Rowland Hill is portrayed.

> *Where Love Begins.* 1995. Crossway, paper. 224 pp. ISBN 0-89107-808-8.
> Evangelist Charles Simeon is portrayed.

> *To Be Worthy.* 1995. Crossway, paper. 255 pp. ISBN 0-89107-809-6.
> Crow constructs a romance around Wilber Wilberforce, who campaigned to end the English slave trade, in the final installment of her Cambridge Chronicles.

✖ ★ MUSSER, JOE. *The Infidel.* 2001. Broadman and Holman, paper. 368 pp. ISBN 0-8054-2480-6. *[Historical]*
The Infidel draws from the writings of John Newton, the mostly self-educated Christian theologian who wrote "Amazing Grace." "Wretch like me" certainly describes Newton, who for most of his life was a seaman and unregenerate slave trader. He raped many slave women and even boasted of the bastards he had fathered into slavery in the New World. Ironically, for a time he became a slave himself, and in part it was that experience that brought him to the other side, becoming a preacher and writing *Thoughts on the African Slave Trade* (1787), which was a direct influence on banning slavery in England. Musser's portrait of Newton as a libertine is frank without being sensational, but it's not for the fainthearted. ■Discussion■

Scotland

SAMSON, LISA

THE HIGHLANDERS
Samson fashions a highly romantic series somewhat in the manner of George MacDonald.

> *The Highlander and His Lady.* 1994. Harvest House, paper. 339 pp. ISBN 1-56507-206-5.
> Jenny Matheson, a young woman with a mysterious past, falls in love with Kyle Maclachlan, a lord who strives to throw off the yoke of the Stuarts and regain his lands.

The Legend of Robin Brodie. 1995. Harvest House, paper. 348 pp. ISBN 1-56507-306-1.
Some years after *The Highlander and His Lady,* another solitary warrior, man of the forest Robin Brodie, battles the English and falls in love with Kyle and Jenny Maclachlin's daughter, Alix.

The Temptation of Aaron Campbell. 1996. Harvest House, paper. 337 pp. ISBN 1-56507-390-8.
Set almost a century after *The Legend of Robin Brodie,* Aaron Campbell's story has little to do with earlier entries in the Highlanders series. Aaron is twin brother to Colin, who because he is 10 minutes Aaron's senior, is heir to a seat in the House of Lords. Aaron, with an uncertain place in society, is supposedly the dissolute brother, and when he is obliged to carry out an oath sworn to in his college days, it seems his reputation may prove true. Then he meets Marie Rosetti and life grows more complicated.

South Africa

CAVANAUGH, JACK

✦ *AFRICAN COVENANT*

Cavanaugh can write lines such as "Let me go, you boorish louse!" for his heroine, Margeurite ("Margot") de Campion, but his subject departs from ordinary Christian fare: the flight to South Africa of French Huguenots and Dutch Protestants, together forming the Dutch-speaking Boers, or *Afrikaans.* Despite Cavanaugh's winning portrait of a stately old Hottentot and other authentic touches, this unusual series never took off, perhaps because of late twentieth century events in Africa and the complicated business of trying to make Israelites out of white colonizers.

The Pride and the Passion. 1996. Moody, paper. 331 pp. ISBN 0-8024-0862-1.
Penniless Margot, an orphan, finds her prince in Jan van der Kemp, son of a plantation owner, but British exploitation of the Boers keeps them from true happiness.

Quest for the Promised Land. 1997. Moody, paper. 287 pp. ISBN 0-8024-0863-X.
In his sequel to *The Pride and the Passion,* Cavanaugh uses another van der Kemp, Christiaan, to portray the Boer flight to the wilderness and their founding of the Orange Free State.

NINETEENTH CENTURY

Australia

HICKMAN, PATRICIA

✦ *LAND OF THE FAR HORIZON*

Voyage of the Exiles. 1995. Bethany, paper. 320 pp. ISBN 1-55661-541-8.
Hickman begins her tale of immigration to Australia in England, where real criminals mix with the destitute poor in what amounts to a slave ship. Romance blooms, but Hickman's most interesting character is Captain Arthur Phillip, a fussy bachelor called out of retirement for the long and perilous voyage.

Angel of the Outback. 1995. Bethany, paper. 319 pp. ISBN 1-55661-542-6.
Two young female prisoners endure their long sentences and then are met with
still more trials. A noble minister intervenes.

The Emerald Flame. 1996. Bethany, paper. 288 pp. ISBN 1-55661-543-4.
A young Irishwoman, forced to emigrate, is caught up in Australia's famous
Battle of Castle Hill.

Beyond the Wild Shores. 1997. Bethany, paper. 288 pp. ISBN 1-55661-544-2.
A young schoolteacher makes the journey to Australia voluntarily, arriving as
friction between colonists and former criminals demanding full emancipation
grows to a fever pitch.

The Treasure Seekers. 1998. Bethany, paper. 320 pp. ISBN 1-55661-545-0.
The energy of the series has dissipated in this mechanical concluding novel,
where the privations of new immigrants Annie Carraway and her widowed
mother are so overwrought, the story so melodramatic, that it's hard to suspend
disbelief. Annie's sassiness, particularly as a child, may have some appeal,
however.

England

⊠ BLACKWELL, LAWANA

GRESHAM CHRONICLES [Historical]
A quiet, preachy Victorian series, though with rich historical detail, about a widow
who takes over management of the family inn when her profligate husband dies. Her
romance with the local parson might best be characterized as polite.

The Widow of Larkspur Inn. 1998. Bethany, paper. 432 pp. ISBN 1-55661-947-X.

The Courtship of the Vicar's Daughter. 1998. Bethany, paper. 400 pp. ISBN
1-55661-948-0.

The Dowry of Miss Lydia Clark. 1999. Bethany, paper. 398 pp. ISBN 0-7642-2149-3.

TALES OF LONDON [Historical]

The Maiden of Mayfair. 2001. Bethany, paper. 432 pp. ISBN 0-7642-2258-9.
Young Sarah Matthews is the ward of St. Matthew Methodist Foundling
Home for Girls in Drury Lane. Though the orphanage is grim, she's lucky, for
abandoned children are everywhere; forced to beg and sleep in the streets. Soon,
she's rescued by a rich widow who suspects that Sarah may be her granddaughter,
daughter of her loutish son.

VICTORIAN SERENADE [Historical]

Like a River Glorious. 1995. Bethany, paper. 333 pp. ISBN 0-8423-7954-1.
Livelier than the series following it, Gresham Chronicles (discussed previously),
but with the same careful re-creation of settings, Victorian Serenade alludes
both to *Jane Eyre* and *Beauty and the Beast* with the characterization of Adam
Burke, a recluse who is almost conned out of his riches by mysterious, beautiful
Corinne Hammond. She's undone by her repressed young servant, however,
for whom true love flowers with Adam.

Measures of Grace. 1996. Bethany, paper. 368 pp. ISBN 0-8423-7956-8.
In the sequel to *Like a River Glorious,* Corinne, along with her daughter, the main character of the series, accepts Christ and tries to atone for her shady past.

Jewels for a Crown. 1996. Bethany, paper. 398 pp. ISBN 0-8423-7960-6.
The third novel in Blackwell's Victorian Serenade series features Jenny Price, a nurse who takes a job caring for a 12-year-old epileptic, Celeste Harrington, and who also tries to break through to Celeste's aloof father.

Song of a Soul. 1997. Bethany, paper. 340 pp. ISBN 0-8423-7965-7.
The series concludes with the story of Deborah Burke, a would-be opera singer who, when offered a once-in-a-lifetime opportunity, worries about compromising her faith.

✠ CROW, DONNA FLETCHER

Encounter the Light. 1997. Crossway, paper. 240 pp. ISBN 0-89107-876-2.
Jennifer Neville and Richard Greystone both volunteer for the Crimean War in this Victorian romance, Jennifer as a nurse and Richard as a soldier. When they return to England the shallowness of Victorian society offends them, and they decide to work with London's poor. Jennifer loves Richard, but he was blinded in the war and feels, despite their mutual faith, that he would be a burden in marriage.

Where Love Calls. 1998. Crossway, paper. 301 pp. ISBN 0-89107-998-X. *[Historical]*
Crow's novel might belong to her Cambridge Chronicles series (p. 63), except that it's set a century later and features the Cambridge Seven, whose evangelical fervor, inspired in part by the American evangelist D. L. Moody, impelled them to follow the leadership of J. Hudson Taylor and become missionaries to China. Crow's heroine is Hilda Beauchamp, and she's full both of romantic and religious machinations, but Crow's carefully re-created China adventures carry the story.

GILLENWATER, SHARON

✠ ***Song of the Highlands.*** 1997. Multnomah, paper. 428 pp. ISBN 0-88070-946-4.
Scotsman Kiernan Macpherson inherits a rundown English estate in this Regency, laboring under the long shadow of George MacDonald. Kiernan meets Lady Mariah Douglas, sister of the deceased owner, to whom he gives employment as a chaperone. The three go adventuring in London until they must retreat again to the estate.

✠ ***Highland Call.*** 1999. Multnomah, paper. 400 pp. ISBN 1-57673-275-4.
Former army officer Gabriel MacPherson has been hired by the British government to spy on Selena Delaroe, a spy for Napoleon, in this Regency set in 1810. Gabriel takes a job as Selena's estate manager and means to unmask her as a traitor, but falls in love with her instead. Fortunately, there are mitigating circumstances to Selena's disloyalty.

✠ JOHNSON, GRACE. ***Tempest at Stonehaven.*** 1997. Tyndale, paper. 251 pp. ISBN 0-8423-6250-9.
Victoria Holt comes to mind in this gothic tale set in 1880s Scotland about Annie Mackinnon, a widowed schoolteacher whose son, like his father, goes off to sea, and a mysterious stranger who appears to be linked to pirates lurking off the wild coast, luring honest sailors to their doom.

PEART, JANE

◀E▶ *Web of Deception.* 1996. Revell, paper. 208 pp. ISBN 0-8007-5598-7.
When her father dies, Rachel Penniston becomes a governess for a rich businessman.

◀E▶ *Shadow of Fear.* 1996. Revell, paper. 176 pp. ISBN 0-8007-5597-9.
A *Wuthering Heights* sort of tale of a young woman who loses her fortune.

ROGERS, JANE. *Mr. Wroe's Virgins.* 1999. Overlook Press. 273 pp. ISBN 0-87951-702-6. *[Historical]*

John Wroe was an actual figure, an English doomsayer who joined the Southcottian sect in Lancashire and later founded a subgroup called the Christian Israelites, whose task was to rally the far-flung tribes of Israel and to reconcile the Jewish and Catholic faiths. He made a number of prophecies, some of which came true. In 1830 he asked his congregation to give him seven virgins, and Rogers constructs her colorful tale around the narratives of each of them.

SAMSON, LISA

◀E▶ *SHADES OF ETERNITY*
The melodramatic fortunes of Earl John Youngblood tie together these three tales set in France, England, and Scotland in the 1860s and featuring appearances from Queen Victoria and several early feminists.

◀E▶ *Indigo Waters.* 1999. Zondervan, paper. 366 pp. ISBN 0-310-22368-7.
Through convoluted, unlikely circumstances, John Youngblood is swept up in a plot to assassinate Sylvie de Courcey, heiress to vast acres of French vineyards. Instead, her husband is killed, freeing her to marry the English evangelist Matthew Wallace. John Youngblood, in love with Sylvie, retreats in disgrace and is given up for dead.

◀E▶ *Fields of Gold.* 2000. Zondervan, paper. 336 pp. ISBN 0-310-22369-5.
John Youngblood, full of contrition for his deeds, reappears in this sequel to *Indigo Waters.* But the story is really about Matthew Wallace's older sister, Miranda, who is entrusted with the care of John Youngblood's illegitimate daughter, Elspeth; and John's Uncle Tobin, a moody musician who has come to Scotland to claim the supposedly dead nephew's estate. Elspeth has a birth defect, Miranda has a birthmark, and Tobin treats them both with scorn because they are, on the surface, without beauty.

◀E▶ *Crimson Skies.* 2000. Zondervan, paper. 351 pp. ISBN 0-310-22370-9.
After serving some time on Devil's Island for his crimes, John Youngblood finds love with a reformed prostitute, Camille, and sees his daughter, Elspeth, happily married.

WICK, LORI

◀E▶ *KENSINGTON CHRONICLES*
The widely popular Wick, perhaps best known for her romantic westerns, tried her hand with Victorian romance in these far-flung adventures all loosely associated with Queen Victoria's palace at Kensington.

The Hawk and the Jewel. 1993. Harvest House, paper. 347 pp. ISBN: 1-56507-101-8.

Wings of the Morning. 1994. Harvest House, paper. 273 pp. ISBN 1-56507-177-8.

Who Brings Forth the Wind. 1994. Harvest House, paper. 396 pp. 1-56507-229-4.

Hawaii

◀▣✕ **CHAIKIN, LINDA.** *For Whom the Stars Shine.* **1999. Bethany, paper. 256 pp. ISBN 1-55661-647-1.**
Young nurse Eden Derrington is a devout Christian and devoted, traditional daughter, but God has called her to help those in the leper colony on Molokai. God also gives his blessing to a man she loves but of whom her family doesn't approve in this conventional romance with an unconventional subject. This is the first in a projected series dramatizing the impact of Christianity on Hawaii, the "Jewel of the Pacific."

Ireland

HOFF, B. J.

◀▣✕ *SONG OF ERIN*
Hoff chronicles the melodramatic but often lyrical fortunes of Terese Sheridan, impoverished, pregnant, and unmarried, who makes her way to America from the famine-stricken Ireland of the 1840s. There she meets Jack Kane, ambitious newspaperman, and her fortunes rise with his. The tale also unfolds in Ireland, where Jack's brother, Brady, the father of Terese's unborn child, forms a relationship with a woman as stormy as the hurricane in which they meet.

Cloth of Heaven. 1997. Tyndale, paper. 400 pp. ISBN 0-8423-1478-4.

Ashes and Lace. 1999.Tyndale, paper. 390 pp. ISBN 0-8423-1479-2.

◀▣✕ THOENE, BODIE, AND BROCK THOENE

★ *GALWAY CHRONICLES [Historical]*
The Thoenes' Gold Medallion-winning series chronicles the Irish troubles with the English in the mid-nineteenth century, precipitating the great Irish migration to the United States.

Only the River Runs Free. 1997. Nelson. 269 pp. ISBN 0-7852-80677.
The title of the first entry in the Galway Chronicles refers to the lot of the Irish under English rule in the 1830s: disenfranchised poverty. The Thoenes use the Irish village of Ballynockanor to stand for all of Ireland under the English tenant laws that divided Catholic from Protestant, landowner from tenant, and caused the Irish to despise the English. An eccentric villager, Mad Molly Fahey, like Cassandra, predicts the return of Joseph Connor Burke to Ballynockanor, inspiring hope among the villagers that Connor's usurped lands will again be used wisely and that prosperity will arrive. Joseph is a seminary student or at least he purports to be, dashing the hopes of Ballynockanor's fair maidens. But the young widow, Kate Garrity, and Joseph seem destined for each other.

Of Men and of Angels. 1998. Nelson. 320 pp. ISBN 0-7852-80685.
The second entry of the Galway Chronicles occurs in 1843. The tenant farmers around the village of Ballynockanor face eviction, deportation to America, or both, from English landlords in league with an oppressive English government. Some choose violent

opposition by joining the secretive Ribbonmen, whereas others, led almost reluctantly by the mild-mannered Joseph Burke, pursue Repeal, or laws to protect tenants' rights and prevent unfair rents. Joseph's romance with Kate Garrity heats up. Mad Molly and wise Father O'Bannon return, broadening the series's appeal even though they are stereotypes.

Ashes of Remembrance. 1999. Nelson. 320 pp. ISBN 0-7852-80693.
Ashes of Remembrance also occurs in 1843, closely following *Of Men and of Angels*. Joseph Burke and Kate Garrity marry but share little marital bliss, for soon Joseph is swept up in the Irish Troubles and deported to America, leaving Kate to do battle alone.

All Rivers to the Sea. 2000. Nelson. 320pp. ISBN 0-7852-80766.
Joseph Burke's return in 1844 and a bumper potato crop seem to herald better times for Ballynockanor in the concluding volume of the Galway Chronicles. But Mad Molly warns of a great blight that will descend upon potatoes, eventually leading to widespread starvation and an Irish diaspora to America.

United States

CHAIKIN, LINDA

◄►✖ *DAY TO REMEMBER*
Various heroines meet with love and peril in this nonsequential series set in different time periods.

Monday's Child. 1999. Harvest House, paper. 437 pp. ISBN 0-7369-0067-5.
Krista von Buren, a Swiss model ("Monday's child is fair of face") discovers that her family may have been involved in confiscating Jewish assets in WWII.

Tuesday's Child. 2000. Harvest House, paper. 335 pp. ISBN 0-7369-0068-3.
The reader journeys to Vichy France, where Valli Chattaine, a ballerina ("Tuesday's child is full of grace"), must flee to Algeria because of her activities as a spy.

Wednesday's Child. 2000. Harvest House, paper. 350 pp. ISBN 0-7369-0069-1.
The woe ascribed to Wednesday's child emanates from the stock market crash of 1929. Spoiled Gemma Alcott and her sister are daughters of a tycoon who has lost everything, and they must adjust. Gemma heads west.

Thursday's Child. 2001. Harvest House, paper. 358 pp. ISBN 0-7369-0070-5.
Paulette Brandt, the child of the week with "far to go," searches for her new husband, whom she married in wartime London, and who goes missing on a business trip to Berlin.

◄►✖ **HOFF, B. J.** *The Winds of Graystone Manor.* **1995. Bethany, paper. 320 pp. ISBN 1-55661-435-7.**
The first and only entry of what was to have been the St. Clare trilogy is set on Staten Island after the Civil War and features troubled Robin St. Clare, who marries as the story ends but has only begun to look for his first wife's murderer.

◀❊✕ **JACOBS, KATHY.** *Never Forsaken.* **1999. Crossway, paper. 272 pp. ISBN 1-58134-110-5.** *[Historical]*

In this first novel, 19-year-old Louisa Shumaker, her younger siblings, and their long-suffering mother slowly make their way from Germany to rejoin Louisa's father. In every little town, the Shumaker women are beset with thieves and confidence men, and they arrive in America penniless. Nor is America quite the promised land they'd hoped for.

KRAUS, JIM, AND TERRI KRAUS

◀❊✕★ *CIRCLE OF DESTINY [Historical]*

The Price. 2000. Tyndale, paper. 300 pp. ISBN 0-8423-1835-6.
The first in this series about four Harvard classmates features Joshua Quittner, son of an Ohio preacher. Joshua's brilliance as a student earns the support of his father's church to study at Harvard's famous seminary. It's a wonderful life for Joshua until he graduates and must fulfill his promise to take up his father's ministry. Ohio seems podunk after Harvard, and Joshua soon wriggles out of his obligations and heads for the California gold fields.

The Treasure. 2000. Tyndale, paper. 300 pp. ISBN 0-8423-1836-4.
The protagonist of the sequel to *The Price* is Joshua Quittner's classmate Gage Davis, the rich New Yorker who, to his three friends, seems to have it made. But Gage finds the going rough, both financially and romantically, when he takes over his father's business.

The Promise. 2001. Tyndale, paper. 403 pp. ISBN 0-8423-1837-2.
Surprisingly, the woman who so fired young Joshua Quittner's imagination in *The Price,* the liberated Hannah Morgan, becomes a submissive, even an abused wife. Her Harvard friends remain true, but her dreams of emancipation are shattered. She does receive her medical degree and eventually finds her place despite her cruel marriage, but only because she gives herself to God.

The Quest. 2002. Tyndale, paper. 300 pp. ISBN 0-8423-1838-0.
In the conclusion to the Circle of Destiny series the Krauses tell of the fourth Harvard friend, Jamison Pike. Jamison loved the rich but unhappy Hanna (of *The Price* and *The Promise*), but when it grew clear that she would marry another, he became a journalist and world-traveler. All his traveling has brought a weariness to his soul, though; a weariness his long-neglected faith may be able to address. And could it be that Hanna is available, after all? In an epilogue, the Krauses—through Jamison—update readers on what happened to the other members of the Circle of Four.

◀❊✕ **MACLEAN, AMANDA (Diane Noble).** *Kingdom Come.* **1997. Multnomah, paper. 257 pp. ISBN 1-57673-120-0.**
Ivy Rose Clayborne leaves her Appalachian home of Kingdom Come to become a doctor. When she returns, she finds that her enemies are not only poverty and ignorance, but also the MacKenzie Coal Mining Company, which is intent on destroying the environment while exploiting workers. But Harrison MacKenzie, the grandson of the company's patriarch, is more progressive, and attracted to Ivy Rose as well.

MORRIS, GILBERT. *Jacob's Way.* 2001. Zondervan, paper. 400 pp. ISBN 0-310-22696-1.

Jacob Dmitri and his granddaughter, Reisa, flee czarist Russia when a pogrom is directed at Jews. In America, they hit upon the colorful scheme of peddling uncommon goods across the Reconstruction South, encountering danger and privation. Jacob, his soul troubled as he nears the end of life, seeks answers in the Christian Messiah. Reisa seeks love but can't be sure that she's found it in Ben Driver, a man with a troubled past.

MORRIS, LYNN, AND GILBERT MORRIS

CHENEY DUVALL, M.D.

The highly popular romantic and medical career of a nineteenth-century woman doctor.

> *Stars for a Light.* 1994. Bethany, paper. 320 pp. ISBN 1-55661-422-5.
>
> *Shadow of the Mountains.* 1994. Bethany, paper. 336 pp. ISBN 1-55661-423-3.
>
> *A City Not Forsaken.* 1995. Bethany, paper. 335 pp. ISBN 1-55661-424-1.
>
> *Toward the Sunrising.* 1998. Unity, ME: Five Star. 408 pp. ISBN 0-78621-436-8.
>
> *Secret Place of Thunder.* 1996. Bethany, paper. 335 pp. ISBN 1-55661-426-8.
>
> *In the Twilight, In the Evening.* 1997. Bethany, paper. 320 pp. ISBN 1-55661-427-6.
>
> *Island of the Innocent.* 1998. Bethany, paper. 320 pp. ISBN 1-55661-698-8-6.
>
> *Driven with the Wind.* 2000. Bethany, paper. 315 pp. ISBN 1-55661-699-6.

NOBLE, DIANE. *The Veil.* 1998. WaterBrook, paper. 400 pp. ISBN 1-57856-014-4.

Noble attacks the Mormon doctrine of blood atonement—or killing of Gentiles—in a romance between a hardscrabble young Missourian, Lucas Knight, and a Mormon girl, Hannah McClary. Lucas's villainous stepfather, John Steel, wants pretty Hannah, too—for his eighth wife. All comes to a climax at the Mountain Meadows Massacre, an actual historical event in which Mormons killed Gentiles; in Noble's version, the murdering is undertaken by a band of vigilantes led by John Steel. Lucas and Hannah are portrayed as good people caught up in the wrong religion, whereas the corrupt John Steel represents the very heart of Mormonism's early days. The novel is in some ways reminiscent of Zane Grey's classic *Riders of the Purple Sage.* ■ Discussion ■

★ RIVERS, FRANCINE. *The Last Sin Eater.* 1998. Tyndale. 380 pp. ISBN 0-8423-3570-6. *[Historical]*

Rivers's title refers to the practice of certain hill people, recent immigrants from Wales, of calling in a "sin eater" upon the death of a relative. The sin eater's task was to take up, like Jesus, the sins of the deceased, thus easing passage to the afterlife. After her grandmother's death, 10-year-old Cadi Forbes looks for the sin eater, but her search is really a search for God, and eventually she leads the community away from the notion of a sin eater and toward Jesus. Rivers writes in a convincing Welsh dialect and vividly reconstructs the harsh life of the Smoky Mountains in the 1850s. And she makes a marvelous character of Cadi, not least because of her imaginary childhood playmate, Lilybet, a sort of angel. A complex, ambitious work informed by Cadi's innocence, free of the self-righteous qualities that sometimes detract from Rivers's surpassing talents. **Discussion**

SNELLING, LAURAINE

◀💊✗★ RED RIVER OF THE NORTH

An Untamed Land. 1996. Bethany, paper. 352 pp. ISBN 1-55661-576-0. *[Historical]*
Snelling's Norwegian Bjorklund family braves the North Atlantic, stumbles uncomprehendingly through the desperate immigrant community of New York City, and after a perilous overland journey is thrown upon the North Dakota prairie. They bust sod, try to make a crop, and somehow survive the fierce, interminable winter in this fine series opener, some scenes of which are the equal of Willa Cather.

A New Day Rising. 1996. Bethany, paper. 368 pp. ISBN 1-55661-577-9.
The much lighter sequel to *An Untamed Land* features Ingeborg Bjorklund, who, after losing her husband in a snowstorm, finds that she manages pretty well on her own. Men may have their uses, but suddenly she's beset with two of them. If she's interested at all, there will be conditions.

A Land to Call Home. 1997. Bethany, paper. 368 pp. ISBN 1-55661-578-7.
Ingeborg and new husband Haaken struggle to make their farm pay, while still more Bjorklunds arrive from Norway and the railroad makes its way through Dakota Territory.

The Reaper's Song. 1998. Bethany, paper. 368 pp. ISBN 1-55661-579-5.
Ingeborg and Haaken's farm is prospering, and Haaken even hires out with his steam thresher. But Ingeborg fears an early winter and undertakes fieldwork herself, hiring a dubious stranger to help.

Tender Mercies. 1999. Bethany, paper. 304 pp. ISBN 0-76422-089-6.
Snelling leaves off tales of Ingeborg and her husband for the quiet story of a young minister, John Solberg, who is endemically girl-shy but at last seems to have found his true love.

Blessing in Disguise. 1999. Bethany, paper. 269 pp. ISBN 0-76422-090-X.
In the formulaic conclusion of Red River of the North, Amanda Bjorklund flees Norway with a broken heart, hoping to join her North Dakota relatives. Not understanding English, she makes a wrong train connection, to arrive in an unknown town where a young rancher greets her as if he knows her.

◀💊✗ RETURN TO RED RIVER

A Dream to Follow. 2001. Bethany, paper. 304 pp. ISBN 0-7642-2317-8.
In this first volume of a reprise of Snelling's popular Red River of the North series, young Thorliff Bjorklund, the son of Ingeborg and Haaken Bjorklund, heads off to college at St. Olaf's to study journalism. His father thinks this is foolishness and wants Thorliff to stay on the farm. Thorliff counters that his younger brother is the real farmer of the new generation, but he feels guilty, nonetheless.

STAFFORD, TIM

◀◗✕★ *RIVER OF FREEDOM* [Historical]

Christianity Today editor Stafford's well-researched series gives life to periods in American history that dramatically affected the workings of democracy.

The Stamp of Glory. 2000. Nelson, paper. 396 pp. ISBN 0-78526-905-3.

That slavery is doomed is symbolized by the last will and testament of Martin Nichols, an Alabama plantation owner who sets his slaves free. This effectively ruins the viability of the plantation and sets his four children to the winds. Young Thomas heads for a successful life in New York City; his stubborn older brother, Martin, hangs on to the plantation, and as it fails he turns to drink. Sister Cecilia manages to marry well, while the youngest sibling, Brady, grows up rootless and arrogant. Meanwhile, the Civil War looms, and abolitionist figures such as Frederick Douglass and Harriet Beecher Stowe make their marks against such historical events as Nat Turner's slave rebellion. In New York, Thomas himself becomes an active abolitionist, linking with the preacher Charles Finney.

Sisters. 2000. Nelson, paper. 367 pp. ISBN 0-7852-6906-1.
Stafford uses the lives of two sisters, Susan and Elizabeth Netherton, named after suffrage heroines Susan B. Anthony and Elizabeth Cady Stanton, to portray the cause of feminism at the turn of the twentieth century. Much like contemporary women, plain Susan and attractive Elizabeth must balance their loyalty to traditional roles with the expanding horizons presented to women in a new era.

The Law of Love. 2001. Nelson, paper. 382 pp. ISBN 0-7852-6908-8.
Stafford jumps forward to the 1910s and 1920s to portray the "noble experiment" of Prohibition in the third entry of his River of Freedom series. His young hero, M. K. Nichols, loses his wife, a glamorous actress, to demon rum, and afterwards Nichols becomes a sworn foe of alcohol, moving to Washington to lobby for enactment of the Eighteenth Amendment.

WILLIAMSON, DENISE

◀◗✕★ *ROOTS OF FAITH* [Historical]

The Dark Sun Rises. 1999. Bethany, paper. 480 pp. ISBN 1-55661-882-4.
This solid, impressively researched series begins with the portrait of an antebellum, rich South Carolinian plantation family, the Callcotts. Their lifestyle and the sincerity of their faith are brought into question by an educated slave named Joseph. Joseph finds love with a fellow slave, but questions how Christianity can justify the ownership of one man by another.

When Stars Begin to Fall. 2000. Bethany, paper. 480 pp. ISBN 1-55661-883-2.
In the sequel to *The Dark Sun Rises*, Joseph makes his way via the Underground Railroad to Philadelphia. There, a Quaker physician trains him for medical practice, even though the color of his skin makes such practice illegal. His already difficult life is further complicated when fate conspires to pair him with Mayleda Callcott Ruskin, a white woman, and both must go on the run to escape slave hunters.

Civil War

⬥ DWYER, JOHN J. *Stonewall.* **1998. Broadman and Holman, paper. 631 pp. ISBN 0-8054-1663-3.**

Dwyer's biographical novel of Stonewall Jackson covers the great Confederate general from impoverished childhood to tragic death. Dwyer does not exaggerate Jackson's deeply religious nature, but his adulatory tone can be wearisome. Still, the heroic Jackson is intrinsically interesting, and so is Dwyer's account.

GAFFNEY, VIRGINIA

⬥ *RICHMOND CHRONICLES*

Southern belle Carrie Cromwell becomes a nurse as the Civil War rages in Virginia and her true love goes off to battle for the Confederacy. But Carrie's sympathies are always divided, and she sometimes openly cheers for the North.

> *Under the Southern Moon.* 1996. Harvest, paper. 375 pp. ISBN 1-56507-507-2.
> In 1850 Carrie Cromwell comes of age on a Virginia plantation. Like Eugenia Price, Gaffney weaves in period documents to illustrate the debate over slavery, which Carrie comes to oppose even though she will remain a Southern loyalist. But she aids two slaves, Moses and Rose, on the road to freedom in Philadelphia.

> *Carry Me Home.* 1997. Harvest, paper. 450 pp. ISBN 1-56507-562-5.
> In the sequel to *Under the Southern Moon,* it is 1861 and the Civil War rages. Carrie's true love, Robert Borden, is a lieutenant for the Virginia army. Moses and Rose struggle with the headiness of freedom, and Carrie, now that all the men are gone, struggles to run the plantation.

> *The Tender Rebel.* 1997. Harvest, paper. 445 pp. ISBN 1-56507-669-9.
> In the sequel to *Carry Me Home,* Carrie, who has always wanted to be a physician, becomes a nurse caring both for Union and Confederate wounded in Richmond. She continues to have things both ways: to serve as a Southerner, but talk as though she's loyal to the Union. Meanwhile, Moses and Rose join the cause of the Union.

> *Magnolia Dreams.* 1998. Harvest, paper. 403 pp. ISBN 1-56507-670-2.
> As it grows clear that the South will lose the war, Carrie marries Robert Borden in the concluding entry of the Richmond Chronicles. Carrie continues caring for the war's casualties and, recovered from his wounds, Lt. Borden must return to battle. As the novel concludes, the war rages toward an end, but the reader is left somewhat in the air.

LACY, AL

⬥ *BATTLES OF DESTINY [Historical]*

Though competing in a large field, Lacy's research skills shine through in this series dramatizing Civil War battles.

> *A Promise Unbroken.* 1993. Multnomah, paper. 307 pp. ISBN 0-88070-581-7.
> War splits the Ruffin family of Rich Mountain, West Virginia, between North and South.

> *A Heart Divided.* 1993. Multnomah. 320 pp. ISBN 0-88070-591-4.
> The battle of Mobile Bay.

Beloved Enemy. 1994. Multnomah. 356 pp. ISBN 0-88070-626-0.
The battle of Bull Run.

Shadowed Memories. 1994. Multnomah, paper. 307 pp. ISBN 0-88070-657-0.
The battle of Shiloh.

Joy from Ashes. 1995. Multnomah, paper. 285 pp. ISBN 0-88070-720-8.
The battle of Fredericksburg.

Season of Valor. 1996. Multnomah, paper. 294 pp. ISBN 0-88070-865-4.
The battle of Gettysburg.

Wings of the Wind. 1997. Multnomah, paper. 300 pp. ISBN 1-57673-032-8.
The battle of Antietam.

Turn of Glory. 1998. Multnomah, paper. 300 pp. ISBN 1-57673-217-7.
The final book in the series tells of the battle of Chancellorsville and includes a
portrait of Stonewall Jackson.

MORRIS, GILBERT

APPOMATOX SAGA
The Rocklin family is torn apart in this highly romantic Civil War series.

Covenant of Love. 1992. Tyndale, paper. 361 pp. ISBN 0-8423-5497-2.

Gates of His Enemies. 1992. Tyndale, paper. 337 pp. ISBN 0-8423-5069-X.

Where Honor Dwells. 1993. Tyndale, paper. 355 pp. ISBN 0-8423-6799-3.

Land of the Shadow. 1993. Tyndale, paper. 338 pp. ISBN 0-8423-5742-4.

Out of the Whirlwind. 1994. Tyndale, paper. 316 pp. ISBN 0-8423-1658-2.

Shadow of His Wings. 1994. Tyndale, paper. 270 pp. ISBN 0-8423-5987-7.

Wall of Fire. 1995. Tyndale, paper. 338 pp. ISBN 0-8423-8126-0.

Stars in Their Courses. 1995. Tyndale, paper. 350 pp. ISBN 0-8423-1674-4.

◄✗ *Edge of Honor.* 2000. Zondervan, paper. 384 pp. ISBN 0-310-22589-2.
Morris recycles elements of earlier efforts in this predictable tale of a surgeon,
Quentin Laribee, who, as the Civil War draws to a close, unintentionally kills a Confederate attempting to surrender. Haunted by his mistake, Quentin bids farewell
both to a lucrative New York practice and a rich sweetheart to seek out the dead
man's widow in primitive Helena, Arkansas. Without divulging his secret, Quentin
does all within his power to help the widow, and falls in love with her. The widow,
as it turns out, was less than grief stricken when she heard of her husband's death.

PRICE, EUGENIA. *The Waiting Time.* 1996. Bantam. 384 pp. ISBN 0-385-47938-7.
Price's last novel recycles earlier plots (see chapter 6, "Sagas") in her familiar setting of coastal southern Georgia. She introduces a northern heroine, Abigail Banes,
whose much-older husband, Eli, is drowned, leaving her as proprietor of not only his
rice plantation but also 100 slaves. Thad Green, the plantation overseer, steps into
the vacuum left by Eli; and his influence, the notions of abolitionist friends, and

Christian values make Abigail decide to free her slaves, even as the news arrives of John Brown's raid.

SNELLING, LAURAINE

✇ *A SECRET REFUGE*

Daughter of Twin Oaks. 2000. Bethany, paper. 282 pp. ISBN 1-55661-839-5.
Young Jesselynn Highwood takes on responsibility for her ruined Kentucky plantation when her father dies at the onset of the Civil War. Accompanied by freed slaves and fleeing an unwanted suitor, she disguises herself as a man and attempts to smuggle her priceless thoroughbred horses to Missouri. When Missouri proves not to be a refuge, she soldiers on along the Oregon Trail, seeking safety in the West.

Sisters of the Confederacy. 2000. Bethany, paper. 304 pp. ISBN 1-55661-840-9.
In the sequel to *Daughter of Twin Oaks* Jesselynn's saintly sister, Louisa, cares for the wounded in Richmond and falls in love with a brave man. For Louisa, the trials placed upon the South strengthen her faith; but for Jesselyn, the atrocities she witnesses call faith into question. Jesselynn falls in love, too, with a half-breed trail boss named Wolf. Her strained faith begins to reassert itself, but the calamitous times throw the would-be lovers apart in bittersweet confusion.

The Long Way Home. 2001. Bethany, paper. 288 pp. ISBN 1-55661-841-7.
The sequel to *Sisters of the Confederacy* finds Jesselynn Highwood still struggling to reach Oregon, and delayed at Fort Laramie. Meanwhile, Jesselynn's sister, Louisa, and their brother, Zachary, fall into Union hands as they attempt to smuggle medical supplies into Richmond.

TWENTIETH CENTURY

Austria

✇ PORTER, DAVID. *Vienna Passage.* 1995. Crossway, paper. 288 pp. ISBN 0-89107-824-X. *[Historical]*
Toby Burgate is a young, naive, stuffy, but rather likable Englishman at the beginning of the twentieth century. He takes a teaching job in Vienna, hoping that exposure to the city's civilizing traditions of art and music will lift him from his family's heritage of determined mediocrity. Unfortunately, Vienna is rife with anti-Semitism, which at first Toby embraces. But as he studies, his horizons expand, and he embraces a joyous new universe that has room both for Christians and Jews.

England

PHILLIPS, MICHAEL *[Historical]*

✇ *SECRETS OF HEATHERSLEIGH HALL*
In frank imitation of his literary hero George MacDonald, Phillips re-creates the intellectual turmoil of Victorian England at the beginning of the twentieth century. Phillips doesn't have MacDonald's quirky imagination or depth and can't deal effectively with ideas he finds heretical. Instead, he relies on romantic conventions such as dark and stormy nights, family curses, and

deathbed confessions—not to mention abandoned heroines. But he does root every story in painstaking historical research.

Wild Grows the Heather in Devon. 1998. Bethany, paper. 320 pp. ISBN 0-7642-2043-8.
The self-consciously modern, upper-class Rutherfords flirt with newfangled ideas such as evolution. Their daughter, Amanda, embraces the emancipation of women but only to meet with disaster when she runs off with a flashy charlatan, Ramsay Halifax.

Wayward Winds. 1999. Bethany, paper. 426 pp. ISBN 0-76422-044-6.
The evil Ramsey whisks Amanda away to Europe as World War I begins.

Heathersleigh Homecoming. 1999. Bethany, paper. 429 pp. ISBN 0-76422-045-4.
At last Amanda understands the mistakes she's made, not only with Ramsey but in finding herself behind enemy lines, where she's learned secrets that could help the English cause. The prodigal daughter escapes what amounts to her cell and, full of penitence and praise for God, makes her way home.

A New Dawn Over Devon. 2001. Bethany House, paper. 448 pp. ISBN 0-76422-440-9.
Phillips's series concludes with Amanda assuming the family legacy at Heathersleigh and features a preacher, Timothy Diggorsfeld, closely modeled on George MacDonald.

France

★ HORTON, DAVID

E⟨ A Legion of Honor. 1995. Victor, paper. 324 pp. ISBN 1-56476-540-7. **Discussion**

E⟨ The Sign of the Cross. 1997. Chariot Victor, paper. 350 pp. ISBN 1-56476-611-X.
See discussion in chapter 15, "Young Adult." **Sequel**

★ MUSSER, ELIZABETH *[Historical]*
The Huguenot cross, symbol of persecuted sixteenth century French Protestants, becomes also the symbol of the *pied-noirs,* the one million French citizens for whom Algeria is native, in Musser's two highly romanticized tales of the Algerian War of Independence in the early 1960s. Musser's experiences as a missionary in France add authenticity.

E⟨ Two Crosses. 1996. Chariot Victor, paper. 467 pp. ISBN 1-56476-577-6.
American Gabriella Madison, the daughter of missionaries to Senegal but studying at a fancy girls' school in southern France, falls in love with her teacher, David Hoffman. But David is deeply involved in espionage for the *pied-noirs* and *harki* (Algerian military loyal to France), and soon Gabriella's fate is intertwined with his. Gabriella's passionate Christianity eventually softens David's professed atheism and bitterness over a violent childhood.

◀█❮ *Two Testaments.* 1997. Chariot Victor, paper. 510 pp. ISBN 1-56476-610-1.
To escape the rising terror in Algeria, Anne-Marie Duchemin flees to France with the aid of her
childhood sweetheart, David Hoffman of *Two Crosses.* There she works in Gabriella's orphanage
with children displaced by the war, struggling at the same time with her love for an Algerian
named Moustafa and to raise her daughter, Ophelie. Ophelie is also David's daughter, the result
of teenage passions, but only Ophelie wants David and Anne-Marie to marry.   ██ Sequel ██

Germany

█❮ **CAVANAUGH, JACK**

YA *SONGS IN THE NIGHT*

While Mortals Sleep. 2001. Bethany, paper. 384 pp. ISBN 0-7642-2307-0.
While Mortals Sleep introduces the Reverend Josef Schumacher, who tries to provide
an alternative to Hitler's Youth Corps by training youngsters in resistance. As the first
entry ends, Josef has been arrested, but knows his anti-Nazi crusade will go on.

★ **GIARDINA, DENISE.** *Saints and Villains.* **1998. Norton. 483 pp. ISBN 0-393-04571-4.
[Historical]**
Giardina, novelist of the American labor movement and lay Episcopal preacher, surpasses
herself in this portrait of the Lutheran theologian Dietrich Bonhoeffer, who spoke out against
the Nazis and joined a plot to assassinate Hitler, the latter of which brought about Bonhoeffer's
own execution in the last days of WWII. Giardina adds characters but otherwise stays close to
the historical record, even drawing from Bonhoeffer's own writings.   ██ Discussion ██

█❮ ★ **SIMON, FRANK.** *Trial by Fire.* **1999. Crossway, paper. 320 pp. ISBN 1-58134-075-3.**
In this original and suspenseful story portraying the difficulties of Christians under the Nazis,
an influential architect, inextricably linked with the Reich, arranges his son's marriage with
the daughter of another prominent family. Erich von Arendt, the son, is pleased at first because
he has from childhood been in love with Johanna Kammler. For her part, Johanna understands
the futility of resisting the match, but she loves someone else, and treats Erich coldly. In despair,
but conscious of his duty, Erich joins his father in his architectural firm, and together they
help design Nuremberg Stadium, the sort of work that comes to the elder von Arendt because
he supports the Nazis. But Erich is a sincere Christian, and everything the Nazis stand for is
anathema to him. Difficulties with Johanna deepen his dilemma.   ██ Discussion ██

Israel

█❮ **THOENE, BODIE, AND BROCK THOENE**
The Zion Covenant and Zion Chronicles series established Bodie Thoene—and her research
collaborator and husband, Brock—as one of the premiere talents of Christian fiction. The two
series demonstrated that evangelical fiction could be well researched, and they spawned literally
dozens of imitations throughout the 1990s.

★ *ZION COVENANT [Historical]*
Zion Covenant dramatizes the plight of European Jews during WWII—living under assumed
identities, always on the run, dreaming of their biblical homeland.

Vienna Prelude. 1989. Bethany, paper. 410 pp. ISBN 1-55661-066-1.

Prague Counterpoint. 1989. Bethany, paper. 380 pp. ISBN 1-55661-078-5.

 Munich Signature. 1990. Bethany, paper. 396 pp. ISBN 1-55661-079-3.

Jerusalem Interlude. 1990. Bethany, paper. 400 pp. ISBN 1-55661-080-7.

Danzig Passage. 1991. Bethany, paper. 413 pp. ISBN 1-55661-081-5.

 Warsaw Requiem. 1991. Bethany, paper. 510 pp. ISBN 1-55661-188-9.

★ *ZION CHRONICLES [Historical]*

Zion Chronicles, published before Zion Covenant but occurring later, is about the pouring of refugees into Israel after WWII.

 The Gates of Zion. 1986. Bethany, paper. 368 pp. ISBN 0-87123-870-5.

A Daughter of Zion. 1987. Bethany, paper. 330 pp. ISBN 0-87123-940-X.

The Return to Zion. 1987. Bethany, paper. 343 pp. ISBN 0-87123-939-6.

A Light in Zion. 1988. Bethany, paper. 352 pp. ISBN 0-87123-990-6.

 The Key to Zion. 1988. Bethany, paper. 351 pp. ISBN 0-87123-034-3.

★ *ZION LEGACY [Historical]*

Zion Legacy is set in the state of Israel, barely coming to its feet in the first entry. Some characters appearing in Zion Covenant and Zion Chronicles appear also in Zion Legacy. All three series are essential holdings.

Jerusalem Vigil. 2000. Viking. 336 pp. ISBN 0-670-88911-3.
The Thoenes return to the territory of their earlier two series in this rousing, Michener-like tale of Israel in its first five days of nationhood. As the British pull out and David Ben-Gurion consolidates power, Arab forces attempt to route Jews from the Holy City, while the poorly armed, nascent Jewish army, composed of almost every nationality, schemes to break through Arab defenses and bring aid to their starving compatriots.

Thunder from Jerusalem. 2000. Viking. 307 pp. ISBN 0-670-89206-8.
In the almost immediate sequel to *Jerusalem Vigil,* the Theones give a fast-paced account of street fighting in Jerusalem between the disciplined Arab Legion and poorly armed Jewish irregulars, led by the shrewd Moshe Sachar. A group of flyboys provide the novel's few moments of levity as they jury-rig a cargo transport to bomb the Egyptian column heading north through the Negev Desert; meanwhile, a band of Jewish commandos inflicts heavy damage on the armored Syrians as they advance from the north.

Jerusalem's Heart. 2001. Viking. 336pp. ISBN 0-670-89487-7.
Most characters return in this third installment of the Zion Legacy series, including hapless Jacob and Lori Kalner. Jacob leads the fight to defend Jerusalem from the Arab Legion—a gallant and successful fight. But as in *Thunder from Jerusalem,* aerial combat steals the show, this time for pilot David Mayer, who rams Israel's one Messerschmitt down the Egyptians' throat. Love affairs continue on hold, as does the fate of young Daoud, the Arab–Jewish boy uncertain where to place his loyalties.

The Jerusalem Scrolls. 2001. Viking. 288 pp. ISBN 0-670-03012-0.
The Thoenes use the frame of a lull in the battle for Jerusalem to drop back in time 2,000 years and tell the story of Mary Magdalene. An independent

woman trying to make her way in a harshly patriarchal world, Mary scandalizes her late husband's family when she has an affair with a Roman officer, Marcus Longinus. Though Marcus loves Mary, his fortunes turn sour when political intrigues go against him. Thus, he cannot protect Mary when the Jewish community brands her a prostitute. Soon, she *is* a prostitute, and so full of despair that she's prepared to kill herself. The teachings and miracles of a gentle new prophet, Yeshua, literally rescue her—and Marcus as well.

Stones of Jerusalem. 2002. Viking. 304 pp. ISBN 0-670-03051-1.
Stones of Jerusalem continues the New Testament story begun in *The Jerusalem Scrolls*. Miryam prospers in her new faith, converting her estate into a refuge for the poor. Marcus, slowly turning toward conversion, undertakes a fact-finding mission for the Roman authority, trying to determine what potential for rebellion Yeshua represents. Accidentally, he's joined by Nakdimon (Nicodemus), undertaking a similar mission for the Sanhedrin. Also seeking Yeshua are three bedraggled, sentimentally drawn children, dragooned into the service of Barabbas, the true revolutionary of the piece. Yeshua himself makes an appearance in the final third of the book. *Stones of Jerusalem* lacks the focus of Miryam's moving story in *The Jerusalem Scrolls*, but, because of the momentous events soon to come, the Thoenes generate suspense, and each of their characterizations is vivid.

Lithuania

SCHUNK, LAUREL

◀▣✖ *LITHUANIAN TRILOGY*

A Clear North Light. 2001. St Kitts. 332 pp. ISBN 0-9661879-6-2.
Schunk's hero is an impoverished stained-glass artisan, a young Lithuanian Baptist named Petras Simonaitis. Petras is striving to make enough money to marry his sweetheart, a Catholic girl named Rima. Unfortunately, it's 1938 and the Nazis are rapidly gaining power. The province's rich man, Baron Pavel Gerulaitis, allies himself with the Nazis but is less interested in politics than lechery. He virtually commands Petras's pretty sister to move into his castle, and he also has designs on Rima. Petras rescues her from the Baron's castle, and they flee to safety, but happiness eludes the young couple, for they are desperately poor and must live in hiding. The Nazis lose their hold, and the Baron is deposed, but then the Soviets gain control and poor Lithuania is even worse off.

Russia

PHILLIPS, MICHAEL R., AND JUDITH PELLA

◀▣✖ *THE RUSSIANS*
The series tells the stories of individual Russians at the end of the nineteenth century through the Revolution. The first installment features a devout peasant girl brought to work for a royal family in St. Petersburg—like all royal families, doomed by the rise of the Bolsheviks. Later episodes feature a love affair between a Russian nurse and an American reporter and the valiant struggles of the Fedorcenko family to maintain their faith under the threat of its extinction. Phillips and Pella collaborated on the first four novels of this popular, ambitious series, and Pella continued thereafter.

[by Phillips and Pella]

The Crown and the Crucible. 1991. Bethany, paper. 410 pp. ISBN 1-55661-172-2.

A House Divided. 1992. Bethany, paper. 350 pp. ISBN 1-55661-173-0.

Travail and Triumph. 1992. Bethany, paper. 400 pp. ISBN 1-55661-174-9.

Heirs of the Motherland. 1993. Bethany, paper. 382 pp. ISBN 1-55661-358-X.

[by Pella alone]

The Dawning of Deliverance. 1995. Bethany, paper. 400 pp. ISBN 1-55661-359-8.

White Nights, Red Mornings. 1996. Bethany, paper. 400 pp. ISBN 1-55661-360-1.

Passage into Light. 1998. Bethany, paper. 400 pp. ISBN 1-55661-869-7.

Scotland

PHILLIPS, MICHAEL

CALEDONIA

Legend of the Celtic Stone. 1999. Bethany, paper. 546 pp. ISBN 0-7642-2250-3.
Using a broad brush, Phillips retells Scottish history through the eyes of Andrew Trentham, an MP and rich bachelor, up from London after being jilted by his lady love. The nation is shocked by a burglary at Westminster Abbey that has political implications, but Andrew is too depressed to ponder the matter. Sulking about in the Scottish Highlands, Andrew stops at the house of an old shepherd who regales him with tales of early Scotland. Andrew begins to feel that understanding his ancestry and the history of Scotland will make him a better legislator for twenty-first-century England.

An Ancient Strife. 2000. Bethany, paper. 530 pp. ISBN 0-7642-2354-2.
In the second volume of the Caledonia series, Andrew Trentham continues to try to get a handle on a present-day political dilemma by researching his noble ancestors. Recovered from his unrequited love affair, he falls for a Scottish woman.

Turkey

KELLY, CLINT

IN THE SHADOW OF THE MOUNTAIN

Deliver Us from Evil. 1998. Bethany, paper. 304 pp. ISBN 1-55661-955-3.
Kelly delivers a vital, even brutal, representation of one of the viler chapters of twentieth century history: the genocide of Armenian Christians during WWI. It's marred by Kelly's cardboard characterizations of every Turk as a pitiless killer; still, he stakes out a piece of history much in need of explication for contemporary readers. In the first novel, Kelly's heroine, Adrine Tevian, disguises her beauty to avoid being raped in a Turkish camp while the love of her life, Tatul Sarafian, joins the more or less futile resistance.

The Power and the Glory. 1999. Bethany, paper. 304 pp. ISBN 1-55661-956.
In this sequel to *Deliver Us from Evil,* Adrine and Tatul, struggling to survive in the shadow lands of Istanbul, join a battered remnant of refugees trying to reconstitute their decimated community. Readers will be reminded of the more recent history of religious minorities in the Balkans.

United States

Great Depression

◄**E**✕ **AUSTIN, LYNN.** *Hidden Places.* **2001. Bethany, paper. 432 pp. ISBN 0-7642-2197-3.**
With the last of the men of her family in the grave, Eliza Wyatt is left to run the orchard, and raise her three children, alone. It's 1930, and striking off for new territories isn't an option. A stranger arrives at her doorstep, and Eliza is mindful of the verse in Hebrews that Christians should "entertain strangers," for they may turn out to be angels. But this stranger seems to be dying, and his knapsack holds a story that is less than angelic.

◄**E**✕ **HATCHER, ROBIN LEE.** *The Shepherd's Voice.* **2000. WaterBrook, paper. 367 pp. ISBN 1-57856-152-3.**

Gabe Talmadge is a broken man. Released from prison after serving 10 years for a murder he didn't commit, he comes home to his father, Hudson, the most powerful man in Ransom, Idaho. But Gabe is no prodigal son, and his father, the one who engineered his son's imprisonment, does not welcome him. Gabe goes to work for Akira Macauley, a sheep rancher whose land Hudson covets. The work is meaningful and he loves Akira, but Gabe's troubles are far from over.

LEON, BONNIE

◄**E**✕ *SOWERS TRILOGY*

YA Russian farmers flee Stalinist terror only to suffer privations in Washington State in this workmanlike series.

> ***Where Freedom Grows.*** 1998. Broadman and Holman, paper. 300 pp. ISBN 0-8054-1272-7.
> The first in the series is a coming-of-age tale about a young Russian Jew, Tatyana Letinov, who, as Stalin's rule grows more ruthless, is sent to the United States by her parents. But although she finds religious freedom in her new homeland, the Great Depression is in full swing, and daily life is hardly easier. Tatyana is lonely and longs for Russia, at least until she meets her husband-to-be, Dmitri Broido.

> ***In Fields of Freedom.*** 1999. Broadman and Holman, paper. 309 pp. ISBN 0-8054-1273-5.
> In the sequel to *Where Freedom Grows,* Dmitri labors mightily to put his new family on solid economic footing. He heads for the timber country of Washington State, but the only job he can find is in a coal mine.

> ***Harvest of Truth.*** 2000. Broadman and Holman, paper. 320 pp. ISBN 0-8054-1274-3.
> In this conclusion to the Sowers Trilogy, conditions have improved for the Broidos. But Tatyana worries for the fate of her brother, Yuri, placed in a concentration camp back in the Soviet Union.

◀E✗ MCCOURTNEY, LORENA. *Escape.* 1996. Multnomah, paper. 258 pp. ISBN 1-57673-012-3.

As the Dust Bowl descends on Oklahoma, Beth Curtis is on hard times. The school where she taught has shut down. Complicating matters, her sister dies in childbirth, leaving Beth strict instructions not to turn her infant son over to her rich but godless in-laws. When a handsome stranger shows up wanting custody, Beth grabs the boy and flees into the night for parts unknown. The stranger trails her.

◀E✗ MILLER, CALVIN

Snow. 1998. Bethany. 144 pp. ISBN 0-76422-152-3.

In 1929, King of Prussia, Pennsylvania is hit by a devastating snowstorm. Erick Mueller, a college professor visiting home for the holidays, takes over when his father, the coal man, can't deliver the town's fuel. Doing the job, he meets Mary Withers, a widow with a young asthmatic daughter, Alexis, and as the weeks pass, the attraction between them grows. There are conflicts—Mary's inability to commit to another marriage, and a feud between Erick's father and the other son, Otto, but everything comes heartwarmingly together on Christmas Eve.

Wind. 2000. Bethany. 159 pp. ISBN 0-7642-2362-3.

When he loses everything, including his Philadelphia house, in the stock market crash of 1929, Ernest Pitovsky moves his sickly wife and his two children into the country near King of Prussia. There, they make a home out of a junk car, and there is no income until Ernest takes a job milking cows from Isabel McCaslin. She's co-owner of a prosperous dairy with her brother, a skinflint who sees Pitovsky's troubles to be of his own making.   **■ Sequel**

Shade. 2001. Bethany. 160 pp. ISBN 0-7642-2363-1.

Erick Mueller, of *Snow*, is about to marry the widow Mary Withers when an event from the past brings them both up short. It's all tied to another couple about to marry, Isabel "Dizzy Izzy" McCaslin of *Wind*, and Erick's son, Otto. And in their case, too, their betrothal is threatened by the past: Dizzy Izzy's old beau, the Bible salesman Benny Baxter, returns. Isabel's story steals the show as her rapturous nature heats up and she flutters between Benny's wild fundamentalism and Otto's solid virtue. It's a hot summer in King of Prussia, and everyone needs a bit of shade.   **■ Sequel**

◀E✗ MORRIS, GILBERT. *A Time to Weep.* 1996. Revell, paper. 336 pp. ISBN 0-8007-5576-6.

Okies and Ozarkers flee the desolation wrought by the Depression and attempt to make their way in Los Angeles and Chicago, maintaining their faith and hope in the face of poverty and despair.

See also Frederick Buechner's *The Wizard's Tide,* p. 220; B. J. Hoff's *The Penny Whistle,* p. 243; and Agnes Sligh Turnbull's *The Bishop's Mantle,* p. 239.

World War II

World War II is one of the most frequently used settings in Christian historical fiction. Robert Funderburk, in his dedication to *The Fires of Autumn* (p. 191), explains why:

> World War II separated us geographically, but it was the last time
> America was truly united as a nation. Men and women believed that
> their country was worth the ultimate sacrifice, that the price of liberty
> was too dear not to be paid. We looked to God for victory, patriotism
> was a quality worthy of praise, and prayer was accepted as an essential
> part of our public and private lives. Husbands and wives treasured
> each other, their children and their homes. (Funderburk 1996)

Funderburk's remarks also suggest why the divisive Vietnam War is not as often treated in Christian fiction, although he himself treats it with sensitivity in his Dylan St. John mystery series (p. 191) and in *The Rainbow's End,* the final volume of his Innocent Years series (p. 89).

See also chapter 6, "Sagas"; chapter 11, "The Christian Life," the nostalgia section; and the chapter 5, "Twentieth-Century" subheadings "Germany" and "France."

⬛✖ ★ BELLIREAU, G. K. *Go Down to Silence.* 2001. Multnomah, paper. 352 pp. ISBN 1-57673-736-5.

When Jacob Horowitz learns that his old friend Pierre is dying, he's overwhelmed with memories. Pierre, a Belgian, got Jacob out of Nazi Germany long ago, and at some risk to himself. Jacob came to New York and grew rich. Ironically, Jacob himself has been diagnosed with terminal cancer. Almost worse, Jacob has come to a time in his life when he should be looking back with satisfaction, but he doesn't like the way business is done these days, and his children are strangers to him. He decides to visit Pierre one last time, but before he goes he summons his estranged son, Alex. Jacob wants reconciliation if not love, and the two cross the ocean together on their sad, cathartic odyssey.   **▌Discussion**

⬛✖ FRENCH, DAVID, AND NANCY FRENCH. *South Pacific Journal.* 1999. Broadman and Holman, paper. 215 pp. ISBN 0-8054-1963-2.

Jacob Levine, an arrogant and highly successful New York lawyer, thinks his older sister, Sarah, has been dead since WWII. Then he receives a mysterious message from the Philippines that she has only just died and has left an "inheritance." He flies to Manila, where he finds Sarah's diary of her wartime experiences, a tale of heroism and sustained faith, which deeply moves him.

⬛✖ JOENS, MICHAEL R. *Triumph of the Soul.* 1999. Baker, paper. 384 pp. ISBN 0-8007-5702-5.

A battle-weary German ace, Roll Schiller, shoots down his naive American counterpart, Billy Hochreiter, in this B-movie rehash graced with some fine aerial combat scenes. Joens traces the spiritual lives of both fliers, and in both cases they are inspired by women: Roll's, his sometime sweetheart, Olga, thoughts of whom are intermingled with his Christian sister's fate and the declining fortunes of the Reich; Billy's, a Christian Frenchwoman, Colette, whom he meets while thrashing about in the woods after bailing out. Colette guides young Billy to a profounder examination of life and the great war against it, but Roll's fortunes continue to worsen.

⬛✖ LARSON, ELYSE J. *Dawn's Early Light.* 1996. Nelson, paper. 240 pp. ISBN 0-7852-7688-2.

Jean Thornton hates the Japanese and is glad to take a job at the Tule Lake settlement camp for Japanese Americans, where she'll pose as a teacher while spying. Soon Jean must confront her own prejudices and reexamine her faith when confronted with the unswerving loyalty of the inmates, their tragic individual stories, and romance.

LARSON, ELYSE J.

◀█✕ *WOMEN OF VALOR*

> ***For Such a Time.*** 2000. Bethany, paper. 352 pp. ISBN 0-7642-2355-0.
> The first in the Women of Valor series features Giselle Munier and Jean Thornton, cousins who are more than ordinarily intimate because they spent much of their childhood together in 1930s France. As the war deepens, Giselle, married to a Jew who has been captured by the Nazis, runs errands for the Resistance and tries to shield her daughters from lustful German soldiers. Then Jean, stationed with the Red Cross in Wales, hears of her cousin's arrest. In a series of unlikely scenes, Larson puts Jean through combat training and drops her into France on a rescue mission a la *The Guns of Navarone*. Giselle gets her man back, and an old beau, wounded in Italy, shows up in Wales to recuperate under Jean's care. Meanwhile, it's D-Day.

> ***So Shall We Stand.*** 2001. Bethany, paper. 352 pp. ISBN 0-7642-2375-5.
> Nella Killian, a minister's daughter and, at 18, a mother and war widow, returns home to Wales with her daughter. She is going wearily and bitterly through the motions of life when she discovers that the death of a young American soldier, ruled a suicide, was actually a murder. Giselle Munier of *For Such a Time* takes a minor role in this sequel.

MINATRA, MARY ANN

◀█✕ *LEGACY OF HONOR*
As the war looms, a young American woman becomes entangled with a Nazi with a conscience.

> ***Before Night Falls.*** 1996. Harvest, paper. 420 pp. ISBN 1-56507-432-7.

> ***Jewel in the Evening Sky.*** 1997. Harvest, paper. 467 pp. ISBN 1-56507-668-0.

◀█✕ THOENE, BODIE, AND BROCK THOENE. *Twilight of Courage*. 1995. Nelson. 512pp. ISBN 0-7852-7596-7.
This rare stand-alone from the Thoenes seems like a pastiche from other books: Essentially, it tells the story of the escape of two journalists from Warsaw as the Nazis tighten their noose. Other elements, such as the tale of a baby's journey to Jerusalem and the efforts of one man to crack the German secret code, are interwoven.

◀█✕ WALES, KEN, AND DAVID POLING. *Sea of Glory*. 2001. Broadman and Holman, paper. 384 pp. ISBN 0-8054-5000-9. *[Historical]*
Wales and Poling offer a "greatest generation" sort of tale of real-life chaplains, one Jewish, one Catholic, one Dutch Reformed, and one Methodist, who in 1943 sailed together on an ill-fated troop ship called the *Dorchester*. The chaplains struck up a friendship based on their lively theological discussions. When the ship was torpedoed in frigid North Atlantic waters, there were not enough lifeboats, and with great patriotic fervor the chaplains volunteered to stay behind.

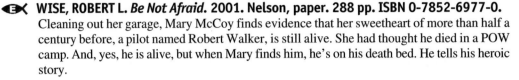 **WISE, ROBERT L.** *Be Not Afraid.* **2001. Nelson, paper. 288 pp. ISBN 0-7852-6977-0.**
Cleaning out her garage, Mary McCoy finds evidence that her sweetheart of more than half a century before, a pilot named Robert Walker, is still alive. She had thought he died in a POW camp. And, yes, he is alive, but when Mary finds him, he's on his death bed. He tells his heroic story.

See also "Germany" in "Twentieth Century" discussed earlier.

Post-War

MUSSER, ELIZABETH. *The Swan House.* **2001. Bethany, paper. 448 pp. ISBN 0-7642-2508-1.**
Mary Swan Middleton, a privileged young white girl in 1960s Atlanta, has her world turned upside down when her mother dies in a Paris plane crash, an historical event that killed Atlanta's most eminent visual artists and funders of art. Though money won't be a problem, Mary's unstable mother leaves behind some mysteries, with which for the moment Mary cannot cope. She falls into a depression that threatens never to lift until the family's black maid takes her in hand and tells her to make something of herself. Mary volunteers for charity work and falls in love with a charismatic young black man, Carl. Sorting through her feelings for Carl and her dead mother, she reaches the threshold of adulthood.

Chapter 6

Sagas

Though the word *saga* may conjure up Vikings wielding axes against their equally valiant foes, in genre terms it simply refers to historical series that extend over generations, or individual novels that tell a generational story, such as Colleen McCullough's *The Thorn Birds* (p. 254).

Evangelical sagas are usually romantic historicals, differing from that subgenre in that the reader may be able to find out what happened after her favorite characters got married and settled down in the castle. As in the previous chapter, *[Historical]* indicates those titles or series where the treatment of history is somewhat rigorous.

AMERICAN SAGAS

AUSTIN, LYNN. *Eve's Daughters.* 1999. Bethany, paper. 448 pp. ISBN 0-7642-2195-7.

Austin traces the fortunes of four women through more than 100 years from Germany to New York, beginning with the sour Louise Schroder. Like each of her descendants, Louise is a difficult wife, but her long-suffering, heroic husband at last wins her obedience and admiration; Suzanne Pulaski, a contemporary woman and Louise's great-granddaughter, is another story, and so is her husband. When he wants to move cross-country, her career is threatened, and she files for divorce. There's a secret in the family that her grandmother, Emma Bauer, knows that may cause her to change her mind.

BERGREN, LISA TAWN

NORTHERN LIGHTS

More than can be said of other series, Northern Lights is really one novel, stretching out the episodic trials of a group of Norwegian immigrants in the 1880s.

The Captain's Bride. 1998. WaterBrook, paper. 384 pp. ISBN 1-57856-013-6.
Elsa Anders marries the seaman Peder Ramstad and begins to wonder if his voyages ever will end in this tale of Norwegian valor at sea set in 1880. Bergren also introduces her other major characters: Elsa's kid sister, Tora, a flirt; and Karl, Peder's friend who also is in love with Elsa.

Deep Harbor. 1999. WaterBrook, paper. 384 pp. ISBN 1-57856-045-4.
Bergren takes up the lives of her characters five years later in *The Captain's Bride.* Elisa's friend Kaatje Jansen occupies center stage as she searches for her missing husband and tries to run a farm carved out of the rainforests in what will become the state of Washington. Tora leads a gay, thoughtless life, while her older sister must cope with the loss of her husband and the taking over of his ship. This leaves an opening for Karl, successful now in his own right but convinced true love will never come his way.

Midnight Sun. 2000. WaterBrook, paper. 366 pp. ISBN 1-57856-113-2.
In the concluding novel of the Northern Lights series, Kaatje treks through the Alaskan wilderness seeking her lost husband, resisting her feelings for her handsome guide. Tora settles down at last, putting her flirtatiousness behind her, and old friends Karl and Elsa wonder about getting together.

BOESHAAR, ANDREA, SALLY LAITY, YVONNE LEHMAN, AND DIANN MILLS. *The Painting.* 2000. Barbour, paper. 347 pp. ISBN 1-57748-640-4.
Beginning in 1860 Pennsylvania and ending in 1994 Wisconsin, four writers spin a romantic legacy around a painting of the Morgan family homestead.

CHAIKIN, LINDA

GREAT NORTHWEST [Historical]
Chaikin's sprawling, Michener-like tales ladle in big dollops of history, from the Chicago Fire to the Battle of the Little Big Horn, but focus on the settlement of the American Northwest.

Empire Builders. 1994. Bethany, paper. 334 pp. ISBN 1-55661-441-1.
In the series opener, the highfalutin ways of a railroad heiress, Ember Ridgeway, crash against the ambitions of a lumber baron, Tavish Wilder.

Winds of Allegiance. 1996. Bethany, paper. 296 pp. ISBN 1-55661-442-X.
In the sequel to *Empire Builders,* Trace Wilder runs afoul of Russian territorial interests and his own feelings for a Russian–English woman in his attempts to secure the Northwest for the United States.

CAVANAUGH, JACK

AMERICAN FAMILY PORTRAIT
This ambitious and, for the most part, highly readable series follows the Morgan family line through American history, from the Puritans through the confusing 1960s, mostly emphasizing wars including the Revolutionary War, the Civil War, the two World Wars, and the Vietnam War. In the first volume, young Drew Morgan becomes a Puritan convert, and his strong faith imprints the family through the years, though sometimes, as in the 1960s, it must endure heavy challenges.

The Puritans. 1994. Chariot Victor, paper. 426 pp. ISBN 1-56476-440-0.

The Colonists. 1995. Chariot Victor, paper. 482 pp. ISBN 1-56476-346-3.

The Patriots. 1996. Chariot Victor, paper. 530 pp. ISBN 1-56476-428-1.

The Adversaries. 1996. Chariot Victor, paper. 500 pp. ISBN 1-56476-535-0.

The Pioneers. 1996. Chariot Victor, paper. 423 pp. ISBN 1-56476-587-3.

The Allies. 1997. Chariot Victor, paper. 500 pp. ISBN 1-56476-588-1.

The Victors. 1998. Chariot Victor, paper. 500 pp. ISBN 1-56476-589-X.

The Peacemakers. 1999. Chariot Victor, paper. 512 pp. ISBN 1-56476-681-0.

COTE, LYN

BLESSED ASSURANCE

Cote follows the interlinked fortunes of two families, the black Duboises and the white Wagstaffs, through 50 years of upheaval, attending the Chicago Fire of 1871, the San Francisco earthquake of 1906, and Prohibition New Orleans.

Whispers of Love. 1999. Broadman and Holman, paper. 280 pp. ISBN 0-8054-1967-5.

Lost in His Love. 2000. Broadman and Holman, paper. 309 pp. ISBN 0-8054-1968-3.

Echoes of Mercy. 2000. Broadman and Holman, paper. 245 pp. ISBN 0-8054-1969-1.

FUNDERBURK, ROBERT

INNOCENT YEARS

★ *Love and Glory.* 1994. Bethany, paper. 304 pp. ISBN 1-55661-460-8.
Love and Glory, Funderburk's first novel, is about a returning war veteran, Lane Temple, a lawyer who moves to the big city of Baton Rouge when he can't find work in his little hometown. He meets with success but also starts living the high life, to the point that his long-suffering wife checks into a hotel to kill herself. Instead, she hears Billy Graham on the radio, comes to God, and rallies her errant husband and confused family.

Those Golden Days. 1995. Bethany, paper. 299 pp. ISBN 1-55661-461-6.
In the sequel to *Love and Glory,* Jessie, Catherine and Lane's oldest daughter, strikes out on her own as a USO singer and is seduced by the lifestyle, much to the dismay of her world-weary parents. Meanwhile, the Korean Peninsula erupts in war, and Lane is called up for service.

Heart and Soul. 1995. Bethany, paper. 298 pp. ISBN 1-55661-462-4.
Lane returns from the Korean War as a hero, but he's shaken up emotionally and is somewhat physically disabled. At the urging of an old friend, he runs for the Louisiana House, but a crooked senator manages to frame him over land designated for the new interstate highway system, and he goes to prison.

★ *Old Familiar Places.* 1996. Bethany, paper. 287 pp. ISBN 1-55661-463-2.
In the delightful and inventive *Old Familiar Places,* Funderburk creates a brief portrait of Elvis, whom Jessie hears in Memphis. She decides to become a rock-and-roll singer, but then a Jimmy Swaggart sort of figure, Billy Pilgrim, offers her a job in his traveling evangelist show. Meanwhile, back in Louisiana, Jessie's younger sister is dying of leukemia.

Tenderness and Fire. 1997. Bethany, paper. 287 pp. ISBN 1-55661-464-0.
Catherine and Lane's son, Dalton, is featured in the fifth installment of the Innocent Years series. He's a running back on the football team at Louisiana State University, assured of a pro career until he hurts his leg, whereupon his superficial girlfriend, a cheerleader, drops him cold. He starts hanging out in the French Quarter, where he meets a fallen woman who has a heart of gold.

The Rainbow's End. 1997. Bethany, paper. 256 pp. ISBN 1-55661-465-9.
Young Cassidy Temple drops out of college to join the Green Berets in the series finale, becoming an advisor in the early days of the Vietnam War (1960). For R&R he romances a USO dancer.

GRANT, JEAN

⬤✖ SALINAS VALLEY
Grant fictionalizes historical highlights of the Salinas Valley, beginning after the Civil War with a portrait of the Salvation Army, and finishing with Cesar Chavez and the strikes of farmworkers in the 1960s.

The Promise of the Willows. 1994. Nelson, paper. 221 pp. ISBN 0-7852-8102-9.

The Promise of Peace. 1994. Nelson, paper. 213 pp. ISBN 0-7852-8104-5.

The Promise of Victory. 1995. Nelson, paper. 221 pp. ISBN 0-7852-8103-7.

The Promise of the Harvest. 1996. Nelson, paper. 228 pp. ISBN 0-7852-8105-3.

LACY, AL, AND JOANNA LACY

⬤✖ SHADOW OF LIBERTY

Let Freedom Ring. 2001. Multnomah, paper. 300 pp. ISBN 1-57673-756-X.
Persecuted Christian Vladimir Petrovna flees from the Cossacks to the more hopeful shores of America is this first of a series celebrating America's immigrants.

MORRIS, GILBERT

⬤✖ AMERICAN ODYSSEY
Generations of the Stuart family experience the major eras of the twentieth century—from the turn of the century through the 1950s.

A Time to Be Born. 1994. Revell, paper. 304 pp. ISBN 0-80075-610-X.

A Time to Die. 1994. Revell, paper. 290 pp. ISBN 0-80075-521-9.

A Time to Laugh. 1995. Revell, paper. 304 pp. ISBN 0-80075-566-9.

A Time to Weep. 1996. Revell, paper. 320 pp. ISBN 0-80075-576-6.

A Time of War. 1997. Revell, paper. 352 pp. ISBN 0-80075-610-X.

A Time to Build. 1998. Revell, paper. 320 pp. ISBN 0-80075-645-2.

HOUSE OF WINSLOW

The Winslow family's adventures range from the American West to Africa, and from the nineteenth century into the twentieth.

The Honorable Imposter. 1987. Bethany, paper. 331 pp. ISBN 0-87123-933-7.

The Captive Bride. 1987. Bethany, paper. 238 pp. ISBN 0-87123-978-7.

The Indentured Heart. 1988. Bethany, paper. 288 pp. ISBN 1-55661-003-3.

The Gentle Rebel. 1988. Bethany, paper. 285 pp. ISBN 1-55661-006-8.

The Saintly Buccaneer. 1989. Bethany, paper. 299 pp. ISBN 1-55661-048-3.

The Holy Warrior. 1989. Bethany, paper. 284 pp. ISBN 1-55661-054-8.

The Reluctant Bridegroom. 1990. Bethany, paper. 303 pp. ISBN 1-55661-069-6.

The Last Confederate. 1990. Bethany, paper. 333 pp. ISBN 1-55661-109-9.

The Dixie Widow. 1991. Bethany, paper. 318 pp. ISBN 1-55661-115-3.

The Wounded Yankee. 1991. Bethany, paper. 304 pp. ISBN 1-55661-116-1.

The Union Belle. 1992. Bethany, paper. 334 pp. ISBN 1-55661-186-2.

The Final Adversary. 1992. Bethany, paper. 301 pp. ISBN 1-55661-261-3.

The Crossed Sabres. 1993. Bethany, paper. 317 pp. ISBN 1-55661-309-1.

The Valiant Gunman. 1993. Bethany, paper. 320 pp. ISBN 1-55661-310-5.

Gallant Outlaw. 1994. Bethany, paper, 288 pp. ISBN 1-55661-311-3.

The Jeweled Spur. 1994. Bethany, paper. 299 pp. ISBN 1-55661-392-X.

The Yukon Queen. 1995. Bethany, paper. 285 pp. ISBN 1-55661-393-8.

The Rough Rider. 1995. Bethany, paper. 303 pp. ISBN 1-55661-394-6.

The Iron Lady. 1996. Bethany, paper. 320 pp. ISBN 1-55661-687-2.

The Silver Star. 1997. Bethany, paper. 304 pp. ISBN 1-55661-688-0.

The Shadow Portrait. 1998. Bethany, paper. 304 pp. ISBN 1-5566-689-9.

The White Hunter. 1999. Bethany, paper. 304 pp. ISBN 1-55661-909-X.

The Flying Cavalier. 1999. Bethany, paper. 318 pp. ISBN 0-76422-115-9.

The Glorious Prodigal. 2000. Bethany, paper. 320 pp. ISBN 0-7642-2116-7.

Amazon Quest. 2001. Bethany, paper. 320 pp. ISBN 0-7642-2117-5.

The Golden Angel. 2001. Bethany, paper. 316 pp. ISBN 0-7642-2118-3.

The Heavenly Fugitive. 2002. Bethany, paper. 320 pp. ISBN 0-7642-2599-5.

NOBLE, DIANE

◆▣✕ *CALIFORNIA CHRONICLES*

When the Far Hills Bloom. 1999. WaterBrook, paper. 384 pp. ISBN 1-57856-140-X.
The Callahan and Byrne families squabble, make peace, and establish dynasties in California toward the end of the Civil War in *When the Far Hills Bloom,* featuring Aislin Byrne. She's courted by the two Dearbourne brothers, Spence and Jamie, who aid her in saving Rancho de la Paloma, the family spread, with their scheme of rounding up mustangs and selling them to the army.

The Blossom and the Nettle. 2000. WaterBrook, paper. 400 pp. ISBN 1-57856-090-X.
Emmy Callahan, a homely though obdurate girl out of place in the Washington society her stepfather, Senator Jamie Dearbourne, must inhabit, pines for California in the sequel to *When the Far Hills Bloom.* She leaps at the opportunity to manage an orange grove planted with a new Brazilian cultivar to prove herself as a businesswoman, at least, though true love seems always to elude her.

PAGE, CAROLE GIFT

◆▣✕ *HEARTLAND MEMORIES*

A creative writing teacher and speaker at conferences, Page had written about 40 books as the twenty-first century began, most of them nostalgic romances in the tradition of Hilda Stahl, her mentor. Settings for the Heartland Memories series range from the Depression to the Vietnam War, but their common denominator is the quintessentially Midwestern town of Willowbrook, not a completely idyllic place, but at the least a respite for troubled women who have run aground in the great big world full of war, social unrest, the unpredictability of careers, and the treacheries of love. These women return to mythic Willowbrook in search of the American Dream, and find it.

The House on Honeysuckle Lane. 1994. Nelson, paper. 286 pp. ISBN 0-8407-6777-3.

Home to Willowbrook. 1995. Nelson, paper. 240 pp. ISBN 0-8407-6778-1.

The Hope of Herrick House. 1996. Nelson, paper. 280 pp. ISBN 0-84407-6780-3.

Storms Over Willowbrook. 1998. Nelson, paper. 275 pp. ISBN 0-7852-7671-8.

A Rose for Jenny. 1999. Nelson, paper. 269 pp. ISBN 0-7852-7672-6.

A Locket for Maggie. 2000. Nelson, paper. 270 pp. ISBN 0-7852-7673-4.

PARKER, GARY E.

◆▣✕ *BLUE RIDGE LEGACY*

Highland Hopes. 2001. Bethany, paper. 400 pp. ISBN 0-7642-2452-2.
On her 100th birthday, Abigail "Abby" Porter sets down the story of her life, a chronicle of faith and travail set in the Blue Ridge Mountains of North Carolina. Her mother dies giving birth to Abby, and her father, Solomon, struggles mightily onward with his farm and raising his children alone. Abby comes slowly into her own in this first entry, as she adapts to a stepmother, poverty, the magic of learning, and to wrenching events in the larger world, such as WWI, the influenza epidemic of 1918, and the Great Depression. Parker is working in fields long played out and always romanticized, but he eschews melodramatic touches and makes a conscientious effort to bring period and place to life.

PEART, JANE

AMERICAN QUILT

The Pattern, set prior to the Civil War, features Joanna Shelby, who marries a doctor and moves to the Appalachians, where the beauty of quilting and the harmony it inspires become integral to her life. Each tale in the series ends with the making of a quilt that passes on a mother's legacy to her daughter, whose life is chronicled in the sequel.

> **The Pattern.** 1996. Zondervan, paper. 208 pp. ISBN 0-310-20166-7.

> **The Pledge.** 1996. Zondervan, paper. 256 pp. ISBN 0-310-20167-5.

> **The Promise.** 1996. Zondervan, paper. 240 pp. ISBN 0-310-20168-3.

BRIDES OF MONTCLAIR

A perennially popular series featuring brides from the earliest days of the Republic through World War II.

> **Valiant Bride.** 1989. Zondervan, paper. 191 pp. ISBN 0-310-21506-4.

> **Ransomed Bride.** 1989. Zondervan, paper. 192 pp. ISBN 0-310-21498-X.

> **Fortune's Bride.** 1990. Zondervan, paper. 269 pp. ISBN 0-310-66971-5.

> **Folly's Bride.** 1990. Zondervan, paper. 192 pp. ISBN 0-310-21466-1.

> **Yankee Bride/Rebel Bride.** 1990. Zondervan, paper. 275 pp. ISBN 0-310-66991-X.

> **Gallant Bride.** 1990. Zondervan, paper. 217 pp. ISBN 0-310-67001-2.

> **Shadow Bride.** 1991. Zondervan, paper. 224 pp. ISBN 0-310-67011-X.

> **Destiny's Bride.** 1991. Zondervan, paper. 214 pp. ISBN 0-310-67021-7.

> **Jubilee Bride.** 1992. Zondervan, paper. 207 pp. ISBN 0-310-67121-3.

> **Mirror Bride.** 1993. Zondervan, paper. 206 pp. ISBN 0-310-67131-0.

> **Hero's Bride.** 1993. Zondervan, paper. 215 pp. ISBN 0-310-67141-8.

> **Senator's Bride.** 1994. Zondervan, paper. 224 pp. ISBN 0-310-67151-5.

> **Daring Bride.** 1997. Zondervan, paper. 288 pp. ISBN 0-310-20209-4.

> **Courageous Bride.** 1997. Zondervan, paper. 256 pp. ISBN 0-310-20210-8.

PELLA, JUDITH

DAUGHTERS OF FORTUNE [Historical]

> **Written on the Wind.** 2002. Bethany, paper. 384 pp. ISBN 0-7642-2421-2. A predictably chauvinist Los Angeles newspaper tycoon, Keegan Hayes, sires three daughters after WWI: an aspiring actress, Blair; a sincere Christian, Jackie; and the heroine of *Written on the Wind,* Cameron. When her father ridicules her skills as a reporter, Cameron signs with a rival paper and heads for Europe to cover the advances of the Nazis. There she reluctantly teams with her father's ace foreign correspondent, Johnny Shanahan. Pella's scenes in Los Angeles are routine, but those on the warfront vividly combine Pella's research with a feeling of urgency.

PETERSON, TRACIE, AND JAMES SCOTT BELL

◀🐟 *THE SHANNON SAGA*

> ***City of Angels.*** 2001. Bethany, paper. 384 pp. ISBN 0-7642-2418-2.
> With "I can do all things through Christ which strengtheneth me" ever foremost in her mind, orphaned Kathleen ("Kit") Shannon journeys to Los Angeles in 1903 to live with her rich aunt and, she hopes, to study law.

> ***Angels Flight.*** 2001. Bethany, paper. 384 pp. ISBN 0-7642-2419-0.
> Now a lawyer with a celebrated case in her dossier, Kit still finds that there are few cases for a 24-year-old woman lawyer. Desperate immigrants turn to her: first, a Chinese woman with green card problems; and then a young Mexican gardener accused of sexual assault of a white woman. Thus, Kit finds herself crusading against racial prejudice, pro bono work at best in the early 1900s and an unlikely scenario, though Bell's legal expertise informs every scene, and there's plenty of action.

PRICE, EUGENIA

Price's four series go over the same ground (e.g., the antebellum South of Georgia; the Civil War). Despite an ability to portray grim reality, her plots veer toward the sentimental, and her dialogue often seems stilted even as a representation of the time. There is always a strong woman character at the center of things, but even though her name changes, she's the same character. In fact, all of Price's characterizations are with broad strokes.

Her many fans don't seem to mind, however, and on the positive side, her research is meticulous to the point of scholarly, drawing upon primary sources such as the letters and journals of real historical figures. Price died in 1996, but should be popular for years to come. See also chapter 4, p. 33.

ST. SIMONS TRILOGY [Historical]

> ***Lighthouse.*** 1999. (Originally published in 1971.) Providence House, paper. 352 pp. ISBN 1-57736-154-7.
> Price so loved St. Simons Island, off the coast of Georgia, that she herself moved there. The first entry in her popular trilogy tells the story of New Englander James Gould, who came to the island in the early nineteenth century and built its famous lighthouse.

> ***New Moon Rising.*** 2000. (Originally published in 1969.) Providence House, paper. 352 pp. ISBN 1-57736-181-4.
> The sequel to *Lighthouse* tells the story of James Gould's son, Horace, whose Northern education has put him at odds with his Georgia heritage. He spends the years leading up to the Civil War and part of the war itself in self-imposed exile, but his love of St. Simons calls him home, at last, to begin life anew.

> ***The Beloved Invader.*** 2000. (Originally published in 1965.) Providence House, paper. 320 pp. ISBN 1-57736-204-7.
> Price concludes her trilogy with a fictional portrait of a real personage, Anson Dodge, St. Simons's beloved Episcopal minister, who comes to the island in 1879.

GEORGIA TRILOGY [Historical]

> ***Bright Captivity.*** 1996. (Originally published in 1991.) St. Martin's, paper. 613 pp. ISBN 0-312-95968-0.
> Price takes up the story of the Coupers and Frasers, actual historical families on St. Simons Island, immediately after the War of 1812. The reader meets young Anne

Couper, a plantation owner's daughter, who dreams of her prince charming. Sure enough, he arrives in the person of a British officer, John Fraser.

Where Shadows Go. 1996. (Originally published in 1993.) St. Martin's, paper. 597 pp. ISBN 0-312-95969-9.

Price chronicles Anne and John's entirely devoted marriage in the sequel to *Bright Captivity,* giving a mostly idyllic portrait of plantation life though with much attention to the scourge of slavery.

Beauty from Ashes. 1995. Doubleday. 627 pp. ISBN 0-385-26703-7.

The conclusion of the Georgia Trilogy is set in the 1850s, after Anne has lost her husband, her parents, and two of her daughters as well. She struggles to survive as the institution of slavery grows more evidently hideous and the Civil War looms.

SAVANNAH QUARTET [Historical]

Savannah. 1997. (Originally published in 1983.) St. Martin's, paper. 608 pp. ISBN 0-312-96232-0.
Newly graduated from Yale, but with his parents dead and nothing to hold him in Philadelphia, Mark Browning sails for Savannah in 1812 to make his fortune. In reality, it is already made because he's the heir to his father's shipping firm and enough riches that at least two of Savannah's young women will want him.

To See Your Face Again. 1997. (Originally published in 1985.) St. Martin's, paper. 512 pp. ISBN 0-312-96233-9.
In the sequel to *Savannah,* young Natalie Browning, Mark and Caroline's spoiled daughter, sets her sights on Burke Latimer, a tycoon who loses everything, and follows him all over Georgia.

Before the Darkness Falls. 1987. (Out of print.)
Natalie and Burke settle into marital bliss.

Stranger in Savannah. 1997. (Originally published in 1989.) Berkley, paper. 744 pp. ISBN 0-515-10344-6.
The Civil War breaks out in the concluding volume of the Savannah Quartet. Mark Browning's family is split: Mark himself sympathizes with the Union from which he came; but his son and daughter back the South, right or wrong. Price draws from actual letters to bring to life historical figures such as Robert E. Lee and W. H. Stiles.

FLORIDA TRILOGY
Northern Florida shared with southern Georgia a plantation economy and fought with the Confederacy, but Price weaves in the state's Spanish and Seminole heritages and emphasizes its history in the eighteenth century. Thus, the series, her least well-known, is also her least typical.

Maria. 1999. (Originally published in 1977.) Providence House, paper. 408 pp. ISBN 1-57736-152-0.
Maria dramatizes the British and Spanish struggle for dominion over Florida as it plays out in the lives of Maria and David Fenwick. David's military obligations take the couple to the British garrison in St. Augustine, where David dies of fever and Maria must make her own impetuous way, rising to eminence in the community and finding a new love as the American Revolution looms.

Don Juan McQueen. 1974. (Out of print.)
Set after the Revolution, *Don Juan McQueen* is the story of Georgia timber baron John McQueen and his wife, Anne. Shifting politics force John, now a "don" because of his holdings in Spanish Florida, to be gone for long periods, while Anne raises the family back in Georgia.

Margaret's Story. 1980. (Out of print.)
The conclusion to the Florida Trilogy sprawls across the nineteenth century, from the 1830s to the 1880s, and features the matronly Margaret Fleming on her Florida planta- tion, Hibernia, which after the Civil War she turns into something on the order of a bed-and-breakfast.

RAO, LINDA RAE

⬤✖ EAGLE WINGS

YA Rao's series ranges from the Revolutionary War through Texas's struggles prior to statehood.

Eagles Flying High. 1995. Baker, paper. 334 pp. ISBN 0-8007-5548-0.
In the early days of the Revolutionary War, Young Jessica "Jess" McClaren must turn over her prize mare, Lady, to a ruthless Tory because of her father's financial obliga- tions. Reluctantly, Jess accompanies Lady to Charleston, from which she is to be shipped to a farm in the West Indies. When her father is injured, Jess accepts help from Andrew "Mac" Macklin, a half-blood Delaware and Continental Army spy.

Ordeal at Iron Mountain. 1995. Baker, paper. 200 pp. ISBN 0-8007-5568-5.
In the sequel to *Eagles Flying High* the Revolutionary War is over, and Jess and Mac are married. Mac's grandmother summons him to the Cherokee mission, Iron Mountain, where Mac did much of his growing up. A land company is trying to take away the mission land and, like Fenimore Cooper's Natty Bumppo and Chingachgook, wife and husband head through the wilderness toward conflict.

Of Eagles and Ravens. 1996. Baker, paper. 288 pp. ISBN 0-8007-5580-4.
Rao dramatizes the War of 1812 in the sequel to *Ordeal at Iron Mountain,* featuring Jess and Mac's daughter, Christiana. Mac has taken up the trade of silversmith, and his apprentice, Stephan Pages, has eyes for Christiana. But she's worried he may be a spy for the British.

The Eagle Stirs Her Nest. 1997. Baker, paper. 254 pp. ISBN 0-8007-5607-X.
Seventeen-year-old Chad Macklin, grandson of Stephan and Christiana, is the hero of the concluding volume of Eagle Wings, set in 1841. Eager to escape a house full of sisters, Chad strikes for Texas to join his uncle, a Texas Ranger, and fight Comanches with him.

RIZZO, KAY

⬤✖ SERENITY INN
The first of these romances features Serenity Pownell, 16, who, a little before the Civil War, is attending a fancy young lady's school. She must quickly adjust to the adult world when her mother dies, but she finds happiness even as the effects of the war grow unavoidable. Serenity takes on a minor presence in later installments, allowing other young women to look for love in the West, much like the women in Jane Peart's Brides of the West series (see chapter 7, "Romancing the West").

Serenity's Desire. 1998. Broadman and Holman, paper. 273 pp. ISBN 0-8054-6373-9.

Serenity's Quest. 1998. Broadman and Holman, paper. 256 pp. ISBN 0-8054-1674-9.

Josephine's Fortune. 1999. Broadman and Holman, paper. 256 pp. ISBN 0-8054-1675-7.

Lilia's Haven. 1999. Broadman and Holman, paper. 256 pp. ISBN 0-8054-1685-4.

Abigail's Dream. 2000. Broadman and Holman, paper. 304 pp. ISBN 0-8054-2131-9.

★ STAHL, HILDA. *The White Pine Chronicles.* 1996. Nelson. 792 pp. ISBN 0-7852-7405-7.
Romances framed around her stock-in-trade, marriages of necessity that turn into love relationships, this trilogy (*The Covenant, The Inheritance,* and *The Dream*) is the late Stahl's best-known work. The overarching, larger-than-life story, set in central Michigan from the Civil War years through the 1920s, is of the Havlick clan's fight to preserve 6,000 acres of virgin pines from rapacious lumbering interests.

STOKES, PENELOPE J. *The Amethyst Heart.* 2000. Word. 400 pp. ISBN 0-8499-3721-3.
Amethyst Noble, 93, figures out that her no-good son, Conrad, plans to sell the ancestral home out from under her and plop her in a rest home in this sentimental tale. Amethyst bars the door and tells the family history to her granddaughter, "Little Am." Little Am learns that Silas Noble, patriarch of the family and a physician, was unique in the community in that he treated blacks the same way he did rich white landowners. Kindness to the needy is the legacy of Noble House, explains Amethyst, hoping to awaken the altruist in Little Am. The reader understands—though may not believe—that Little Am will defend Noble House and her grandmother against her weak and venal father.

THOENE, BODIE

SHILOH LEGACY [Historical]
Christian fiction's most respected team treats WWI as a noble enterprise, bringing together ordinary men and women from places like Shiloh, Arkansas, to vanquish a great evil. Afterwards, black and white, poor and privileged, struggle alike in a rapidly changing country. Full of melodrama, plot shifts, and dashes of humor, the Shiloh Legacy is a crowd-pleaser, but it's also discursive and derivative.

Bodie Thoene's husband, Brock, given a research credit throughout the series, shares authorship in the fourth volume, *Shiloh Autumn.*

In My Father's House. 1992. Bethany, paper. 430 pp. ISBN 1-55661-189-7.
As smoothly as her fictional master, James Michener, would have done, Bodie Thoene follows her phalanx of characters from the trenches in France through the Armistice and home again, where they fall in love, struggle with their careers, and run from the law. There's the idealized black character, Jefferson Canfield, a hero on the battlefield but persecuted by the Klan back home; New Yorker Max Meyer, mingling with the common lot of man in France, but destined to make his way into high finance; Ellis Warne, a doctor's son who comes home without one leg but finds hope; and Birch Tucker, an Arkansas farm boy. Birch is the nearest thing to the major character, and appears throughout the series. His path crosses Jefferson Canfield's as he aids in the black man's escape from the Klan into Oklahoma. Even so, there is no white-hot focus to this plot; rather, it's an episodic saga portraying a generation.

A Thousand Shall Fall. 1992. Bethany, paper. 428 pp. ISBN 1-55661-190-0.
The wild prosperity of the 1920s is drawing to a close as the second entry in the Shiloh Legacy opens; the reader knows the Stock Market Crash is looming and that Max Meyer, who has become a financial columnist for the *New York Times,* will be hurt by it. Max discovers he has a son, David, and turns all of his attention to protecting the boy's future. Meanwhile, Jefferson Canfield struggles against racial injustice and a mighty tornado to hold his head high, while Birch Tucker, who has spent most of the weary years since the War working in the Oklahoma oilfields, at last returns to Shiloh to take over the family farm.

Say to This Mountain. 1993. Bethany, paper. 447 pp. ISBN 1-55661-191-9.
Thoene brings some of her myriad plot strands together in the conclusion to her Shiloh Legacy series, which occurs in the early years of the Great Depression. Ellis Warne, introduced in *In My Father's House* as a disabled veteran, does his best to practice good medicine in the midst of a violent labor strike. A mission ministering to hungry, out-of-work men is portrayed with care. In New York, panic has set in, and then despair, but in little Shiloh life goes on, not much harder than it already was. Jefferson Canfield and Birch Tucker again cross paths, though their stories are not so much concluded as stopped.

Shiloh Autumn. 1996. Nelson. 470 pp. ISBN 0-7852-8066-9.
The Thoenes shifted publishers after *Say to This Mountain,* and thus Shiloh Autumn is not officially part of the Shiloh Legacy. The novel is set in Shiloh, Arkansas, at the crest of the Depression. The town had mostly escaped economic disaster, but following a mini-panic in Memphis it, too, spirals downward. Birch and Trudy Tucker, staunch Christians, lose their farm and strike off for the Promised Land of California. The novel is a personal favorite of the Thoenes.

WICK, LORI

A PLACE CALLED HOME
A perennially popular, often-reprinted series, A Place Called Home chronicles the romantic lives and adventures of the Cameron family at the turn of the twentieth century in Baxter, Wisconsin.

A Place Called Home. 1990. Harvest House, paper. 240 pp. ISBN 1-56507-588-9.

A Song for Silas. 1990. Harvest House, paper. 195 pp. ISBN 1-56507-589-7.

The Long Road Home. 1990. Harvest House, paper. 190 pp. ISBN 1-56507-590-0.

A Gathering of Memories. 1991. Harvest House, paper. 250 pp. ISBN 1-56507-591-9.
See also Delbert Plett's *Sarah's Prairie,* p. 281, and Mormon writer Virginia Sorenson's *The Evening and the Morning*, p. 287.

EUROPEAN SAGAS

DE GRAAF, ANNE

HIDDEN HARVEST
De Graaf uses the fortunes of the German–Polish Piekarz family to portray Poland from the dark years of Nazi subjugation through the equally repressive period of Stalinist rule through Solidarity and freedom.

Bread Upon the Waters. 1995. Bethany, paper. 350 pp. ISBN 1-55661-618-X. Hanna Muller, a German whose family sympathizes with the Poles, falls in love with Tadeusz Piekarz, an engineer conscripted by the Nazis, and they find a measure of happiness even as the world unravels around them.

Where the Fire Burns. 1997. Bethany, paper. 320 pp. ISBN 1-55661-619-8. The American spy Jacek Duch, introduced in *Bread Upon the Waters,* defects to the Communists, or seems to. Complicating his life, and forcing him to make some long-delayed decisions, his American-born daughter, Amy, journeys to Poland. Naive Amy soon must choose between the loves of both sons of Tadeusz and Hanna, one of whom is religious, the other of whom fights with the Underground to rid his country of Stalinism.

 Out of the Red Shadow. 1999. Bethany, paper. 352 pp. ISBN 1-55661-620-1. In the conclusion to the Hidden Harvest trilogy, the old spy Jacek must at last make peace with his conscience as he confronts his grandson, Tomasz. Tomasz is a passionate soldier for Solidarity.

★ CROW, DONNA FLETCHER

 The Banks of the Boyne. 1998. Moody, paper. 818 pp. ISBN 0-8024-7737-2. *[Historical]*
The frame for Crow's massive, noble attempt to understand the conflict in Ireland is the story of young American Mary Hamilton and her fiance Gareth, a divinity student. She joins him in Scotland with visions of living in an ivy-covered English cottage, but he's sent to Belfast to work as a mediator between Catholics and Protestants. Mary follows, but their relationship is soon overrun by the intensity of conflict. Into this sad story Crow weaves a series of novellas that explicate key events in 300 years of bloody Irish history.

 Glastonbury: The Novel of Christian England. 1992. Crossway, paper. 859 pp. ISBN 0-89107-660-7. *[Historical]*
Crow brings the Michener technique to bear on the history of Christianity in England, fictionalizing about 1,500 years from the time of the Druids through the dissolution of Glastonbury Abbey in 1539.

HOWATCH, SUSAN

★ *STARBRIDGE NOVELS*
Romance writer Howatch upped the ante with these historicals about the Church of England in the twentieth century, spanning from the time of disillusionment after WWI through the tumultuous 1960s. Howatch focuses on three clerics in and around Starbridge Cathedral: the Catholic monk and psychic Jonathan Darrow; the conservative Anglican Charles Ashworth (whose conservatism doesn't inhibit his libido); and the Protestant Neville Aysgarth. Sprawling, sexy epics, the novels are also a parade of the ideas buffeting the Church, and reflect Howatch's own spiritual journey. Howatch's sequence is a good follow-up to Colleen McCullough's *The Thorn Birds* (p. 254).

Glittering Images. 1988. (Originally published in 1987.) Ballantine, paper. 434 pp. ISBN 0-44921-436-2.

Glamorous Powers. 1989. (Originally published in 1988.) Ballantine, paper. 403 pp. ISBN 0-44921-728-0.

Ultimate Prizes. 1990. (Originally published in 1989.) Ballantine, paper. 436 pp. ISBN 0-44921-811-2.

Scandalous Risks. 1991. (Originally published in 1990.) Fawcett, paper. 385 pp. ISBN 0-44921-982-8.

Mystical Paths. 1993. (Originally published in 1992.) Fawcett, paper. 504 pp. ISBN 0-44922-122-9.

Absolute Truths. 1996. (Originally published in 1994.) Ballantine, paper. 624 pp. ISBN 0-44922-555-0.

HUNT, ANGELA ELWELL

⬛✕ *HEIRS OF CAHIRA O'CONNOR*

A modern O'Connor woman, Kathleen, stumbles onto the fact several O'Connor women of the past have risen in battle to save the day. These O'Connor women are insistently strong, donning male clothing, and male roles, in rebellion at history itself.

The Silver Sword. 1998. WaterBrook, paper. 400 pp. ISBN 1-57856-012-8.
During the time of the Bohemian Hussite Wars of 1419, an O'Connor woman, Anika of Prague, dons male clothing and becomes a knight to fight for religious reformation.

The Golden Cross. 1998. WaterBrook, paper. 412 pp. ISBN 1-57856-053-8.
Aidan O'Connor, a waif working in a tavern in 1642 Java, is a talented artist. She disguises herself as a boy to work for Schuyler Van Dyck, a Dutch cartographer who has been commissioned to chart new seas and lands.

The Velvet Shadow. 1999. WaterBrook, paper. 400 pp. ISBN 1-57856-131-0.
In the third volume of the Heirs of Cahira O'Connor, Flanna O'Connor, a medical student in 1860 Boston, disguises herself as a boy to serve for the Union cause deep in the South.

The Emerald Isle. 1999. WaterBrook, paper. 389 pp. ISBN 1-57856-180-9.
Hunt returns to the story of Cahira O'Connor in her final volume of the Heirs of Cahira O'Connor, interleaving it with Kathleen's own story in contemporary Ireland. Cahira, superb archer, fights against the Normans in 1234 while Cahira comes to terms both with her romantic and intellectual lives.

MORRIS, GILBERT

⬛✕ *THE WAKEFIELD DYNASTY [Historical]*

The tireless Morris spins tales of an Elizabethan family caught up in the Protestant Reformation, the formative period of modern Christianity that introduced the Tyndale Bible and *Pilgrim's Progress.*

Sword of Truth. 1994. Tyndale, paper. 409 pp. ISBN 0-8423-6228-2.

The Winds of God. 1994. Tyndale, paper. 380 pp. ISBN 0-8423-7953-3.

The Shield of Honor. 1995. Tyndale, paper. 394 pp. ISBN 0-8423-5930-3.

The Fields of Glory. 1996. Tyndale, paper. 376 pp. ISBN 0-8423-6229-0.

The Ramparts of Heaven. 1997. Tyndale, paper. 361 pp. ISBN 0-8423-6233-9.

The Song of Princes. 1997. Tyndale, paper. 386 pp. ISBN 0-8423-6234-7.

A Gathering of Eagles. 1998. Tyndale, paper. 320 pp. ISBN 0-8423-6237-1.

RIOLS, NOREEN

◀▣✕ *HOUSE OF ANNANBRAE*

Where Hope Shines Through. 1994. Crossway, paper. 320 pp. ISBN 0-89107-790-1.
An espionage caper toward the end of WWII sweeps up a well-born young
Englishwoman, Katherine De Montval, into mostly tragic events, including the
death of her mother and her father's desertion of the family. He didn't desert, it
turns out, but is serving his country secretly. Doing her own part for the war,
Katherine meets a brave young officer, and after much travail, the two marry.

To Live Again. 1995. Crossway, paper. 313 pp. ISBN 0-78527-413-8.
In the sequel to *Where Hope Shines Through,* Katherine's husband is killed,
and it seems that the tragedies in her life will never end. They do, along with
the war. She marries a rich man, Maxime, in part to solidify family fortunes at
Annanbrae, the family estate, and her future seems secure.

Before the Dawn. 1996. Crossway, paper. 320 pp. ISBN 0-89107-872-X.
Riols leaves behind her vivid re-creation of wartime England for conventional
melodrama, trading on the disappearance of Katherine's father and Maxime's
seeming abandonment of the marriage.

Where Love Endures. 1998. Crossway, paper. 304 pp. ISBN 0-89107-779-0.
The conclusion of the House of Annanbrae series is set 15 years after *Before
the Dawn,* with Katherine and Maxime settled into a contented middle age.
Riols relegates them to the background and instead tells the story of Laura
Denning, who repairs to Annanbrae to sort out the problems of her marriage.

THOENE, JAKE, AND LUKE THOENE

◀▣✕ *PORTRAITS OF DESTINY*
The sons of Brock and Bodie Thoene trace several generations of the Sutton family
from Scotland to America at the time of the Revolutionary War. The Thoenes have
also written a juvenile series, Baker Street Mysteries (p. 298).

Heart of Allegiance. 1998. Nelson, paper. 289 pp. ISBN 0-7852-7145-7.

Eyes of Justice. 1999. Nelson, paper. 324 pp. ISBN 0-7852-7146-5.

Hands of Deliverance. 2000. Nelson, paper. 305 pp. ISBN 0-7852-7147-3.

Chapter 7

Romancing the West

The good news is that there are a number of Christian westerns, so that reader demand for them, pretty much overlooked in recent years by mainstream publishers, can be addressed to a degree. However, following the mainstream trend, the majority of them are romantic historicals, which offer little to appeal to men.

Mainstream publishers sharply curtailed their publication of traditional westerns in the early 1990s because the readership had fallen off. Younger men didn't pick up westerns as their fathers and grandfathers had. Traditionally, women didn't like westerns.

Thus, the new primacy of the romantic western, but—for public libraries, in particular—the problem remains: how to find enough traditional westerns to satisfy those readers still asking for them. Although Christian fiction isn't a total solution, it does address the problem, particularly under the category, "traditional."

CONTEMPORARY WESTERNS

AARSEN, CAROLYNE. *The Cowboy's Bride.* 1999. Harlequin (Love Inspired), paper. 256 pp. ISBN 0-373-87067-1.
A struggling rancher meets a bank manager and the two reluctantly allow that they are made for each other.

BALL, KAREN. *Reunion.* 1996. Multnomah, paper. 265 pp. ISBN 0-88070-951-0.
Connor Alexander, a wildlife biologist trying to census the wolves that he suspects have returned to Wyoming, takes a job as a ranch hand for Taylor Sorenson, a widow who also wants to protect the wolves.

BLY, STEPHEN

◆✗ *AUSTIN-STONER FILES*
Lynda Austin is a New York editor who, now 30, has never been able to find the right guy in this witty adventure series.

> ***The Lost Manuscript of Martin Taylor Harrison.*** 1995. Crossway, paper. 349 pp. ISBN 0-89107-852-5.
> A seeming lunatic bursts into Lynda Austin's office, raving about a lost manuscript that would prove the find of the century if authentic. As Lynda realizes that the manuscript is real, the lunatic is killed, sending Lynda on a frantic trip to Arizona to secure the original manuscript. There, her guide is the drawling Brady Stoner, a rodeo rider and, just maybe, Lynda's soul mate.

> ***The Final Chapter of Chance McCall.*** 1996. Crossway, paper. 368 pp. ISBN 0-89107-903-3.
> Lynda and Brady chase through Montana, ruthless men in pursuit, after the last chapter of yet another manuscript, this one giving directions to lost treasure.

> ***The Kill Fee of Cindy LaCoste.*** 1997. Crossway, paper. 361 pp. ISBN 0-89107-954-8.
> Lynda and Brady finally get married in the conclusion to the Austin-Stoner series, but not before speeding through half the West in search of a missing friend.

◆✗ ★ **COLSON, CONSTANCE.** *Chase the Dream.* **1996. Multnomah, paper. 448 pp. ISBN 0-88070-928-6.**
🆈🅰 See discussion in chapter 15, "Young Adult."

◆✗ **JOENS, MICHAEL R.** *The Dawn of Mercy.* **1996. Moody, paper. 301 pp. ISBN 0-8024-1711-6.**
Though not as lyrical or passionate as *The Breaking of Ezra Riley* (discussed later), Joens's
🆈🅰 novel, also set in Depression-era Montana ranch country, has a charm all its own. His hero, young Tyler Hochreiter, wants to go off to college in Chicago and become a minister. But he can't bear to bring the news to his powerful father, Henry, who has battled to hold on to the ranch through the lean years and needs every hand he can get. Tyler must also do battle with a local bully, son of an unscrupulous rancher and the embodiment of meanness, if not outright evil. He finds solace in his wise girlfriend, Kate, though she is yet another reason he finds it so hard to leave Montana.

◆✗ **LIVINGSTON, JOYCE.** *The Bride Wore Boots.* **2000. Barbour, paper. 170 pp. ISBN 1-57748-956-X.**
By the terms of her father's will, Rose Kinsey must leave the big city and learn how to run the ranch in Kansas, staying for at least one year. She must also agree to the instructions of Bane Jacob, her father's foreman.

◆✗ **MOORE, JOHN L.** *Bitter Roots.* **1993. Nelson, paper. 223 pp. ISBN 0-8407-6759-5.**
Long ago, Alistair McColley, the agnostic, sheep-ranching patriarch of a strong but troubled family in eastern Montana, "killed the Swede." He needed killing, but the act proved to be a curse for Alistair's sons. As they gather to mark the old man's passing, they confess their frustrations and spiritual yearnings to Reba, Alistair's daughter-in-law, who draws them into a narrative with her husband, Donald, and herself at the center, but with Alistair dominating every scene. Not as well focused as *The Breaking of Ezra Riley* (discussed later), but Moore's

dry wit and earthy detail—Alistair wears long johns and woolen trousers year-round and keeps a dog that smells as bad as he—have considerable appeal.

MOORE, JOHN L.

◀️📖✖★ *EZRA RILEY TRILOGY* **Discussion**

YA This exceptional trilogy, a contemporary classic, portrays the ranching country of eastern Montana, from the disastrous 1930s that scarred Ezra's father through the 1980s, a period of drought almost as devastating.

The Breaking of Ezra Riley. 1990. Nelson, paper. 266 pp. ISBN 0-8407-6760-9.
Ezra Riley is a sensitive young man who, fleeing his harsh father and wanting to become an artist, strikes out on the road to find the meaning of life. He experiments with drugs and alternative lifestyles in a search reminiscent of *On the Road.* He meets the extraordinary Jubal Lee Walker, a confused young preacher's son with a gift for music. Jubal means trouble, but also kindles Ezra's spiritual awakening.

Leaving the Land. 1995. Nelson, paper. 245 pp. ISBN 0-7852-8288-2.
Ezra has settled down in this sequel to *The Breaking of Ezra Riley,* but his spirit is not at ease. Jubal shows up, much older, and revitalizes Ezra's home church with a fiery revival. Jubal is magnificent but has not overcome his youthful shallowness or his intrinsic dishonesty, and ultimately Ezra must reject him—once again, ironically, leading to Ezra's spiritual growth. Overarching the story of Jubal and Ezra is Ezra's beautiful, heartbreaking struggle to make the ranch pay—a ranch he owns with his two feuding sisters.

The Limits of Mercy. 1996. Nelson, paper. 276 pp. ISBN 0-7852-8299-0.
Ezra's struggles with the land—not to mention his struggles with his quarreling sisters and the bank—seem at last to be resolved in the concluding volume of the Ezra Riley Trilogy. Ezra's life is devoted to the outdoors, writing, and an occasional attempt at preaching. Then a seductive young woman lands in his household, wanting either his counseling or his love, and perhaps representing the dissolution of all that he has worked for. Simultaneously, a radical environmentalist holes up in the hills, gunning for Ezra. Through it all, Moore's knowledge of ranching—of horses, cattle, and the capriciousness of nature—shines through in naturalistic passages worthy of John Steinbeck.

◀️📖✖ **WOLVERTON, CHERYL.** *For Love of Zach.* 1999. Harlequin (Love Inspired), paper. 254 pp. ISBN 0-373-87076-0.
Detective Laura Walker wakes up in a hospital with no memory of why she's come to the ranch town of Hill Creek, Texas. But something links her to Zachary McCade, a local rancher and, like Laura, a Christian.

See also Constance Colson's *Chase the Dream,* p. 307.

MYSTERIES

Who killed whom is often a part of westerns, but the following feature sleuths on the puzzling trails of killers.

◉✖ MITCHELL, SARA. *Ransomed Heart.* **1999. Bethany, paper. 320 pp. ISBN 1-55661-499-3.**
Rosalind Hayes has come to Denver in 1896 to search for her missing brother, but is drawn into companionship with a stalwart Pinkerton detective when she witnesses a jewel robbery. He helps her find her brother, and she helps him find the dashing thief in this romantic suspense novel in western gear.

MORRIS, ALAN, AND GILBERT MORRIS

◉✖ *KATY STEELE ADVENTURES*

YA   *Tracks of Deceit.* 1996. Tyndale, paper. 256 pp. ISBN 0-8423-2039-3.
This likable though short-lived series features special agent Katy Steele, hired in *Tracks of Deceit* to investigate the death of her father, himself a detective for the Central Pacific Railroad. Katy partners with a sometime actor, Sam Bronte, to find the killer, in this Old West version of the elder Morris's Danielle Ross mystery series (p. 192).

Imperial Intrigue. 1996. Tyndale, paper. 225 pp. ISBN 0-8423-2040-7.
In the sequel to *Tracks of Deceit,* Katy and Sam find work escorting an Austrian prince across Texas to his ranch, which seems simple enough until they find themselves embroiled in foreign politics and gunplay.

RODDY, LEE

◉✖ *LADY PINKERTON*
In the first installment, Laurel Bartlett works as a Union spy in search of her fiancé somewhere in the South at the start of the Civil War. Roddy stretches out the romance as Laurel moves West to take on Pinkerton assignments.

Days of Deception. 1998. Chariot Victor, paper. 320 pp. ISBN 1-56476-635-7.

Yesterday's Shadows. 1999. Chariot Victor, paper. 335 pp. ISBN 1-56476-687-X.

Tomorrow's Promise. 2000. Chariot Victor, paper. 363 pp. ISBN 1-56476-688-8.

WALKER, JIM

◉✖★ *WELLS FARGO TRAIL*
Walker's Wells Fargo investigator, Zachary Cobb, is an avenger out of a Randolph Scott movie, and the series is both witty and varied throughout.

The Dreamgivers. 1994. Bethany, paper. 217 pp. ISBN 1-55661-428-4.
Zachary Cobb is a bitter veteran of the Civil War, slowly finding peace through his relationship with God. He has a ranch in California, but his "other occupation," investigating for Wells Fargo, pleases him most. His first case takes him to the Mojave Desert down a dangerous trail involving the opium trade and illegal trafficking in Chinese railroad workers.

The Nightriders. 1994. Bethany, paper. 271 pp. ISBN 1-55661-429-2.
In the second entry of the Wells Fargo Trail series, Zachary Cobb investigates stolen gold shipments in the California gold fields, encountering a band of vigilantes who are worse than the outlaws, as well as a crooked federal judge who commanded the prison where Zach's brothers were held during the Civil War.

The Rail Kings. 1995. Bethany, paper. 301 pp. ISBN 1-55661-430-6.
In the third entry of the Wells Fargo Trail series, Zachary Scott rescues the
president of the Denver and Rio Grande Railroad from kidnappers, then must
fend off gunmen as well as the amorous intentions of the president's daughter.

The Rawhiders. 1995. Bethany, paper. 334 pp. ISBN 1-55661-431-4.
Zachary is sent undercover to investigate the robbery of cattle payrolls in Kansas
in the fourth entry of the Wells Fargo Trail series. But Zachary's brother, Joe,
assumes the starring role as he comes to the aid of the remnant of a Mennonite
family, the Reddiger sisters, who struggle to drive their cattle north from Texas
to the railhead in Dodge City, plagued all the way by the violent Rawhiders.

The Desert Hawks. 1996. Bethany, paper. 336 pp. ISBN 1-55661-700-3.
Zachary is in Arizona investigating the robbery of army payrolls in the fifth
entry of the Wells Fargo Trail series. But again one of his brothers, Julian, is a
main character, an outlaw still fighting the Civil War.

The Oyster Pirates. 1996. Bethany, paper. 336 pp. ISBN 1-55661-701-1.
Zachary Scott seems finally to have settled on a sweetheart, Jenny Hays, after
turning down several applicants in previous entries of the Wells Fargo Trail
series. Borrowing a bit from the mythology of Jack London's rough childhood,
Walker sketches out the waterfront culture of San Francisco in a plot involving
stolen bullion and paddleboats on the Sacramento River.

The Warriors. 1997. Bethany, paper. 352 pp. ISBN 1-55661-702-X.
In the seventh entry of the Wells Fargo Trail series, Zachary heads south of the
border with his brothers, Joe and James, to rescue their bandit brother, Julian,
who holds a secret the federal government regards as vital.

The Ice Princess. 1998. Bethany, paper. 288 pp. ISBN 1-55661-703-8.
Zachary returns home to San Luis Obispo in the eighth entry of the Wells
Fargo Trail series to find that Jenny Hays, now elevated to the status of
fiancée, has sailed for Alaska because of a family crisis. Zachary follows her.

NATIVE AMERICANS

★ **GROSECLOSE, ELGIN.** *The Kiowa.* **1978. Cook. (Out of print.)**
With realism and the attentiveness to Native American culture found in Don
Coldsmith's Spanish Bit series, Groseclose portrays Sanjak, an intelligent, misun-
derstood Kiowa brave. Partly through the influence of a captive white woman,
Sanjak comes to believe in the white man's God, but with tragic consequences.

★ **JACKSON, DAVE.** *Lost River Conspiracy.* **1995. Good Books, paper. 218
pp. ISBN 1-56148-183-1.**
See discussion in chapter 15, "Young Adult."

KIRKPATRICK, JANE

◀▣✕★ *DREAM CATCHERS [Historical]*   `Discussion`
This sprawling, loosely sequential series, covering big chunks of the story of Oregon settlement, draws together lyrical, realistic novels that can be read independently. Each treats traditional western themes with a woman's sensibility.

> ***A Sweetness to the Soul.*** 1995. Multnomah, paper. 452 pp. ISBN 0-88070-765-8.
> Kirkpatrick tells an archetypal story of the Northwest in the first volume of her trilogy about the wanderer Joseph Sherar, who seeks his fortune in California, and then in Oregon. He marries teenager Jane Herbert and carves out an exemplary life on the frontier, building roads, operating a historic inn, and relating with fairness to local Native Americans. Jane's lifelong friendship with Sunmiet, a Native American from the Confederated Tribes of Warm Springs, is portrayed with great care and insight.

> ***Love to Water My Soul.*** 1996. Multnomah, paper. 380 pp. ISBN 0-88070-939-3.
> A frontier girl is adopted by the Modocs when her caravan leaves her behind. Later, Shell Flower is traded to the Paiutes for an obsidian knife, not as an expression of abuse, but of her precise value; later, still, she rejoins the white culture and studies the Christian God. Shell Flower's story is enormously appealing, in large part because of Kirkpatrick's complete immersion in the Native American cultures of Oregon.

> ***A Gathering of Finches.*** 1997. Multnomah, paper. 300 pp. ISBN 1-57673-082-4.
> Again using historical sources, Kirkpatrick tells the story of the New York debutante Cassie Simpson in the last volume of her trilogy. Tempestuous and self-centered, she marries a well-heeled engineer for his money and for the adventure of moving to San Francisco. Then she has an affair with Louis Simpson, a timber baron on the Oregon coast, and takes up with him. Eventually, the second marriage works, but both Louis and Cassie are self-indulgent people, not entirely likable, and peace is a long time coming. In her later years, Cassie became something of an environmentalist and left a beautiful garden to posterity, preserved today as an Oregon state park.

LEON, BONNIE

◀▣✕ *NORTHERN LIGHTS*

> ***Journey of Eleven Moons.*** 1995. Nelson, paper. 274 pp. ISBN 0-7852-7974-1.
> A lonely Civil War veteran, Erik Engstrom, befriends a young Aleut woman, Anna, and her little sister, Iya, when a tsunami wipes out their village. Soon another person joins the group: Anna has a baby by her intended husband, who was killed in the disaster. She names her daughter Luba. The group battles for survival as they attempt to reach safety before winter comes on; Anna's knowledge of the land often saves the day. Slowly, Erik and Anna fall in love, and Anna puzzles over Erik's strange faith. Though Leon is no Jack London, she's done her research and her far northern setting comes vividly to life.

> ***In the Land of White Nights.*** 1996. Nelson, paper. 324 pp. ISBN 0-7852-7668-8.
> Erik and Anna marry in the sequel to *Journey of Eleven Moons.* But Erik is crazy to find gold. When he heads up-country to make a claim, he's forced to deposit Anna in a Sitka boarding house, an inadvertently cruel act. Anna remains boundlessly cheerful despite the prejudice she encounters, full of love for her newly discovered Jesus but also with a puzzled, naive sadness at her inability to fit in.

Return to the Misty Shore. 1997. Nelson, paper. 324 pp. ISBN 0-7852-7413-8.
In the loose sequel to *In the Land of White Nights,* Anna's daughter, Luba, marries an Aleut and encounters prejudice from the opposite direction, as well as the difficulty of living with an unbeliever.

A Sacred Place. 2000. Broadman and Holman, paper. 310 pp. ISBN 0-8054-2152-1.
Set in 1917 as the United States enters WWI, *A Sacred Place* concludes Leon's series, though it is not strictly a sequel. It's the story of the arranged marriage of Irishman Sean Calhoun and Mary Matroona, Luba's daughter. They spend the first year of their marriage caretaking a "fox island"—that is, an island where foxes are commercially harvested—and nearly die from winter's severity.

◀✝ WHITSON, STEPHANIE GRACE

Whitson's pioneer women seem contemporary, but her research into the lore of the Lakota Sioux is impressive.

DAKOTA MOONS

Valley of the Shadow. 2000. Nelson, paper. 295 pp. ISBN 0-7852-6822-7.
Genevieve "Gen" LaCroix, half French, half Dakota Sioux, comes reluctantly to the white mission in northern Minnesota just a few years before the Dakota Sioux Uprising of 1862, brought on by land-grabbing settlers. Gen makes many friends at the mission and even begins to fall in love with Two Stars, a young Dakota warrior. But the Uprising tears the lovers apart and Gen marries Simon Dane, missionary to the Sioux, in this highly romantic tale that strives mightily to portray the Sioux with respect.

Edge of the Wilderness. 2001. Nelson, paper. 288 pp. ISBN: 0-7852-6823-5.
In the sequel to *Valley of the Shadow,* Gen and Simon move their ministry to a Sioux prison camp, while Two Stars, whom Gen presumes to be dead, becomes an army scout.

Heart of the Sandhills. 2002. Nelson, paper. 288 pp. ISBN 0-7852-6824-3.
In the third entry of the Dakota Moon series, Gen LaCroix and Two Stars strike out for the Sandhill country of Minnesota and begin their married life. The two are the brunt of prejudice of the white community toward the Sioux, and have a tough time making it on their rented farm. Two Stars takes a job scouting for the army, throwing the young marriage into crisis.

PRAIRIE WINDS

Walks the Fire. 1995. Nelson, paper. 301 pp. ISBN 0-7852-7981-4.
Jesse King, traveling the Oregon Trail through Nebraska, loses her baby and husband, then is captured by the Lakota Sioux. "Captured" may be too strong a word because the Sioux are sympathetic and agreeable, particularly Rides the Wind, a Christian brave who wants Jesse to nurse his motherless infant son, Soaring Eagle. Rides the Wind christens Jesse Walks the Fire, marries her, and fathers their daughter, LisBeth.

Soaring Eagle. 1996. Nelson, paper. 312 pp. ISBN 0-7852-7617-3.
In the sequel to *Walks the Fire,* Whitson follows the fortunes of Soaring Eagle and LisBeth, the children of Rides the Wind and Jesse King. Soaring Eagle is a fierce brave admired by the estimable Sitting Bull, but at the Battle of Little Bighorn he discovers a locket that turns him toward the white side of his heritage.

He goes in search of his sister, made a widow by the battle. LisBeth, in turn, is embittered by the events of her life, and looks for love.

Red Bird. 1997. Nelson, paper. 288 pp. ISBN 0-7852-7484-7.
In the conclusion of Whitson's trilogy, Soaring Eagle has secured a white man's education in the East, and even lectures on Indian affairs. Carrie Brown, whom readers first met in *Soaring Eagle,* takes her schoolgirl's crush on Soaring Eagle back to Nebraska. She's a grown woman now and hopes her love will be returned.

ROMANTIC WESTERNS

Romantic westerns are simply romances with western settings. They feature heroines rather than heroes—strong Christian women who, nonetheless, don't wish to brave life without husbands. They talk like contemporary women, and as in contemporary Christian romances, the unsaved suitor is often a cad. Of course, the man the heroine marries must be a Christian. And, usually, the heroine faces some trial other than finding true love: she battles disease or saves a ranch. Historical events are used as a backdrop and are seldom portrayed in depth.

◄ BLY, STEPHEN

BELLES OF LORDSBURG

The Senator's Other Daughter. 2001. Crossway, paper. 256 pp. ISBN 1-58134-236-5.
Grace Denison arrives in rundown Lordsburg, New Mexico, and holdups, runaway horses, shoot-outs, and mysteries ensue. Grace is on the run from the stifling life her father, a U.S. Senator, would have her live. She has a secret, too, which the reader will be a while in learning. Meanwhile, Grace works as a telegraph operator on the late shift—not a woman's job, several men point out. Local hero "Colt" Parnall courts Grace but doesn't exactly sweep her off her feet. And yet Lordsburg is much in need of a woman's touch—as is Colt—and Grace eventually climbs down from her high horse.

The General's Notorious Widow. 2001. Crossway, paper. 240 pp. ISBN 1-58134-280-2.
In the sequel to *The Senator's Other Daughter,* Lixie Miller, widow of a general caught with his pants down, comes to backwater Lordsburg to escape publicity. But men immediately circle around her, including Charles Noble, a dime novelist wanting her story, and Jefferson Carter, the interesting lawyer from Santa Fe.

HEROINES OF THE GOLDEN WEST

Sweet Carolina. 1998. Crossway, paper. 223 pp. ISBN 0-89107-973-4.
Carolina Cantrell, who drives a hard bargain for the family business back in Maryland, comes with irritation to the gold country of Montana when her brother is killed. She aims to settle his affairs and leave again, but the rough store her brother ran with a drunken partner shows promise for a good businesswoman. She goes wittily and cleverly to work, and soon they're calling the town Cantrell.

The Marquesa. 1998. Crossway, paper. 224 pp. ISBN 1-58134-025-7.
The loose sequel to *Sweet Carolina* features actress Isabel Leon, who comes to Cantrell with plans to build a hotel. Shootings, robberies, and the orneriness of her contractor provide obstacles.

Miss Fontenot. 1999. Crossway, paper. 224 pp. ISBN 1-58134-074-5.
Oliole Fontenot is accomplished in the newfangled art of photography, and she comes to Cantrell, Montana, to explore photography's possibilities in perfect freedom. She becomes friends with Isabel Leon and Carolina Cantrell, but there are also desperadoes on the prowl, and a handsome cowboy who complicates her notions of freedom.

OLD CALIFORNIA

Red Dove of Monterey. 1998. Crossway, paper. 224 pp. ISBN 1-58134-004-4.
Alena Tipton, daughter of Bostonians, has grown up in Old Monterey because of her father's hide business. It's hardly a romantic trade, but Alena wants to take it on when her father dies. She's called a red dove because of her red hair.

Last Swan in Sacramento. 1999. Crossway, paper. 221 pp. ISBN 1-58134-109-1.
Set in 1865, *Last Swan* features plain Martina Swan, mother of an infant and proprietress of a failing dry-goods store in the absence of her adventurer husband. When the bank forecloses, Martina, an angry woman, goes in pursuit of her husband, meeting with adventures along the way and encountering truths she's not prepared for.

Proud Quail of the San Joaquin. 2000. Crossway, paper. 240 pp. ISBN 1-58134-152-0.
Proud Quail's heroine is schoolteacher Christina Swan, daughter of Martina of *Last Swan in Sacramento.* Christina, a beauty, loses her job when two suitors fight over her on school grounds, but she hits the ground running and takes over the management of her uncle's ranch. Then she locks horns with her neighbor, Kern Yager, but before long the two share a common enemy.

BLY, STEPHEN, AND JANET BLY

CARSON CITY CHRONICLES
Stephen Bly teams with his wife for these woman-centered westerns set in frontier Nevada, featuring the upright Judge Hollis Kingston, who is nearing retirement, and his feisty wife, Judith.

Judith and the Judge. 2000. Servant, paper. 258 pp. ISBN 1-569551-58-8.

Marthellen and the Major. 2000. Servant, paper. 251 pp. ISBN 1-569551-59-6.

Roberta and the Renegade. 2000. Servant, paper. 251 pp. ISBN 1-569551-23-5.

COPELAND, LORI

◀▣✕★ BRIDES OF THE WEST
Three Michigan sisters become mail-order brides in *Faith, June,* and *Hope.* Copeland's conception isn't fresh, but her cornpone humor and the earthy simplicity of her heroines turn this into a likable series.

Faith. 1998. Tyndale, paper. 350 pp. ISBN 0-8423-0267-0.
The three Kallahan sisters decide to become mail-order brides in the first installment of Brides of the West. A Texas rancher answers Faith's ad, and at first they don't hit it off, in part because of Faith's prospective mother-in-law.

June. 1999. Tyndale, paper. 272 pp. ISBN 0-8423-0268-9.
June, the second sister in Copeland's Brides of the West series, gets along all right with her new husband, a pastor in Washington State. But his grandiose plans for a big tabernacle are at odds with the community, and soon June wonders about them, too.

Hope. 1999. Tyndale, paper. 304 pp. ISBN 0-8423-0269-7.
Heading west to meet her man, Hope Kallahan, the third sister in Copeland's Brides of the West series, falls in love with a kindhearted outlaw instead.

Glory. 2000. Tyndale, paper. 320 pp. ISBN 0-8423-3749-0.
Disguised as a boy, Glory—she doesn't have a last name—hitches a ride west with a wagonload of would-be wives and falls in love with the wagon master.

DOW, ROSEY. *Lisa's Broken Arrow.* **2000. Barbour, paper. 170 pp. ISBN 1-57748-957-8.**
Love plays Lisa Feiklin false, and she finds herself stranded in Silverville, South Dakota, cooking for a big hotel.

FELDHAKE, SUSAN

ENDURING FAITH

In Love's Own Time is a prairie romance (discussed later) set in Illinois, but the emphasis of the series gradually changes from prairie romance to romantic western. In any case, though Feldhake is more emotional and didactic, readers of Janette Oke will also enjoy Feldhake.

In Love's Own Time. 1993. Zondervan, paper. 176 pp. ISBN 0-310-48111-2.

Seasons of the Heart. 1993. Zondervan, paper. 200 pp. ISBN 0-310-48121-X.

For Ever and Ever. 1993. Zondervan, paper. 191 pp. ISBN 0-310-48131-7.

Hope for the Morrow. 1993. Zondervan, paper. 191 pp. ISBN 0-310-48141-4.

From This Day Forward. 1994. Zondervan, paper. 208 pp. ISBN 0-310-47931-2.

Joy in the Morning. 1994. Zondervan, paper. 208 pp. ISBN 0-310-47941-X.

Serenity in the Storm. 1996. Zondervan, paper. 249 pp. ISBN 0-310-20261-2.

The Darkness and the Dawn. 1996. Zondervan, paper. 203 pp. ISBN 0-310-20262-0.

GROTE, JOANN. *The Unfolding Heart.* **1997. Barbour, paper. 192 pp. ISBN 1-55748-994-7.**
Grote tells a realistic tale of Milicent Strong, a woman who travels west and meets a minister.She is attracted to the minister but doesn't want to live as primitively as he does and, what's more, doesn't believe in his God.

HEITZMANN, KRISTEN

ROCKY MOUNTAIN LEGACY
Life on the Wyoming frontier for Abbie Farrel is strewn with tragedies that test her own and others' sense of honor, but there's no shortage of suitors.

Honor's Pledge. 1998. Bethany, paper. 288 pp. ISBN 0-7642-2031-4.

Honor's Price. 1998. Bethany, paper. 288 pp. ISBN 0-7642-2032-2.

Honor's Quest. 1999. Bethany, paper. 288 pp. ISBN 0-7642-2033-0.

Honor's Disguise. 1999. Bethany, paper. 288 pp. ISBN 0-7642-2203-1.

Honor's Reward. 2000. Bethany, paper. 317 pp. ISBN 0-7642-2204-X.

DIAMOND OF THE ROCKIES
Nothing seems to go right for pouty Carina DiGratia, who in 1880 buys a house in
Crystal City, Colorado, a mining town filled with rough men. One, a lawyer, pretends to come to her aid; another, a freight hauler, turns out nobler than she'd
thought, and she marries him. Then her troubles really begin.

The Rose Legacy. 2000. Bethany, paper. 320 pp. ISBN 0-7642-2381-X.

Sweet Boundless. 2001. Bethany, paper. 400 pp. ISBN 0-7642-2382-8.

The Tender Vine. 2002. Bethany, paper. 384 pp. ISBN 0-7642-2417-4.

LACY, AL

ANGEL OF MERCY
Lacy's series is a hybrid mix of nurse and western motifs that readers of the Morrises'
Cheney Duvall series may also enjoy, though this series is far more preachy.

A Promise for Breanna. 1995. Multnomah, paper. 319 pp. ISBN 0-88070-797-6.

Faithful Heart. 1995. Multnomah, paper. 307 pp. ISBN 1-57673-835-2.

Captive Set Free. 1996. Multnomah, paper. 278 pp. ISBN 1-57673-872-7.

A Dream Fulfilled. 1996. Multnomah, paper. 300 pp. ISBN 1-57673-940-5.

Suffer the Little Children. 1997. Multnomah, paper. 300 pp. ISBN 1-57673-039-5.

Whither Thou Goest. 1997. Multnomah, paper. 300 pp. ISBN 1-57673-078-6.

Final Justice. 1998. Multnomah, paper. 300 pp. ISBN 1-57673-260-6.

Not by Might. 1999. Multnomah, paper. 300 pp. ISBN 1-57673-2442-8.

Things Not Seen. 1999. Multnomah, paper. 320 pp. ISBN 1-57673-413-7.

Far Above Rubies. 2000. Multnomah, paper. 337 pp. ISBN 1-57673-499-4.

HANNAH OF FORT BRIDGER
Hannah Cooper's husband is killed on the way west, and she must fend for her children
and herself at rough Ft. Bridger, Wyoming, in the years immediately after the Civil War.

Under the Distant Sky. 1997. Multnomah, paper. 300 pp. ISBN 1-57673-033-6.

Consider the Lilies. 1997. Multnomah, paper. 320 pp. ISBN 1-57673-422-6.

No Place for Fear. 1998. Multnomah, paper. 322 pp. ISBN 1-57673-083-2.

A Pillow of Stone. 1998. Multnomah, paper. 300 pp. ISBN 1-57673-234-7.

The Perfect Gift. 1999. Multnomah, paper. 300 pp. ISBN 1-57673-407-2.

Touch of Compassion. 1999. Multnomah, paper. 320 pp. ISBN 1-57673-422-6.

Beyond the Valley. 2000. Multnomah, paper. 318 pp. ISBN 1-57673-618-0.

Damascus Journey. 2000. Multnomah, paper. 286 pp. ISBN 1-57673-630-X.

LACY, AL, AND JOANNA LACY

◀E✕ *MAIL ORDER BRIDES*
Young women go to husbands in the West.

Secrets of the Heart. 1998. Multnomah, paper. 301 pp. ISBN 1-57673-278-9.

A Time to Love. 1998. Multnomah, paper. 312 pp. ISBN 1-57673-284-3.

The Tender Flame. 1999. Multnomah, paper. 278 pp. ISBN 1-57673-399-8.

Blessed Are the Merciful. 1999. Multnomah, paper. 300 pp. ISBN 1-57673-417-X.

Ransom of Love. 2000. Multnomah, paper. 300 pp. ISBN 1-57673-609-1.

Until the Daybreak. 2000. Multnomah, paper. 313 pp. ISBN 1-57673-624-5.

LAVO, NANCY. *Lessons in Love.* 2000. Barbour, paper. 170 pp. ISBN 1-57748-967-5.
With the Civil War over, and with no better prospects, Deborah Marbury heads to Texas with her little brother to prove up on a homestead her uncle left her. Trouble is, her house is already occupied.

MORRIS, ALAN

◀E✕ *GUARDIANS OF THE NORTH*
Though set in Canada as the Mounties are begun, Guardians of the North otherwise has all the features of romantic westerns.

By Honor Bound. 1996. Bethany, paper. 288 pp. ISBN 1-55661-692-9.

Heart of Valor. 1996. Bethany, paper. 256 pp. ISBN 1-55661-693-7.

Bright Sword of Justice. 1997. Bethany, paper. 256 pp. ISBN 1-55661-694-5.

Between Earth and Sky. 1998. Bethany, paper. 288 pp. ISBN 1-55661-695-3.

Wings of Healing. 1999. Bethany, paper. 270 pp. ISBN 1-55661-696-1.

MORRIS, GILBERT, AND J. LANDON

◀E✕ *CHRONICLES OF THE GOLDEN FRONTIER*
Jennifer Hamilton makes her way in the gold-rich Nevada of the 1860s.

Riches Untold. 1998. Crossway, paper. 368 pp. ISBN 1-58134-014-1.

Unseen Riches. 1999. Crossway, paper. 368 pp. ISBN 1-58134-022-2.

Above the Clouds. 1999. Crossway, paper. 360 pp. ISBN 1-58134-108-3.

The Silver Thread. 2000. Crossway, paper. 320 pp. ISBN 1-58134-212-8.

ORCUTT, JANE

★ *HEART'S TRUE DESIRE*

Strong characterizations and a vivid sense of scene raise this series above other romantic westerns.

> ***The Fugitive Heart.*** 1998. WaterBrook, paper. 352 pp. ISBN 1-57856-022-5.
> Samantha Martin waits for her childhood sweetheart, Nathan Hamilton, fully six years while the Civil War drags on. Her family and home are destroyed. Yet when Nathan returns he's a distant, embittered man, an outlaw who may be beyond redemption.

> ***The Hidden Heart.*** 1998. WaterBrook, paper. 352 pp. ISBN 1-57856-053-5.
> Elizabeth Cameron is a sanctimonious, stubborn, but somehow endearing young woman. She takes the Indian boy she's grown to love like a son and heads to Texas for a colony of women, the Sanctificationists, who want to live independently of men. But at least for the journey she needs the protection of a man, ex-gunfighter Caleb Martin, brother of Samantha in *The Fugitive Heart.* He agrees to accompany her in exchange for a pardon from the governor.

PEART, JANE

WESTWARD DREAMS

Young single women find their way in the West in Peart's predictable though often witty series.

> ***Runaway Heart.*** 1994. Zondervan, paper. 250 pp. ISBN 0-310-41271-4.

> ***Promise of the Valley.*** 1995. Zondervan, paper. 282 pp. ISBN 0-310-41281-1.

> ***Where Tomorrow Waits.*** 1995. Zondervan, paper. 221 pp. ISBN 0-310-41291-9.

> ***A Distant Dawn.*** 1995. Zondervan, paper. 240 pp. ISBN 0-310-41301-X.

> ***Undaunted Spirit.*** 1999. Zondervan, paper. 208 pp. ISBN 0-310-22012-2.

> ***A Tangled Web.*** 2001. Zondervan, paper. 192 pp. ISBN 0-310-22013-0.

PETERSON, TRACIE

YUKON QUEST

> ***Treasures of the North.*** 2001. Bethany, paper. 384 pp. ISBN 0-7642-2378-X.
> It's 1897. Because of the financial difficulties of her father, Chicago debutante Grace Hawkins is about to be forced into marriage with Martin Paxton, a villain so crudely drawn he might as well be called Snidely Whiplash. Grace's governess, Karen Pierce, suggests they flee to Alaska, where Karen's father is a missionary. Astoundingly, the evil Paxton follows. More believably, Karen searches for her father among the Tlingit Indians, who are sympathetically portrayed as a people trying to cope with the intrusive gold rush that will change Alaska forever.

> ***Ashes and Ice.*** 2001. Bethany, paper. 384 pp. ISBN 0-7642-2379-8.
> Karen Pierce takes center stage in the sequel to *Treasures of the North.* She escapes a fire in which she loses her beloved aunt, as well as everything material. It appears as though the villainous Martin Paxton set the fire, but there's nothing to do

except pack up with the two teenagers she's raising and her new beau, Adrik Ivanov, and head for the gold fields. Karen joins Grace, who has troubles of her own in her new marriage to Peter Colton, a better man than Paxton but nonetheless an unbeliever.

Rivers of Gold. 2002. Bethany, paper. 384 pp. ISBN 0-7642-2380-1.
New characters arrive in the Yukon Quest series. Principal among them is Miranda Colton, whose wilderness trek leaves her presumed dead. But she survives under the tender care of an English botanist, Teddy Davenport, who's in Alaska to study its unique flora. Miranda may have found a life for herself, but something in her past troubles her.

◀✕ PHILLIPS, MICHAEL

JOURNALS OF CORRIE BELLE HOLLISTER
The popular, sentimental, first-person account of a teenage girl who comes to California via wagon train, grows up, and marries.

My Father's World. 1990. Bethany, paper. 286 pp. ISBN 1-55661-104-8.

Daughter of Grace. 1990. Bethany, paper. 299 pp. ISBN 1-55661-105-6.

On the Trail of the Truth. 1991, Bethany, paper. 319 pp. ISBN 1-55661-106-4.

A Place in the Sun. 1991. Bethany, paper. 300 pp. ISBN 1-55661-222-2.

Sea to Shining Sea. 1992. Bethany, paper. 320 pp. ISBN 1-55661-227-3.

Into the Long Dark Night. 1992. Bethany, paper. 297 pp. ISBN 1-55661-300-8.

Land of the Brave and the Free. 1993. Bethany, paper. 317 pp. ISBN 1-55661-308-3.

A Home for the Heart. 1994. Bethany, paper. 313 pp. ISBN 1-55661-440-3.

Grayfox: A Companion Reader to the Journals of Corrie Belle Hollister. 1993. Bethany, paper. 297 pp. ISBN 1-55661-368-7.

JOURNALS OF CORRIE AND CHRISTOPHER
The continuation of Corrie's journals, now as a married woman.

The Braxtons of Miracle Springs. 1996. Bethany, paper. 272 pp. ISBN 1-55661-635-X.

A New Beginning. 1997. Bethany, paper. 256 pp. ISBN 1-55661-933-2.

◀✕ PELLA, JUDITH, AND TRACIE PETERSON

RIBBONS OF STEEL
Love finds destinations on the rapidly expanding western railroad lines.

Distant Dreams. 1997. Bethany, paper. 349 pp. ISBN 1-55661-862-X.

A Hope Beyond. 1997. Bethany, paper. 320 pp. ISBN 1-55661-863-8.

A Promise for Tomorrow. 1998. Bethany, paper. 368 pp. ISBN 1-55661-864-6.

RIBBONS WEST
A spin-off from the authors' Ribbons of Steel series.

Westward the Dream. 1999. Bethany, paper. 352 pp. ISBN 0-7642-2071-3.

Separate Roads. 1999. Bethany, paper. 320 pp. ISBN 0-7642-2072-1.

Ties That Bind. 2000. Bethany, paper. 320 pp. ISBN 0-7642-073-X.

PETERSON, TRACIE

◼️ *WESTWARD CHRONICLES*

Young women find adventure and love as Harvey Girls.

A Shelter of Hope. 1998. Bethany, paper. 256 pp. ISBN 0-76422-112-4.

Hidden in a Whisper. 1999. Bethany, paper. 284 pp. ISBN 0-76422-113-2.

A Veiled Reflection. 2000. Bethany, paper. 288 pp. ISBN 0-76422-114-0.

STOKS, PEGGY

◼️ *ABOUNDING LOVE*

Olivia's Touch. 2000. Tyndale, paper. 300 pp. ISBN 0-8423-1942-5.
A Colorado frontier midwife, Olivia Plummer, who learned the gift of healing from her legendary grandmother, gets her dander up when the town of Tristan hires a real physician from Boston, Ethan Gray. Ethan gave up his lucrative but unsatisfying practice because he wanted to help "real" people, rather than rich hypochondriacs. He takes the practice of medicine seriously, and the mere idea of Olivia is an affront to him, but he must modify his thinking when his hand is cut and she's the only one qualified to stitch him up.

Romy's Walk. 2001. Tyndale, paper. 262 pp. ISBN 0-8423-1943-3.
The second entry in Stoks's Abounding Love series is linked to the first by the friendship of its heroine, Romy, with Olivia Plummer. Romy's walk is a walk of faith, severely tested literally and figuratively when she loses a foot in a violent accident. A quiet schoolteacher, Romy's inhibitions disappear as she lies near death, and she declares her love for a shy local storekeeper. Thinking she's about to die, he declares his love, too, and the two are married on the spot. And then Romy survives.

◼️ WICK, LORI

THE CALIFORNIANS

The missionary Donovan family returns from Hawaii and establishes itself in the California of the 1870s in this extremely popular, often-reprinted series.

Whatever Tomorrow Brings. 1992. Harvest, paper. 323 pp. ISBN 0-89081-969-6.

As Time Goes By. 1993. Harvest, paper. 279 pp. ISBN 0-736902-562-1.

Sean Donovan. 1993. Harvest. 269 pp. ISBN 1-56507-046-1.

Donovan's Daughter. 1994. Harvest. 312 pp. ISBN 1-56507-129-8.

ROCKY MOUNTAIN MEMORIES
Unconnected tales of romance in frontier Colorado.

> *Where the Wild Rose Blooms.* 1996. Harvest, paper. 342 pp. ISBN 1-56507-391-6.

> *Whispers of Moonlight.* 1996. Harvest, paper. 423 pp. ISBN 1-56507-483-1.

> *To Know Her by Name.* 1997. Harvest, paper. 300 pp. ISBN 1-56507-574-9.

> *Promise Me Tomorrow.* 1997. Harvest, paper. 400 pp. ISBN 1-56507-695-8.

YELLOW ROSE TRILOGY

> *Every Little Thing About You.* 1999. Harvest, paper. 300 pp. ISBN 0-7369-0104-3.
> Set in Shotgun, Texas, *Every Little Thing About You* is the didactic tale of Texas Ranger
> Slater Rawlings, whose nascent faith tugs at his consciousness to the point that he quits his
> job and looks for a quiet town in which to worship. Ironically, he's arrested by diminu-
> tive Deputy Liberty Drake for displaying a weapon in a public place. Tweaking western
> stereotypes, Wick makes her ex-Ranger the gentle one, and her law woman fierce; but
> both characters suffer from believability.

> *A Texas Sky.* 2000. Harvest, paper. 300 pp. ISBN 0-7369-0187-6.
> Dakota Rawlings, Slater's brother, also a Texas Ranger and a new believer, recovers
> from the wounds he suffered in *Every Little Thing About You* on a mission escorting his
> boss's niece, Darvi Wingate, to the town of Stillwater. This seems simple enough, but
> Dakota hadn't bargained on Darvi's stubbornness or her knack for getting into trouble.

> *City Girl.* 2001. Harvest, paper. 300 pp. ISBN 0-7369-0255-4.
> Another Rawlings brother, Cash, falls for the "city girl," stubborn Reagan Sullivan, out
> on the Texas range in the final entry of the Yellow Rose Trilogy.

WILBEE, BRENDA

◆▧ SEATTLE SWEETBRIAR
Long-running series about the founding of Seattle.

> *Sweetbriar.* 1983. Harvest, paper. 206 pp. ISBN 0-8908-1336-1.

> *Sweetbriar Bride.* 1986. Harvest, paper. 238 pp. ISBN 0-89081-482-1.

> *Sweetbriar Spring.* 1989. Harvest, paper. 254 pp. ISBN 0-89081-661-1.

> *Sweetbriar Summer.* 1997. Revell, paper. 288 pp. ISBN 0-8007-5619-3.

> *Sweetbriar Autumn.* 1998, Revell, paper. 271 pp. ISBN 0-8007-5661-4.

> *Sweetbriar Hope.* 1999. Revell, paper. 304 pp. ISBN 0-8007-5695-9.

Prairie Romance

In the classic prairie romance—the classic as formulated by Janette Oke in the 1980s—a
schoolmarm heads west, draws nearer to God through a series of trials, and finds her man. One might
say that the romantic western leans toward more melodramatic plotting and that in the prairie romance
the setting plays a more important role—that is, the story is more often, and more distinctly, set in
farming communities, and these tend to be in pioneer Kansas, Iowa, and Nebraska. But other than the
setting—the prairies—and Oke's extraordinary example, the actual difference between prairie romances
and romantic westerns is slight.

BACHER, JUNE MASTERS

The late Bacher's romances grow older and are mostly out of print. But they circulate vigorously, a good alternative for the reader who has read all of Janette Oke.

HEARTLAND HERITAGE

> *No Time for Tears.* 1992.

> *Songs in the Whirlwind.* 1992.

> *Where Lies Our Hope.* 1992.

> *Return to the Heartland.* 1993.

PIONEER ROMANCE SERIES 1

> *Love Is a Gentle Stranger.* 1983.

> *Love's Silent Song.* 1983.

> *Diary of a Loving Heart.* 1984.

> *Love Leads Home.* 1984.

> *Love Follows the Heart.* 1990.

> *Love's Enduring Hope.* 1990.

PIONEER ROMANCE SERIES 2

> *Journey to Love.* 1985.

> *Dreams Beyond Tomorrow.* 1985.

> *Seasons of Love.* 1986.

> *My Heart's Desire.* 1986.

> *The Heart Remembers.* 1990.

> *From This Time Forth.* 1991.

PIONEER ROMANCE SERIES 3

> *Love's Soft Whisper.* 1986.

> *Love's Beautiful Dream.* 1987.

> *When Hearts Awaken.* 1987.

> *Another Spring.* 1988.

> *When Morning Comes Again.* 1988.

> *Gently Love Beckons.* 1989.

GLOVER, RUTH

The Saskatchewan prairie that Glover writes of is also where she grew up, and her unadorned prose has the same quiet authority and religious passion of Janette Oke.

SASKATCHEWAN SAGA

A Place Called Bliss. 2001. Revell, paper. 239 pp. ISBN 0-8007-5743-2.
Two pregnant Scottish women, the peasant Mary Morrison and Sophia Galloway with her claims to quality, come to Canada in the 1870s. Mary and her husband look for a new start on the frontier, while Sophia and her husband carve out a niche among the movers and shakers of Toronto.

With Love from Bliss. 2001. Revell, paper. 240 pp. ISBN 0-8007-5744-0.
The sequel to *A Place Called Bliss* features Kerry Fane, a young woman seeking revenge; she blames the death of a friend on a young man in Bliss.

WILDROSE SERIES

★ ***The Shining Light.*** 1994. Beacon Hill, paper. 214 pp. ISBN 0-83911-514-X.
Abbie Rooney struggles with the harsh frontier after her husband dies, battling loneliness and searching for love even as the shining light of the West seems to die.

★ ***Bitter Thistle, Sweet Rose.*** 1995. Beacon Hill, paper. 206 pp. ISBN 0-83411-528-X.
The frontier itself, with all of its harshness, is the main character in the sequel to *The Shining Light*. Linn Graham is the brave, trusting young woman looking for love, but after being jilted twice, she can't trust the man who loves her sincerely.

A Time to Dream. 1996. Beacon Hill, paper. 191 pp. ISBN 0-83411-572-7.
Life was already hard for homesteader's wife, Cassie Quinn. But now her husband is dead, and she's expecting a baby.

Turn Northward, Love. 1997. Beacon Hill, paper. 216 pp. ISBN 0-83411-590-5.
A plain woman, Hannah Vaughn, is convinced that men will only be interested in her money. Then she finds a kindred spirit.

Second Best Bride. 1998. Beacon Hill, paper. 208 pp. ISBN 0-83411-628-6.
Meg Shaw loves fickle Royce Ferguson, but he loves Meg's shallow but beautiful sister, Marlys. Royce leaves for the Saskatchewan frontier, confident that Marlys will follow, but Marlys wants no part of such hardship. Meg, swallowing her pride, goes in her sister's place.

Place to Call Home. 1999. Beacon Hill, paper. 204 pp. ISBN 0-83411-753-3.
Young Lolly Dalton's father moves the family to an abandoned homestead in the concluding volume of the Wildrose series. Life is hard, but the place feels like home to Lolly and her siblings. To thwart her father's restless ways, Lolly does all she can to interest a widower neighbor in marrying her. Meanwhile, a poor but honest young farmer strives to make his modest case for Lolly's hand.

HATCHER, ROBIN LEE

◀E▶ COMING TO AMERICA
Hatcher reworked this popular mainstream series for the evangelical market, and because the mainstream novels were published in the late 1990s, it's often possible to find them beside the Zondervan editions on library shelves.

Dear Lady. 2000. Zondervan, paper. 303 pp. ISBN 0-310-23083-7.
Beth Wellington, though titled and with her future secure, flees England and an arranged marriage for the wilds of Montana in 1897. She has a pen pal there, Janie Steele, and a teaching job. Soon, Lady Beth is attracted to young Janie's father, Garrett, and is running as fast as she can from another man, Owen Simpson, mayor of the town.

R *Patterns of Love.* 2001. Zondervan, paper. 320 pp. ISBN 0-310-23105-1.
Swede Inga Linberg becomes a housekeeper for Iowa rancher Dirk Bridger in 1897, then marries him, not realizing that Dirk is only marrying out of family necessity and really wants to go fortune hunting in the great wide world.

In His Arms. 2001. Zondervan, paper. 304 pp. ISBN 0-310-23120-5.
Woebegone Mary Malone, an unwed mother, flees Ireland with her small son for New York City in the last of Hatcher's Coming to America novels. Mary finds work as a maid, but when her employer makes a pass, she deals him such a hard blow that he falls down dead. Mary grabs her son and buys a ticket to Omaha. Then she is befriended by a dying woman on her way home to Whistle Creek, Idaho, where, perhaps, Mary's fortunes will improve.

MCREYNOLDS, MARY. *Wells of Glory.* **1996. Crossway, paper. 304 pp. ISBN 0-89107-889-4.**
Oklahoma Sooner Ben Reuben's wife dies, leaving him with four children. The kindness of strangers and the attentions of a new schoolmarm, a Christian, lifts his sorrow.

MORGAN, KATHLEEN

BRIDES OF CULDEE CREEK

Daughter of Joy. 1999. Revell, paper. 336 pp. ISBN 0-8007-5718-1.
Abby Stanton, a grieving widow, comes to Culdee Creek, Colorado, as a housekeeper and tutor in this mildly salacious ranch romance. Rancher Conor MacKay's daughter proves willful, and the rancher himself is amorous.

Woman of Grace. 2000. Revell, paper. 304 pp. ISBN 0-8007-5727-0.
Hannah Cutler, a reformed prostitute, struggles to overcome her past and make ranch life, and married life, a path of grace.

Lady of Light. 2001. Revell, paper. 336 pp. ISBN 0-8007-5755-6.
In the third entry of the Brides of Culdee Creek series, Evan MacKay is jilted in Colorado. He finds a bride on a trip to his Scottish ancestral home, but will she fit in on the ranch?

Child of Promise. 2002. Revell, paper. 320 pp. ISBN 0-8007-5761-0.
Beth MacKay earns her medical degree and takes over her aging father's practice in Culdee Creek. She has enough to do battling prejudice against female physicians, but finds herself falling in love with a troubled Episcopal rector, Noah Starr.

★ OKE, JANETTE

Oke, who grew up on the prairie of Alberta to become a pastor's wife, is the gold standard for prairie romances, and indeed for all of Christian fiction. Her titles, both in regular editions and large print, will be read for many years to come. All of Janette Oke's titles are excellent for young adults—for girls, at least, because she often uses teenage girls and young women barely out of adolescence for her protagonists.

There's little original in Oke's story lines, but her authentic settings and intimate characterizations strike a realistic note with women readers, in part because, in sequels, she moves beyond courtship into the hardships and rewards of marriage itself. Oke's religious message is clear and uncompromising, but never seems like an uneasy appendage to the story.

Beyond the Gathering Storm. 2000. Bethany. 256 pp. ISBN 0-7642-2401-8.

Following up her Canadian West series (discussed later) Oke sets *Beyond the Gathering Storm* in her favorite Canadian province of Alberta a little before WWI. It's a quiet story about brother and sister Christine and Henry Delaney, adopted children who strike out from their parents on new courses. Christine finds a clerical job in Edmonton, while Henry, a Mountie like his father, assumes his first command at a small post in the far north. Christine's tale develops into the familiar one of a Christian woman who falls in love with an unbeliever. In this case, the unbeliever happens also to be the boss's son, and when Christine reaffirms her faith, the romance, not to mention the job, heads south. Henry's less instructional story may be more satisfying: In his lonely outpost, he connects again with a widow to whom several years before, as a rookie, he had to deliver the news of her husband's death.

When Tomorrow Comes. 2001. Bethany, paper. 288 pp. ISBN 0-7642-2555-3.

In the sequel to *Beyond the Gathering Storm,* Oke turns her focus to Christine Delaney, still suffering from the emotional effects of her unfortunate romance. There's a new man pursuing her, but, in passages that are unusually preachy even for Oke, Christine seeks the Lord's will as to whether she should head to Canada's North.

CANADIAN WEST

The Canadian West series, set in 1891, begins as Elizabeth Thatcher, a well-educated young woman from Toronto, heads west to become a schoolteacher. Though she has vowed never to fall in love with a ruffian of the frontier, she finds that she can't resist a certain Mountie.

When Calls the Heart.1983. Bethany, paper. 221 pp. ISBN 0-87123-611-7.

When Comes the Spring. 1985. Bethany, paper. 255 pp. ISBN 0-87123-795-4.

When Breaks the Dawn. 1986. Bethany, paper. 223 pp. ISBN 0-87123-882-9.

When Hope Springs New. 1986. Bethany, paper. 222 pp. ISBN 0-87123-657-5.

LOVE COMES SOFTLY

Not only did this series introduce Janette Oke, but it also virtually founded evangelical fiction.

Set on the Iowa prairie, the series begins with woe and ends in a triumph of faith and married love. Nineteen-year-old Marty comes west to homestead with her new husband, but he promptly dies. On the day of his funeral the destitute young woman must decide on marriage to Clark Davis, whose wife died over a hard winter, leaving him with a little girl to raise. Slowly, the family of a painfully ridiculous necessity becomes a real family.

Love Comes Softly. 1979. Bethany, paper. 188 pp. ISBN 0-87123-342-8.

Love's Enduring Promise. 1980. Bethany, paper. 206 pp. ISBN 0-87123-345-2.

Love's Long Journey. 1982. Bethany, paper. 200 pp. ISBN 0-87123-315-0.

Love's Abiding Joy. 1983. Bethany, paper. 217 pp. ISBN 0-87123-401-7.

Love's Unending Legacy. 1984. Bethany, paper. 224 pp. ISBN 0-87123-616-8.

Love's Unfolding Dream. 1987. Bethany, paper. 222 pp. ISBN 0-87123-979-5.

Love Takes Wing. 1988. Bethany, paper. 220 pp. ISBN 1-55661-035-1.

Love Finds a Home. 1989. Bethany, paper. 221 pp. ISBN 1-55661-086-6.

PRAIRIE LEGACY

Oke tells the story of Virginia Simpson, granddaughter of Marty and Clark Davis of *Love Finds a Home* and daughter of Belinda Simpson—all of whom make frequent appearances in the series.

The Tender Years. 1997. Bethany, paper. 384 pp. ISBN 0-7642-2953-7.
Struggling against the rigid morality of her parents, high school girl Virginia Simpson falls under the influence of a "big city" girl, Jenny, whose reckless ways indirectly lead to a drowning.

A Searching Heart. 1999. Bethany, paper. 256 pp. ISBN 0-7642-2139-6.
Having survived her late adolescence, Virginia graduates from high school as valedictorian, but though college beckons, her future seems confused. Her friend from *The Tender Years,* Jenny, spirals downward in troubles, and Virginia's high school sweetheart, Jamison Curtis, finds someone else to marry. Then Virginia meets Jonathan Lewis, who wants to be a rancher.

A Quiet Strength. 1999. Bethany, paper. 256 pp. ISBN 0-7642-2156-6.
Virginia and Jonathan's romance heats up, and they marry. Jenny's troubles continue, to the point she wants to give up her daughter, Mindy, for adoption. Virginia and Jonathan take Mindy in, even as Jonathan struggles to make the ranch pay.

Like Gold Refined. 2000. Bethany, paper. 251 pp. ISBN 0-7642-2162-0.
Virginia's grandparents begin to fail, but the ranch is doing fine, and Jonathan and Virginia have several children. Mindy goes back to her mother for a time, but the wages of sin finally catch up to Jenny. She dies with a deathbed conversion, sending Mindy back to Virginia to be raised as a Lewis.

SEASONS OF THE HEART

Oke creates Josh, a 12-year-old orphan on the frontier who finds mother, sister, and sweetheart in his lovely, 18-year-old Aunt Lou, who raises him and then gets married and moves away. Restless Josh at last accepts his place in God's universe and becomes a farmer.

Once Upon a Summer. 1981. Bethany, paper. 203 pp. ISBN 0-87123-413-0.

The Winds of Autumn. 1987. Bethany, paper. 218 pp. ISBN 0-87123-946-9.

Winter Is Not Forever. 1988. Bethany, paper. 218 pp. ISBN 1-55661-002-5.

Spring's Gentle Promise. 1989. Bethany, paper. 224 pp. ISBN 1-55661-059-9.

WOMEN OF THE WEST

Oke presents the adventures of different women on the frontier who seek love and find solace in their faith when difficulties beset them, from the ugly duckling sister in *The Bluebird and the Sparrow* to the lonely Indian girl at the white man's school in *Drums of Change.*

The Calling of Emily Evans. 1990. Bethany, paper. 288 pp. ISBN 0-76422-098-5.

Julia's Last Hope. 1990. Bethany, paper. 204 pp. ISBN 1-255661-153-6.

Roses for Mama. 1991. Bethany, paper. 222 pp. ISBN 1-55661-185-4.

A Woman Named Damaris. 1991. Bethany, paper. 288 pp. ISBN 0-76422-018-7.

They Called Her Mrs. Doc. 1992. Bethany, paper. 222 pp. ISBN 1-55661-246-X.

The Measure of a Heart. 1992. Bethany, paper. 219 pp. ISBN 1-55661-296-6.

A Bride for Donnigan. 1993. Bethany, paper. 223 pp. ISBN 1-55661-327-X.

Heart of the Wilderness. 1993. Bethany, paper. 239 pp. ISBN 1-55661-362-8.

Too Long a Stranger. 1994. Bethany, paper. 288 pp. ISBN 0-76422-385-2.

A Gown of Spanish Lace. 1995. Bethany, paper. 251 pp. ISBN 1-55661-683-X.

The Bluebird and the Sparrow. 1995. Bethany, paper. 251 pp. ISBN 1-55661-612-0.

Drums of Change. 1996. Bethany, paper. 235 pp. ISBN 1-55661-812-3.

PALMER, CATHERINE

◀❚✖ *A TOWN CALLED HOPE*

Palmer's popular series, set in Kansas and Missouri, centers on the struggles of a blended family to come together as they battle the hardships of homesteading. Readers may want also to look for "The Christmas Bride," a novella featuring some of the same characters, in the anthology *Prairie Christmas* (p. 214).

Prairie Rose. 1997. Tyndale, paper. 272 pp. ISBN 0-84237-056-0.
Rosie Mills, an orphan, heads for the Kansas prairie to care for the young son of a widower, Seth Hunter. Soon, Rosie's real task is revealed: bringing together a blended family, each member of which has cause for bitterness.

Prairie Fire. 1999. Tyndale, paper. 288 pp. ISBN 0-84237-705-7.
Jack Cornwall, the sworn enemy of Seth Hunter of *Prairie Rose,* hits bottom near Topeka in 1865. But Jack is a misunderstood man, and there's good in him. A good woman, Caitrin Murphy, and a prairie fire may be enough to redeem him.

Prairie Storm. 1999. Tyndale, paper. 272 pp. ISBN 0-84237-058-7.
The last in Palmer's Town Called Hope series features characters who had prominent roles in the first two books, but the main story is about another blended family: the Reverend Elijah Book, who discovered a baby at the sight of an Indian massacre, and Lily Nolan, who has just lost her child.

STAHL, HILDA

◀❚✖ *PRAIRIE SERIES*

The popular Stahl died in 1993. Set in Nebraska in the 1890s, this series, similar to Oke's Love Comes Softly series, features desperate spinster schoolmarms and mail-order brides who vault into marriages by necessity, finding love later.

Blossoming Love. 1991. Bethel, paper. 224 pp. ISBN 0-934998-42-6.

The Stranger's Wife. 1992. Bethel, paper. 200 pp. ISBN 0-934998-44-2.

The Makeshift Husband. 1993. Bethel, paper. 172 pp. ISBN 0-934998-48-5.

WHITSON, STEPHANIE G.

◆ KEEPSAKE LEGACIES

Whitson draws from her own family's history for these tales of hardship on the Nebraska prairie.

> **Sarah's Patchwork.** 1998. Nelson, paper. 287 pp. ISBN 0-7852-7185-6.
> *Sarah's Patchwork* is an orphan train story about Sarah Biddle and her younger brother, Tom, who are shipped west to work in Lincoln, Nebraska.

> **Karyn's Memory Box.** 1999. Nelson, paper. 266 pp. ISBN 0-7852-7186-4.
> Karyn Ritter copes with living in a soddy and the vicissitudes of wild prairie weather as she tries to build a marriage and a family.

> **Nora's Ribbon of Memories.** 1999. Nelson. paper. 288 pp. ISBN 0-7852-7187-2.
> The characters from the first two novels of Whitson's trilogy make appearances in *Nora's Ribbon of Memories.* But the principal story is of an abandoned child, Elnora O'Dell, who begins her career as a housekeeper in a brothel in Lincoln but finds a path to happiness.
> See also Quaker writer Susan McCracken's Friends Trilogy, p. 282.

TRADITIONAL WESTERNS

What is a traditional western? In library terms, it's a western that men like, and often, nowadays, old men. If this seems sexist, then ask yourself how many men check out Janette Oke's books.

Zane Grey and Louis L'Amour, still by far the bestselling western writers, are the standards. Louis L'Amour's authentic settings and macho heroes secured his fame. Although Zane Grey's novels are all romances modeled after Walter Scott's, and his heroines are not delicate, his dialogue between men and women is so quaint that the love stories date him. But his understanding of horses, his naturalist's eye for western landscapes, and the part of his romantic approach that glorified what he called the Code of the West are as popular as ever.

Traditional westerns feature decent, hard men fighting to do right, and brutal men who oppose them. Women stay mostly in the background. The lore of the West runs deep, and the physical stubbornness of the land and weather are ever present. There's always some ordeal to be borne. There's much wildlife, clean water, and privacy. Although the stories may be far-fetched, you have the feeling that the settings are on the mark.

Of course, there are many exceptions to this formula, such as Elmer Kelton's emblematic tales of aimless modern cowboys and Cynthia Haseloff's fine stories of the beleaguered Plains Indians. Following are *somewhat* traditional westerns. Ernest Haycox, like the West he rhapsodized, is gone forever.

See also Willa Cather's classic, *Death Comes for the Archbishop,* p. 248.

◆ ★ BLY, STEPHEN

CODE OF THE WEST

Bly is the name that springs first to mind with Christian westerns. Though sometimes didactic and overplotted, they are also witty and full of the deep lore of the West that readers expect from Louis L'Amour. And there's plenty of action.

Code of the West is perhaps Bly's most successful series. It's about ex-gunfighter Tap Andrews, his wife Paige, and their attempt to leave their colorful pasts behind by building up a Colorado ranch.

It's Your Misfortune and None of My Own. 1994. Crossway, paper. 192 pp. ISBN 0-89107-997-9.

Bly introduces Pepper Paige, ex-dance-hall girl from Denver, and Tap Andrews, ex-gunfighter, more or less from Arizona. They fall in love pretending that their pasts are clean. But when, after many a witty exchange, each penetrates the other's disguise, they are still a couple, intent on marrying and starting a ranch in Colorado.

One Went to Denver and the Other Went Wrong. 1995. Crossway, paper. 183 pp. ISBN 0-89107-834-7.

Though the reader will find Tap's battles with bad hombres entertaining, Tap is sick of them, and he's determined to go back to Arizona and clear up that business about a murder he didn't commit. But first he has to go to Denver where Pepper's dark past lies, and she can't make herself go there with him.

Where the Deer and the Antelope Play. 1995. Crossway, paper. 192 pp. ISBN 0-89107-850-9.

Tap and Pepper prepare to marry in the third entry of the Code of the West series. But then there are rustlers to deal with, and it seems Tap missed a payment on his mortgage. The wedding looks a bit doubtful.

Stay Away from That City . . . They Call It Cheyenne. 1996. Crossway, paper. 192 pp. ISBN 0-89107-890-8.

Tap and Pepper, married at last in this fourth entry of the Code of the West series, lose their Colorado ranch and move to Cheyenne, where Tap becomes deputy sheriff and Pepper becomes pregnant.

My Foot's in the Stirrup . . . My Pony Won't Stand. 1997. Crossway, paper. 192 pp. ISBN 0-89107-898-3.

Having lost his job as deputy in *Stay Away from That City,* Tap tries his hand as brand inspector for the cattle association in the fifth entry of the Code of the West series. So once again he's fighting with rustlers and other miscreants, all the while longing for that ranch Pepper and he lost.

I'm Off to Montana for to Throw the Hoolihan. 1997. Crossway, paper. 208 pp. ISBN 0-89107-953-X.

In the concluding entry of the Code of the West series, Tap and Pepper finally have a ranch—and a big one. It's a partnership, though, not a perfect arrangement, and there are outlaws and Indians to be fought off. Still, Tap's name is cleared at last, and Pepper and he seem to have found what they were looking for.

FORTUNES OF THE BLACK HILLS

The witty Bly relates the fortunes of the Fortunes, a stalwart and long-suffering family in the Dakotas headed by a tough hombre named Brazos.

Beneath a Dakota Cross. 1999. Broadman and Holman, paper. 224 pp. ISBN 0-8054-1659-5.

Shadow of Legends. 2000. Broadman and Holman, paper. 212 pp. ISBN 0-8054-2174-2.

The Long Trail Home. 2001. Broadman and Holman, paper. 272 pp. ISBN 0-8054-2356-7.

SKINNERS OF GOLD FIELD

 Fool's Gold. 2000. Crossway, paper. 264 pp. ISBN 1-58254-155-5.
Bly recaptures the wit of his Code of the West series in this disarming tale of the God-fearing, seemingly foolhardy family of Orion Tower ("O. T.") Skinner. They are pilgrims bound for California after a tornado wiped out what little they had back east. They only mean to pass through Goldfield, Nevada, the site, in 1905, of the last great American gold rush. O. T. is the chief attraction, specializing in the ignorance that confounds wisdom, but his naiveté, reminiscent of Jeeter Lester's in *Tobacco Road,* always results in good.

Hidden Treasure. 2000. Crossway, paper. 272 pp. ISBN 1-58134-199-7.
In the sequel to *Fool's Gold,* the Skinner family has determined that the Lord wants them for Christian witness in lawless Goldfield. O. T. heads off looking for lost Spanish treasure, while Dola Mae, his wife, runs the Miner's Delight Cafe.

Picture Rock. 2001. Crossway, paper. 252 pp. ISBN 1-58134-254-3.
O. T. helps out a miner friend whose crew stumbles onto "picture rock," or gold that is nearly pure metal, in the third entry of the Skinners of Goldfield. The miner thinks his Mexican workers are trying to rob him, but self-effacing O. T. finds out what's really riling them. Meanwhile, all the family pines for California, but the Goldfield townsfolk, seeing the value of having the peacemaking Skinners around, beg them to stay.

BROUWER, SIGMUND

★ GHOST RIDERS

This series was reissued under different titles (*Morning Star* became *Evening Star; Moon Basket* became *Silver Moon*) by Bethany in 2000, under the series title Sam Keaton: Legends of Laramie.

Morning Star. 1994. Victor, paper. 307 pp. ISBN 1-56476-340-4.
The first in this interesting series is among the best Christian westerns ever written. Drifter Samuel Keaton, on his way to Laramie to become sheriff, meets an English-speaking Sioux woman named Morning Star, who is drawn mysteriously but inexorably to the Lakota Sioux homeland of the Black Hills. Throughout most of the novel, she is disguised as an "Injun," filthy, male, and silent. This is a shopworn device, but Brouwer builds it into his action so carefully that it becomes a powerful commentary. Masquerading as a man, Morning Star observes Keaton as he breaks up a buffalo-hunting camp where white men have corrupted the Sioux by trading them whiskey for squaws. This is the moment when Morning Star's love for Keaton begins. The two plunge deeper into Brouwer's magnificently rendered Sioux country, and the Sioux are sympathetically portrayed as a great people reeling under the onslaught of the whites.

Moon Basket. 1994. Victor, paper. 314 pp. ISBN 1-56476-341-2.
In this sequel to *Morning Star,* set in Laramie in 1874, Keaton becomes Laramie's marshall and solves a series of murders in his laconic, self-effacing manner. There are compassionate portrayals of an overworked physician and of the sturdy character of a frontier widow, besieged by suitors and shysters.

SunDance. 1995. Victor, paper. 276 pp. ISBN 1-56476-427-3.
By the time of this third entry in the Ghost Riders series, Brouwer is observing as many conventions of the mystery as of the western. The love story also takes an odd turn: Apparently, Rebecca has married, and Sam has a new girlfriend.

Thunder Voice. 1995. Victor, paper. 280 pp. ISBN 1-56476-426-5.
At the end of *Thunder Voice,* Sam and Rebecca are together again, but Brouwer's plot tricks in *SunDance* may cause the reader to distrust their reunion.

DAVIS, WALLY

◗✕ *VALLEY OF THE PEACEMAKER*
Valley of the Peacemaker is a solid, unpreachy, witty series about a drifter who, after the Civil War, finds a job as sheriff in the California gold fields.

The Gathering Storm. 1996. Crossway, paper. 448 pp.ISBN 0-89107-887-8.

The Proving Ground. 1996. Crossway, paper. 368 pp. ISBN 0-89107-884-3.

The Refining Fire. 1997. Crossway, paper. 336 pp. ISBN 0-89107-936-X.

◗✕ ★ JACKSON, DAVE. *Lost River Conspiracy.* 1995. Good Books, paper. 220 pp. ISBN 1-56148-183-1. *[Historical]*
See discussion in chapter 15, "Young Adult."

KIRKPATRICK, JANE

◗✕★ *KINSHIP AND COURAGE*   ▐ Discussion ▌

All Together in One Place. 2000. WaterBrook, paper. 416 pp. ISBN 1-57856-232-5.
Kirkpatrick bases her series on a tantalizing historical reference to a wagon train in which every man had died, and characterizes 12 stalwart female survivors. In the beginning there are men: Jeremy Bacon, for instance, who sells his Wisconsin farm over the protestations of his wife, Mazy. They bicker until the moment of Jeremy's death. A toughened Mazy bonds with the others, all of them suddenly single, in this feminist view of how it really must have been heading down the Oregon Trail in the early 1850s, threatened by Indians and brutal weather, and without men.

No Eye Can See. 2001. WaterBrook, paper. 400 pp. ISBN 1-57856-233-3.
In the sequel to *All Together in One Place,* the death of Jeremy continues to haunt Mazy, but her respectable widowhood gives her the chance to become the leader of the wagon train's valiant band of widows, who eventually reach Shasta City, California, and establish new lives. Several Chinese women join the band, and particularly with the characterization of Zilah, Kirkpatrick brilliantly conveys the sense of coping with an alien culture. But the convincing internal lives of all her characters makes Kirkpatrick's series a standout.

LACY, AL

◗✕ *JOURNEYS OF THE STRANGER*
Lacy draws upon an old motif of the traditional western, the mysterious stranger, appearing out of nowhere to right wrong.

Legacy. 1994. Multnomah, paper. 317 pp. ISBN 0-88070-619-8.

Silent Abduction. 1994. Multnomah, paper. 320 pp. ISBN 0-88070-674-0.

Blizzard. 1995. Multnomah, paper. 277 pp. ISBN 0-88070-702-X.

Tears of the Sun. 1995. Multnomah, paper. 270 pp. ISBN 0-88070-838-7.

Circle of Fire. 1996. Multnomah, paper. 269 pp. ISBN 0-88070-893-X.

Quiet Thunder. 1996. Multnomah, paper. 248 pp. ISBN 0-88070-975-8.

Snow Ghost. 1997. Multnomah, paper. 300 pp. ISBN 0-88070-047-6.

MILLER, JANICE

◆✕ *ELK HEAD CREEK*

Miller draws on her own family history for this authentic series set in northwestern Colorado.

> *Winter's Fire.* 1995. Moody, paper. 312 pp. ISBN 0-8024-7921-9.
> *Winter's Fire* occurs in 1886 during a hard winter in the life of rancher Courtney McCannon, who faces debt, a roundup interrupted by early storms, and a wife, Caroline, far along in a difficult pregnancy. Then rustlers strike, and a range war erupts.

> *McCannon's Country.* 1996. Moody, paper. 276 pp. ISBN 0-8024-7922-7.
> *McCannon's Country* is a prequel to *Winter's Fire.* It's a mountain-man tale featuring a company of trappers, among whom are Jim Bridger and Mike Fink, bound up the Missouri River in 1822 to establish a fur trading post. In boy's clothing, impetuous young Emily Davidson stows away, chasing after one of the trappers, Courtney McCannon's grandfather, Corrin. She hopes to drag him back to St. Louis, but instead they make a home in wild Colorado.

MORRIS, GILBERT

◆✕ *JIM RENO*

Drifter Jim Reno fights corrupt cattle barons, cleans up mining camps, rescues white boys raised as Indians, and generally befriends the friendless in this sturdy series first published in the 1980s, reprinted and added to in the 1990s.

> *Reno.* 1992. Tyndale, paper. 258 pp. ISBN 0-8423-1058-4.

> *Rimrock.* 1992. Tyndale, paper. 257 pp. ISBN 0-8423-1059-2.

> *Ride the Wild River.* 1992. (Originally published in 1987 as *The Runaway.*) Tyndale, paper. 339 pp. ISBN 0-8423-5795-5.

> *Boomtown.* 1992. Tyndale, paper. 261 pp. ISBN 0-8423-7789-1.

> *Valley Justice.* 1995. Tyndale, paper. 258 pp. ISBN 0-8423-7756-5.

> *Lone Wolf.* 1995. Tyndale, paper. 226 pp. ISBN 0-8423-1997-2.

PELLA, JUDITH

◆✕★ *LONE STAR LEGACY*

Pella's Texas tales dust off the time-honored western themes of the cattle baroness and the Indian caught between two cultures.

> *Frontier Lady.* 1993. Bethany, paper. 398 pp. ISBN 1-55661-293-1.

Deborah Graham comes to Texas as the Civil War rages, where she marries into the Stoner clan, a fearsome lot of ranchers; soon enough, she's accused of killing her cruel husband. Deborah Stoner is rescued from the gallows by an outlaw who has a grudge against the Stoners, and in the outlaw camp, ironically more humane than the Stoner household, she meets another captive: the ex-ranger and preacher, Sam Killion. But in an involved plot indeed, Deborah and Sam don't get together until Deborah, free also of the outlaws, is again rescued, this time by Broken Wing's band of Cheyennes. Deborah marries the noble Broken Wing and thinks of herself as Cheyenne. But Broken Wing is killed in the raging Indian wars and Deborah is once more without a husband. Sam marries Deborah, and along with her two children, Carolyn and Blue Sky, they take up ranching.

Stoner's Crossing. 1994. Bethany, paper. 383 pp. ISBN 1-55661-294-X.
The sequel to *Frontier Lady* tells the story of Deborah Killion's son, Blue Sky, who is caught between the white and the Cheyenne cultures as was his own father, Broken Wing.

Warrior's Song. 1996. Bethany, paper. 400 pp, ISBN 1-55661-655-4.
Carolyn, Deborah Killion's daughter from her first marriage, pursues her troubled heritage in the conclusion to Lone Star Legacy.

◖🅔✕★ *UNTITLED SERIES*

Texas Angel. 1999. Bethany. 320 pp. ISBN 0-7642-2278-3.
Texas Angel is a lively tale set in 1836 Texas. Elise Hearne, who has married into a fine family and borne a child, is revealed to be an octaroon, daughter of a "stolen" New Orleans prostitute. She, too, is doomed for prostitution, first in New Orleans and then on the woebegone Texas coast. Meanwhile, the sanctimonious Methodist preacher, Bostonian Benjamin Sinclair, drags his delicate wife, Rebekah, and family west to save Mexican-owned Texas from savages and Catholics. At last Rebekah can bear no more and prevails upon Benjamin's brother, Haden, to return her to Boston, but she dies on the trail. As heartbroken Benjamin attempts to struggle on as head of a family that hates him, Elise escapes her own captor in search of Rebekah, who once did her a kindness. In sorrow and humility, both Elise and Benjamin welcome a second chance at life.

Heaven's Road. 2000. Bethnay, paper. 331 pp. ISBN 0-7642-2279-1.
In the sequel to *Texas Angel,* Benjamin's son, Micah, leads a drifter's life down Mexico way, first as a soldier fighting for Texan independence, then as an outlaw. He despises his father and refuses any overtures of reconciliation. He has no use for religion but, while rustling cattle, saves the life of young Lucie Maccallum. He's lovestruck, but her religion scares him off. Even so, he goes straight, taking up the company of his Uncle Haden and joining the Texas Rangers. And he can't stay away from Lucie.

RICHARDSON, H. L.

◖🅔✕★ *SAM DODD*
Somewhat like Stephen Bly in his Code of the West series but with a tougher tone, Richardson stakes out a Colorado and Montana territory that is all his own in these tales of gun-savvy Marshall Sam Dodd.

The Devil's Eye. 1995. Word, paper. 299 pp. ISBN 0-8499-3855-4.
In the old days, Civil War veteran Sam Dodd practiced eye-for-an-eye, Old Testament Christianity in his battles with violent hombres. Now he just wants to run his ranch and raise his family, but a killing on the range makes him strap on his gun again.

The Shadows of Crazy Mountain. 1996. Word, paper. 307 pp. ISBN 0-8499-3856-2.
Once again with reluctance, Sam Dodd straps on his gun in this sequel to *The Devil's Eye.* In part because of his own foolishness, Sam's son, David, is in bad trouble up in Montana.

THOENE, BODIE, AND BROCK THOENE

◀▣✕★ *SAGA OF THE SIERRAS*

The Thoenes' fine series chronicling the early days of Americans in California was written in the spirit of Louis L'Amour, with his lone gunmen righting wrongs and settling down after much travail.

The Man from Shadow Ridge. 1990. Bethany, paper. 239 pp. ISBN 1-55661-098-X.
Tom Dawson, who left Missouri because of his Union sympathies, is waiting out the Civil War in a valley of the Sierras when word comes of a murder undertaken by Southern sympathizers. Reluctantly, he takes up his gun and the Union cause.

Riders of the Silver Rim. 1990. Bethany, paper. 204 pp. ISBN 1-55661-0-998.
Like Tom Dawson of *The Man from Shadow Ridge,* Joshua Roberts, a blacksmith by trade, is running from his past. After almost perishing in the desert, he takes up blacksmithing in the town of Garson, working for the Silver Rim Mine. But things aren't as they should be at the mine, and Tom must stand up for what's right, or run again.

Gold Rush Prodigal. 1990. Bethany, paper. 224 pp. ISBN 1-55661-162-5.
In the third entry of the Saga of the Sierras series, David Bollin rejects the life of his missionary parents to seek fame and fortune in Boston and then on the high seas. Misadventures land him in the California gold fields, where the faith he rejected may be the only answer to the troubles he soon finds himself in.

Sequoia Scout. 1990. Bethany, paper. 239 pp. ISBN 1-55661-165-X.
Seeking to improve his fortunes, Will Reed, a mountain man, heads through the remotest corners of the Sierras and into Spanish California in the fourth entry of the Saga of the Sierras.

Cannons of the Comstock. 1992. Bethany, paper. 203 pp. ISBN 1-55661-166-8.
Though fifth in the series, *Cannons of the Comstock* is the direct sequel to *The Man from Shadow Ridge,* and again features Tom Dawson thrust against his will into the Civil War, as he protects his brother's ranch and family after his brother is killed.

Year of the Grizzly. 1992. Bethany, paper. 192 pp. ISBN 1-55661-1-676.
Though sixth in the series, *Year of the Grizzly* is the sequel to Will Reed's wandering adventures in *Sequoia Scout.* Will has found happiness on a big ranch near Santa Barbara, but his life is threatened by the impending squabble over California between Mexico and the Americans now occupying California.

Shooting Star. 1993. Bethany, paper. 206 pp. ISBN 1-55661-320-2.
The final entry in the Saga of the Sierras features old-timer Andrew Jackson Sinnickson, who recollects the story of legendary outlaw Jake Slade during the reckless, gold-mad days of the Bear Flag Republic.

★ **THOENE, BROCK.** *The Hope Valley War.* **1997. Nelson, paper. 228 pp. ISBN 0-7852-8071-5.**

News of his brother's lynching brings drifter John Thornton back to Hope Valley, Utah, in 1858 in this tough tale of a range war, reminiscent of Walter Van Tilburg Clark's classic *The Ox-Bow Incident.*

Chapter 8

Romance

Christian romances are much like mainstream romances, and many of the field's leading names, such as Terri Blackstock, Francine Rivers, and Catherine Palmer, are crossovers.

It is not putting things too strongly to say that, in Christian romances, Christ is the love interest. Still, one encounters the tried-and-true formula of a woman being duped or exploited by Mr. Wrong, while Mr. Right, when the heroine first meets him, doesn't *seem* to be right. As in a mainstream romance, Mr. Wrong is revealed as less than sensitive, and Mr. Right's true, princely character establishes itself. Mr. Right, however, must be a Christian, and often the blindness of the heroine to true love is the same as her blindness to the will of God.

Featured here are romances other than romantic westerns and historical romances, treated in previous chapters. For humorous romances, see chapter 11, "The Christian Life." For a discussion of Grace Livingston Hill, see chapter 3, "Christian Classics," p. 19.

CONTEMPORARY ROMANCE

AUSTIN, LYNN. *Fly Away*. 1996. Beacon Hill of Kansas City, paper. 206 pp. ISBN 0-8341-1595-6.
When his cancer diagnosis becomes terminal, retired Air Force pilot Mike Dolan seeks solace in the company of Wilhemina Brewster, a retired, embittered professor of music.

BAER, JUDY

TRILOGY

Jenny's Story. 2000. Tyndale, paper. 260 pp. ISBN 0-8423-1922-0.
The first installment of this trilogy about three women who were childhood friends features Jenny Owens, an almost statistically average, even boring middle-class wife. Jenny's comfortable world is shattered when her husband of 12 years is accidentally killed. Tia Warden and Libby Morrison, Jenny's childhood friends, provide support, but then the other shoe drops: In the most interesting scenes of the novel, readers learn that Jenny's husband was a secret sinner, addicted to fast women and gambling.

Libby's Story. 2001. Tyndale, paper. 250 pp. ISBN 0-8423-1923-9.

In the second installment of Baer's trilogy, Tia and Jenny take a backseat as Libby Morrison courses through her romantic problems. A quiet woman and single, she gives all her time to her aging parents. The other character is self-pitying Reese Reynolds, whom a gunshot has paralyzed.

Tia's Story. 2001. Tyndale, paper. 275 pp. ISBN 0-8423-1924-7.

Baer concludes her trilogy with the story of a businesswoman, Tia Warden. Tia is doing well in her gift business and at last has a romantic prospect: her handsome partner, Brandon Ainsley. Jenny and Libby cheer her on. But not all is as it seems, and even before her business prospects crash, Tia is wondering if there isn't something more meaningful to do in life. She volunteers for work with abused women.

BERGREN, LISA TAWN. *The Bridge.* 2000. WaterBrook, paper. 240 pp. ISBN 1-57856-272-4.

Jared Conway, a commodities broker, comes home to find his ex-wife—with whom he had been trying to reconcile—in bed with another man in this emotional tale. Deeply disillusioned, and feeling guilty toward his son, Nick, Jared heads west with the boy to Montana, where he has inherited a cabin high in the mountains. Jared wants to fix up the place and sell it for a handsome profit, but then he meets Eden Powell, a Christian potter who was left at the altar not long before. Still, love isn't all of it. Jared is almost mystically drawn to a bridge over the wild trout stream near his cabin, where his mother drowned long ago, saving her son in her last conscious effort. Placed in a contemplative mood, Jared, the materialist, stumbles toward spiritual renewal.

⬛◣ BLACKSTOCK, TERRI. *Emerald Windows.* 2001. Zondervan, paper. 256 pp. ISBN 0-310-22807-7.

Brooke Martin, a stained-glass artist, returns to her hometown when her former high school art teacher, Nick Marcello, offers her a job remodeling an old church. Brooke fled the town at her high school graduation because of accusations that she was having an affair with Nick. Nick lost his job, but refused to leave. The two were innocent but attracted to each other; their current romance is threatened by the machinations of a prudish local matron. Small towns can be completely irrational, sometimes, but not without *some* justification. It's hard to believe Blackstock's premise, that Brooke and Nick were completely innocent—or if they were, that they could not have found a way to prove it.

BLACKSTOCK, TERRI

⬛◣ SECOND CHANCES

Crossover talent Blackstock reworked for the Christian market some of her mainstream romances in this series, each entry of which features disappointed men and women who give love another try. It's a second chance for the novels as well, but this has been an exceptionally popular series.

Blind Trust. 1997. Zondervan, paper. 208 pp. ISBN 0-310-20710-X.

In *Blind Trust,* Sherry Cranston's old boyfriend appears after a long absence, the explanation for which is slow in coming. The old boyfriend declares his undying love, but Sherry doesn't know whether to believe him.

Broken Wings. 1998. Zondervan, paper. 224 pp. ISBN 0-310-20708-8.

Pilot Erin Russell is shaken when a colleague goes down in an airline crash that kills all on board. Erin's friend is blamed, but she doesn't buy it, and teams with an investigator to prove his innocence, in the process falling in love and renewing her faith in God.

Never Again Good-bye. 1996. Zondervan, paper. 336 pp. ISBN 0-310-20707-X. Beset with guilt and impelled by her revitalized faith, Laney Fields tracks down the daughter she gave up for adoption and finds her being raised by a lonely widower.

When Dreams Cross. 1997. Zondervan, paper. 208 pp. ISBN 0-310-20709-6. Young Andi Sherman's father dies and bequests to her a half-completed amusement park. Reluctantly, she enlists the aid of a Christian animator who was once her boyfriend.

BUNN, T. DAVIS. *The Book of Hours.* 2000. Nelson, paper. 318 pp.

The wide-ranging Bunn tries his hand with a romance. Brian Blackstone, still grieving for his dead wife, retreats to an inherited castle near a small English village. There a local woman doctor helps to repair his spirits as he explores the past of the castle, in the process growing passionate about its preservation.

CARLSON, MELODY. *Homeward.* 1997. Multnomah, paper. 450 pp. ISBN 1-57673-029-8.

 Coming home is a spiritual journey for Meg Lancaster, weary down to the soul with San Francisco. But her assumptions about her halcyon small town in Oregon, which she hasn't seen in 20 years, will have to be adjusted to accommodate some family secrets. She can't go home again, except with God's help.

★ FELL, DORIS ELAINE

SAGAS OF A KINDRED HEART

Blue Mist on the Danube. 1999. Revell, paper. 432 pp. ISBN 0-8007-5677-0. Fell tells the thoughtful story of an accomplished violinist, Kerina Rudzinski, who, near the end of her career and perhaps her life, sifts through her haunting memories and comes to a deeper understanding of God. Part of what she must reconcile is the loss of her son, also claimed as a son by another woman, the wife of an American pastor.

Willows on the Windrush. 2000. Revell, paper. 348 pp. ISBN 0-8007-5732-7. The second tale in Fell's Sagas of a Kindred Heart series features Sydney Barrington, a rather unpleasant executive whose love life isn't going well. When the news arrives that she's inherited an old estate in the English Cotswolds, she's eager to take some time off. The Cotswolds, she soon discovers, don't conform to her hard-charging lifestyle: The locals seem standoffish and even somewhat secretive. A local attorney offers still more challenges.

HATCHER, ROBIN LEE. *Whispers from Yesterday*. 1999. WaterBrook, paper. 416 pp. ISBN 1-57856-151-5.

Socialite Karen Butler takes a fall when her father kills himself rather than face financial ruin. Without friends or money—much less a faith to lean on—Karen goes to live with her grandmother, Sophia, hoping to inherit her ranch. But the dilapidated ranch is not what Karen expects, and her uncanny resemblance to Sophia's dead sister, Esther, forces Sophia to confront the tragic mistakes of her own past by giving Esther's diaries to Karen. As Karen grows to love the ranch and the ranch manager, Dusty Stoddard, she also has to confront family secrets.

HICKS, BARBARA JEAN

◀🖪✕ *Coming Home.* 1996. Multnomah, paper. 280 pp. ISBN 0-88070-945-6.
Coming Home, Hicks's first novel, is the bittersweet love story of childhood friends Keith Castle and Katie Brannigan, who take far different paths as adults but find each other at last.

◀🖪✕ *Snow Swan.* 1997. Multnomah. 286 pp. ISBN 1-57673-107-3.
The sequel to *Coming Home* follows the trail of a minor character in the first novel, Toni Ferrier, who has fallen on hard times after a glamorous youth. A recovering addict with a son to raise, she doesn't know if she'll ever find love again.

◀🖪✕ **HIGGS, LIZ CURTIS.** *Mixed Signals.* **1999. Multnomah, paper. 450 pp. ISBN 1-57673-401-3.**
Belle O'Brien, a 32-year-old disc jockey, is lured from a big station in Chicago to a small Virginia station by an old friend whom she hopes will become her one-and-only. But the old spark isn't there anymore, and Belle turns to David Cahill, her engineer. Unfortunately, David carries some baggage from his teenage affair with the local banker's daughter. Because David hails from the wrong side of the tracks with a locally famous reprobate for a father, the woman moved away rather than marry David. David, however, is noble to the point of self-parody, never missing a month of child support in the nine years his ex-lover has been gone. If that isn't enough, Higgs makes him perform mighty feats of heroism to win Belle's heart. Belle, in fact, isn't worthy of him.

◀🖪✕ **JONES, ANNIE.** *Deep Dixie.* **1999. Multnomah, paper. 343 pp. ISBN 1-57673-411-0.**
Eager beaver Jake Walker and cheeky Dixie Fulton-Leigh lock horns over a family business that holds the key to the future for Fulton's Dominion, Mississippi. Opposites attract, but then Dixie discovers a branch in the family tree that complicates matters even further in this smooth, flippant romance.

◀🖪✕ **JONES, ANNIE.** *The Prayer Tree.* **1998. Multnomah, paper. 374 pp. ISBN 1-57673-239-8.**
Naomi Beauchamp returns home to New Bethany, Tennessee, from her unhappy life in Maine to care for her aged mother. In part because of her mother, she joins the town's tradition of a prayer tree. The tradition began in World War II, when women gathered in a grove to plant trees and pledged to pray for each other, and for New Bethany, through the coming year. But the tradition has fallen on hard times, and now only three women, each troubled in her own way, join Naomi. They form powerful friendships and look for love in a Christian version of the film *Steel Magnolias* (1989).

◀🖪✕ **JONES, ANNIE.** *Saving Grace.* **1998. Multnomah, paper. 364 pp. ISBN 1-57673-330-0.**
In the sequel to *The Prayer Tree,* Naomi Beauchamp, now happily married, gathers her women friends to pray for Grace Grayson-Wiley, an old woman in a rest home whom many in the town think is crazy.

JONES, ANNIE. *The Snowbirds*. 2001. Multnomah, paper. 336 pp. ISBN 1-57673-623-7.

Along with her sisters, single mom Nicolette ("Nic") Dorsey is a "snowbird," every December returning to the home place down in Persuasion, Alabama. This year Nic has a mission: She wants to sell her interest in the house to finance schooling for her daughter, Willa, a special-needs child. But Nic hadn't counted on the simultaneous return of bad boy Sam Moss, her childhood sweetheart and just maybe Willa's father.

PALMER, CATHERINE. *Finders Keepers*. 1999. Tyndale, paper. 252 pp. ISBN 0-8423-1164-5.

Antiques dealer Elizabeth Hayes hopes to expand her shop by purchasing and refurbishing an historic house. Zachary Chalmers, an architect who recently inherited the house, wants to tear it down and build an office. The resulting feud drags the town into a battle of progress versus history, but love and the innocence of Nikolai, the Romanian adopted son of Elizabeth, eventually softens the battle.

ROPER, GAYLE

SEASIDE SEASONS

Spring Rain. 2001. Multnomah, paper. 350 pp. ISBN 1-57673-638-5.

Set on the New Jersey shore, the first entry in Roper's series brings Leigh Spenser, a teacher and single mother, in unwilling contact with her son's father, Clay Wharton. Clay got Leigh pregnant one wild night but somehow has blocked out that he's actually the father of their son, Billy. Clay, a career naval officer, had retired from active service and is coming home to tend to his mother and his twin brother, Ted, who is dying of AIDS. Roper goes light on the sin, heavy on the compassion, for Ted, a genuinely likable character and a remarkable personage for evangelical fiction, which seldom portrays homosexuals and even less seldom portrays them favorably.

SMITH, DEBRA WHITE. *Best Friends*. 1999. Chariot Victor, paper. 347 pp. ISBN 1-56476-721-3.

Beth Alexander, owner of a bed-and-breakfast, has been waiting for Mr. Right. A mysterious stranger arrives, and she thinks he may be the one. Old friend Scott Caldwell, who would like to be Mr. Right if only Beth would let him, knows better.

SMITH, DEBRA WHITE

SEVEN SISTERS

Smith's series follows the lives of seven friends from college.

Second Chances. 2000. Harvest House, paper. 334 pp. ISBN 0-7369-0276-7.

Marilyn Thatcher and her four-year-old daughter, Brooke, retreat to Marilyn's hometown when her husband, Gregory, finds another woman. Marilyn has no use for men for a time, until she meets Josh Langham, a local evangelical minister. Slowly, she begins to trust Josh—and God. Then she learns that Josh has a checkered past.

The Awakening. 2000. Harvest House, paper. 332 pp. ISBN 0-7369-0277-5.
The second in the Seven Sisters series features Kim Lowery, a supermodel whose celebrity makes finding true love difficult. To escape an unwanted suitor, she signs up for a trip to Vietnam, but the tour guide, handsome Mick O'Donnel, doesn't want her along because of the trail of glamour she leaves behind.

A Shelter in the Storm. 2001. Harvest House, paper. 314 pp. ISBN 0-7369-0278-3.
Sonsee LeBlanc's father is killed and an old beau is the prime suspect in the third entry of Smith's Seven Sisters series.

◖E◗ THRASHER, TRAVIS. *The Watermark.* 2001. Tyndale, paper. 237 pp. ISBN 0-8423-5445-X.
Thrasher tells the simple love story of a college student, Sheridan Blake, who meets a nice girl, Genevie Liu. Well, it's almost simple. Long ago, Sheridan did something awful, and was gone from college for a long time. He's reformed, but can't bear to tell Genevie what he did for fear that she'll reject him. Thrasher teases out this slight plot almost unbearably, but love stories from men are rare, and because of that this one may have some appeal.

◖E◗ WICK, LORI. *Pretense.* 1998. Harvest House, paper. 702 pp. ISBN 1-56507-945-0.
Though packaged like a fat romance from Nora Roberts or Janet Dailey, Wick's contemporary story is really a fairy tale. It's about the two supremely talented and beautiful Bishop sisters, black-haired Mackenzie and blonde Delancey, whose childhoods are spent moving about a great deal because of their father's military career. After dabbling in tastefully rendered sin as young women, they meet with dazzling literary, marital, and spiritual success.

◖E◗ WICK, LORI. *Sophie's Heart.* 1995. Harvest House, paper. 425 pp. ISBN 1-56507-311-8.
Czechoslovakian Sophie Velikonja emigrates to America, where the best job she can find is as a housekeeper, even though she is well educated and her English is good. Her employer is a lonely widower, however, and soon Sophie's tenderhearted ways win his love.

◖E◗ WINTERBOURN, SALLY BRICE. *Autumn Return.* 2001. Bethany, paper. 288 pp. ISBN 0-7642-2394-1.
Against the wishes of her sons and their wives, widow Lucy Summers moves to a house on the coast of Cornwall. Lucy and her husband were missionaries, but her husband was the outgoing one, and now all Lucy wants is a quiet, solitary life free of church concerns. Unfortunately, the local villagers overwhelm her with kindness, and a lonely vicar comes calling.

HISTORICAL ROMANCE

(See chapter 5, "Historical Christian Fiction.")

LIGHT CONTEMPORARY ROMANCE

Readers can count on things working out in the highly formulaic genre of light romances. There is often an element of the fairy tale, with faith in God standing in for magic; humor, too, born of a heroine thrust into absurd situations reminiscent of Doris Day's bedroom farces, can play a role, though of course explicit sex is absent. The heroine's faith sees her through, or we learn the reason she has lost her way is that she has lost her faith. The reader's own faith, that "God's in His Heaven, and all's right with the world," is reinforced.

AIKEN, GINNY

◀ЕХ *BELLAMY'S BLOSSOMS*
The parents of the three Bellamy sisters, modern Southern belles, thought their daughters' names were cute. The daughters all think the names undermine their seriousness as modern women in this treacly trilogy featuring each of the sisters in turn, each a sleuth in a gentle mystery.

> *Magnolia.* 2000. Tyndale, paper. 280 pp. ISBN 0-8423-3559-5.

> *Lark.* 2000. Tyndale, paper. 304 pp. ISBN 0-8423-3560-9.

> *Camellia.* 2001. Tyndale, paper. 300 pp. ISBN 0-8423-3561-7.

◀ЕХ ALEXANDER, KATHRYN. *The Forever Husband.* **Harlequin (Love Inspired), paper. 254 pp. ISBN 0-373-87083-3.**
Hope Granston has loved her husband, Eric, since childhood, but now they are separated and moving toward divorce. Setbacks and tragedies have caused Eric to lose his faith. Hope's faith also wavers. Circumstances throw them together in a setting where they are forced to get along, and Hope wonders, is their marriage still possible?

◀ЕХ ALEXANDER, KATHRYN. *Twin Wishes.* **2000. Harlequin (Love Inspired), paper. 252 pp. ISBN 0-373-87102-3.**
Julianne Quinn can't have children. Widower Luke O'Hara is father to two of them, perhaps a bit more than Julianne wants to take on.

◀ЕХ BALL, KAREN. *Wilderness.* **1999. Multnomah, paper. 384 pp. ISBN 1-57673-552-4.**
Mady Donovan, whom everyone describes as "cute," and Jason Tiber, who has little tolerance for cuteness, have signed up for a supervised wilderness trek in the Cascades. An accident separates them from their group, and they are thrown upon their own resources. Lost, forced to rely on each other, they search for the way home, making a spiritual journey as well.

◀ЕХ BRAND, IRENE. *Tender Love.* **2000. Harlequin (Love Inspired), paper. 253 pp. ISBN 0-373-87101-5.**
Widow Alice Larkin comes to the aid of Mark Tanner, a grieving former minister, and his two children.

◄∈✕ **BULOCK, LYNN.** *Looking for Miracles.* **Harlequin (Love Inspired), paper. 254 pp. ISBN 0-373-87103-1.**
Lori Harper is a recent widow with a young son to care for and another baby on the way. A fireman comes to her rescue.

◄∈✕ **CARLSON, MELODY.** *Heartland Skies.* **1998. Multnomah, paper. 241 pp. ISBN 1-57673-264-9.**
Jayne Morgan's boyfriend jilts her for an old love after Jayne has moved to his hometown of Paradise, Texas. So, Paradise it isn't, but maybe it's horse heaven. Jayne loves horses, and, lucky her, she wins one. But Bailey's an Arabian, and the local cowpokes think only quarter horses matter. Will Jayne ever find happiness, either with horses or men?

CARLSON, MELODY

◄∈✕ *WHISPERING PINES*

A Place to Come Home To. 1999. Harvest House, paper. 300 pp. ISBN 0-7369-0053-5.
Burned-out Maggie Carpenter, a single mother embittered by her failed marriage, takes a job as newspaper editor in a small Oregon town. Soon she discovers that the town may be doomed because of a rerouted highway.

Everything I Long For. 2000. Harvest House, paper. 268 pp. ISBN 0-7369-0062-4.
In the sequel to *A Place to Come Home To,* Maggie and her son, Spencer, have found a measure of peace in their lives when suddenly a young runaway, Leah, appears. She's looking for her biological father and her own shot at happiness.

Looking for You all My Life. 2000. Harvest House, paper. 304 pp. ISBN 0-7369-0063-2.
The third entry of the Whispering Pines series chronicles the continuing adventures of Leah, and Maggie has a new chance at love.

◄∈✕ **DAVIS, MARY.** *Newlywed Games.* **2000. Multnomah, paper. 367 pp. ISBN 1-57673-268-1.**
To satisfy her mother that she's making progress on the courtship-and-marriage front, Meghann Livingston pretends that her boss is her boyfriend. Then her little white lie escalates, and she's forced to pretend—with his bemused cooperation—that he's her husband.

GUNN, ROBIN JONES

◄∈✕ *GLENBROOKE*
Young women seek love in Glenbrooke, Oregon, often overcoming obstacles they themselves have erected, in this nonsequential series drawing together earlier Gunn efforts.

Secrets. 1999. Multnomah, paper. 287 pp. ISBN 1-57673-420-X.

Whispers. 1999. Multnomah, paper. 288 pp. ISBN 1-57673-327-0.

Echoes. 1999. Multnomah, paper. 270 pp. ISBN 1-57673-648-2.

Sunsets. 2000. Multnomah, paper. 242 pp. ISBN 1-57673-103-0.

Clouds. 2000. Multnomah, paper. 268 pp. ISBN 1-57673-113-8.

Waterfalls. 1999. Multnomah, paper. 267 pp. ISBN 1-57673-221-5.

Woodlands. 2000. Multnomah, paper. 326 pp. ISBN 1-57673-503-6.

HICKS, BARBARA JEAN. *An Unlikely Prince.* **1998. WaterBrook, paper. 256 pp. ISBN 1-57856-122-1.**
Suzie Wyatt starts a day-care facility in her parents' house as they embark on a missionary assignment. Suzie longs for life to be like a fairy tale, and, sure enough, a prince arrives in the person of a shy history professor, Harrison Hunt. Harrison has rented the house next door in hopes of a quiet summer in which to write his book, but, of course, the kids are noisy, and Suzie and he are thrown together in mild conflict.

HIGGS, LIZ CURTIS. *Bookends.* **2000. Multnomah, paper. 400 pp. ISBN 1-57673-611-3.**
Emilie Getz, at 36, is neat, compulsive, and much taken with herself, though she's worried that she has become an old maid. A history professor, she's come to Lititz, Pennsylvania, to pursue a minor historical discrepancy regarding the Moravian Church. She runs afoul of Jonas Fielding, a developer whose scheme for a golf course at first seems to threaten Emilie's historical shrines, but the two are attracted even so. Shallow characterizations and an anemic story are offset with the banter between Emilie and Jonas and a winning subplot featuring Jonas's attempts to care for his kid brother, Nate, a golf pro who has a problem with alcohol.

KASTNER, DEBRA. *Beloved.* **1998. Multnomah, paper. 236 pp. ISBN 1-57673-331-9.**
Kate Logan runs a wedding chapel east of Denver. She interviews a number of candidates for her part-time pastor's position, but can't resist young Father Todd Jensen, who falls for her immediately as well.

KASTNER, DEBRA. *Daddy's Home.* **1999. Harlequin (Love Inspired), paper. 254 pp. ISBN 0-373-87055-8.**
Soap opera about Chris Jordan's betrayal of the long-suffering Jasmine Enderlin: He married her sister, then abandoned her during her first pregnancy. However reluctantly, Jasmine is still linked to Chris because her sister dies and Jasmine becomes guardian of her nephew. Enter the penitent Chris with lots of stories to explain his absence, and despite herself, Jasmine finds she still loves him.

MACDONALD, SHARI

Diamonds. 1996. Multnomah, paper. 235 pp. ISBN 0-88070-982-0.
An aging minor league pitcher, Tucker Boyd, gets what is probably be his last shot at the majors, but he may turn it down for love of Casey Foster, the new team owner.

Stardust. 1997. Multnomah, paper. 286 pp. ISBN 1-57673-109-X.
When she was a girl, starry-eyed Gillian Spencer fell in love with Max Bishop. Max was a student of Gillian's astronomer father, and too old for her. Circumstances change once Gillian finishes school and becomes an astronomer, too.

⬛✕ MARR, PATT. *Angel in Disguise*. 2000. Harlequin (Love Inspired), paper. 254 pp. ISBN 0-373-87104-X.

Basketball coach Sunny Keegan is left at the altar. Through the scheming of friends, she shortly finds herself on a TV show called *Dream Date,* where she meets her angel, a carpenter who wants to build her a house.

⬛✕ MCCOURTNEY, LORENA. *Dear Silver*. 1987. Multnomah, paper. 286 pp. ISBN 1-57673-110-3.

McCourtney turns in a comedy of errors starting with an identity mix-up: Her heroine, Silver Sinclair, receives a Dear John letter from a developer in Seattle whom she's never met. The "right" Silver Sinclair lives in Portland, but the Seattle Silver, indignant at the man's effrontery with the other woman, decides to answer.

⬛✕ ★ MITCHELL, SARA. *Montclair*. 1997. Bethany, paper. 252 pp. ISBN 1-55661-963-4.

Sabrina Mayhew is an accomplished young equestrienne who takes a bad fall in a show and then fears to mount a horse again. After several years in the doldrums, she consents to help from Hunter Buchanan, a Colorado trainer who happens also to be a Christian. A sense of humor, a graceful style, and a gruff minor character, a desert recluse named Gabe Wisniewski, combine to lift this pleasant but otherwise conventional romance above the ordinary.

⬛✕ MORRIS, LYNN. *The Balcony*. 1997. Bethany, paper. 244 pp. ISBN 1-55661-981-2.

Accountant Johnnie James loves the old castle in which Esteban Ventura, her rich new client, hosts her. She is particularly enamored of the high balcony of her room overlooking the sparkling Caribbean. Thus wooed, it's all her practical nature can manage to avoid being swept away by Latin lover Esteban, an alluring but infuriating man who seems to be involved in shady dealings and possibly even piracy.

⬛✕ MURRAY, VICTORIA CHRISTOPHER. *Temptation*. 2000. Warner Books (Walk Worthy), paper. 353 pp. ISBN 0-446-52792-0.

Kyla Blake and her physician husband, Jefferson, have been together 16 years. They have a fine daughter and a shared faith. But the staunchest of Christians can be tempted, as Kyla learns when her old friend Jasmine, newly divorced, shows up with her sights on Jefferson.

⬛✕ PALMER, DIANA. *Blind Promises*. 1999. Harlequin (Love Inspired), paper. 252 pp. ISBN 0-373-87061-2.

A nurse romance about Dana Steele, caring for a depressed blind man, who is not only blind physically but also blind to the good life he still can lead.

⬛✕ RANEY, DEBORAH. *Kindred Bond*. 1998. Bethany, paper. 280 pp. ISBN 1-55661-999-5.

Claire Anderson, a teacher, comes to Hanover Falls hoping to put her difficult romantic past behind her. But as she cares for her failing grandmother, she crosses paths with Michael Meredith, the director of the local nursing home, who also has painful memories.

RICHER, LOIS

◆ *BRIDES OF THE SEASON*
Caitlin Andrews gets pregnant and has no one to marry her, but still she trusts in God. Eventually, she finds a husband and a father for her child.

> ***Baby on the Way.*** 1999. Harlequin (Love Inspired), paper. 253 pp. ISBN 0-373-87073-6.

> ***Daddy on the Way.*** 1999. Harlequin (Love Inspired), paper. 254 pp. ISBN 0-373-87079-5.

> ***Wedding on the Way.*** 2000. Harlequin (Love Inspired), paper. 254 pp. ISBN 0-373-87085-X.

◆ RUTLEDGE, CYNTHIA. *Unforgettable Faith.* 2000. Harlequin (Love Inspired), paper. 252 pp. ISBN 0-373-87108-2.
Fleeing from a crisis in faith in Kansas City, Faith Richards, a teacher, piles up her motorcycle in rural Nebraska and is rescued by a handsome preacher.

◆ SAMSON, LISA. *The Moment I Saw You.* 1998. Harvest, paper. 246 pp. ISBN 1-56507-759-8.
The owner of a bed-and-breakfast in the Blue Ridge Mountains, Natalie St. John, entertains a shy professor.

◆ SATTLER, GAIL. *On the Road Again.* 2000. Barbour, paper. 172 pp. ISBN 1-57748-964-0.
A schoolteacher, off for the summer, decides to help out her uncle in his trucking business and meets a Christian trucker.

◆ ★ SCHMIDT, ANNA. *Caroline and the Preacher.* 1999. Harlequin (Love Inspired), paper. 252 pp. ISBN 0-373-87082-8.
Caroline Carson is a sort of fancy secretary to her boss, a gruff Manhattan developer. When he runs aground trying to buy All Souls, a historic but rundown church, he sends Caroline to flirt with the handsome young pastor of All Souls, John Barrows, and to try to close the deal. He promises a vice presidency if she does. Over the years, as a single woman in a male-dominated field, Caroline has become a tough customer, but her resolve and managerial acumen dissolve when she witnesses the gallant work John is doing.

TURNBULL, AGNES SLIGH. *The Two Bishops.* 1980. Houghton Mifflin. (Out of print.)
The story is appealing enough: the attempt of an old, much beloved Episcopal bishop, Larry Ware, to bring along his overly formal young protege, Julian Armstrong. But Turnbull, who wrote several fine novels set earlier in the century, is hopelessly old-fashioned when she must deal with "contemporary" love. After shy Julian finally kisses his amazingly patient sweetheart, Cicely, Turnbull exclaims of their ecstatic talk: "O sweet vocables of love!"

◆✗ **WALSH, KATE.** *Never Lie to an Angel.* **1999. Harlequin (Love Inspired), paper. 255 pp. ISBN 0-373-87069-8.**
Detective Greg Peterson's angel is Angelica DeVoe, who has dedicated her life to a Christian mission in a tough part of town. Greg must lie to his angel because he suspects drug trafficking in the mission—even, at first, suspects Angelica. Her sweetness and sincerity gradually soften his battle-scarred soul.

◆✗ **WICK, LORI.** *The Princess.* **1999. Harvest, paper. 300 pp. ISBN 0-7369-0034-9.**
A contemporary woman, Shelby Parker, marries the prince of a small modern kingdom, not out of love but patriotism because the prince in question is required to marry by age 26. Though man and wife are strangers, Shelby's faith in God provides the basis for a solid marriage over time.

◆✗ ★ **WILLIAMS, SUSAN DEVORE.** *Sunset Coast.* **1995. Crossway, paper. 320 pp. ISBN 0-89107-854-1.**
A witty, subtle romance about Sally Alexander, who over the years has recovered from a messy divorce, raising her son by herself and becoming a writer. Along comes Mac McDonald, a friend from high school whom Sally always thought to be dull. Maybe not.

◆✗ **WINDSOR, LINDA**

Hi Honey, I'm Home. 1999. Multnomah, paper. 352 pp. ISBN 1-57673-556-7.
Kathryn Sinclair's husband, a journalist, comes home about five years after it was reported he'd died. In his mind and in the minds of their children, married life can pick up where it was interrupted, but Kathryn isn't so sure.

◆✗ *It Had to Be You.* 2001. Multnomah, paper. 300 pp. ISBN 1-57673-765-9.
Dan Jarrett is a busy rancher who reluctantly leaves his work to investigate his new stepfather, whom Dan is convinced is a con artist. On the airplane to Miami he meets accident-prone Sunny Elders, a cheery soul who has had to bear more than her share of sorrow. Both Dan and Sunny find themselves on a Caribbean cruise.

◆✗ **WORTH, LENORA.** *Ben's Bundle of Joy.* **2000. Harlequin (Love Inspired), paper. 251 pp. ISBN 0-373-87105-8.**
A baby is abandoned on the doorstep of Reverend Ben Hunter's church. He doesn't know what to do, but his day-care teacher, Sara Conroy, comes to his aid.

UNEQUALLY YOKED

This quaint subheading is drawn from 2 Corinthians 6: 14: "Be ye not unequally yoked together with unbelievers: for what fellowship hath righteousness with unrighteousness? and what communion hath light with darkness?" Many Christian romances portray love between a believer and an unbeliever; the unbeliever must be saved for the romance to succeed. Sometimes it doesn't happen, as in Janette Oke's *Beyond the Gathering Storm* (p. 122). Usually it does, but in either case the lesson of the verse in Corinthians is brought home.

See also chapter 11, the section, "Morality Tales."

BLAIR, ALMA. *Circle of Love.* 1995. Barbour, paper. 170 pp. ISBN 1-55748-607-7.

Ellen Scott, radio personality, finds herself drawn to the new manager of her station when the beloved old manager dies. That's Steven Markham, a bottom-line businessman and a ladies man, but Ellen is determined to reform him so they may join together in God's love.

DARTY, PEGGY. *Seascape.* 1996. Multnomah, paper. 286 pp. ISBN 0-88070-927-8.

Jessica Thorne slowly rebuilds her life after her husband's death by throwing herself into the establishment of a seaside bed-and-breakfast. A chance meeting with lawyer Mark Castleman finds her reconsidering romance, but he has a dark past that the two may not be able to overcome.

FROEMKE, MARCY. *A Family Man.* 1999. Harlequin (Love Inspired), paper. 255 pp. ISBN 0-373-87068-X.

Single mother Maggie Gould reluctantly comes home to care for her own mother and meets her sweetheart from long before, Adam Morgan. Adam is also a single parent, and feelings stir. But he's a devout Christian, and Maggie has rejected her childhood faith.

GILLENWATER, SHARON

Antiques. 1995. Multnomah, paper. 253 pp. ISBN 0-88070-801-8.

Widower Grant Adams, a cowboy of sorts, has sworn off women forever because of his late wife's infidelities. That may change with the arrival in West Texas of an antiques dealer, Dawn Carson. There are fireworks, but the cowboy isn't saved, Dawn is, and marriage is problematical.

Love Song. 1995. Multnomah, paper. 252 pp. ISBN 0-88070-747-X.

Country singer Andi Carson goes home to Texas to recuperate from persistent bouts with pneumonia, where old friend Wade Jamison, a Christian, awakens feelings of nostalgia, love, and faith. Trouble is, Andi wants to resume her career.

GUNN, ROBIN JONES. *Echoes.* 1996. Multnomah, paper. 280 pp. ISBN 0-88070-773-9.
Spiritual problems break up Lauren Phillips' longtime romance, but she begins a new one on a Christian chat club.

JOHN, SALLY D. *In the Shadow of Love.* 1998. Crossway, paper. 224 pp. ISBN 0-89107-983-1.
Reporter Tori Jeffers has had bad luck in love, but sparks fly when she meets a rich businessman named Erik Steed. As the two pursue a mutual interest, MIAs, their initial hostility for each other dissolves, but Erik isn't a Christian.

◄✗ **JOHN, SALLY.** *Surrender of the Heart.* 1999. Crossway, paper. 224 pp. ISBN 1-58134-047-8.

Kendall O'Reilly, who prides herself on being the consummate fifth-grade teacher, is perplexed that a new transfer student, Caitlin Zukowski, doesn't like her. She gets to know both the child and his father, a minister, and falls in love with them. But she is not a firm believer, a great obstacle for the father.

◄✗ **SCHULTE, ELAINE.** *Voyage.* 1996. Multnomah, paper. 245 pp. ISBN 1-57673-011-5.

Anne Marie takes a Christian Holy Land cruise ("Follow in the footsteps of the Apostle Paul") because of her aunt, who has recently died and had already paid for the trip. Her aunt always wanted for Anne Marie to connect with Jon Burnett, a Christian lawyer. She also wanted her to become a Christian. Jon's on the trip, so maybe she'll have her wish still, but Anne Marie is thinking of Alex, the Greek exchange student who stayed with her parents eight years ago. She had a crush on him and plans to look him up.

◄✗ **THRASHER, TRAVIS.** *The Promise Remains.* 2000. Tyndale, paper. 224 pp. ISBN 0-8423-3621-4.

Sara Anthony has turned 30, and her parents and friends pressure her to accept Bruce Erickson's proposal for marriage. Bruce is perfect, but Sara still pines for the chemistry she had with Ethan Ware nine years ago. Ethan wasn't a Christian, but he made a promise he'd try to find God, and Sara promised she'd wait.

PROBLEM ROMANCE

Problem romances tackle some tough issues, and love can have a hard time surviving. But any problem the world presents, no matter how enervating or physically difficult, is a problem of faith: One must be strong enough, through belief and prayer, either to overcome or accept. (See also chapter 11, the section "Morality Tales.")

◄✗ **COPELAND, LORI.** *Child of Grace.* 2001. Tyndale, paper. 230 pp. ISBN 0-8423-4260-5.

Eva Jean "E. J." Roberts, a successful businesswoman in Los Angeles, comes home to the little town of Cullen's Corner, North Carolina, to get an abortion after a date rape leaves her pregnant. Happy families, relatives, physicians, and new babies conspire to convince E. J. to have her baby, and in the bargain she finds romance, too.

COYLE, NEVA

◄✗ *SUMMERWIND*

🅈🄰 Graduates of Summerwind High School face life in the 1950s, often with great difficulty.

A Door of Hope. 1995. Bethany, paper. 288 pp. ISBN 1-55661-475-6.

Because their families disapprove, high school sweethearts Karissa and Michael Andrews marry secretly. Michael is a popular boy and Karissa feels blessed, but then Michael becomes abusive, and, exacerbating Karissa's dilemma, she's pregnant.

Inside the Privet Hedge. 1996. Bethany, paper. 249 pp. ISBN 1-55661-547-7.
Young Retta McCarron fights to save the family orange grove from developers.

Close to a Father's Heart. 1996. Bethany, paper. 256 pp. ISBN 1-55661-548-5.
When her mother dies, Amy Weaver confronts the sad mystery of her parents' past.

COYLE, NEVA. *Sharon's Hope.* 1996. Nelson, paper. 288 pp. ISBN 0-7852-7660-2.
Finally free of her abusive husband, Sharon Frances Mason Potter struggles to raise
her two children. She's not looking for love, but then finds herself attracted to a
Vietnam War veteran, Kenneth—a wounded soul as well. Can two hurt people heal
each other, with the help of God's love?

CROW, DONNA FLETCHER

◆✕ *VIRTUOUS HEART*

All Things New. 1997. Beacon Hill, paper. 210 pp. ISBN 0-8341-1674-X.
In the first entry of this thematic series, devout Debbie Jensen, a homebody, wants
nothing from life but to become a wife and mother. Then her father remarries,
and she has to look for a job for the first time in her life. Visiting her cousin,
she meets Gregory Masefield, a theologian, and finds herself both with Gregory
and his young daughter.

Roses in Autumn. 1998. Beacon Hill, paper. 208 pp. ISBN 0-8341-1713-4.
Frank discussions of sexual problems inside marriage follow when Laura James,
a romance writer who considers her marriage perfect except for the minor problem
of sex, discovers her husband with another woman. The counseling sessions
are somewhat facile, perhaps, but Crow tackles a tough subject courageously.

◆✕ **DUCKWORTH, MARION. *Remembering the Roses.* 1998. Multnomah, paper. 282 pp. ISBN 1-57673-236-3.**
When Sammie Sternberg's seemingly secure life falls apart, she opens an antiques
shop in a Washington small town. Sammie is a Jew who has become a Christian, and
many in the town discriminate against her, but she finds solace in the company of
her new Christian boyfriend, an artist named Brad MacKenzie. Brad, too, has been
hurt by life, and happiness for the two is not automatic. **❚Discussion❚**

◆✕ **EASTON, PATRICIA HARRISON. *A Bridge to Hope.* 1996. Servant, paper.
231 pp. ISBN 0-89283-950-3.**
Marty Harris, a middle-age widow with two children, is forced to return to her parents'
farm in Pennsylvania when her husband dies. Two men express interest in her, but
life isn't simpler on the farm, nor immediately more blissful, because Marty must
work through her grief, and her children have trouble adjusting.

◆✕ ★ **HATCHER, ROBIN LEE. *The Forgiving Hour.* 1999. WaterBrook, paper.
384 pp. ISBN 1-57856-150-7.**
Claire Conway's husband left her for another woman, and she has distrusted men
ever since. Get over it, friends say, but even the exemplary life her son, Dakota,
leads won't temporize her distrust. Meanwhile, the younger woman Claire's ex had

his affair with crosses paths with Dakota, and the two fall in love. Though such a coincidence seems far-fetched, it nicely illustrates Hatcher's theme. Claire must at last forgive—or lose her son.   ■ Discussion ■

★ **HICKS, BARBARA JEAN.** *China Doll.* **1998. Multnomah, paper. 256 pp. ISBN 1-57673-262-2.**
Georgine Nichols wants children but cannot conceive, and because of it her marriage breaks up. She hits upon the scheme of adopting, as a single woman, a Chinese girl, a complicated process that Hicks researched well, and more interesting than the sidebar of Georgine's new romance (with a man who doesn't want children, adopted or otherwise).   ■ Discussion ■

★ **HUNT, ANGELA ELWELL.** *Gentle Touch.* **1997. Bethany, paper. 244 pp. ISBN 1-55661-944-8.**
Jacquelyn Wilkes is a dedicated oncology nurse who is faced with breast cancer. She had always found Dr. Jonah Martin forbidding, but he is wonderful in her time of crisis, and as patient and doctor join in battle against the disease, the two fall in love. As the doctor cures the body, the patient cures the soul, because Jonah is not a Christian. The romance makes a depressing subject more palatable, no doubt, but the real story is one woman's battle against cancer, and it's admirably brought off.

KINGSBURY, KAREN

A Moment of Weakness. 2000. Multnomah, paper. 411 pp. ISBN 1-57673-616-4.
Kingsbury's melodramatic tale is as titillating as evangelical fiction gets, though in the service of a moral imperative: Don't have sex before you marry. Poor girl Jade Conner and rich kid Tanner Eastman seem star-crossed, in love even as children, but family scandal tears them apart. Chance reunites them. Their desire is so powerful that, even though Tanner is a zealous Christian and talks constantly of abstinence, the two make love. Jade is all but immediately pregnant, but because Tanner has gone overseas for two months of missionary work, Jade appeals to his evil mom for help. She ends up taking Dear Mother's hush money and marrying a man she hates. Will poor Jade and Tanner never get together?

A Time to Dance. 2001. Word, paper. 328 pp. ISBN 0-8499-4282-9.
Though Abby and John Reynolds seem like a model couple, they aren't. John is the high school football coach in a small Illinois town, and Abby is the quintessential soccer (football) mom, but John is obsessed with work, Abby feels neglected, and there are financial problems. Abby suspects John of having an affair and brings up the subject of divorce. But Kingsbury wants to show that these universal problems have solutions if taken to God, and thus Abby and John start talking things through in what is perhaps the most realistic of Kingsbury's morality tales.   ■ Discussion ■

When Joy Came to Stay. 2000. Multnomah, paper. 322 pp. ISBN 1-57673-746-2.
Maggie Stovall, a self-righteous columnist and foster mother to two boys, longs for her own baby, but otherwise seems to have an idyllic life married to Ben, an attorney. Then visions of an angelic blonde girl plague her, and she begins doing crazy and dangerous things. When she imperils her (foster) boys and the county takes them away, Maggie breaks down and turns herself in to a Christian psychiatric clinic, where she sinks into clinical depression. Turns out that before Ben and Maggie were married, she had a baby with a violent man who abandoned her.

E⟨ *Where Yesterday Lives.* 1998. Multnomah, paper. 401 pp. ISBN 1-57673-285-1.
Though her marriage seems to be on the rocks, *Miami Times* reporter Ellen Barrett feels she must go home to Michigan when her father dies. She sees an old beau and wonders if she should have married him. She visits with her sisters and discovers their problems are worse than her own. Somehow, her faith is renewed, and she heads back to Florida to do battle with her professional life and the vicissitudes of modern marriage.

E⟨ ★ MCCOURTNEY, LORENA. 1998. *Canyon.* **Multnomah, paper. 256 pp. ISBN 1-57673-287-8.**

YA As Kit Holloway and Tyler McCord are about to be married, Kit's father leaves her mother for Tyler's widowed stepmother. The four have worked together for years running tourist excursions down the Grand Canyon, and so Kit and Tyler's dilemma is whether to forgive their parents their sins or consign them to hellfire. Kit chooses hellfire, shrilly breaking her relationship with her father and hovering over her mother, who has been thrown into an almost catatonic state. Tyler cannot abandon his stepmother, however, and breaks up with Kit.   **[Discussion]**

E⟨ NORDBERG, BETTE. *Serenity Bay.* **2000. Bethany, paper. 319 pp. ISBN 0-7642-2396-8.**
Never having met the right man, Patricia Morrow lives a serene but lonely life on beautiful Puget Sound. She finally lands a doctor, Russell Koehler, and bears two children. But Russell, a decent enough fellow in some respects, is a perfectionist, and over time turns abusive. You don't have to take it, says Susan, Patricia's new friend in Christ. So Patricia leaves Russell, but he "abducts" their children and heads for parts unknown. Once again, seeking her lost children, Patricia is full of sorrow. Though clearly meant as a cry against spouse abuse, Nordberg does a good job portraying Russell, so much so that readers may have more sympathy for him than Patricia.

E⟨ ★ ORCUTT, JANE. *The Living Stone.* **2000. WaterBrook, paper. 352 pp. ISBN 1-57856-292-9.**
Leah Travers walls off emotions like a stone when her husband and two-year-old son are killed in a car crash. Things change, though slowly and with great pain, when Leah meets Jacobo Martinez, the brother-in-law of the drunken driver who ran her family down. Orcutt uses stock romance elements but has a superior sense of characterization and scene building. For instance, moments prior to the accident, Leah and her husband argue, making the accident itself the more affecting. And Orcutt develops the drunk driver's family with great care and compassion; they are as devastated as Leah.

E⟨ PETERSON, TRACIE. *The Long-Awaited Child.* **2001. Bethany, paper. 272 pp. ISBN 0-7642-2290-2.**
Tess Holbrook, in her 30s now, has tried for years to have a baby with her husband, Brad, but she seems to be infertile. She doesn't want to adopt because she was adopted herself, but then she crosses paths with Sherry Macomber, an unhappy, pregnant teenager.

◄▣✕ **RIVERS, FRANCINE.** *The Scarlet Thread.* **1996. Tyndale, paper. 352 pp. ISBN 0-8423-3568-4.**
Offered a new, high-paying job, dowdy housewife Sierra's husband moves his family to Los Angeles from their comfortable if modest life in a small, northern California town. He proceeds to go off the deep end, buying BMWs and having affairs with debutantes. Grief-stricken Sierra begins reading the journal of an ancestor, Mary, that was given to her by her dying mother. Sierra is symbolically linked to Mary by a scarlet thread—the faith of ages—in an old quilt. The two stories never satisfactorily merge, but Rivers's scenes are so passionate and authentic that, as always, she's worth reading.

◄▣✕ **RUSHFORD, PATRICIA H.** *Morningsong.* **1998. Bethany, paper. 256 pp. ISBN 1-55661-993-6.**
Patricia Rushford, best known for her young adult mysteries, tells of a country singer, Shanna O'Brian, who has painfully rebuilt her life after her husband walked out. In poverty and despair, she gave up her baby for adoption. Now her husband is back swearing eternal love, and she doesn't know what to do.

SCOTT, KATHLEEN. *A Test of Love.* **2002. Kregel, paper. 224 pp. ISBN 0-8254-3664-8.**
Scott introduces us to Juliet Nelson as an old married woman—that is, she's still young and stunningly beautiful, but her husband, Michael, is no longer interested in sex. What's wrong? Juliet prays about it, but her marriage seems about to break apart, even so. Then Michael kills the family dog, and although the death is accidental, Juliet can't forgive him. Michael needs to be more sensitive, she thinks, and he agrees, and seeks counseling. *A Test of Love* is a well-written, rather preachy story about an ordinary marriage with ordinary problems, and may appeal to some women for that very reason.

◄▣✕ **STEVENS, KELLY R.** *Ragdoll.* **1995. Barbour, paper. 170 pp. ISBN 1-55748-661-1.**
Rebecca Wesbrook's uncle rapes her on the night of her graduation. She flees, unable to tell her parents, and her life comes to a standstill until she meets Trevor Houston, whose steadiness and faith in God slowly returns Rebecca to normalcy. Now she has the courage to confront her uncle.

◄▣✕ **STOKES, PENELOPE J.** *The Amber Photograph.* **2001. Word, paper. ISBN 0-8499-3722-1.**
The truth about Cecilia's McAlister older sister, Amber, has always been a taboo subject. She left North Carolina long ago and is presumed dead. But when Cecilia discovers an old photograph of Amber that looks hauntingly like herself, she begins to press for information. On her deathbed, Cecilia's mother offers tantalizing clues that the man Cecilia has always called father is unrelated to her and that there is something odd about her sister as well. Seeking the truth, Cecilia heads for Seattle with a friend. Meanwhile, Amber struggles with her life on the opposite side of the continent, unaware of who's coming to see her.

◄▣✕ ★ **TATLOCK, ANN.** *A Place Called Morning.* **1998. Bethany, paper. 320 pp. ISBN 1-55661-922-7.**
Tatlock's offbeat love story features Mae Demaray, a widow nearing 70, whose fiction about herself is that she takes care of Roy Hanna, a retarded fellow who has been her lifelong companion. There's truth to Mae's fiction, but it's also true that Roy takes care of Mae, and only late in life

does she come to realize this. Roy fixes things around the house, but he is also Mae's great emotional solace, and through him she's at last able to forgive herself for that day many years ago when her negligence resulted in her grandson's death.   **Discussion**

ROMANTIC ADVENTURE

Romantic adventure may also be suspenseful (discussed later), but this grouping of novels offers pure escape, flinging heroines into exotic locations and putting them through the perils of Pauline.

BERGREN, LISA TAWN

❿ *FULL CIRCLE*
Some characters reappear in Bergren's loosely connected series.

> **Refuge.** 1994. Multnomah, paper. 336 pp. ISBN 0-88070-621-X.
> San Franciscan Beth Morgan answers a personal ad on a dare and ends up married to a Montana rancher. Her friend Rachel Johanssen comes to visit and ends up falling in love with yet another rancher. Then there's Jake Rierdon, who also likes Montana and a woman named Emily Walker. The first entry in this adventure series isn't terribly adventurous; it's a gathering of couples who put their pasts behind them for the refuge of Montana.

> **Torchlight.** 1994. Multnomah, paper. 249 pp. ISBN 0-88070-669-4.
> The sister of Jake Rierdon from *Refuge,* Julia Rierdon, heads to Maine to attend to her inheritance, a lighthouse and mansion. She intends to turn the place into a sort of bed-and-breakfast and enlists the aid of a mysterious, motorcycle-riding handyman, Trevor Kenbridge.

> **Pathways.** 2001. WaterBrook, paper. 288 pp. ISBN 1-57856-462-X.
> Bryn Bailey, cousin to Trevor Kenbridge of *Torchlight,* runs into an old flame, Eli Pierce, in Alaska. Ten years before, she rejected him because of his Christianity, but now coincidence makes her dependent on him as her pilot in the backcountry. She finds she still likes him and has, if she's candid with herself, also grown curious about his faith. The plane goes down in the wilderness, injuring Eli but leaving Bryn whole. Her search for pathways to safety turns out to be a spiritual search as well.

> **Treasure.** 1995. Multnomah, paper. 273 pp. ISBN 0-88070-725-9.
> The fourth entry in the Full Circle series features Dr. Christina Alvarez, who wants to solve an ancestral mystery lodged in a ship sunken off the coast of Maine. She enlists the aid of a salvage expert, Mitch Crawford. Mitch thinks Christina is gorgeous but also that she has no part in such dangerous work. Christina works fiercely and indignantly to gain his respect, and the two fall in love as they dodge various greedy miscreants who also covet Christina's treasure.

> ★ **Chosen.** 1996. Multnomah, paper. 292 pp. ISBN 0-88070-768-2.
> The fifth and most atypical entry in Bergren's Full Circle series features archeologist Aleksana Rourke. She has an old boyfriend who is Palestinian, Khalil al Aitam, and he's not just any Palestinian but a leader in Hamas. Aleksana is in Israel to pursue an excavation project, Solomon's Stables, and hopes for Khalil's protection. She's hindered, then helped, by glamour boy Ridge McIntyre of CNN.

Soon the threats begin from Hamas, putting Aleksana's longtime friendship with Khalil to the test and giving Ridge a chance to prove his mettle. Aleksana is an unpleasant character, and whether her pursuit is for her own or God's glory is an open question. But her edginess gives some unpredictability to Bergren's novel, as does the fair treatment of Palestinian issues—almost unheard of in an evangelical novel, and this one's chief virtue.

Firestorm. 1996. Multnomah, paper. 257 pp. ISBN 0-88070-953-7.
The Full Circle series comes full circle with this sequel to *Refuge*. Reyne Oldre, a friend of Rachel Tanner and Beth Morgan of that novel, used to be a fearless smoke jumper, but on her last mission some colleagues were killed, and she has retreated into a cautious life. Logan McCabe, a smoke jumper new on the scene, lights her inner fire, but she can't quite bring herself to jump. Then she's faced with a choice.

CHAIKIN, LINDA. *Endangered.* **1997. Bethany, paper. 255 pp. ISBN 1-55661-977-4.**
Sable Dunsmoor, who has returned to Kenya to help her widowed father protect endangered animals, endangers her heart every time she nears handsome Kash Hallet, once an ally in the cause and her suitor, but now turned into a poacher. Or so Sable thinks, doing her best to love Dr. Vince Adler instead. Lush descriptions of the Kenyan outback grace this otherwise routine adventure.

METZER, PATTY. *Lights of the Veil.* **2001. Multnomah, paper. 400 pp. ISBN 1-57673-627-X.**
Erica Tanner returns to India, where her parents were missionaries, to get to the bottom of her sister's death. Her sister, Ellyn, was also a missionary, and the bane of existence for extremist Sikhs. Several operatives race about in unconvincing fashion in this heavily plotted tale as Erica eventually unravels the mystery surrounding Ellyn, in the process falling in love with a Hindu prince named Sajah. Happily for Erica, Sajah converts to Christianity after the miraculous healing of Betul, Ellyn's son and Sajah's nephew.

PALMER, CATHERINE

TREASURES OF THE HEART

A Kiss of Adventure. 2000. Tyndale, paper. 272 pp. ISBN 0-8423-3884-5.
Palmer touches bases with the flippancy and plot of the film *Romancing the Stone* (1984) as Tillie Thornton, to avoid being kidnapped by the fierce Tuaregs, is forced to rely on the wits of adventurer Graeme McLeod. The novel is a retitled version of Palmer's 1997 novel *The Treasure of Timbuktu*.

A Whisper of Danger. 2000. Tyndale, paper. 262 pp. ISBN 0-8423-3886-1.
The second entry in Palmer's Treasures of the Heart series is set on an island, where Jessica Thornton pursues her inheritance at peril of her life, while her ex-husband pursues her.

 A Touch of Betrayal. 2000. Tyndale, paper. 275 pp. ISBN 0-8423-5777-7.
The third entry of the Treasures of the Heart series is set in Kenya. Again Palmer leans on *Romancing the Stone* as fashion designer Alexandra Prescott reluctantly teams up with Grant Thornton, a wisecracking anthropologist.

✦ ★ RISPIN, KAREN. *African Skies*. 2000. Multnomah, paper. 384 pp. ISBN 1-57673-626-1.

Laurel Binet goes to Kenya to work on a project researching baboons under the supervision of a famous conservationist, Joan Doyle, a stern personage seemingly modeled on Jane Goodall. Laurel is convinced God's work can be done through caring for his creatures, and Rispin's fine scenes with animals make them seem superior to humankind. Rispin's true theme, however, is that if a choice must be made between endangered animals and desperate people, people matter more. Before Laurel learns that lesson, she must confront Darren Grant, a pragmatic former conservationist now involved in poverty relief and education.

✦ WINDSOR, LINDA. *Not Exactly Eden*. 2000. Multnomah, paper. 284 pp. ISBN 1-57673-445-5.

Jenna Marsten travels to the Peruvian Amazon to seek out the truth of her medical missionary father's apparent death in this variation on the 1984 film *Romancing the Stone*. The spoiled rich girl persona Windsor attempts to give Jenna is unconvincing juxtaposed with her bedrock faith; and the reader will sympathize with the contempt of Dr. Adam DeSanto, the jungle doctor assigned to pick her up at the airport. Windsor did her homework on the great river and its people, but as a romantic couple these two seem stitched out of stereotypes and are never convincing.

ROMANTIC SUSPENSE

BLACKSTOCK, TERRI

✦ *SUNCOAST CHRONICLES*

Mainstream romance writer Blackstock broke into the Christian market with this highly popular series of romantic mysteries.

Evidence of Mercy. 1995. Zondervan, paper. 368 pp. ISBN 0-310-20015-6.
Attorney Lynda Barrett must sell her plane when her debt-ridden father dies, even though flying is her favorite pastime. On a test flight with a potential buyer, rich man Jake Stevens, the plane goes down, injuring Stevens. Lynda and Jake are drawn together in an uncertain romance, even as Lynda discovers that her plane was sabotaged and that someone wants her dead.

Justifiable Means. 1996. Bethany, paper. 304 pp. ISBN 0-310-20016-4.
The second in Blackstock's mystery series features Detective Larry Millsap, called in to investigate what seems clearly to have been a rape. Then he begins to suspect that the victim, Melissa Nelson, may have planted the evidence in a plot to convict the rapist, who killed her sister. Millsap is attracted to Melissa, even so.

Ulterior Motives. 1996. Zondervan, paper. 314 pp. ISBN 0-310-20017-2.
Ben Robinson's boss is found dead, but Ben's ex-wife, Sharon, doesn't believe he did it. She pays his bail, lines up a lawyer, and shelters him in part to prove to her daughter that her Christianity is not lip service but a compassionate conviction she acts upon daily. Troubles ensue.

Presumption of Guilt. 1997. Zondervan, paper. 352 pp. ISBN 0-310-20018-0.
Reporter Beth Wright investigates a nasty story about abuse at the St. Clair Children's Home, and someone equally nasty doesn't want her to.

☒ **BULOCK, LYNN.** *Island Breeze.* **1999. Multnomah, paper. 299 pp. ISBN 1-57673-398-X.**
Computer whiz Bree Trehearn sees something she shouldn't have on a client's hard drive and runs for her life. On a Florida island she meets an ex-cop and slowly turns him into a Christian. He helps her solve her problems.

COTE, LYN

NORTHERN INTRIGUE
A sheriff and a nurse team to solve mysteries in Steadfast, Wisconsin.

Winter's Secret. 2002. Tyndale, paper. 268 pp. ISBN 0-8423-3556-0.

HENDERSON, DEE

☒★ *Danger in the Shadows.* 1999. Multnomah, paper. 352 pp. ISBN 1-57673-577-X.
Sara Walsh is a writer almost by default: She's in the witness protection program and must lay low. Fully 25 years ago, she was kidnapped along with her twin sister. Her sister died, and Sara has never fully recovered from the trauma. As she starts to have a real life, having fallen in love with a football player named Adam Black, she thinks one of the kidnappers is stalking her. Adam doesn't believe her. When she wants to retreat into her shell, he won't let her. Gritty detail, characteristic of Henderson's work, authenticates this scary tale.

☒★ *O'MALLEY SERIES*
The O'Malleys are seven orphans or abandoned children who band together as adults in a fierce family, seemingly all of them devoted to law enforcement.

The Negotiator. 2000. Multnomah, paper. 379 pp. ISBN 1-57673-608-3.
Jaded Kate O'Malley is a legendary hostage negotiator who meets a character from Henderson's *Danger in the Shadows,* Dave Richman. (Thus fans of this series might also wish to read that novel.) Like Kate, Dave's an FBI agent, and as the two work a bank holdup, they are drawn together. Dave is a Christian, Kate isn't, but the handling of faith is subtle, the suspense strong, the police procedural detail convincing.

The Guardian. 2000. Multnomah, paper. 352 pp. ISBN 1-57673-642-3.
The sequel to *The Negotiator* features U.S. Marshall Marcus O'Malley, introduced as a minor character in that novel. He's assigned to security at a judicial conference in Chicago, out of which may come the next Supreme Court appointee. Marcus has to track down a potential assassin while courting Shari Hanford, a lawyer whose brief for the potential appointee may carry the day. The romance proceeds in fits and starts as the complex plot ticks cleverly toward its conclusion, nearly turning the love story into an afterthought. Kate O'Malley returns as a minor character.

The Truth Seeker. 2001. Multnomah, paper. 245 pp. ISBN 1-576-73-753-5.
The third in the O'Malley series brings forth two minor characters from *The Guardian:* forensics investigator Lisa O'Malley, and U.S. Marshall Quinn Diamond. Lisa, nursing herself back to health after an on-the-job injury, is given light duty for a time. She immediately turns it into active duty as she ponders an arson death that looks more like

murder, and she comes up missing. Meanwhile, when he's not busy rescuing Lisa, Quinn pursues a new lead in the murder of his father 20 years ago.

The Protector. 2001. Multnomah, paper. 350 pp. ISBN 1-57673-846-9.
The Protector is the fourth in the O'Malley series, but the series is flexible enough to accommodate this firefighter story that could be read without reference to other entries. It's about Jack O'Malley, a solid guy faced with combating a series of arson fires; and a woman firefighter, Cassie Ellis, who works with Jack and isn't so sure he's not the arsonist. As usual with a Henderson story, the milieu—firefighting—is authentically detailed.

JOHN, SALLY. *To Dream Again*. 2000. Crossway, paper. 256 pp. ISBN 1-58134-186-5.
Cat St. Clair is a frail, naive young woman working as the assistant manager of a medium fancy resort motel on the California coast. She dreams of a big house, an ideal husband, and children. Lately, however, since her rich, seemingly perfect fiancé dumped her for another woman, she's been suffering from migraines, recurring nightmares, and memory lapses. Like a knight-errant, the drifter Dominick D'Angelo appears and hires on as a handyman. Dominick solves many of Cat's woes, but unknown to her he's a government agent whose mission is to break a narcotics ring that seems to be centered at the resort. Cat is a suspect because of her mysterious trips to Tiajuana.

KOK, MARILYN. *Stillpoint*. 1996. Bethany, paper. 254 pp. ISBN 1-55661-821-2.
Kylie Austin works in the import and export business. She uncovers a smuggling operation running out of Hong Kong and teams with a handsome company officer to run down the mystery through a variety of coincidental plot turns.

MACDONALD, SHARI. *Forget Me Not*. 1996. Multnomah, paper. 266 pp. ISBN 0-88070-769-0.
Hayley Buckman, a young American woman, takes a job in England as a gardener on an old estate. The previous gardener, also a young woman, left abruptly, so Hayley has a mystery to solve a la *Jane Eyre*. Meanwhile, the suitors line up.

MARTINUSEN, CINDY MCCORMICK

Winter Passing. 2000. Tyndale, paper. 369 pp. ISBN 0-8423-1906-9.
Darby Evans drives around Salzburg, Austria, trying to fulfill her Jewish grandmother Celia's deathbed wish: to give "her name back" to a prewar friend named Tatianna and to discover what happened to priceless family heirlooms. Brant Collins, an Austrian American who investigates the property claims of Holocaust survivors, is drawn to Darby, though he doubts her story; Richter, his storm trooper of a cousin, also turns on the charm. Both share a link to Tatianna through her recently deceased husband, Gunther. Martinusen's characterizations are shallow, but she effectively teases out the mystery of the missing heirlooms, Gunther's odd legacy, and who actually died in the concentration camp.

⬤✕★ *Blue Night*. 2001. Tyndale, paper. 399 pp. ISBN 0-8423-5236-8.

Martinusen strikes a steady, serious tone in her loose sequel to *Winter Passing*. The characters change, but the novel is a sequel in the sense that it again frames a modern story around events of the Holocaust. While on vacation in Venice, Kate Porter's husband, Jack, disappears as she leaves the room to find breakfast. There is no clue what has happened except a small piece of blue tile lying on his pillow. Three years later, five old—very old—German soldiers gather in Phoenix, breaking a pact they made during WWII never to meet again. Shortly thereafter, as she is about to close the book on Jack forever, Kate receives a package containing another blue tile fragment. The package is from Phoenix.   ■ Sequel ■

NOBLE, DIANE

⬤✕ *Distant Bells*. 1999. Zondervan, paper. 368 pp. ISBN 1-57673-400-5.

In Spain to be married, Elliot Gavin, a scholar studying a Spanish religious cult, loses his fiancée, K. C. Keegan. Has she abandoned him? Has she been kidnapped? As Elliot searches frantically for his lost love, it grows clear that the cult is actually a front for a radical political group bent on overthrowing the Spanish government. K. C. may be their first victim.

⬤✕ *Tangled Vines*. 1998. Multnomah, paper. 335 pp. ISBN 1-57673-219-3.

K. C. Flynn, a small-town publisher, grows concerned when her aunt, a mystery writer, disappears. She trails her to the Napa Valley, where she joins forces with an old flame, now the local sheriff, to investigate a suspicious local winery.

PETERSON, TRACIE

⬤✕★ *Controlling Interests*. 1998. Bethany, paper. 256 pp. ISBN 0-76422-064-0.

No one loves Denali Deveraux, despite her beauty and education. So she throws herself into the family business, designing theme parks, but the business is controlled by her grandfather, who seems to blame Denali for her mother's suicide and her father's disappearance. Almost contemptuously, he orders her to Dallas to work on a tricky account. There she can at least confide in another designer, Michael Copeland, who also has a painful past, but after a while she suspects he has a hidden agenda. Maybe the future holds peace for Denali, but only if she can unravel the truth behind her tortured family history.

⬤✕ *Entangled*. 1997. Bethany, paper. 244 pp. ISBN 1-55661-936-7.

Entangled is the strange tale of Cara Kessler, a young widow of a prominent man who is coerced into running for the office of Kansas attorney general. Cara enlists the help of a handsome state trooper, Harry Oberlin, to help her expose the corruptions of the governor that she, riding her late husband's reputation, helped to elect.

⬤✕ *Framed*. 1998. Bethany, paper. 256 pp. ISBN 1-55661-992-8.

Gabrielle Fleming, in Great Britain to do a series of travel articles, plunges into a mystery with international implications when her sister disappears. She must rely on the wits and skills of the photographer assigned to her, Jarod Wells, a good-looking man she somehow doesn't trust, to find out what happened.

⬤✕ SCHUNK, LAUREL. *The Voice He Loved*. 1995. Nelson, paper. 277 pp. ISBN 0-7852-8082-0.

Paige Brookings' high-rolling life as a New York model has brought her near collapse in this first novel, made interesting by Schunk's portrait of Wichita, the hometown to which Paige retreats, and by the creepy stalker who follows her. But Paige's old flame, Paul Sherman, seems too good to be true, nor is Paige herself quite credible.

WOLFE, SUZANNE. *Veiled Images.*1996. Nelson, paper. 288 pp. ISBN 0-7852-8242-4.

Veiled Images is an able first novel about an American art historian, Rachel Piers, who journeys to Italy to restore a valuable panel of paintings and finds herself embroiled in corrupt political intrigues. Giovanni Donati, an assistant, helps her extricate herself and provides love interest as well.

SHORT STORIES

AIKEN, GINNY, LORI COPELAND, DIANNA CRAWFORD, AND CATHERINE PALMER. *With This Ring.* 1998. Tyndale, paper. 368 pp. ISBN 0-8423-7822-7.

A multicultural anthology both of historical and contemporary wedding stories: Lori Copeland's "Something Old," about the conflict of an immigrant culture with the American Way; Dianna Crawford's "Something New," about an arranged marriage in 1895 San Francisco; Ginny Aikin's "Something Borrowed," set in 1880s west Texas; and Catherine Palmer's "Something Blue," the tale of a Norwegian on the Louisiana bayou in 1876.

AIKEN, GINNY, RANEE MCCOLLUM, JERI ODELL, AND DEBRA WHITE SMITH. *A Bouquet of Love.* 1999. Tyndale, paper. 400 pp. ISBN 0-8423-3848-9.

Both lighthearted love and marital difficulties are explored in these four novellas aimed at Valentine's Day: Ginny Aiken's "The Wrong Man," Ranee McCollum's "His Secret Heart," Jeri Odell's "Come to My Love," and Debra White Smith's "Cherish."

AIKEN, GINNY, JERI ODELL, AND ELIZABETH WHITE. *Dream Vacation.* 2000. Tyndale, paper. 316 pp. ISBN 0-84231-899-2.

The ideal vacation combines with love in Aiken's "A Single's Honeymoon," Odell's "Love Afloat," and White's "Miracle on Beale Street."

BALL, KAREN, JENNIFER BROOKS, AND ANNIE JONES. *Fools for Love.* 1998. Multnomah, paper. 246 pp. ISBN 1-57673-235-5.

Ball's character, Kitty Hawk, always gets depressed on April Fools' Day in "Jericho's Walls"; Caleb Murphy tries to pick up a donation of books for his library but finds himself ensnared by the donor's granddaughter in "Cat in the Piano"; and Professor Ginny Sanborn is all through with love, but love isn't through with her, in "Fool Me Twice."

BALL, KAREN, BARBARA JEAN HICKS, AND DIANE NOBLE. *Heart's Delight.* 1997. Multnomah, paper. 256 pp. ISBN 1-57673-220-7.

A young woman goes along with a blind date set up by her sisters in Ball's "Valentine Surprise" and discovers she went out with the wrong man; children interfere with their parents' silly romance in Barbara Jean Hicks's "Cupid's Chase," and in Diane Noble's "Birds of a Feather," two bird-watching seniors set aside their differences to save a park, and fall in love.

BERGER, EILEEN M., COLLEEN COBLE, DENISE HUNTER, AND JANICE POHL. *Reunions: Four Inspiring Romances of Friends Reunited.* 2000. Barbour, paper. 344 pp. ISBN 1-57748-728-1.

Reunions collects four buoyantly optimistic novellas around a theme or place: a family reunion (Berger's "That Special Something"); the meeting of two long-lost friends, both storm chasers (Coble's "Storm Warning"); a high school reunion that throws together a one-time cheerleader with the jock who rejected her (Hunter's "Truth or Dare"); and a man and woman brought together at the deathbed of a third party (Pohl's "Too Good to Be True").

BERGREN, LISA TAWN, CONSTANCE COLSON, AND AMANDA MACLEAN. *A Mother's Love.* 1997. Multnomah, paper. 276 pp. ISBN 1-57673-106-5.

When his wife dies, a father tries to cope with his daughter's grief in Bergren's "Sand Castles." Colson's "A Mother's Miracle" brings old sweethearts together, and MacLean's "Legacy of Love" features newlyweds facing parenthood.

BERGREN, LISA TAWN, BARBARA JEAN HICKS, JANE ORCUTT, AND SUZY PIZZUTI. *Porch Swings and Picket Fences.* 1999. WaterBrook, paper. 352 pp. ISBN 1-57856-226-0.

This popular anthology features four novellas about love in idyllic small towns: "Tarnished Silver," by Lisa Tawn Bergren; "Twice in a Blue Moon," by Barbara Jean Hicks; "Texas Two-Step," by Jane Orcutt; and "The Boy Next Door," by Suzy Pizzuti.

BLACKSTOCK, TERRI, ELIZABETH WHITE, AND RANEE MCCOLLUM. *Sweet Delights.* 2001. Tyndale, paper. 350 pp. ISBN 0-8423-3513-0.

Three tales of chocolate and romance: Blackstock's "For Love of Money," White's "The Trouble with Tommy," and McCollum's "What She's Been Missing."

HICKS, BARBARA JEAN, ANNIE JONES, DIANE NOBLE, AND LINDA WINDSOR. *Unlikely Angels.* 1999. Multnomah, paper. 352 pp. ISBN 1-57673-589-3.

There is nothing to do with angels in these four novellas, unless dogs and horses are angels: Each story features an animal that somehow brings lovers together: Hicks's "Cupid's Chase" involves a cat; Jones's "Fool Me Twice" features Ralphie the greyhound; Noble's "Birds of a Feather" brings two octogenarian birdwatchers together; and Windsor's "A Season for Love" is a story of homecoming involving a horse.

HIGGS, LIZ CURTIS, CAROLYN ZANE, AND KAREN BALL. *Three Weddings and a Giggle.* 2001. Multnomah, paper. 352 pp. ISBN 1-57673-656-3.

Three well-known Christian romance writers offer comedies of errors about weddings and matchmaking, some jokes, and the recipe for a burrito casserole.

WICK, LORI. *Beyond the Picket Fence.* 1998. Harvest, paper. 180 pp. ISBN 1-56507-817-9.

Eight short stories set in small towns.

Chapter 9

Fantasy and Science Fiction

Two of Christian science fiction's best-known contemporary talents are Stephen Lawhead and Orson Scott Card, major, mainstream writers who also publish in the Christian press: Lawhead with Zondervan and Card with Mormon publishers such as Deseret. Lawhead is better known for his medieval historical fantasies than for science fiction. Card's books with Deseret are not science fiction, but directly religious titles, such as *Stone Tables* (p. 37).

Both are major voices, so much so that neither really owes much of a debt to C. S. Lewis, except possibly Lawhead early in his career, which is a long way of saying that everyone else does. One cannot read Madeleine L'Engle's *A Wrinkle in Time*—or its several sequels—without being reminded of Lewis's Narnia stories.

The influence of J.R.R. Tolkien, George MacDonald, and Charles Williams is also apparent among Christian science fiction writers but with nothing like the magnitude of Lewis. Elements of his science fiction trilogy, *Out of the Silent Planet, That Hideous Strength,* and *Perelandra* (see chapter 3, "Christian Classics"), as well as the Narnia Tales and *Screwtape Letters,* appear repeatedly in fantasies, apocalyptic fiction, allegories, and spiritual warfare novels. Often, Christian science fiction writers deliberately and forthrightly imitate Lewis. Even if they do not, he is so widely revered that he has become an unavoidable, perhaps unsurpassable, prototype. C. S. Lewis made the rules.

The other major influence on Christian science fiction is politics. Here's one of the places where that right-wing agenda that some readers fear can be found. A handful of writers try to prove the literal truth of the Bible by constructing fiction around the Garden of Eden, or the Flood, or the blood of Jesus. Others write dystopian, latter-day fantasies of the collapse of civilization and the Second Coming, all brought on by big government, the United Nations, a general breakdown in morality, and, of course, the inevitability of biblical prophecy.

See also chapter 12, "Catholic Fiction," the sections on apocalypse and science fiction.

ALLEGORIES

Most Christian fantasy is allegorical in the sense that characters stand for some virtue or sin, and Christian lessons can be taken. But the following titles are strict allegories in the tradition of *Pilgrim's Progress*.

ALCORN, RANDY

E✖ *Edge of Eternity*. 1998. WaterBrook. 336 pp. ISBN 1-57856-085-3.
Monsters abound in Alcorn's scary mystical landscape, full of tributes to Bunyan such as "The Chasm," "The Endless Night," and "The Imposter." The journey of his sinful hero, Nick Seagrave, is a bit confusing, however. It's plain that he has cheated on his wife, and Alcorn manages some extraordinary scenes in which Nick must look down on his own infidelity. But otherwise, Alcorn is so intent on his allegory that he neglects to develop a story, and the result makes the reader's head swim.

E✖ *Lord Foulgrin's Letters*. 2000. Multnomah. 300 pp. ISBN 1-57673-679-2.
Deliberately imitating the structure of C. S. Lewis's *The Screwtape Letters,* Alcorn alternates the letters from Hell of the demon Lord Foulgrin to a subordinate with scenes portraying materialistic Jordan Fletcher and his unhappy family. Angels also battle for Jordan's soul.

E✖ ALCORN, RANDY, ANGELA ALCORN, AND KARINA ALCORN. *The Ishbane Conspiracy*. **Multnomah, paper. 300 pp. ISBN 1-57673-817-5.**
Though placed here for convenience, the Alcorns really intend this sequel to *Lord Foulgrin's Letters* to be a youth novel. Unable to woo away Jordan Fletcher, Lord Foulgrin goes after the Fletcher kids, tempting them with alcohol, drugs, sex, and the occult. ▰ Sequel ▰

HAMILTON, DAN

E✖ *TALES OF THE FORGOTTEN GOD* ▰ Discussion ▰
Hamilton's trilogy is composed of parable-like vignettes loosely linked by the appearance throughout of characters with the allegorical names Beauty, Covenant, Damon, and the Ancient Enemy. Hamilton sets his spare meditations in some faraway, more or less biblical land, and narrative isn't his strong suit, but his trilogy makes for wonderful discussion group material.

> *The Beggar King*. 1993. InterVarsity. (Out of print.)

> *The Chameleon Lady*. 1994. InterVarsity. (Out of print.)

> *The Everlasting Child*. 1994. InterVarsity. (Out of print.)

E✖ HAWKINS, DON. *flambeau@darkcorp.com*. **Kregel, paper. 138 pp. ISBN 0-8254-2868-8.**
As Hawkins notes, C. S. Lewis described Hell as "a thoroughly nasty business concern." Hawkins runs with this notion, renaming Screwtape and Wormword of *The Screwtape Letters* as Scraptus and Flambeau, respectively, subaltern and functionary for Satan, CEO of Hell. Like many another imitation, Hawkins's exercise has neither the subtlety nor the humor of the original, but his forthright homage may earn Lewis new readers.

HURNARD, HANNAH

E✖ *Hinds' Feet in High Places*. 1997. Tyndale, paper. 317 pp. ISBN 0-8423-1429-6.
This semiautobiographical (Hurnard was herself, like her major character, disabled) homage to Bunyan features the crippled Much Afraid, who lives in the village of Much-Trembling in the Valley of Humiliation and, to escape a forced marriage to her cousin, Craven Fear, flies with the Good Shepherd to the high places. There her crippled state is healed, and she is given strong hind feet to frolic about in her Master's joyful domain. First published in 1955, *Hinds'*

Feet has become an evangelical classic and sells steadily every year, even though Hurnard herself, a British missionary to Israel, in later years became a sort of evangelical apostate, embracing New Age tenets such as vegetarianism and universalism and dabbling in the occult (Fisher 1996). The unusual title is from 2 Samuel 22: "He maketh my feet like hinds' feet: and setteth me upon my high places."   **Discussion**

E✗ *Mountains of Spices.* 1983. (Originally published in 1973.) Tyndale, paper. 250 pp. ISBN 0-8423-4611-2.

In the sequel to *Hinds' Feet in High Places,* Much Afraid, now called Grace and Glory, joins in the effort to bring her former friends out of the Valley of Humiliation and into the high places, more or less through positive thinking. For instance, Mrs. Dismal Foreboding hasn't had a cheery thought in her life, but through the efforts of Grace and Glory, the Good Shepherd, and Mrs. Valiant she becomes Mrs. Thanksgiving. The title comes from the nine spices and nine fruits of the spirit mentioned in the Song of Solomon.

E✗ **MACLEAN, AMANDA (Diane Noble).** *Everlasting.* **1996. Multnomah, paper. 320 pp. ISBN 0-88070-829-4.**

Sheridan O'Brian, a young Irishwoman, hires a handsome detective to help her find her brother. Their search takes them to the California gold fields of the 1850s in this heavy-handed Christian pilgrimage, beset with trials but ending in the joy to be found in the town of Everlasting.

E✗ **MURRAY, KATHERINE.** *Jake.* **1995. Nelson, paper. 186 pp. ISBN 0-7852-8095-2.**

YA See discussion in chapter 15, "Young Adults."

MYRA, HAROLD

E✗ *CHILDREN OF THE NIGHT*

Myra's are vivid, passionate tales about an underground, blind people who slowly emerge into the light. Their mysterious but apparently glorious destiny lies with outcasts—the leader, Yosha, and the blind girl, Mela. Mela gives birth to a maimed, strange child, and the promise of the people, and their future in the light, is vested in the child in this allegorical retelling of the gospel story.

> *Children in the Night.* 1991. Zondervan. (Out of print.)
>
> *The Shining Face.* 1993. Zondervan. (Out of print.)
>
> *Morning Child.* 1994. Zondervan. (Out of print.)

PECK, M. SCOTT. *In Heaven As on Earth.* 1996. Little, Brown. 192 pp. ISBN 0-7868-6204-1.

In this weak effort at fiction from the popular psychiatrist, Daniel Turpin enters the afterlife and is guided by several friendly spirits through Heaven's various realms, each deepening his spiritual and psychological awareness.

◀▣✗ **PHILLIPS, MICHAEL.** *The Garden at the Edge of Beyond.* 1998. Bethany, paper. 144 pp. ISBN 0-7642-2042-X.

Mimicking George MacDonald's nineteenth century fantasies and C. S. Lewis's *The Great Divorce,* and in some instances quoting from his own work, Phillips conjures up a sort of Purgatory through which he's guided by MacDonald and Lewis. The narrator sorts out the life he led by smelling flowers; each flower's odor causes him to recall a set of events on Earth. Phillips tries for something special here, but he's not the equal of his mentors, and the result is pedantic and fawning.

FABLES

◀▣✗ ★ **HUGGINS, JAMES BYRON.** *A Wolf Story.* 1993. Harvest, paper. 250 pp. ISBN 1-56507-126-3.

YA *Wolf Story* is a crisp allegorical fable reminiscent of *Watership Down* (1972). Deep in the woods at the beginning of time, a colony of hares loyal to Silver Wolf and the Lightmaker live peacefully. But these Christians cannot hide forever, for the kingdom of light is in retreat, and the Dark Council of wolves is nearly victorious. Saul can pass on his wisdom, but he may be too old for the fight. When the monstrous wolves arrive, courageous young Windgate rises in his place.

YA **SUHAY, LISA.** *Tell Me a Story.* 2000. Paraclete. 164 pp. ISBN 1-55725-247-5.

Suhay is a newspaper columnist whose bedtime stories for her three boys slowly grew into these contemporary fables drawing on Christian practice, New Age philosophy, and common sense. None has the spare quality of Aesop, but many use animals, such as the tale of the grackle and the rabbit, to illustrate the necessity for thankfulness and optimism. Suhay's most interesting effort may be "Eagle's Fight to Heaven's Fall," ostensibly a retelling of the Icarus myth but with a feminist subtext: The eagle's high climb is all male vanity; his poor wife is left to keep up with him, and suffers almost unto death. ▣ Discussion ▣

WANGERIN, WALTER, JR.

◀▣✗★ *The Book of the Dun Cow.* 1978. HarperSanFrancisco, paper. 256 pp. ISBN 0-06-250937-3.

Wangerin tells an adult story here, but his gentle consciousness seems closer to E. B. White's and A. A. Milne's than Orwell's or Richard Adams's, and some see his tale as a children's fable. **YA** His hero is a vain rooster, Chaunticleer, who slowly discovers that the henhouse over which he rules is being stalked by a fearsome blacksnake, Wyrm. A classic battle of good and evil ensues, with the survival of the henhouse—its eggs—at stake. Though in some ways a comic tale, the sorrow of the hens is real, Chaunticleer's anguish is real, the weasel is weaselly, and the self-effacing dog, Mundo Cani, will remind the reader of Eeyore from Winnie the Pooh stories. Winner of the American Book Award.

◀▣✗★ *The Book of Sorrows.* 1996. (Originally published in 1985.) Zondervan, paper. 352 pp. ISBN 0-310-21081-X.

In the equally fine sequel to *The Book of the Dun Cow,* the barnyard is victorious but deci- **YA** mated. Chaunticleer slowly gathers his forces and his resolve, fighting his own demons even as Wyrm organizes another assault. ▣ Sequel ▣

ALTERNATE UNIVERSE

⬛ ★ **BENTZ, JOSEPH.** *Song of Fire.* 1995. Thomas Nelson, paper. 438 pp. ISBN 0-7852-7882-6.

A musician named Jeremy awakens as a prophet in another world, though he isn't sure what he's the prophet of. For a time he becomes the stooge of a clever ruler and his daughter, who, succumbing to sensual delights and joining the ruling class, regularly retire to their chambers to lose themselves in visions brought on by soporific "vapors." Eventually, Jeremy understands his new world and becomes the leader of a suppressed cult called the Emajians. The struggle is resolved in a great, ingenious battle between good and evil, suggestive of Armageddon. With its strange machines and alternative Messiahs, Bentz's world of marvels is reminiscent both of Lewis's *Perelandra* (p. 24) and Edgar Rice Burroughs's Mars stories.

⬛ **BROWN, GRAYSON WARREN.** *Jesusgate.* 1997. Crossroad, paper. 226 pp. ISBN 0-8245-1601-X.

Brown mixes the gospels with current events in this alternative history. He sets the Crucifixion in contemporary Israel, but the Roman Empire still exists, complete with its cruel King Herod. There is a United Nations, jet travel, uplinks to satellites, and so forth. Jesus is known worldwide, not as a Messiah but as a folk hero and prophet of the people. News media gather to cover the arrest and trial of Jesus, and both a beautiful American reporter and a Roman soldier are moved to conversion. Such an astounding approach never quite suspends disbelief.

⬛ ★ **JOHNSON, SHANE.** *The Last Guardian.* 2001. WaterBrook, paper. 512 pp. ISBN 1-57856-367-4.

🔲 Naive grad student T. J. Shoss finds himself on the world of Noron, a vividly rendered parallel Earth where dinosaurs stalk the steamy swamps, and the ruling race of giants, while protesting its refinement, practices cannibalism. T. J. settles into an official, seemingly vital post for the rulers, but gradually realizes he's being duped. His real, daunting purpose is to assume the role of Christ.

⬛ ★ **MYERS, BILL.** *Eli.* 2000. Zondervan, paper. 304 pp. ISBN 0-310-21803-9.

🔲 Conrad Davis, a TV producer, lies in a coma after an automobile crash, but seems also to live again in a Santa Monica nearly the same as the one he's accustomed to. But now it's the 1960s and his ex-wife of both universes, always religious, is drawn to a charismatic young teacher named Eli. Eli rises to prominence as a champion of the poor and oppressed, is opposed by established religion (represented by a corrupt televangelist), dies, and is resurrected. Possibly this happens, in one alternative world after another. But it could be that all of this is Conrad's near-death experience, in which he affirms in one universe the Messiah he rejected in another, and thus, a Christian, is readied for death.   **▮Discussion▮**

PHILLIPS, MICHAEL

◄❯✗ *Rift in Time.* 1997. Tyndale, paper. 480 pp. ISBN 0-8423-5500-6.
Phillips attempts to lend credence to biblical accounts of creation and the ancient history of humankind through the discoveries of an Indiana Jones sort of character named Adam Livingstone. Interweaving speculation, history, and research, Phillips contrives for his Adam to discover Noah's Ark, the Garden of Eden, and the Tree of Life. The Garden changes as it is viewed, seemingly with apocalyptic implications.

◄❯✗ *Hidden in Time.* 2000. Tyndale, paper. 492 pp. ISBN 0-8423-5501-4.
In the sequel to *Rift in Time,* Adam is joined by his fiancée, Juliet Halsay, in a search for the Ark of the Covenant.   ▄▄ Sequel ▄▄

APOCALYPSE

See also chapter 12, "Catholic Fiction."

◄❯✗ **BALIZET, CAROL.** *Plague.* **1994. Baker, paper. 350 pp. ISBN 0-8007-9213-0.**
Those who are HIV-positive have been quarantined in huge settlements in the "O-Zone" of Florida. Readers are treated to an imaginative rendering of life in the O-Zone with its "death games" and suicide parlors. The nation is in a state of near anarchy. Balizet's tale plays out as a Christian family's two children are abducted by petty criminals who hope to sell the kids to child molesters in the O-Zone. Mom and Dad arm themselves to the teeth and team with two soldiers to chase the criminals down central Florida and into the Everglades in this muddled but genuinely scary novel that brings to mind both Pat Frank's *Alas, Babylon* (1959) and Ayn Rand's *Atlas Shrugged* (1957).

◄❯✗ **BAUER, S. WISE.** *The Revolt.* **1996. Word, paper. 425 pp. ISBN 0-8499-3935-6.**
Sometime in the near future, Virginia and North Carolina secede from the Union to form a theonomy, a state governed by the Ten Commandments. These Reformed American States issue demands to the federal government, such as a nine percent flat tax and the revocation of homosexual rights, that have more to do with right-wing politics than theonomy. Shortly, a civil war erupts, appropriately enough, from Lynchburg.

BEAUSEIGNEUR, JAMES

★ *CHRIST CLONE TRILOGY*   ▄▄ Discussion ▄▄
The Christ Clone trilogy went unreviewed in mainstream and evangelical media alike but has enjoyed a considerable underground success. Its almost fanatically loyal readers claim it to be the best of the End Times novels for several reasons: its meticulous research (the novels are footnoted); the evil that arises has a certain subtlety about it and is convincing, unlike the cardboard variety appearing in many strictly evangelical novels; and BeauSeigneur delivers his message in techno-thriller style, throwing in scholarly details about the Russian Revolution and junk DNA while still pumping the suspense.

> *In His Image.* 1997. SelectiveHouse, paper. 384 pp. ISBN 0-9656948-5.
> BeauSigneur goes into detail about actual events surrounding the scientific examination of the Shroud of Turin in the 1970s, thereby setting up an elaborate verisimilitude for his larger story: the cloning of Christopher Goodman from the blood of Christ. As a

child, Christopher is bright, shy, lonely, and occasionally prescient. His childhood grows more serious when the scientist dies—simultaneous to certain bizarre events around the world.

Christopher joins Decker Hawthorne, a journalist who has lost his family in the Rapture. Christopher becomes like a son to Decker. He grows to be a fine young man as Decker comes to prominence working for the United Nations. Logically and inevitably, Christopher rises to become Secretary-General of the United Nations, surrounding himself with clever sycophants and the well-meaning Decker, his tireless publicist. Meanwhile, evil stalks the Earth, even as Christopher, seemingly the savior of humankind, does good.

Birth of an Age. 1997. SelectiveHouse, paper. 241 pp. ISBN 0-9656948-6-0.
Birth of an Age, sequel to *In His Image,* could as well be called the *Book of Plagues.* Christopher Goodman makes his case for the illegitimacy of a jealous God, wreaking revenge on a humankind destined to rise to a new level of consciousness, becoming godlike itself. He is so entirely reasonable that the reader will often sympathize with him, particularly when BeauSeigneur presents his maniacally detailed plagues: meteors that strike Earth, and the tsunamis and dead oceans they create; locusts that attack with the ferocity of scorpions; and streams that run with blood—blood that soon begins to decay and fester with vermin.

Acts of God. 1998. SelectiveHouse, paper. 384 pp. ISBN 0-9656948-7-9.
Decker Hawthorne is kidnapped by a band of resistant Christians and converted Jews who attempt to show him how deep Christopher's subterfuge runs and how Decker has done the Devil's bidding without realizing it. As if reluctantly, Christopher imposes the communion of his cloned blood on all humankind, and then the mark of the beast. New plagues arise, the most hideous of which is a terrible heat wave in which millions perish. At last Decker understands the enormity of his sins and repents, even as Christopher beheads him. After all this, the Battle of Armageddon seems almost anticlimactic, but it, too, is brilliantly rendered.

BULWER-LYTTON, EDWARD. *The Last Days of Pompeii.* 1834.
See discussion in chapter 3, "Christian Classics," p. 19.

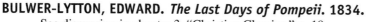 BUNN, T. DAVIS

The Warning. 1998. Nelson, paper. 315 pp. ISBN 0-7852-7516-9.
In *The Warning,* Buddy Korda, a banker, receives a revelation from God about the imminent economic collapse of the United States. He wants to cast off the revelation as a bad dream because it flies against conventional wisdom and he doesn't want to endure public ridicule. Worse, he's having trouble getting along with the aggressive new manager of his branch and could lose his job. But the warning grows so compelling that he has no choice but to spread the word, evangelist-style, until he has a great following. The market rises as never before, seeming to prove Buddy wrong. Then the market crashes, and he is a national hero.

The Ultimatum. 1999. Nelson, paper. 310 pp. ISBN 0-7852-7086-8.
In this sequel to *The Warning,* the world has plunged into depression, but there has been a great revival and churches have become refuges for the poor and displaced. Buddy receives a second message: he is to do all he can to amend the U.S. Constitution to protect religious freedom. There's resistance from the federal government, which Bunn clearly has little use for, but the will of the people is too strong.

BURKETT, LARRY. *Solar Flare.* **1997. Northfield Publishing. 436 pp. ISBN 1-881273-07-5.**
Solar Flare is a cross between two classic science fiction novels: Pat Frank's *Alas, Babylon* (1959) and Philip Wylie's *When Worlds Collide* (1934). How would we survive, it asks, if a solar flare of gigantic proportions, with its lethal radiation and potential for electronic disruptions, shot toward Earth? The best and brightest construct new communities in rural areas, where they learn self-sufficiency and trust in God; when at last the crisis abates, they don't want to return to their old ways. A terrific premise, though Burkett's strident conservatism will irritate some readers. The novel also suffers from incompetent editing: it's full of repetitions, inconsistencies, and bizarre typographical errors.

◄ CUNNINGHAM, WILL. *Sins of the Fathers.* **1997. Nelson, paper. 274 pp. ISBN 0-7852-8129-0.**
Here's a Christian version of Philip K. Dick's classic *Do Androids Dream of Electric Sheep?* featuring an America in 2038, when overpopulation has led to abortion as the chief means of birth control, love is a quaint concept, natural conception is a crime, and lives are terminated at 50 years of age. The action centers around John Nash, a "tag-man" thrown into ethical conflict when he is assigned to kill his own father.

◄ DOLAN, DAVID. *The End of Days.* **1995. Baker, paper. 330 pp. ISBN 0-8007-5630-4.**
Syrians mount an armored attack across the Golan Heights and follow ground assaults with chemical artillery. Suffering great losses, and over objections from the American president, Israel drops an atomic bomb on Damascus. This brings the Syrians to their knees, but the Israelis hadn't counted on the rancor of the Russians, Syrian allies still deeply resentful of their fallen status in world politics. The revitalized Russians form a vanguard for the Antichrist, a smooth talker who quickly brings the world, now suffering from unprecedented natural and ecological disasters, under his control. It's a mystery why Dolan's wooden, unctuous Antichrist wouldn't realize he's no match for Yeshua, who, like the cavalry, arrives when the battle is all but lost.

◄ EVANS, MIKE, AND ROBERT WISE. *The Jerusalem Scroll.* **1999. Nelson. 342 pp. ISBN 0-7852-6915-0.**
With acts of terrorism and apocalyptic murmurings in the background, three scholars, a Jew, a Catholic, and a Muslim, set about to translate a message for the ages from Jerusalem's ancient king, Melchizedek. Evans and Wise use the confluence of the scholars to examine the three separate, opposed points of view regarding the end times, and they do so fairly and engagingly. In fact, this near-scholarly colloquy may prove more interesting for readers than the translation itself.

◄ HUGGINS, JAMES BYRON. *The Reckoning.* **1994. Harvest, paper. 473 pp. ISBN 1-56507-181-8.**
An ancient prophecy foretells the coming of the God-Man, or Antichrist. The prophecy also tells of the God-Man's lineage and birthplace and offers instructions to those evil enough to want him in power. The one copy of the prophecy is stolen from an old priest, who, about to die, summons a trained assassin named Gage whom the priest set upon a righteous path. Now Gage must be a killer again, and he's as adept as any character in a Don Pendleton yarn.

HUNT, ANGELA ELWELL. *The Immortal.* 2000. Word. 390 pp. ISBN 0-8499-1630-5.

Jury consultant Claudia Fischer, one of the best in the country, is hired for a lucrative job screening employees for Global Union, an Italian consortium advocating world peace. Before long she finds herself entangled in the provocative legend of the Wandering Jew, or Asher Goldman, who was destined at the Crucifixion never to die. Instead he must spend his lonely eternity seeking out the Antichrist and attempting to convert him to Christ before he has completely given himself to Satan. As the power of Global Union grows, Claudia comes to understand that Asher's preposterous story is true and that her seemingly reasonable and virtuous boss, Darien Synn, may really be the Antichrist.

JEFFREY, GRANT R., AND ANGELA ELWELL HUNT

Flee the Darkness. 1998. Word. 363 pp. ISBN 0-8499-4063-X.

Flee the Darkness was probably the scariest of the numerous Y2K novels appearing at millennium's end because it linked the bug with the Last Days. Computer whiz Daniel Prentice, the hero, provides a killer cure: embedding a computer chip in every citizen's wrist that links medical, financial, and legal records. Daniel actually means well, but then he meets the Antichrist, who thanks Daniel from the bottom of his heart, such as it is.

C *By Dawn's Early Light.* 2000. Word. 368 pp. ISBN 0-8499-3781-7.

After saving the world from what turned out to be (in the real world) the nonexistent threat of the Y2K bug in *Flee the Darkness,* Daniel Prentice returns to battle against an invasion of Israel by Arab and Russian forces, aiding an American security officer and his Israeli counterpart, Devorah Cohen. But if this looming invasion is a fulfillment of a prophecy in Ezekiel, there will be no stopping it.   ■ Sequel ■

JENKINS, JERRY, AND TIM LAHAYE

✦★ *LEFT BEHIND*

This famous series, the most successful Christian fiction series ever, caught the imagination of the general reading public and appeared week after week on the *New York Times* bestseller lists. Given its transformations into audios, a video, and a juvenile series, Left Behind may exceed 50 million copies sold by the time it's done.

Several apocalyptic series are more interesting as fiction, notably, the trilogies of Bill Myers (discussed later) and James BeauSeigneur (discussed previously). Jenkins, certainly, has elsewhere written thoughtful fiction with well-drawn characters, most notably in *Hometown Legend* (p. 233). But his skill with characterization isn't in evidence when he's teamed with LaHaye. The two main characters are believable, but the evil characters seem derived from B movies—they are one-dimensional, and they aren't evil enough.

Unlike BeauSeigneur's Antichrist, Jenkins and LaHaye's creation seems crippled by verses in Revelation and is without nuance. He's about as scary as Lex Luthur in Superman comic books, and as predictable. Of course, he carries much heavier freight than a comic book villain, and a series as full of action as Left Behind may not need careful characterizations. And at times, Jenkins and LaHaye can be funny.

Tyndale's marketing was magnificent: Because the year 2000 had always been loosely associated with Christ's return, a series of novels describing events from the Rapture forward appealed to millions of readers filled with apocalyptic wonder. And no question, for secular readers in particular, the events of the first novel are startling.

Left Behind. 1995. Tyndale. 320 pp. ISBN 0-8423-2911-0.
The series begins on a transatlantic flight as the pilot, Rayford Steele, is turning over in his mind whether to begin an affair with one of his stewardesses. Suddenly, she bursts into the cabin to tell him that a number of the passengers have disappeared. Radio contact with New York confirms the same development all over North America. Rayford is overwhelmed with sadness, guilt, and apprehension, knowing that his wife is a Christian, already understanding what has happened. He isn't interested in the stewardess anymore. What will happen to Rayford—a decent man, but not a believer—and the millions of others like him, now that the born-again have been swept away?   **◼ Discussion▮**

Tribulation Force. 1996. Tyndale. 450 pp. ISBN 0-8423-2913-7.
In the sequel to *Left Behind,* Ray Steele and Buck Williams begin an underground resistance to the Antichrist, Nicolae Carpathia, who has the power to convince his adherents that the evil he commits is actually good; only those in the Tribulation Force can see through him.

Nicolae: The Rise of the Antichrist. 1997. Tyndale, 450p. ISBN 0-8423-3905-1.
In the third entry of the series, Nicolae becomes the focus as he continues to consolidate his power, unifying both political and religious realms as prophesied in Revelation. Rayford Steele and Buck Williams have their hands full protecting their families and themselves as global war spreads and natural disasters strike.

Soul Harvest. 1998. Tyndale. 448 pp. ISBN 0-8423-2915-3.
By the fourth entry the seven years of Tribulation are in full bloom. Having survived a global earthquake, Rayford and Buck search for their separated loved ones and try to mount an effective resistance, even as prophecies come true all around them.

Apollyon. 1999. Tyndale. 416 pp. ISBN 0-8423-2916-1.
Plagues such as demon locusts descend upon those who do not have the mark of God on their foreheads in the fifth entry. Believers join forces using the Internet and gather according to prophecy in Jerusalem. There, in a stadium rally, they face off with smooth-talking Nicolae.

Assassins. 1999. Tyndale. 448 pp. ISBN 0-8423-2920-X.
In the sixth entry, Rayford Steele, now a fugitive, puts together a plan to assassinate Nicolae, while his cohort Buck Williams founds a cyberzine called *The Truth* and preaches to masses. A seeming double agent infiltrates the Tribulation Force as Hattie, formerly Nicolae's mistress. Nicolae is assassinated.

(GM) *The Indwelling: The Beast Takes Possession.* 2000. Tyndale. 400 pp. ISBN 0-8423-2928-5.
Some believers are killed in the seventh entry, while others come forward. Newly converted Chicago lies in ruins, and the safe house is safe no longer. The mystery of who killed Nicolae is revealed, though it wasn't much of a mystery and is undercut in any case because Nicolae returns from the dead at his own funeral. Still, the funeral is among the best-set pieces of the series.

The Mark: The Beast Rules the World. 2001. Tyndale. 400 pp. ISBN 0-8423-3225-1.
In the eighth entry, Nicolae rises from the dead, and his religion, Carpathianism, sweeps the world. Followers of the Antichrist have to take the mark of the beast, as well as an electronic implantation that ensures no citizen can escape detection. But it is still possible to resist, and the Tribulation Force knows that yielding to Nicolae dooms them upon the return of Christ—three-and-a-half years, and several books, away.

Desecration. 2001. Tyndale. 400 pp. ISBN 0-8423-3225-1.
The Great Tribulation has begun, and Nicholae is supreme ruler. Plagues and abominations descend per Revelation, however, and he's driven to bloody reprisals to maintain control. Members of the Tribulation Force, suffering mightily, do their best to resist, but are in a holding action until Nicholae's dubious kingdom, at last beginning to unravel, is plunged into Armageddon.

★ **MADDOUX, MARLIN. *The Seal of Gaia*. 1998. Word, paper. 480 pp. ISBN 0-8499-3715-9.**
In Maddoux's chilling scenario of the end times, one-world government comes about because of the desperate state of Earth and the hope of its fragmented few for survival. With explanations the equal of any appearing in the best science fiction—and really, that's what the *Seal of Gaia* is, a fine science fiction novel—Maddoux piles ecological disaster upon brushfire nuclear war upon famine upon mass annihilation from AIDS to portray a scary world full of scared people. They are willing to accept—in fact, they clamor for—the rule of the all-knowing, possibly sentient computer, Omega. Omega is the heartbeat of the New World Order, governing from Geneva. Almost anticlimactically, the AntiChrist arises. He can levitate over every region of the Earth, and his mad proclamations seem the sanest thing left in a dehumanized, hopeless, dying world. ■Discussion■

MARZULLI, L. A. *Nephilim*. 1999. Zondervan, paper. 352 pp. ISBN 0-310-22011-4.
The X-Files meets Christian fiction when Art Mackenzie, a reporter whose father disappeared at Roswell, stumbles onto a ward of mental patients who speak—who scream—of flying saucers and a race of giants. Art has been boozing it since the tragic death of his own son. He hasn't much to live for. But this story sobers him up, and soon he's off to Israel and Peru to verify what the mental patients say. Yes, there are aliens among us. They are the Nephilim. They are a race of giants who were described in Genesis. Their appearance prefigures the Second Coming.

MEIER, PAUL. *The Third Millennium*. 1993. Nelson, paper. 300 pp. ISBN 0-8407-7571-7.
The Angel Michael narrates this less-than-subtle end-times tale that leans both on Revelation and Daniel for its prophetic underpinnings. The U.S. President Damian Gianardo is the Antichrist. His nefarious policies lead to the Battle of Armageddon in 2000. Meier's predictions of political events in the Mideast, based on Revelation and carried past the fictional narrative with his long afterword, date the novel rather more than other such efforts.

MEIER, PAUL, AND ROBERT WISE

The Fourth Millennium. Nelson, paper. 320 pp. ISBN 0-7852-8149-2.
The sequel to *The Third Millennium* is set near the end of Christ's 1,000-year reign. War and disease have been banished, and it's possible to grow as old as Methusaleh. Now, it's 999 N.E., Christ has disappeared, and 1,034-year-old Ben Feinberg and his friend Jimmy Harrison (who also appeared in the first novel) must deal with the rise of a cult that worships Marduk, an ancient Iranian god who is really Satan. ■Sequel■

◼✝ *The Secret Code.* 1999. Nelson, paper. 324 pp. ISBN 0-7852-7090-6.
A cabalistic interpretation of Scriptures foretells a nuclear explosion in Israel in 2006. The requisite computer whiz, Benjamin Meridor, and his girlfriend Judy Bithell have only five days to prevent the catastrophe.

◼✝ **MOORE, JOHN L.** *The Land of Empty Houses.* **1998. Broadman and Holman, paper. 266 pp. ISBN 0-8054-1648-X.**
A plague has befallen the Earth. Various malcontents wander the wasteland of the interior United States. One such is Daniel, an Army Ranger who went AWOL when the U.S. Army came under United Nations command. A missionary named Deborah seeks him out as a guide so that she may bring the gospel to fractured humanity, and the West may be settled again. Moore, author of the fine contemporary western *The Breaking of Ezra Riley* (p. 105), excels at describing western landscapes, and often his characters, such as the "babbler" who survives by eating prairie dogs, are appealing. Some readers will respond to his broad satire of New Age philosophy, which descends into cannibalism. But his dystopia, like David Brin's *The Postman* (1985), which it somewhat resembles, is never quite plausible.

★ **MUSTIAN, MARK.** *The Return.* **2000. Pineapple. 304 pp. ISBN 1-56164-190-1.**
Reporter Michael Mason, who over the years has become a sort of devil's advocate in his exposés of false Messiahs, is dispatched to Brazil for a story on Zhezush da Bahia, a woman from the streets, perhaps even a prostitute, who attracts thousands with her simple message of love and her ability to heal. Is she real, an unusually clever charlatan, or the Antichrist? Mustian's frank sexuality and open questioning will be off-putting to evangelical readers, but he knows how to create suspense, intriguingly explores the political implications of the return of Christ, and his portrait of the back streets of Sao Paulo seems to come from firsthand knowledge.

MYERS, BILL

◼✝★ *UNTITLED SERIES*
Myers's series is superior to other apocalyptic novels because of his superbly drawn, sorrowful characters; his grasp of the intricacies of DNA, not to mention the frontiers of quantum mechanics and psychokinetic research; and his fine, passionate style.

Blood of Heaven. 1996. Zondervan, paper. 304 pp. ISBN 0-310-20119-2.
In *Blood of Heaven,* a biotech firm happens upon an ancient blood sample that possibly is from Christ. As experiments produce gentler mice and baboons, the researchers make a Faustian bargain with a death-row inmate, who is indeed transformed into a gentle, insightful man. He dies for humankind, destroying the unholy experiment in the process.

Threshold. 1997. Zondervan, paper. 304 pp. ISBN 0-310-20120-0.
Though it is the second entry of Myers's series, *Threshold* is only loosely a sequel. It concerns Brandon Martus, a rootless blue-collar kid from northern Indiana who begins having visions. At first he ascribes these to his guilt over the deaths of family members—for which he was partly responsible. But Brandon's visions are extraordinarily detailed and may be prophecies of the Last Days.

Fire of Heaven. 1999. Zondervan, paper. 415 pp. ISBN 0-310-21738-5.
Brandon Martus, introduced in *Threshold,* and his wife, Sarah, become the two prophets spoken of in the Book of Revelation. They do battle with the rising Antichrist, but it is foreordained that they lose and ascend to Heaven. Meanwhile, Sarah's son, channeling with the Antichrist, is drawn down to utter ruin.

≡✕ ROBERTSON, PAT. *The End of the Age.* **1995. Word. 300 pp. ISBN 0-84991-290-3.**
The most durable of televangelists tries his hand at end times, rolling in much of the same kind of material covered in the more popular, and more artful, Left Behind series, including natural disasters, the rise of an Antichrist, and the Battle of Armageddon.

≡✕ VAN KAMPEN, ROBERT. *The Fourth Reich.* **1997. Revell. 445 pp. ISBN 0-8007-1745-7.**
A Jewish brother and sister, the prophets spoken of in Revelation, are drawn into the web of the Antichrist, who rises to power as the populist president of a weak Russia hungry for strong leadership. He at first pretends to be pro-Israeli, but the reader knows that he was born of a woman impregnated with Hitler's DNA.

≡✕ WADE, KENNETH R. *The Orion Conspiracy.* **Pacific, paper. 199 p4. ISBN 0-8163-1195-1.**
Computer hackers receive transmissions from extraterrestrials, an American president becomes the dupe of evil forces, an imposter assumes the Pope's robes, and New Age spiritual leaders lock horns with evangelicals a la Peretti. And, in a rare narrative ploy, Jesus actually appears in Wade's final chapters.

FANTASY

In the case of Christian fantasy, it has all been done before: the visit to Heaven, the visit to Earth from Jesus, the tales of a persecuted people staunch in their faith. Still, the quality of writing among contemporaries is high, comparable to that of fantasy writers in the mainstream. And some writers, such as Orson Scott Card, reinvent the genre.

≡✕ BELL, KATHERINE. *Jonathan's Journey.* **1994. Nelson, paper. 146 pp. ISBN 0-7852-8040-5.**
Jesus comes to visit a child with severe disabilities and takes him on a magical journey where he learns of the great figures of faith, such as Abraham and David. He learns that God has a place for him and a plan no matter how capricious and futile life may sometimes seem.

CARD, ORSON SCOTT

Treasure Box. 1996. HarperCollins. 310 pp. ISBN 0-06-017654-7.
Card enters the outskirts of Stephen King territory with his story of software genius Quentin Fears, who may be worth millions but is still an itinerant recluse. Then he falls in love with a wonderful girl, Madeleine, who is as naive and eccentric as he is. But there are problems: her strange family, and an age-old malevolence to which Madeleine is key. Quentin must face up to his inadequacies and make a stand in this solid effort splitting the difference between realism and horror.

YA ★ *Wyrms.* 1987. Arbor House. (Out of print.)
The coming of Christos, or Christ, has long been predicted and prayed for on the faraway planet Imakulata. Also prophesied is that the "seventh seventh seventh daughter" of the Heptarch, or ruler, will either destroy or save Imakulata. That daughter is Patience, groomed by her father both for diplomacy and assassination from the age of five. In her young womanhood, Patience must quest the Christ by doing battle with a grotesque, near-omniscient creature called the Unwyrm, the great mother of all. Like knight-errants, Patience and her companions make their way to the final confrontation. Readers will puzzle over the shocking ending of *Wyrms* and Card's curious portrait of evil, suggestive of *Speaker for the Dead* in Card's Ender Saga, and yet uniquely repulsive.

YA *Songmaster.* 1994. (Originally published in 1980.) Severn House. 338 pp. ISBN 0-7278-4654-X.
In a subtle retelling of the story of old King Saul and young David, Card evokes the tragedy of Emporer Mikal, a conqueror of worlds who, in his old age, requires the poetry of Ansset, a nine-year-old orphan whose singing has never been equaled. He treats the boy as his son, but the tenderness awakened in him is also a weakness exploited by his enemies, as they kidnap Ansset and use his powerful songs against Mikal. At last, Mikal, like King Saul, is no more, and Ansset ascends to power. Like David's, Ansset's hands are not entirely clean.

DODSON, DEANNA JULIE

EX *UNTITLED SERIES*

In Honor Bound. 1997. Crossway, paper. 320 pp. ISBN 0-89107-909-2.
In this medieval fantasy with a seemingly British setting, young Rosalynde enters into an arranged marriage with the man she has always loved, Prince Philip. Philip is indifferent to her, however, having lost the love of his life, a servant girl whom his ruthless father arranged to have killed.

By Love Redeemed. 1997. Crossway, paper. 272 pp. ISBN 0-89107-947-5.
Dodson reverses the plot of *In Honor Bound* in its sequel. Prince Chastelayne, Philip's demon-slaying brother, tries to express his love for his wife, Elizabeth, but she's cold to the touch.

HARDY, ROBIN

EX *ANNALS OF LYSTRA*
Hardy uses a vaguely Romanesque, vaguely British setting, the loosely federated "continent" of Lystra, and a strong romance plot to tell the tale of courageous Chataine (a sort of princess) Deirdre and her Christian husband, Roman. Roman was assigned as her bodyguard when Dierdre was 10 years old. She fell in love with him and married him, despite her father's opposition and the troubles it causes them both. Dierdre and Roman, middle-class Americans to the core, become doting parents and rise in status. But their kingdom still is threatened, and they join a great battle, led by Galapos, against the threat of supreme power wielded by an evil wizard.

Chataine's Guardian. 1994. NavPress, paper. 269 pp. ISBN 0-89109-836-4.

Stone of Help. 1994. NavPress, paper. 267 pp. ISBN 0-89109-837-2.

Liberation of Lystra. 1994. NavPress, paper. 393 pp. ISBN 0-89109-838-0.

HOUGHTON, JOHN. *A Distant Shore.* **1994. Thomas Nelson, paper. 237 pp. ISBN 0-7852-8228-9.**

Houghton imagines a future world in which most people live on boats, alone or in loosely linked communities. People are kept from their full flowering by a massive, unscalable black rock that is universally speculated about but of which little is known. One day a painter named Ewan Jones witnesses a mysterious green light emanating from the rock and is overcome by a desire to track it to its source. He is beset with temptation by a dark figure called the Hunter, but God also speaks, and at last Ewan reaches his distant shore and builds a sturdy faith on the rock in this parable suggestive of C. S. Lewis.

KEMP, KENNY. *I Hated Heaven.* **1998. Alta Films, paper. 288 pp. ISBN 1-92442-10-8.**

Construction worker Tom Waring dies suddenly of pancreatic cancer in the midst of a full, more or less happy life. He goes to "Paradise," not a purgatory but a staging area for Heaven—and where Kemp works out his imaginative theology. Trouble is, Waring left a lot of bills, a trusting young son, and a loving wife whose agnosticism is only strengthened by the sorrows thrust upon her. What kind of God, in other words, would call away a good man leading a worthwhile and vital life?   ∎**Discussion**

 LAWHEAD, STEPHEN

YA ★ *PENDRAGON CYCLE*

In his most famous series, Lawhead combines the legend of Arthur, the myth of Atlantis, and Celtic myth in a time at the end of the Roman Empire.

GM *Taliesin.* 1990. (Originally published in 1987.) Morrow/Avon, paper. 486 pp. ISBN 0-380-70613-X.

Taliesin is the enchanting love story of Taliesin of Britain and Princess Charis of Atlantis. Taliesin must die but not before fathering Merlin. Merlin comes to manhood with a fantastic, druidic heritage of magic.

Merlin. 1990. (Originally published in 1988.) Morrow/Avon, paper. 448 pp. ISBN 0-380-70889-2.

In the sequel to *Taliesin,* Merlin becomes the mentor of Arthur, who will be king.

Arthur. 1990. (Originally published in 1989.) Morrow/Avon, paper. 448 pp. ISBN 0-380-70890-6.

The third volume of the Pendragon Cycle chronicles the reign of Arthur as Christianity arrives in the British Isles and druidism falls away.

Pendragon. 1995. (Originally published in 1994.) Morrow/Avon, paper. 448 pp. ISBN 0-380-71757-3.

Arthur embraces Christianity and fights great wars against the Vandals and the Irish.

Grail. 1998. (Originally published in 1997.) Morrow/Avon, paper. 400 pp. ISBN 0-380-78104-2.

The ordinary and the supernatural continue side by side in the Pendragon Cycle's conclusion, which is told from the point of view of an enlisted man, Gwalchavad. Good triumphs over monsters, sorceresses, spells, zombies, and Arthur's own shortcomings as the Grail is protected.

SONG OF ALBION

The Paradise War. 1998. (Originally published in 1991.) Zondervan, paper. 416 pp. ISBN 0-310-21792-X.

Two graduate students at Oxford, Britisher Simon Rawnson and American Lewis Gillies, go exploring their passion, Celtic lore, in the north of Scotland. Simon disappears, and about four months later Lewis figures out where: to magical Albion, a wild Celtic kingdom in which four months in present-day time equals four years. He finds himself thrown into battle, from which Simon rescues him, but they are thereafter on opposite sides: Lewis with the forces of light, singing Albion's holy song; and Simon with Lord Nudd, king of the Otherworld, or Albion's version of Hell.

The Silver Hand. 1998. (Originally published in 1992.) Zondervan, paper. 399 pp. ISBN 0-310-21822-5.

The sequel to *The Paradise War* is narrated by the bard Tegid, who crowns as king Lewis the great warrior, now known as Llew. But Llew's evil rival Meldron cuts off his hand, usurping the throne because only an unblemished man may rule. As Albion staggers songlessly on, and Meldron bloodily extends his kingdom, Llew and Tegid flee to Caledon, where they prepare for a last stand. Meldron defeats Llew's forces, and Llew is condemned. But it what amounts to a *deus ex machina,* Llew magically acquires a silver hand, with which he captures the Singing Stones that contain the goodness of Albion, and becomes king.

The Endless Knot. 1998. (Originally published in 1993.) Zondervan, paper. 416 pp. ISBN 0-310-21901-9.

If the reader had not guessed, Llew becomes the savior of Albion, restoring its song in the conclusion to the Song of Albion. Llew marries Goewyn and loves her mightily, but the kingdom is still poisoned, and he must sacrifice himself to save it. Thus, Christianity comes to Albion, and Llew can become Lewis again.

◆✕ PORTER, CARYL. *A Child Among Us.* 1995. Thomas Nelson. 145 pp. ISBN 0-7852-9096-0.

A five-year-old boy, mute, appears out of nowhere in a small Nebraska town and leaves behind him a trail of miracles. An old woman at last accepts her Jewish daughter-in-law, for instance, and a fetus is cured of a birth defect. Good deeds done, the child disappears.

◆✕ SEBANC, MARK. *Flight to Hollow Mountain.* 1996. Eerdmans. 402 pp. ISBN 0-8028-3794-8.

The great harp that the legendary King Ardiel used to tune the harmony of Middle Earth has been stolen by dark powers in this Tolkien-like opus featuring dwarves, angels, good and evil, and a noble, vital quest. Young Kalaquinn must find the harp, else all the world will grow dark. The first in a projected trilogy, the concluding volumes of which never appeared, this is a beautifully imagined novel that often, even so, bogs down under the weight of its complex mythology.

WILLIAMS, THOMAS

◆✕ THE SEVEN KINGDOMS CHRONICLES

Crown of Eden. 1999. Word, paper. 436 pp. ISBN 0-8499-1610-0.

The first entry in this homage to Tolkien and C. S. Lewis turns on the tired device of babies switched at birth but otherwise vividly creates its medieval world, called the Seven

Kingdoms. Life here has been in a slow decline since the loss of the Crown of Eden—or, allegorically, since the Fall of Man and the rise of the dark powers. Young Princess Volanna, sworn to a political marriage but in love with a young blacksmith, and the blacksmith himself, Aradon, do unwitting and then conscious battle against the forces of evil, attempting to restore the glory of righteous Eden.

The Devil's Mouth. 2001. Word, paper. 434 pp. ISBN 0-8499-4267-5.
Deceived by a smooth-talking minstrel, young Evalonne loses her house and dowry, and is pregnant. She's forced to become a tavern maid. Unfortunately, all this happens in the Kingdom of Lochlaund, ruled by a legalistic church that punishes the slightest infractions with death—or by flinging into the cave called the Devil's Mouth, surely the equal of death. Meanwhile, young Prince Lanson flees for his life, and regroups, when conspirators kill his father. He falls in love with Evalonne, but he's troubled by her past. On the other hand, she may prove crucial to the kingdom that's his to win.

HARD SCIENCE FICTION

(See also chapter 12, "Catholic Fiction," the "Science Fiction" and "Andrew Greeley" sections; and chapter 14, "Mormon Fiction," the "Science Fiction" section.)

Hard science fiction is the stuff that writers such as Robert Heinlein, Arthur C. Clarke, and Hal Clement, with a nod to Jules Verne and H. G. Wells, brought into a full flowering after WWII. Rather than constructing a world out of whole cloth, as fantasy writers sometimes do—or at least, as hard science fiction writers accuse them of doing—hard science fiction takes a speculative but scientifically plausible concept and spins a story around it.

This kind of definition perhaps demonstrates the difficulty of writing evangelical science fiction. If you, as a writer, believe literally in the Genesis account of Creation, then much of science is closed off to you. If you try to portray such a belief, secular science fiction writers won't take you seriously.

Moreover, the future is foretold in Revelation (and Daniel). Although all manner of apocalyptic fiction can be written drawing upon Revelation, seeing the future as divinely ordered limits speculations. The way around this, as C. S. Lewis demonstrated in *Out of the Silent Planet,* is to tell the story of Christ as he appears on another world or in an alternative universe. When this is done (as in Kathy Tyers's trilogy, discussed later, or Bill Myers's *Eli,* discussed earlier), distinctions between genres and subgenres dissolve, resulting in stories that are not quite fantasy but not as "hard" as what is usually thought of as hard science fiction.

The titles described below are an eclectic mix. Some are mainstream, some are evangelical, some are Mormon (Orson Scott Card), and some are profane. Altogether, they make it clear that hard science fiction that is also Christian is an emerging genre, popping with experiments and ideas.

BAYLY, JOSEPH. *Winterflight.* **2000. (Originally published in 1981.) Chariot Victor, paper. 216 pp. ISBN 1-56476-786-8.**
Controversy swirled around the late Bayly's cry against euthanasia, abortion, and infanticide—not in the mainstream, where the book is scarcely known, but in evangelical circles, where some thought its language excessive and its ending harsh. The story is a pointed but effective tale of a couple, Jon and Grace Stanton, trying to find medical treatment for their son, Stephen, a hemophiliac. Trouble is, they had the boy illegally, because in the future all such birth defects are screened in utero, and fetuses

with defects are aborted. Because Stephen is illegal, any treatment of him would be illegal. The state descends on the Stantons with Orwellian vengeance.

⬛ BUNN, T. DAVIS. *The Dream Voyagers.* **1999. Bethany, paper. 350 pp. ISBN 0-7642-2180-9.**

A young man, Rick, and a young woman, Consuela, are transported to a faraway world where they join Wander, a "sensitive," with their quasitelepathic abilities to sense the pirate ships of a dark power, attacking the ships of the powers of light whom they serve. The novel is a kinder, gentler *Starship Troopers* (1959) and quite similar to Orson Scott Card's Ender series (discussed later) as well, though Bunn is a master of suspense and his love story between Consuela and Wander is beautifully done. Originally published under Bunn's pen name, Thomas Locke, in 1995.

YA ★ BYERS, STEPHEN J. *The Life of Your Time.* **2001. Selah, paper. 151 pp. ISBN 1-58930- 008-4.**

This send-up of quantum physics assumptions that there is no causality results in a sort of cross between Alan Lightman's *Einstein's Dreams* (1993) and Douglas Adams's *Restaurant at the End of the Universe* (1980). There's a protagonist, sort of: sixth-grader Percival Weckbaugh of Central City, Missouri, an extremely polite young man. Percival begins to wonder about the meaning of life when a random number, whom Byers treats as a character with the name 1314, willfully rebels against the tyranny of Blind Chance and Chaos and causes several coincidences. Each of these coincidences corresponds with crucial moments in the lives of Byers' several small-town characters, all of whom are affectionately and subtly drawn.

CARD, ORSON SCOTT (See also chapter 14, "Mormon Fiction," the "Science Fiction" section.)

EMPYRION SAGA

★ *The Search for Fierra.* 1996. (Originally published in 1985.) Zondervan, paper. 480 pp. ISBN 0-310-20509-3.

Orion Treet, a journalist, arrives on the planet Fierra through a wormhole, commissioned to observe and record goings-on in a new colony, Empyrion. Turns out that Empyrion is not a new colony but an old, dying civilization on the brink of civil war. Orion and his odd companions land at Dome, a domed city at the edge of a great desert. It grows clear that Dome is not only decadent but also evil, having for generations opted not for utopia but for collectivization and repression. Orion strikes off over the desert to enlist the aid of the possibly mythical Fieri to fight against Dome. The Fieri are a reasonable, peaceful race—the Christians, following the Infinite Father. They cannot believe war in imminent—and if it is, they still want no part of it.

The Siege of Dome. 1996. (Originally published in 1986.) Zondervan, paper. 480 pp. ISBN 0-310-20508-5.

Card relates the sequel to *The Search for Fierra* from several points of view as the battle between good and evil is joined. Orion becomes a voice in the wilderness, left alone to cry out that the Fieri will soon be annihilated by the Dome. He steals back into the dark city to study its past, where he finds clues to enable him to reverse the downward trends of the present. With the help of the Infinite Father, he resists the powerful mind-control forces of the evil one, Trabant Animus, and rallies the rebels of Empyrion.

YA ★ *ENDER WIGGINS SAGA*

Ender's Game. 1985. Tor, paper. 226 pp. ISBN 0-3128-5323-8.
Because of the imminent threat of attack, young Andrew "Ender" Wiggin is robbed of his childhood to train as a soldier in the battle school orbiting above his planet in *Ender's Game.* He is respected by his peers and his teachers alike, excels in strategic games, and rises to the top of his class. Soon he is promoted to the Command School, but he suffers from loneliness and fear of the aliens, and he misses his sister, Valentine, the only person who has ever seemed to understand him. Though Card's tale is a clever one bringing to mind the best of Robert Heinlein, its appeal is really that of a lonely boy making his way, a precocious boy who is not always likable. There is also an ongoing philosophical argument about when war is justified, rendered horrifically ironic when the race Ender all but exterminates turns out not to have been hostile. Winner of the Nebula and Hugo Awards.

Speaker for the Dead. 1986. Tor, paper. 382 pp. ISBN 0-8125-5075-7.
Ender is called to a planet settled by Portuguese Catholics to learn the secrets of an intelligent porcine race, the Pequeninas, or "Piggies." He hopes to redeem himself for his mistakes in *Ender's Game.* His unique ability is to divine the true natures of others, even of dead others, and take forth their essential messages in an almost godlike way. Winner of the Nebula and Hugo Awards.

Xenocide. 1991. Tor, paper. 592 pp. ISBN 0-8125-0925-0.
Xenocide continues the chronicles of conflict with the virus-plagued Pequeninas on the planet Lusitania, tying up plot lines, seemingly ending the series as a trilogy.

Children of the Mind. 1996. Tor, paper. 370 pp. ISBN 0-8125-2239-7.
A series that seemed to have ended with *Xenocide* continues with the imminent death of Ender. He moves his consciousness into other bodies, named after his brother and sister, to continue his work. The virus decimating Lusitania rages on, and a fleet from Earth is on its way to eradicate it by destroying the planet.

Ender's Shadow. 1999. Tor, paper. 379 pp. ISBN 0-3128-6860-X.
Ender's Shadow retells *Ender's Game* from a different point of view: that of a street kid, Bean, from a grim Rotterdam of the future. Bean is the illegal product of genetic experiments but, like Ender, a bona fide prodigy who takes over a street gang by the sheer power of his intelligence and then turns the gang toward good. His talents bring him to the attention of Battle School recruiters, and he becomes Ender's ally.

Shadow of the Hegemon. 2001. Tor. 384 pp. ISBN 0-312-87651-3.
In the sequel to *Ender's Shadow,* Bean is the military strategist for Peter, Ender's brother, who becomes hegemon, or ruler, of Earth.

HUGGINS, JAMES BYRON. *Leviathan.* 1995. Nelson. 400 pp. ISBN 0-7852-7709-9.
Scientists, tampering with the DNA of a Komodo dragon, fashion a monster of great intelligence, power, and evil.

HUNT, ANGELA ELWELL. *The Truth Teller*. 2000. Bethany, paper. 400 pp. ISBN 0-7642-2155-8.

Devin Sloane, a eugenics fanatic, secures a sample of a frozen early man he's convinced is genetically superior. Then he bribes a DNA researcher to clone the sample into Lara Godfrey, who, in her grief, has decided to bear a child from the frozen sperm of her late husband. Eventually, as a mother, Lara learns of the scheme and goes on the run to protect her child, Hunter, from the malevolent Sloane. Hunter is not the perfect expression Sloane imagined. But he's clearly extraordinary and possibly even divine, because he can tell when anyone is lying and seems able to deduce the innate truth of any circumstance. Though Hunt's characterizations are thin, she grapples provocatively with the ethical issues of cloning, eugenics, and even the perfectibility of man.

LANE, CHRISTOPHER. *Eden's Gate*. 1994. Zondervan, paper. 383 pp. ISBN 0-310-41161-0.

When, precisely, did humankind appear on Earth? In Lane's attempt to refute Darwin, an archaeologist discovers remnants of the first man and shortly thereafter, peering through a chimera, a gateway into the Garden of Eden.

★ LAWHEAD, STEPHEN R. *Dream Thief*. 1996. (Originally published in 1983.) Zondervan, paper. 480 pp. ISBN 0-310-20552-2.

To research the effects of prolonged space travel on sleep patterns, Spence Reston journeys to Earth's first space colony. Then his own sleep grows deeply troubled to the point that he feels his life is endangered. He knows this has something to do with the paraplegic, mystically powerful Dr. Hocking and flees the station for Mars, but his horrific dreams attack him again. Near death, he awakens deep inside the planet, and, in a stunning set of scenes in which he learns of life on ancient Mars, Spence discovers the truth about Dr. Hocking and of God's ultimate plan for him.

LEDFORD, JAN JOADARMEL. *The Cloning*. 2001. Millennium III, paper. 346 pp. ISBN 0-962522-06-6.

Elaina Gambrel, yet another of those fearless women reporters populating Christian fiction, agrees to "mother" the first cloned baby so she can write the story of the century. Meanwhile, a scientist once committed to cloning humans puts forth the evangelical case against it. The child is born, and seems to be perfectly healthy. Elaina is deeply moved, and leaves behind her agnosticism for deep belief. None of Ledford's characters are believable, but she lays out the cases for and against cloning with care.

MORROW, JAMES. *Towing Jehovah*. 1994. Harcourt. 371 pp. ISBN 0-15-190919-9.

Nebula Award-winner Morrow's *Towing Jehovah* is the mournfully satiric tale of a disgraced oil tanker captain hired by the angel Raphael to haul the two-mile-long corpse of God, floating in the Atlantic, to a grave in the Arctic. Morrow throws in send-ups of radical feminism, the Vatican, and hucksters both secular and religious. But despite Morrow's beautiful style, his novel never really ascends from shock value.

E ★ **OLSON, JOHN B., AND RANDALL INGERMANNSON.** *Oxygen.* **Bethany, paper. 288 pp. ISBN 0-7642-2442-5.**

YA Valkerie Jansen, a Christian physician, is a last-minute replacement for a crew undertaking the first mission to Mars. The mission has been heavily criticized in Congress, and, under great pressure to succeed, NASA cuts some corners. The launch and then the bootstrap toward Mars go wrong, and the spacecraft's ability to generate power, and thus to produce oxygen, are compromised. Olson and Ingermannson's rigorous attention to detail will bring to mind the *Apollo13* flight as Valkerie and Bob Kaganovske, the flight's "mechanic," battle time and a waning oxygen supply to reach a safe habitat on Mars.

E **SEDDON, ANDREW M.** *Red Planet Rising.* **1995. Crossway, paper. 240 pp. ISBN 0-89107-825-8.**

Seddon's wild Mars is in the process of being domesticated with hydroponics, biotechnology, and the slow manufacture of an atmosphere, but it is afflicted with many of the issues bedeviling Mother Earth. A New Age cult has arisen to take over the government by cloning key officials and imprinting the clones with instructions to persecute the planet's small band of Christians.

SCOTT, JEFFERSON

E *ETHAN HAMILTON*

YA *Virtu@lly Eliminated.* 1996. Multnomah, paper. 333 pp. ISBN 0-88070-885-9.
Scott introduces the Christian cyberhero Ethan Hamilton, who battles Patriot, a killer hiding out in virtual reality programs sometime in the near future and who, as Ethan draws nearer, threatens Ethan's own family. Scott draws the battle in black-and-white terms, with Ethan refining his faith in God even as Patriot grows more Satanic, and thus *Virtu@lly Eliminated* becomes a kind of spiritual warfare novel.

Terminal Logic. 1997. Multnomah, paper. 358 pp. ISBN 1-57673-038-7.
Ethan Hamilton, Christian cyberwarrior, returns for a second time, and again it seems he's fighting an evil genius. Instead, the renegade artificial intelligence programs appearing all over GlobeNet, sometimes causing death, appear to be generated by machine. As he pursues the matters still further, Ethan begins to suspect a malevolent intelligence after all, maybe even the Antichrist.

Fatal Defect. 1998. Multnomah, paper. 339 pp. ISBN 1-57673-452-8.
In league with Tamara Mark, a Christian bioengineer working for the GeneSys Corporation, Ethan Hamilton battles the spread of biological weapons in his third adventure. Tamara refuses orders to transform *botulin viris* into an airborne vector, the first skirmish in a battle against unscrupulous bioengineers, terrorists, and the nefarious White Corporation.

TYERS, KATHY

E *FIREBIRD*

YA Tyson is a busy writer and arrays too many characters and settings to do them all justice. Sometimes, one seems to be reading yet another episode of Star Wars—the print expression of which she has written for. Still, this is a solid series. The planet Netaia's rigid religion, with its terrestrial parallels, is intriguing, and Tyson's working out of a culture based on ruthless eugenics, an update of *Brave New World*, is conceptually clever.

Firebird. 1999. Bethany, paper. 240 pp. ISBN 0-7642-2214-7.
Lady Firebird Angelo, from the rich, powerful, but decadent planet Netaia, was born a
wastling, doomed to a glorious death in combat against the Ehretan Federate. But she's
captured and falls in love with General Brennen, a telepath of high order and member of
the Sentinels—the good guys of this galaxy.

Fusion Fire. 2000. Bethany, paper. 288 pp. ISBN 0-7642-2215-5.
Firebird joins the Sentinel cause to defeat a renegade band of powerful telepaths called
the Shuhr; the Sentinels are also allied with the "Eternal Speaker," or the "One" who
sang all worlds into existence.

Crown of Fire. 2000. Bethany, paper. 320 pp. ISBN 0-7642-2216-3.
The great war concludes in this last volume of Tyson's trilogy, featuring Terza, a young
eugenics technician who, in support of the war effort, is forced to bear a child the
old-fashioned way.

SPIRITUAL WARFARE

Whether he actually invented the form seems doubtful, but certainly the concept of spiritual
warfare was popularized by Frank Peretti in the mid-1980s, founding an entire subgenre of Christian
fiction. Though somewhat similar to apocalypse, that genre is mainly concerned with biblical prophecy.
Spiritual warfare has to do with the demons who are among us right now, often speaking with New
Age tongues.

DESERMIA, HELEN. *Shadow People.* **1995. Nelson, paper. 288 pp. ISBN 0-7852-7920-2.**
There are dead cats galore in San Diego, and reporter Susan Walker suspects cultists.

★ **GANSKY, ALTON.** *The Prodigy.* **2001. Zondervan, paper. 352 pp. ISBN 0-310-23556-1.**
Toby Matthews is a poor Appalachian boy with a supernatural talent for healing. Though his
empathy is highly developed, he's naive in most ways, and vulnerable. His mother tries to protect him, but at last the cruel world closes in, and she flees with Toby to California. Toby and
his mother are touchingly authentic through most of the novel, then they are swept up by an
unscrupulous promoter in scenes that could have come from a Frank Peretti novel.

HOFF, B. J. *Masquerade.* **1996. Bethany, paper. 222 pp. ISBN 1-55661-860-3.**
Danni St. John, a journalist, returns to her hometown of Red Oak, Alabama, to investigate the
criminal doings of one Reverend Ra, head of a New Age cult, the Colony, vaguely like the
Mooneys. She takes a job editing the Colony's newspaper, doing her best to mouth the party
line while snooping for dirt in her off-hours. At first Danni keeps her secrets from Sheriff Logan
McGarey, who also is suspicious of the cult. But as their paths cross, they fall in love and soon
are doing their investigating together. Hoff's tale lacks the bite and menacing intensity of
This Present Darkness, the novel it seems modeled after.

YA **KING, STEPHEN.** *Desperation.* **1999. (Originally published in 1996.) Diane Publishing. 690 pp. ISBN 0-7881-6597-6.**
Reviewers were universally in awe of *Desperation,* a companion to *The Regulators* (1996) and containing many of the same characters (who can die in one novel, and live in the other). *The Regulators* is a horror novel, and full of goo. But *Desperation* introduces, almost for the first time from King, God, who works his Old Testament will through 11-year-old David Carver. David is trapped with his parents and a worn-out but noble writer in Desperation, Nevada, and he battles against the demon Tak from *The Regulators.*

MCCUSKER, PAUL. *Catacombs.* **1997. Tyndale, paper. 296 pp. ISBN 0-8423-0378-2.**
Sometime not far in the future, a group of fugitive Christians running from persecution takes shelter in an abandoned mountain church, only to find their lives threatened by snow and a food shortage as they await the Christian underground's assistance. A scary, paranoid, but remarkably well-written exercise.   **▮Discussion▮**

MOSER, NANCY

▶ MUSTARD SEED

The Invitation. 1998. Multnomah, paper. 420 pp. ISBN 1-57673-115-4.
A group of ordinary people receives invitations to journey to Haven, Nebraska, for reasons that are initially mysterious, but they are enjoined to have faith like the mustard seed of Matthew 13:31. In Haven, the sojourners are each assigned a mentor, or angel, to identify the central problem in their lives, to correct it through the application of lots of Bible verses, and to journey into the world again on their divinely inspired missions.

The Quest. 1998. Multnomah, paper. 399 pp. ISBN 1-57673-410-2.
In the sequel to *The Invitation,* Haven has disappeared. But the sojourners pursue their new lives diligently and with qualified success: A would-be writer decides not to have an abortion; a TV station director takes stands against immoral programming; and, most grandly, the former governor of Minnesota becomes president. At one point, a la Peretti, Satan takes the form of a horrible demon, but by faith in God the group defeats him.

The Temptation. 1998. Multnomah, paper. 400 pp. ISBN 1-57673-734-9.
In the last volume of Moser's trilogy, the group gathers in Lincoln, Nebraska, for a reunion. Complacency has set in, and the Mustard Seeders take a dangerous pride in their own achievements. This is the essence of their temptation, inevitable and insidious, and their challenge is to bend themselves again to God's will and defeat Satan.

▶ ★ PERETTI, FRANK E.
YA A former Assembly of God minister with a degree in writing from the University of Iowa's prestigious Writers' Workshop, Peretti extended the range of Christian fiction from the gentle reads of Janette Oke to the anything-but-gentle realm of spiritual warfare with Crossway's publication of *This Present Darkness* in 1986. The novel was reviewed in publications as far from the evangelical camp as *The New Republic,* and pulled a readership of men and women alike.

Ironically, the stark originality of Peretti's graphic depiction of sin had grown stale 10 years later, after scores of imitators had tried their hand at spiritual warfare and Peretti had not significantly varied his formula: (1) a New Age threat, masking itself as tolerance and free thinking, arrives in a small town, (2) sinners and fence straddlers embrace the threat's rationalizations, (3) fundamentalist opposition rises, seemingly too late, and (4) the New Age threat, now seen to be a familiar evil, is defeated. But Peretti, often compared to Stephen King, can't be topped for horrific evangelical fantasy, and he's probably the best recommendation of all for Christian teenage boys.

The Oath. 1995. Word. 549 pp. ISBN 0-8499-1178-8.
Back in the 1880s, when Hyde River was a booming mining town, a fire-and-brimstone preacher was hanged, and the perpetrators then signed an oath embracing Reason as their god. After more than 100 years, their sins have grown into a monster—or, to be literal, a fire-breathing dragon. A wildlife biologist, Steve Benson, tracks the chimerical dragon, which toys with him and lets him go. Steve is himself the embodiment of reason but feels the weight of sin when he begins an affair with a married woman, a local deputy named Tracy. Judgment Day arrives and Steve, at last a believer, stands alone to do battle against the dragon, rather like Bilbo Baggins of the Lord of the Rings trilogy, except that Peretti writes with a grim fervor rather than playfulness.

Prophet. 1992. Crossway, paper. 416 pp. ISBN 0-89107-618-2.
By Peretti's standards a quiet novel and something of a departure, *Prophet* is about John Barrett, a TV news anchor and indifferent Christian who, in covering the political rally of a proabortion governor, is embarrassed when his father shows up in the crowd as an unruly pro-life demonstrator. Then his father is killed, and John can't buy the TV station's spin that the death was accidental. Challenged by his estranged son, John pursues the matter, and in the process begins to hear voices. Maybe he's crazy, or maybe God has a plan for him, but either way he's about to lose his job.

★ ***This Present Darkness/Piercing the Darkness.*** 1997. Inspirational Press. 813 pp. ISBN 0-88486-178-3.
In *This Present Darkness* a reporter, Bernice Krueger, and a minister, Hank Busche, suspect something has gone awry in their little college town when New Age courses pop up on the syllabus, there's a suicide, and a mysterious, malevolent stranger appears. They stumble onto a battle between horrid demons and tall, handsome angels right off a felt board. Not only is Ashton at stake but so is the entire world. Peretti juxtaposes his scary demons with the sad, realistic stories of the doomed for a genuinely creepy effect.

Bernice also appears in the sequel, but it is set in another small town and features Sally Beth Roe, an ex-hippie, who has tried every sort of pop solution to assuage her sad heart and is trying to put her demons, both literal and figurative, behind her. She's drawn into the plot of a New Age organization, thinly modeled on the ACLU, to shut down a Christian school on a trumped-up charge of child abuse. **Discussion**

The Visitation. 1999. Word. 400 pp. ISBN 0-8499-1179-6.
A miracle worker comes to a small Washington town, and a dispirited former pastor, Travis Jordan, slowly gathers his courage to fight against what at first only he sees to be a false prophet. Soon there are sightings of angels, supernatural communications in the sky, and most of the town rallies behind the frighteningly logical and effective false Christ (though not the Antichrist). Other false Christs arrive. There's a carnival atmosphere. Then things turn serious as the miracle worker's miracles go sour and his murderous nature is revealed. Travis Jordan, his faith renewed and with a small band of the faithful gathered around him, joins the battle.

TRAYLOR, ELLEN GUNDERSON. *The Priest.* 1998. Word, paper. 384 pp. ISBN 0-8499-4099-0.

Archaeology professor David Rothmeyer responds to a call from a group called "The Temple Consortium" that seeks to find a descendant in the line of Aaron—the only person qualified to be the High Priest of Israel in the proposed new temple. Because the temple would be erected on the site of the Dome of the Rock, Islamic groups are opposed to David's research. His life is threatened as he moves from Dachau to Oxford and back to the Mideast, piecing together clues. Thankfully, romance eases David's tensions with a British reporter after the Temple Consortium story, and with a Jewish woman on the run from a Montana militia that sees Jews as a threat to all things godly and white. In fact, the men of the militia are the most original part of Traylor's fast-paced tale; they are portrayed with intimacy and considerable detail.

WHITLOW, ROBERT. *The List.* 2000. Word. 400 pp. ISBN 0-8499-1640-2.

Renny Jacobson, a young lawyer distinguished only for his greed, has been relying on his expectation of a large inheritance upon his father's death, but the old man leaves only a membership in a mysterious group called the Covenant. Even then, there are some initiations to pass, but Renny, sensing millions at his disposal, is eager to pass them. The Covenant, he learns, was a pact rich Southern families made during the Civil War to ensure that they held onto their money. That sounds fine, but then Renny learns that the pact was really with the Devil. Renny isn't sure he cares until members of the Covenant start turning up dead, and he finds himself in love with a Christian woman mistakenly invited into the Covenant. Now the Covenant won't let him go, and Renny's life, not to mention his soul, is on the line.

TIME TRAVEL

CARD, ORSON SCOTT. *Pastwatch: The Redemption of Christopher Columbus.* 1996. Tor, paper. 416 pp. ISBN 0-8125-0864-5.

In the midst of the Columbus-debunking of the 1990s Card wrote this intriguing tale about the attempt of an academic group, Pastwatch, to alter their own miserable present (in the future, where the world is dying from environmental degradation) by changing the past. Three time travelers go in search of Christopher Columbus with a vision of how he should have treated the Indians, the key to establishing sequences to alter the rape of the Earth, which follows Columbus's famous voyages. But central is Columbus himself: a tormented, flawed, larger-than-life, but basically decent man who matures through the novel, entertains a deeply Christian vision, and grows wise.

★ **INGERMANSON, RANDALL.** *Transgression.* 2000. Harvest, paper, 406p. ISBN 0-7369-0195-7.

Ingermanson, a physicist, devises a playful first novel about time travel to the first century and a maniac, Damien West, who wants to kill Paul. West has determined, with the aid of that great scholar the Unabomber, that without Paul, Christianity would never have spread, and he despises Christianity for how it has persecuted Jews. Ingermanson's hero is Ari Kazan, a shy orthodox Jew of lapsed faith who is the time machine's inventor. Ari finds himself falling in love with Rivka Meyers, a Messianic Jew whom Damien sends into the past in the time machine's first trial.

Ari dives into the time machine to save Rivka, who is on the trail of Damien in an attempt to ruin his plot.

MOORCOCK, MICHAEL. *Behold the Man.* **1966. MoJo Press, paper. 130 pp. ISBN 1-885418-05-1.**

Karl Glogauer, an indecisive modern man plagued with a Christ complex, skips back to the time of Jesus and is befriended by John the Baptist and the Essene sect. But he cannot find Jesus and ends up standing in for him in this dour, often blasphemous, "New Wave" classic.

VIDAL, GORE. *Live from Golgotha.* **1992. Random. (Out of print.)**

A TV crew goes back in time to cover the Crucifixion in Vidal's irreverent, sometimes funny, decidedly unsubtle send-up of the gospel story, in this case supposedly related by Timothy.

Chapter 10

Mysteries and Thrillers

Christian mysteries mirror the concerns of mainstream efforts and break into the same categories. The quality of writing is comparable, though the field lacks any dominating presence, such as a Patricia Cornwell or Mary Higgins Clark.

In recent years, theoretically to appeal to men, Christian publishers have been marketing more thrillers, most of them written by men. The problem these thriller writers encounter is that the mainstream model for thrillers—and for many mysteries—presents a tough world, full of unsavory characters who drink, curse, and fornicate. Can one write a believable thriller without such elements? The answer is yes, but barely. Christian thriller writers walk a tightrope, with the ideal of sin-free writing on one side, sin on the other.

MYSTERIES

See also chapter 8, "Romance," the section "Romantic Suspense."

BENREY, RON, AND JANET BENREY. *Little White Lies.* **2001. Broadman and Holman, paper. 320 pp. ISBN 0-8054-2371-0.**

Britisher Pippa Hunnechurch, a one-woman headhunting firm, teams with the overly ambitious Marsha Morgan in the rather small lie of embellishing resumes. Then Pippa drowns in what is at first thought to be an accident. Another death inspires the interest of the police, and Pippa and Marsha's little fibs may have relevance. Another woman friend, a Christian, tells Pippa she has to come clean. But if Pippa admits she lied, she will do damage to her clients, not to mention her own career.

BLACKSTOCK, TERRI

⬛✝ *NEWPOINTE 911*

Blackstock's melodramatic series centers on emergency services in a small Mississippi town.

Private Justice. 1998. Zondervan, paper. 384 pp. ISBN 0-310-21757-1.
Firemen grumble about having to appear in the annual Fat Tuesday parade wearing clown outfits. But as a Christian, fireman Mark Branning objects to the parade because of the paganism of Mardi Gras. That paganism ties into the murder of two firemen's wives even as the parade proceeds. Mark goes running to see after his estranged wife, Allie, and together they solve the mystery and rediscover their faith in God.

Shadow of Doubt. 1998. Zondervan, paper. 304 pp. ISBN 0-310-21758-X.
Police officer Stan Shepherd dies from arsenic poisoning. Suspicions immediately are cast on his wife, Celia, because her first husband died much the same way.

Word of Honor. 1999. Zondervan, paper. 350 pp. ISBN 0-310-21759-8.
Attorney Jill Clark is taken hostage by a suspect in a bombing who swears his innocence. Meanwhile, Jill's boyfriend, fireman Dan Nichols, prays for Jill's deliverance but is frustrated in his desire to rescue her.

BLY, STEPHEN, AND JANET BLY

⬛✝ *HIDDEN WEST*

Husband-and-wife writers Tony and Price Shadowbrook, clearly modeled on the Blys, seek out less-traveled areas of the modern West to portray them for vacationers in this light, almost frolicsome series. The pair solve mysteries that partake both of the modern and historic West, and Stephen Bly's wit often shows through, spoofing Tony's other career—writing westerns.

Fox Island. 1996. Servant, paper. 245 pp. ISBN 0-89283941-4.

Copper Hill. 1997. Servant, paper. 242 pp. ISBN 0-89283973-2.

Columbia Falls. 1998. Servant, paper. 250 pp. ISBN 1-56955-069-7.

⬛✝ BROUWER, SIGMUND. *Out of the Shadows.* 2001. Tyndale. 350 pp. ISBN 0-8423-3037-2.

Several scenes in Brouwer's old-fashioned mystery—the attack of a rottweiler and a near drowning—will leave the reader in a cold sweat, though in many ways this is a mechanical effort for the accomplished Brouwer. He tells the story of Nick Barrett, an embittered man who returns from Arizona to his home in Charleston when summoned by an unsigned letter. Nick wants to solve the mystery of his mother's disappearance; he's been told she abandoned him to run off with another man. There's also the matter of the manslaughter death of a high school friend for which Nick took the rap.

⬛✝ BUNN, T. DAVIS. *One False Move.* 1997. Nelson, paper. 400 pp. ISBN 0-7852-7368-9.

Corporate executive Donovan Stone and reporter Claire Kingsbury join forces to investigate a mysterious conspiracy linking the use of a drug called Nova to an Internet game called Babylon. There's a love story, and Claire's faith is rekindled through her explorations, but teenagers as a race seem misrepresented here as unsavory and stupid, and Bunn sees the Devil in the cupboards and under every bush.

DICKSON, ATHOL

 GARR REED

Dickson's Texas accent and unpreachy, witty style will appeal to men and women alike. Garr Reed, a middle-aged, whimsical man, is drawn into mysteries that are almost Southern gothic.

> **Whom Shall I Fear?** 1996. Zondervan, paper. 349 pp. ISBN 0-310-20760-6.
> The pace of Garr Reed's lazy, enjoyable life is turned up a notch when he finds a fishing buddy dead and is accused of the murder. His wife, Mary Jo, a Christian who has suffered from his near agnosticism for years, stands by her man as he pieces out the truth.

> **Every Hidden Thing.** 1998. Zondervan, paper. 416 pp. ISBN 0-310-22002-5.
> Garr Reed is a new Christian in the sequel to *Whom Shall I Fear?* His faith is tested when Mary Jo is diagnosed with breast cancer and almost simultaneously charged with the murder of a priest and wounding of a doctor associated with an abortion clinic. Dickson takes the high road: examining all points of view and developing his quirky characters in depth.

GUTTERIDGE, RENE. *Ghost Writer.* 2000. Bethany, paper. 384 pp. ISBN 0-7642-2343-7.

In her first novel Gutteridge devises a powerful hook: Jonathan Harper, a highly successful fiction editor, begins to receive installments of a novel depicting his own life. Because his life is teetering on disaster, and because the serial novel's account of his childhood is so accurate, Jonathan is reduced to panic as he awaits scenes of the present. If all Gutteridge offered were this device, her novel would be a letdown, but she also turns in winning portraits of two minor characters: an old western writer, a friend of Jonathan's whose last novel Gutteridge serializes alongside Jonathan's life story; and a wonderfully idiosyncratic ghost writer, who can tackle anything from murder to grandparenting skills.

HALL, LINDA

April Operation. 1997. Bethel, paper. 268 pp. ISBN 0-934998-70-1.

New Brunswick Mountie Roger Sheppard investigates when Douglas Shanahan, a doctor who pioneered in setting up Canadian abortion clinics, is shot dead tending his flower garden. Simultaneously, the daughter of Emma Knoll, manager of Shanahan's clinic, is abducted. The Christian group responsible isn't very Christian, Hall concludes, in this fair-minded novel that deeply opposes abortion but considers all sides of the question and presents Sheppard and Knoll as multifaceted, caring people.

Island of Refuge. 1999. Multnomah, paper. 308 pp. ISBN 1-57673-397-1.

Like a dark Ann Tyler, Hall focuses on the misspent, unlucky lives of a handful of residents of an abandoned church on Lamb's Island, a quiet, unspoiled place off the coast of Maine. There's a minister who no longer preaches; an ex-flower child who tries to mother everyone; and a young woman, Jo, devoted to her baby. Almost accidentally, woebegone Peter arrives, acquitted of a murder charge but haunted all the same. Jo is kind to him, and then she's killed. Did Peter do it? If not Peter, who? Margot Douglas, owner of a fabric shop in nearby Vermont, hears of the murder, remembers poor Jo, and investigates.

◀▣✗★ *Katheryn's Secret.* 2000. Multnomah, paper. 305 pp. ISBN 1-57673-614-8.
Sharon Colebrook, called home to settle her aunt's estate, finds some unsettling references in the deceased woman's journals—a long-lost brother must be located, for one thing—but it seems that long ago there was a murder. As Sharon and her husband investigate, Sharon must deal with her father after their many years of estrangement, and she finds that his religious views, though still narrow and alienating, at last have some resonance.

◀▣✗★ *Margaret's Peace.* 1998. Multnomah, paper. 308 pp. ISBN 1-57673-216-9.
When Margaret Collinwood was a child, her sister fell to her death from an upstairs porch. Margaret inherits the family home, the scene of this tragedy, and welcomes life there for the escape it will offer. Her daughter has died, and her husband, angry and bereaved, has left. Hoping for solace in a quiet life by the Maine seashore, Margaret instead stumbles onto the true narrative of her sister's death, an ugly story that nonetheless brings an epiphany.

HOFF, B. J.

◀▣✗ *DAYBREAK MYSTERIES*
Jennifer Terry becomes executive assistant at a Christian radio station in Virginia, where she falls in love with her boss, Daniel Kaine. Daniel is a former Olympic gold medalist in swimming, now a Christian songwriter, and he's blind. The two marry and solve various tough mysteries, often putting their lives at risk.

> *Storm at Daybreak.* 1996. Tyndale, paper. 208 pp. ISBN 0-8423-7192-3.
>
> *The Captive Voice.* 1996. Tyndale, paper. 208 pp. ISBN 0-8423-7193-1.
>
> *The Tangled Web.* 1997. Tyndale, paper. 192 pp. ISBN 0-8423-7194-X.
>
> *Vow of Silence.* 1997. Tyndale, paper. 192 pp. ISBN 0-8423-7195-8.
>
> *Dark River Legacy.* 1997. Tyndale, paper. 189 pp. ISBN 0-8423-7196-6.

◀▣✗ ★ **LONG, DAVID RYAN.** *Ezekiel's Shadow.* 2001. Bethany, paper. 432 pp. ISBN 0-7642-2443-3.
Horror writer Ian Merchant's recent conversion fills him with guilt over the novels that have made his reputation. He has writer's block on his new novel. Then someone starts stalking him, and Ian suspects that the stalker is one of his characters. How can that be? A sculpture that alludes cryptically to a verse in Ezekiel may provide the answer.

★ MILLER, JANICE

◀▣✗ *ALEXIS ALBRIGHT*
This fine but short-lived series features a subtle interweaving of Hawaiian and traditional Japanese cultures as amateur sleuth Alexis Albright, a middle-aged woman whose husband has recently died, comes to terms with her nascent Christianity while thoughtfully examining Shinto traditions.

> *The Plum Blossoms.* 1994. Nelson, paper. 319 pp. ISBN 0-7852-8208-4.
>
> *The Jade Crucible.* 1995. Nelson, paper. 315 pp. ISBN 0-7852-7706-4.

NORDBERG, BETTE. *Pacific Hope.* 2001. Bethany, paper. 320 pp. ISBN 0-7642-2397-6.

Mike Langston, computer executive, and his wife, Kate, lead luxurious if hectic lives in Sausalito. Then someone mails Kate some photos showing Mike with another woman, Cara Maria Calloruso, a beautiful financial officer at Mike's company. There's more bad news: Kate's father has had a heart attack back home in Kansas. She hurries to join him, and Mike tries to regroup. But Kate won't talk to him, and now there's something criminally amiss at his company that Cara Maria and Mike's partner of 25 years seem responsible for. Nordberg doesn't know much about computers, and her idea of danger is eating doughnuts and bacon, but Mike and Kate's marriage seems real.

ROPER, GAYLE

◀▶ *AMHEARST MYSTERIES*

Merrileigh "Merry" Kramer, a reporter for a small paper in Pennsylvania, blunders through murder investigations in these light, amusing entertainments.

> *Caught in the Middle.* 1997. Zondervan, paper. 256 pp. ISBN 0-310-20995-1.

> *Caught in the Act.* 1998. Zondervan, paper. 272 pp. ISBN 0-310-21909-4.

> *Caught in a Bind.* 2000. Zondervan, paper. 320 pp. ISBN 0-310-21850-0.

RUSHFORD, PATRICIA

◀▶ *HELEN BRADLEY MYSTERIES*

Best known for her Jennie McGrady mystery series for juveniles, Rushford portrays the other end of life with Helen Bradley, a newly married grandmother who takes on freelance writing assignments that keep her on the trail of murder—and ghosts.

> *Now I Lay Me Down to Sleep.* 1997. Bethany, paper. 288 pp. ISBN 1-55661-730-5.

> *Red Sky in Mourning.* 1997. Bethany, paper. 239 pp. ISBN 1-55661-731-3.

> *A Haunting Refrain.* 1998. Bethany, paper. 254 pp. ISBN 1-55661-732-1.

> *When Shadows Fall.* 2000. Bethany, paper. 320 pp. ISBN 1-55661-733-X.

YA ★ **SCHUNK, LAUREL.** *Black and Secret Midnight.* 1998. St. Kitts. 239 pp. ISBN 0-9661879-0-3.

A literary mystery with strong allusions to *Macbeth* and *To Kill a Mockingbird,* Schunk's second novel features the nostalgic voice of 12-year-old Beth Anne Crane, a northern girl visiting her grandparents in 1951 Georgia. What at first seems mere eccentricity in her family at last shows itself to be insanity, and events take a racist and murderous turn. Although the story may be too short to bear such heavy freight, Schunk nonetheless brings her backwater time and place admirably to life, condemning it, loving it, and mourning its passing.

◀▶ ★ **SHAW, LOU.** *Honor Thy Son.* 1994. Abingdon, paper. 240 pp. ISBN 0-68709-982-X.

YA See discussion in chapter 15, "Young Adults." **█ Discussion**

SLEEM, PATTY. *Second Time Around.* **1995. PREP, paper. 336 pp. ISBN 1-885288-05-0.**
A seemingly content, married woman, Kathryn Haddad, begins a torrid affair with her ex while on a business trip. Sleem then spins the reader into cornucopian talk of relationships, middle age, and what serving God means in a chaotic world. Before the reader can quite make out what all this means, Kathryn returns home and is murdered. Which man did it, or was it either of them?

★ **SPRINKLE, PATRICIA**

◆✕ *MACLAREN YARBROUGH MYSTERIES*
The considerable charm of Sprinkle's series is all due to the narration of MacLaren Yarbrough, a brash and for Christian fare, salty, commentator on small-town Southern mores. She's the owner of Yarbrough Seed, Feed, and Nursery in Hopewell, Georgia.

> *When Did We Lose Harriet?* 1997. Zondervan, paper. 304 pp. ISBN 0-310-21194-4.
> Teenager Harriet Lawson comes up missing, and MacLaren Yarbrough isn't satisfied with the explanation why.

> *But Why Shoot the Magistrate?* 1998. Zondervan, paper. 320 pp. ISBN 0-310-21324-X.
> The popular youth pastor, Luke Blessed, becomes a suspect when a woman is murdered. The magistrate, MacLaren Yarbrough's husband, Joe Riddley Yarbrough, warns MacLaren off the case, but then he's shot and lies comatose, and she really goes to work.

STALLSMITH, AUDREY

◆✕ *The Body They May Kill.* 1995. Nelson, paper. 204 pp. ISBN 0-7852-7713-7.
A beloved minister, sipping from the Communion cup, falls dead from poison, and the local, reasonably competent police officer investigates. Stallsmith has the wit and knack for characterization of English cozies: In particular, there's the quirky Genna Leon, a down-to-earth woman who, when courted by a local farmer, can't understand why he'd be interested.

◆✕ ★ *THYME WILL TELL*

> *Rosemary for Remembrance.* 1998. WaterBrook, paper. 294 pp. ISBN 1-57856-040-3).
> Whether with the heroine's catty sister or the small-town cop who affects arrogance but used to stutter, Stallsmith is deft at creating real characters. And her sleuth, the mild Regan Culver, can't utter a line that isn't ironic: She laments the fact that she can't "even occupy center stage at her own arrest"—this for the alleged murder of her own father with poisoned tea. Speaking of a nosy reporter who "had come from a big-city paper" to Culver's small Pennsylvania town, she suggests that "tact was not an important element in her style."

> *Marigolds for Mourning.* 1998. WaterBrook, paper. 290 pp. ISBN 1-57856-054-3.
> Following the opener, Stallsmith turns her dry wit to the death of a football star.

> *Roses for Regret.* 1999. WaterBrook, paper. 291 pp. ISBN 1-57856-145-0.
> Regan Culver presides over the offbeat, in the end deadly, feud between rival factions of a rose society.

◆✕ ★ **VAUGHN, ELLEN.** *The Strand.* **1997. Word. 320 pp. ISBN 0-8499-1328-4.**
A repressed suburban woman, Anne Lorelli, is confronted with the Capitol's seamy side when a mugging escalates and her husband is murdered. Recovering from shock, Anne feels surprise and guilt that she doesn't miss her late, rather secretive husband. She pays a visit to the Holocaust Museum, is deeply moved, and resolves to do something useful with her life.

She volunteers at an inner-city school, becomes involved with several of the students, and find herself enjoying life again. Romance is slowly kindled with the detective working the murder case, even though he at first suspects Anne. A solid, graceful effort by Charles Colson's sometime collaborator.

Gumshoe Detective

◄E► ★ **BELL, JAMES SCOTT.** *Blind Justice.* 2000. Broadman and Holman, paper. 384 pp. ISBN 0-8054-2161-0.

Like many a gumshoe before him, Jake Denny, a lawyer, has a problem with alcohol. His wife has divorced him because of it, and he teeters on being disbarred because of one too many drunken court appearances. A childhood friend, Howie Patino, appeals to Howie to defend him on the charge he murdered his wife. The case seems open and shut against Howie, a slightly retarded fellow, and when Jake shows up drunk once more, he dooms his client. Chided by Howie's pretty sister, Lindsay, and overwhelmed with guilt, Jake finally pulls himself together. He finds himself in the midst of Devil worship and black magic—and sees a clear path toward establishing Howie's innocence. Lindsay by his side, Jake goes on the spiritual warpath.

DAVIS, WALLY

◄E► *GIL BECKMAN*

Ex-cop Gil Beckman, a bachelor down on his luck, takes a job as security guard for what turns out to be the most accident-prone amusement park in the world. The series is charming, nonetheless, mostly because of Beckman's laconic, self-deprecatory wit. The atmosphere of the series is lent great authority by Davis's many years in law enforcement.

> *Suspended Animation.* 1994. Crossway, paper. 192 pp. ISBN 0-89107-802-9.
>
> *Victim of Circumstance.* 1995. Crossway, paper. 208 pp. ISBN 0-89107-843-6.
>
> *Black Dragon.* 1995. Crossway, paper. 192 pp. ISBN 0-89107-870-3.
>
> *Drastic Park.* 1997. Crossway, paper. 190 pp. ISBN 0-89107-962-9.

FUNDERBURK, ROBERT

◄E► ★ *DYLAN ST. JOHN*

Funderburk models Dylan St. John on Raymond Chandler's Philip Marlowe. He's a master of sarcastic one-liners, has a weakness for the bottle, and yet also he's a knight-errant, determined to behave honorably in a corrupt world. That world is the violent city of New Orleans, and the wider world of the late 1960s, where every value Dylan has thought worth fighting for is under attack from the draft-dodging, drug-addicted, left-leaning young.

> *The Fires of Autumn.* 1996. Bethany, paper. 253 pp. ISBN 1-55661-614-7.
> Dylan tries to win back his beautiful wife, Susan, who could take no more of his boozing or his soul-searching over the misbegotten conduct of the Vietnam War, of which he is a veteran. Dylan loves his wife deeply, and eventually he pulls himself together while running down the mystery of why one-time offender juveniles are disappearing, and why high state officials are involved.

All the Days Were Summer. 1997. Bethany, paper. 205 pp. ISBN 1-55661-615-5.
Dylan patches things up with Susan in the sequel to *The Fires of Autumn*. Eager for a fresh start, the two move to Cajun Country, which Funderburk portrays authentically and with much affection. But then someone assassinates the mayor, and the sleepy country life veers into the fast lane.

Winter of Grace. 1998. Bethany, paper. 221 pp. ISBN 1-55661-616-3.
By the third entry of the Dylan St. John series, Dylan counts on his solid marriage. Susan is about to give birth. Dylan's old devils are mostly vanquished, so he can track down bank robbers with his self mostly intact.

The Spring of Our Exile. 1999. Bethany, paper. 221 pp. ISBN 1-55661-617-1.
By the series's last entry, however, Dylan's marriage is strained once again when he saves a woman from assault. She turns out to be his old high school sweetheart, an actress returned to Louisiana to scout locations. Funderburk's years of experience as a probation officer and his deep love of Louisiana shine through.

MORRIS, GILBERT

◆⧓★ *DANIELLE ROSS*
Danielle "Dani" Ross takes over her father's private investigation agency with trusty, taciturn Ben Savage at her side. Dani feels the need to witness to criminals, which grows tiresome at times, and strains credulity. But the New Orleans setting, which Morris knows well, gumshoe conventions, and Dani's cases involving headliner issues such as right-wing militia and environmental abuses make this an easy series to like. Mild romances arise in each entry.

Crossway reprinted two of the Dani Ross mysteries in 2000: *The Final Curtain* became *The End of Act Three*, and *Guilt by Association* became *One by One*. Crossway also issued two titles new to the series, noted below.

Guilt by Association. 1991. Revell, paper. 348 pp. ISBN 0-8007-5395-X.

The Final Curtain. 1991. Revell, paper. 320 pp. ISBN 0-8007-5411-5.

Deadly Deception. 1992. Revell, paper. 320 pp. ISBN 0-8007-5419-0.

Revenge at the Rodeo. 1993. Revell, paper. 316 pp. ISBN 0-8007-5457-3.

The Quality of Mercy. 1993. Revell, paper. 312 pp. ISBN 0-8007-5474-3.

Race with Death. 1994. Revell, paper. 288 pp. ISBN 0-8007-5498-0.

And Then There Were Two. 2000. Crossway, paper. 285 pp. ISBN 1-58134-193-8.

Four of a Kind. 2000. Crossway, paper. 264 pp. ISBN 1-58134-244-6.

Historical Mysteries

 DOW, ROSEY. *Reaping the Whirlwind.* **2000. Wine Press, paper. 408 pp. ISBN 1-57921-296-4.**

 No mainstream publication reviewed Dow's novel, but it certainly didn't pass unnoticed in the evangelical community, winning a Christy in 2001. Dow revisits the Scopes, or "monkey," trial of 1923, wrapping it in a murder mystery and portraying both John Scopes, the high school teacher who was the focus of the trial, and fundamentalist lawyer William Jennings Bryan with great sympathy.

MITCHELL, SARA

⬤✕ *SHADOW CATCHERS*

Mitchell's series features Pinkerton detectives. A third novel, *Ransomed Heart* (p. 106) seems part of the series but was not designated as such; it is more of a western than a mystery.

> ***Trial of the Innocent.*** 1995. Bethany, paper. 336 pp. ISBN 1-55661-497-7.
> In 1893, Eve Sheridan grows suspicious of the man her sister has married when he whisks her away to a remote part of England. When her sister's letters begin to seem guarded and fearful, Eve teams with Pinkerton detective Alexander MacKay to ferret out what's going on.

> ***In the Midst of Lions.*** 1996. Bethany, paper. 320 pp. ISBN 1-55661-498-5.
> The second entry of the Shadow Catchers series features a new heroine, Elizabeth Granger, a Southern governess struggling to overcome a blemish on the family name, and a new Pinkerton detective, Simon Kincaid, who is on the trail of evil associated with Elizabeth's employer, railroad man Horatio Crump.

WALKER, JIM

⬤✕ *MYSTERIES IN TIME*

YA

> ***Murder on the Titanic.*** 1998. Broadford & Holman, paper. 487 pp. ISBN 0-8054-0198-9.
> Walker is always entertaining, and his research skills are impressive, though sometimes his reliance on stock plot devices does him in, as in the first of this likable series. A young American reporter, the upright (and rich) Morgan Fairfield, falls in love with the daughter of a lord, but she throws him over for a snobbish Britisher. As he tries to figure how to win the lady back, Morgan is drawn into a spy plot with a courier for the American War Department. The courier is murdered, and the great ship goes down, more or less at the same time. Later, melodrama triumphs as Morgan learns the true identity of the courier.

> ***Voices from the Titanic.*** 1999. Broadman and Holman, paper. 480 pp. ISBN 0-8054-1771-0.
> In the sequel to *Murder on the Titanic,* survivor Morgan reports on the aftermath of the disaster for the *New York Herald,* interviewing other survivors. Then he teams with a veteran reporter to investigate a series of murders that seem connected to the disaster and possibly to the intrigue he found himself involved with in the first book.

> ★ ***Murder at Gettysburg.*** 1999. Broadman and Holman, paper. 480 pp. ISBN 0-8054-1970-5.
> The third in Walker's series is a first-rate mystery. It's about young April Wolff, who learns that her father has been murdered, possibly by a Confederate general, as the Confederate army moves toward Gettysburg. April rides to the Confederate camp and demands an investigation. Major Will Chevalier, a straight shooter who is in some ways defending Southern honor, does his best. April is at his side and the two are attracted despite the circumstances, and even as the battle rages.

Murder at Pearl Harbor. 2000. Broadman and Holman, paper. 480 pp. ISBN 0-8054-2160-2.
A Christian naval intelligence officer, Gwen Williams, is tracking the origin of a Hono-
lulu radio transmission regarding the location of U.S. ships when her colleague, Japanese
American Aki Kawa, is murdered. Gwen joins forces with her sweetheart, hard-hitting
reporter Sam Diamond, and Aki Kawa's sweetheart, Navy Lieutenant Brian Picard, to
find the killer. Walker offers up an array of spies, spoiled rich kids, native Hawaiians,
and historical figures such as the beleaguered commander of the Pacific Fleet, Admiral
Husband Kimmel. All are all thinly drawn, but Walker skillfully evokes the climate of
racism toward Japanese Americans in pre-war Hawaii.

★ *October Dawn.* 2001. Broadman and Holman, paper. 480 pp. ISBN 0-8054-2324-9.
The fifth in Walker's Mysteries in Time series features Johnny Pera, a WWII hero who
experienced a battlefield conversion, renounced the business of his Mafioso family and
became a minister. The death of his father, possibly involved in a plot to kill Fidel Castro
shortly after the Bay of Pigs, draws Johnny back to his family as he seeks the truth among
Cuban Freedom Fighters in the Everglades. Meanwhile, the Cuban Missile Crisis boils
over, which Walker effectively portrays with scenes in the Oval Office between President Kennedy and Soviet Foreign Minister Andrei Gromyko, leaving off with the hint
that a future novel in the series may concern the Kennedy assassination.

Medical Mysteries

CUTRER, WILLIAM, AND SANDRA GLAHN

◀█✕ *Lethal Harvest.* 2000. Kregel, paper. 417 pp. ISBN 0-8254-2371-6.
Cutrer and Glahn's thriller centers on the disappearance of Tim Sullivan, a partner with three
physicians running a fertility clinic in Washington, D.C. Sullivan is related to the current
president, and like him carries a recessive gene for akenosis, a neurological disease that results
in quick deterioration of motor function. When the disease begins to affect the president,
Sullivan's death is faked by government operatives, and he begins accelerated research into
akenosis using DNA implantation techniques, becoming a sort of mad scientist in the process.
In a subplot, one of Sullivan's partners confuses clones of discarded eggs (which, unknown to
him, Sullivan was using for research) with the correct eggs for implantation, and twins that
are clones of their mother result. A lawsuit arises, and the clinic is bombed, the mysteries of
which fall to the third partner, Ben McCay, an obstetrician and chaplain, to unravel.

Deadly Cure. 2001. Kregel, paper. 384 pp. ISBN 0-8254-7047-1.
In the sequel to *Lethal Harvest,* Ben McCay acquires a disease that only Tim Sullivan's procedures of cell regeneration, verified illegally and resulting in his death, can treat.   ■ Sequel ■

GANSKY, ALTON

◀█✕ *RIDGELINE MYSTERIES*
Dr. Gates McClure, a single woman who hasn't had time for love, operates a general practice in a
small town named Ridgeline. Her cases turn into mysteries built around hot-button ethical topics.

Marked for Mercy. 1998. Chariot Victor, paper. 326 pp. ISBN 1-56476-678-0.
Dr. Gates McClure meets an acquaintance from medical school, Dr. Norman Meade.
Norman has changed. Gansky models him after Dr. Kavorkian, or "Dr. Death," because
Norman now undertakes going about the country assisting with highly publicized
mercy killings. Gates doesn't approve but sets her feeling aside when her old acquain-
tance is accused not of a mercy killing, but of murder.

A Small Dose of Murder. 1999. Chariot Victor, paper. 323 pp. ISBN 1-56476-679-9.
In the second Ridgeline Mystery, several of Dr. Gates McClure's patients die. Because their illnesses had not appeared fatal, she's baffled, and the autopsy reports don't shed new light. She begins to suspect murder, but if so, someone has found the perfect method. Could the curious deaths have anything to do with a local biotech firm?

KRAUS, HARRY LEE

Kraus, a practicing surgeon, always turns in crisp, authentic hospital scenes, and he never forgets what, in the end, motivates doctors: the desire to help their patients.

His first two novels, *Stainless Steal Hearts* and *Fated Genes* (discussed in this section), feature creaky plots and strained imagery. Kraus is didactic, and his love stories often are less than memorable. But beginning with *Lethal Mercy,* his characterizations become more personal and finely textured, the stories themselves somewhat subtler, the didacticism in better control.

★ *The Chairman.* 1999. Crossway, paper. 496 pp. ISBN 1-58134-038-9.
The title character is Ryan Hannah, a neurosurgeon working on a radical new nerve generation therapy that may have an immediate application for Nathan McAllister, a quadriplegic cop whose spine was severed by a bullet in a drug raid. Nathan steals the show as he struggles with the simplest of physical tasks. He sinks into depression, wondering if his wife, Abby, wouldn't be better off without him. Ironically, before Nathan was injured, Abby was having an affair with his best friend, but Nathan doesn't remember any of it. He has amnesia—a weak bit of plotting, but it gives great depth both to Abby's guilt and Nathan's plight. Questions of faith are posed realistically as Nathan wonders why God could have allowed him to be crippled and whether—when it begins to seem the chairman's therapy will not be successful—he should seek out a faith healer.

Fated Genes. 1996. Crossway, paper. 382 pp. ISBN 0-89107-877-0.
Brad Forrest, a smart young resident, saves the life of Web Tyson's son and is shortly on the fast track for employment at Crestview Women's and Children's Hospital, where Tyson is head of Surgery. Meanwhile, the ruthless Lenore Kingsley, who heads up a nasty pharmaceutical firm doing research with fetal tissue, has engineered the murder of the current surgeon-general so that she can install someone more sympathetic to her aims in the post, namely, Web Tyson. Can Brad risk his fledgling career to blow the whistle on all this and everything else he knows is wrong? As in his first novel, Kraus's didactic asides on health care rationing (which seemed a bigger issue when the novel was written than it turned out to be), insurance companies, abortion, and the like grow shrill. But the medical procedures, the doctors, the nature of medical marriage all ring true.

★ *Lethal Mercy.* 1997. Crossway, paper. 384 pp. ISBN 0-89107-821-1.
There's never much doubt who killed outspoken right-to-lifer Dr. Jake Hampton's pregnant wife, nor who Jake's next wife will be. On the other hand, the culprit, a paranoid schizophrenic thrown to the winds when funding for indigent care wanes, is sensitively drawn, Kraus's medical scenes are compelling, and Jake's grief is movingly evoked.

★ *The Stain.* 1997. Crossway, paper. 424 pp. ISBN 0-89107-972-6.
One truly feels the agony of Seth Berringer as he struggles in vain to save a wounded boy. Berringer himself is appealing, as a man unlucky in love, dissatisfied with his practice, and barely ahead of the hounds of managed care. Fearing his career is about to go down, Berringer makes two bad decisions and plunges into disaster.

Stainless Steal Hearts. 1994. Crossway, paper. 412 pp. ISBN 0-89107-810-X.
The awkward title is the first clue to the awkwardness of the novel itself: Kraus's didactic handling of the themes of abortion and DNA research using fetal tissue, wooden dialogue between lovers, and far-fetched plot twists. The story is about a corrupt doctor, overcome by ambition, who arranges with a doctor who performs abortions to keep the fetuses for research—and to "steal" their hearts to transplant into infants with heart defects. The politician, running for governor, needs an abortion for one of his mistresses, and he needs it quick. Christian practitioner Matt Stone intervenes when the pregnant woman dies in an accident, but he saves the baby.

◀█✕ **STEWART, ED.** *Terminal Mercy.* **1999. Tyndale, paper. 368 pp. ISBN 0-8423-7039-0.**
The medical plot here, of crazed surgeons doing mercy killings of patients with bad DNA, seems contrived in the extreme, but Stewart's hero, Jordan Keyes, is an interesting study. Jordan is a fine surgeon, but abrupt and self-righteous with his colleagues. He was fired in Los Angeles and now is trying to make his way in Oregon, while his wife, still in Los Angeles, wonders if there is anything worth saving in their marriage. The reader may wonder that, too, but Jordan becomes more sympathetic as his story unfolds, and when his patients begin dying in post-op, the reader will rally to his dilemma.

Pastors As Sleuths

DELFFS, D. J.

◀█✕ *GRIFFIN REED*
Father Griffin Reed ("Father Grif") is the widowed rector for a small college in the theoretically bucolic Tennessee hills, but murders keep happening. The amiable Grif is aided by Dr. Caroline Barr, an English professor whose steady support gradually turns to love.

> ***The Martyr's Chapel.*** 1998. Bethany, paper. 319 pp. ISBN 0-7642-2086-1.
> The victim is a famous playwright, writer-in-residence at the school, whose body is found in the Martyr's Chapel, a place of refuge and rest for pilgrims.
>
> ***The Judas Tree.*** 1999. Bethany, paper. 320 pp. ISBN 0-7642-2087-X.
> Another academic is found dead in the sequel to *The Martyr's Chapel.* He's hanging from a famous old oak tree, and his death seems linked to the quiet Amish community nearby.

GANSKY, ALTON. *By My Hands.* 1996. Victor, paper. 325 pp. ISBN 1-56476-534-2.
In Gansky's first novel, miraculous healings at San Diego Regional Hospital have everyone puzzled. Then those healed begin to disappear, adding to the puzzlement. Pastor Adam Bridgers undertakes an investigation that soon turns dangerous.

KRITLOW, WILLIAM

◀█✕ *LAKE CHAMPLAIN MYSTERIES*
Bumbling, likable Win Brady is gently kicked out of seminary to become an assistant pastor in cold Vermont, on the shores of Lake Champlain.

> ★ ***Crimson Snow.*** 1995. Thomas Nelson, paper. 320 pp. ISBN 0-7852-8098-7.
> As Win Brady fumbles about trying to discover what he's supposed to do as assistant pastor of Sugar Steeple Church, he's confronted with a murder on church grounds. Win solves the murder and in the process falls in love with a local cop, attracted to him despite his seeming incompetence in this endearing opener to the series.

Fire on the Lake. 1996. Nelson, paper. 288 pp. ISBN 0-7852-8099-5.
Even as Win and his fiancée, Ginger, the cop he met in *Crimson Snow,* plan their wedding, Win is drawn into an investigation of the drowning of a parishioner on Lake Champlain. If the sudden appearance of DEA agents means anything, the drowning was a murder, and drugs are involved.

Blood Money. 1997. Nelson. 288 pp, ISBN 0-7852-8027-8.
Kritlow's series runs out of gas in this third entry of the Lake Champlain mysteries. Win and Ginger, still planning their marriage, come to the aid of a friend, Bray Sanderson. Bray has received a wonderful inheritance, but it seems to make him a target for murder.

PARKER, GARY E.

⧫✕★ *BURKE ANDERSON*
Burke Anderson is a bachelor pastor in Georgia whose congregation votes away his position when he's accused of murder. Parker shows an understanding of a broad range of characters, but it's really his assured settings, as compelling in portraits of the small-town South as with the complicated politics of Atlanta, that make this a superior series.

Beyond a Reasonable Doubt. 1994. Nelson, paper. 253 pp. ISBN 0-8407-4148-0.
On the night of Burke Anderson's birthday, his old college roommate—who became a pro football player with the Falcons—mysteriously appears, then whisks Burke away to deposit him at the door of a beautiful prostitute. Next thing Burke knows, he's home, and he sees on TV that the prostitute has been murdered—and that his Bible was lying beside her! A mystery unfolds as Burke races to establish his innocence, but what may be the most winning quality of Parker's story is his gentle satire—of Burke's congregation, as they meet to oust their pastor, and of the behind-the-scenes maneuvering of two reporters, who are only slightly less cynical than their criminal quarries.

Death Stalks a Holiday. 1996. Nelson, paper. 288 pp. ISBN 0-7852-7784-6.
As Burke is settling into marriage with Debbi, the journalist he met in *Beyond a Reasonable Doubt,* he's startled by the news of four women's murders on four consecutive Sundays. The police are stumped, but Burke understands that the wounds of the victims resemble those Jesus received on the cross. Still, what does it mean, and can he figure it all out before another woman dies?

Dark Road to Daylight. 1997. Nelson, paper. 252 pp. ISBN 0-7852-7785-4.
In the last of the Burke Anderson mysteries, Burke gets in the middle of a child-custody battle and an apparent kidnapping when Bethany Chapman's daughter comes up missing.

See also chapter 12, "Catholic Fiction," the section "Nuns and Priests as Sleuths," and chapter 11, the section "Pastors."

Serial Killers

⧫✕ ★ **BROUWER, SIGMUND.** *Blood Ties.* **1996. Word. 304 pp. ISBN 0-8499-1294-6.**
In 1973, Clay Garner, rookie FBI agent, comes to Kalispell, Montana, to investigate a train derailment and finds himself on the trail of a serial killer. After a grueling,

scary manhunt, the killer is apprehended, or is he? Brouwer jumps to 1995 when the killings begin again in this compelling examination of absolute evil and the steadfast, good actions that can overcome it.

◆✕ **MINSHULL, EVELYN.** *Familiar Terror.* **1997. Baker, paper. 240 pp. ISBN 0-8010-5698-5.**
Paula, a minister's wife, is exhibiting her paintings at a craft fair when she and her friend Dee discover the brutally murdered body of a retired church organist. In the wake of other recent murders, it soon becomes clear that a serial killer is at work. Minshull does a fine job portraying her quintessential small town, shaken to its roots when it realizes the killer is one of its own.

THRILLERS

◆✕ **BELL, JAMES SCOTT.** *The Nephilim Seed.* **2001. Broadman and Holman, paper. 375 pp. ISBN 0-8054-2438-5.**
Lawyer Janice Ramsey is battling for custody of her daughter, Lauren, when Lauren is kidnapped. All signs point to Janice's strange ex, a rich sinner who has been experimenting with his own genes. The didactic Bell equates such manipulation with demon possession, and Janice's ex is therefore devilish. In a subplot, a saintly creationist is killed by an evil scientist who is in the business of DNA experimentation. The creationist's brother, a bounty hunter named Jed Brown, tracks the killer, and Janice joins forces with him along the trail because the evil scientist appears also to be the kidnapper.

◆✕ **BRIGGS, DEAN.** *The God Spot.* **1999. Word, paper. 480 pp. ISBN 0-8499-37334-5.**
Briggs fashions his slow-moving political/medical thriller around the notion that a pineal gland anomaly sometimes expresses one's conversion to Christianity or one's longtime faith. His researchers measure the growth of new cells in a deceased Arab researcher, Abu Hasim El-Saludin, after his conversion, leaving open the question of whether this "scientific" anomaly excludes Jews, Mormons, Catholics, and Hindus.

◆✕ **BURKETT, LARRY, AND T. DAVIS BUNN.** *Kingdom Come.* **2001. Nelson. 336 pp. ISBN 0-7852-6770-0.**
FBI agent Ben Atkins is dispatched to investigate Kingdom Come, a religious community in North Carolina that is walling itself off from the world Waco-style, fencing in its considerable properties, buying out businesses for miles around. But is Kingdom Come a dangerous cult, or simply a band of devout evangelicals brought together in momentous times? Evil doings are afoot, but Ben soon sees they aren't coming from the 6,000 families of the compound; another force entirely is trying to bring down Kingdom Come.

GANSKY, ALTON

◆✕ *BARRINGSTON RELIEF*

★ *Terminal Justice.* 1998. WaterBrook, paper. 356 pp. ISBN 1-57856-023-3.
After his wife leaves him for another worker in the church, David O'Neal, demoralized, hires on as a speechwriter for A. J. Barrington, director of the international food charity, Barringston Relief. O'Neal soon discovers not all is as it seems: There are murders in

Somalia and mysterious deaths at sea, and Barringston himself may be involved. Soon O'Neal finds himself working with the FBI and against his own boss.

Tarnished Image. 1998. WaterBrook, paper. 358 pp. ISBN 1-57856-046-2. In the less-satisfying sequel to *Terminal Justice,* O'Neal has become head of Barringston Relief. He soon finds himself in much the same situation as his predecessor, involved in a seemingly irrefutable frame implicating him in the smuggling of illegal aliens, and having an illicit affair.

◆✕ *J. D. STANTON MYSTERIES*
Gansky's J. D. Stanton is a retired naval officer turned sleuth in this series that is long on suspense but short on characterization.

A Ship Possessed. 1999. Zondervan, paper. 329 pp. ISBN 0-312-21944-2. Out of nowhere, a missing WWII submarine reappears.

Vanished. 2000. Zondervan, paper. 352 pp. ISBN 0-310-22003-3. A top secret military base suddenly disappears.

GOFF, WALTER. *Chain of Command.* 1998. Word. 360 pp. ISBN 0-8499-1454-X.
Bill Chandler is so shaken by his wife's death that he can hardly do his job. He's a computer geek working for the Defense Department who has invented a radical new form of communications. Cautioning him he needs to pull himself together soon, his boss sends Bill to a seaside cabin to recuperate, where immediately he rescues a beautiful woman, Holly James, from drowning. But is her appearance wholly an accident? Bill nurses her back to health, and she's the cure for what's been ailing him. She also has ties to the State Department and some ugly Middle-eastern men who are very interested in Bill's invention.

◆✕ ★ HALL, LINDA. *November Veil.* 1996. Evangel, paper. 247 pp. ISBN 0-934998-68-X.
The murder of a televangelist forces a small-town school principal, Mary Jones, to confront her bitter past: When she was a young single woman, she found herself pregnant, and no help was forthcoming from her father, a preacher and the dead televangelist-to-be. Events escalate when Mary discovers she is being stalked, and suspects the stalker to be the son she gave up for adoption. Hall tells a suspenseful tale that rebukes a legalistic religion that would cause a young woman's mistakes to cast her out of her church.

JACOBSEN, CLAY

◆✕ *The Lasko Interview.* 1998. Broadman and Holman, paper. 392 pp. ISBN 0-8054-1660-9.
Wade Bennett, eminent director of *The John Herald Show,* is dead, apparently by his own hand. Rick Treadway, a down-on-his-luck TV director, is almost ashamed of the hope he feels when he's given Wade's job. But it's still a piece of luck, and combined with his new understanding of what it means to be a Christian, it seems he's turning his life around. Before long, he's drawn into danger as two tenacious detectives demonstrate that Bennett's death resulted from murder, not suicide. Wade was about to air an interview exposing the network's connection to a kingpin of pornographic movies and prostitution, and more than one highly placed mogul didn't want him to.

◀▷ *Circle of Seven.* 2000. Broadman and Holman, paper. 392 pp. ISBN 0-8054-2283-8.
In the loose sequel to *The Lasko Interview,* Jacobsen takes up the much-ballyhooed issue of liberal bias in the media. The story again features Rick Treadway, his girlfriend Cassie, and the amazing, voyeuristic Samantha Steel, who tempted the incorruptible Rick in the first novel. But the main character is Mark Taylor, a Christian reporter who risks his life to expose the Circle of Seven. They are a conspiratorial group of media moguls who maneuver political polling to falsely represent public opinion to legislators. ■ **Sequel** ■

LANE, CHRISTOPHER

◀▷ *Appearance of Evil.* 1997. Zondervan, paper. 432 pp. ISBN 0-310-21567-6.
Lane tells a bizarre tale, somewhat imitative of *The Silence of the Lambs,* the twist being that Lane's death-row inmate, Craig Hanson, is innocent. The one person who believes Craig is the naive public defender, Susan Grant, assigned to represent him in an 11th hour appeal. Craig is accused of satanic ritual abuse and animal abuse, but Suzan uncovers a malevolent plot on the part of the Christian psychiatric institute where Craig used to work. The institute reconstructs memories of Satanic abuse, then peddles them on the Internet as pornography. Behind all this is a nasty fellow calling himself Satan. As Satan harasses Susan, she finds the strength to resist by drawing upon her childhood faith.

◀▷ *Tonopah.* 1999. Zondervan, paper. 400 pp. ISBN 0-310-21568-4.
Tonopah is a desert north of Las Vegas. A Christian high school teacher, Melissa Lewis, stumbles into a restricted section of it called Quad 217, where one of her geology students discovers a T. rex and what appears to be a human bone. Someone is awfully angry about this, and marines, generals, and freelance thugs descend upon the area and attempt to steal Melissa's prehistoric trophies. *Tonopah* is a snappy and sometimes amusing thriller, though Lane seems obsessed with providing credibility for the science of creationism.

LOCKE, THOMAS (T. Davis Bunn)

◀▷ *The Delta Factor.* 1994. Bethany, paper. 240 pp. ISBN 1-55661-501-9.
The Pharmacon Corporation hides the dark side effects of their DNA treatments of viral disease, but brave researchers shine a light.

◀▷ *The Omega Network.* 1995. Bethany, paper. 250 pp. ISBN 1-55661-502-7.
Gambling interests get nasty for amateur sleuth Chase Bennett, on the trail of murder in Florida.

International Thrillers

◀▷ AUSTIN, LYNN. *Wings of Refuge.* 2000. Bethany, paper. 400 pp. ISBN 0-7642-2196-5.
On the brink of divorce following her husband's infidelity, sheltered Abby MacLeod, an Indiana history teacher, embarks for an archaeological dig in Israel hoping to clear the air. But in the airport the gracious man she talked to on the flight is gunned down, and she becomes a suspect in a Palestinian plot. As Abby proceeds to her dig, getting to know Messianic Jews, orthodox Jews, and Arabs, a plot unfolds back home in Indiana, bringing Abby's ex-husband into her life again as he strives to protect their children.

BADKE, WILLIAM

BEN SYLVESTER
Ben Sylvester is a "political consultant" for Libertec, a company specializing in aiding third-world countries in democratic development, but with his wise-cracking, the knifings and shootings he endures, and Badke's fast pacing, he seems more like a gumshoe detective.

> **The Search.** 1995. Multnomah, paper. 209 pp. ISBN 0-88070-719-4.
> Ben is kidnapped even as he learns that his wife and son have been kidnapped, but his captor isn't what he seems.

> **Saluso's Game.** 1996. Multnomah, paper. 273 pp. ISBN 0-88070-866-2.
> Ben heads to Africa on holiday, but once more he's kidnapped, this time by a ruthless would-be dictator.

> **Avenger.** 1997. Multnomah, paper. 205 pp. ISBN 0-88070-031-X.
> Ben heads to Central America to monitor an election, but someone who doesn't like elections wants him dead.

BAMBOLA, SYLVIA. *Refiner's Fire.* 2000. Multnomah, paper. 320 pp. ISBN 1-57673-694-6.
Bambola's improbable thriller, centering on two brothers who smuggle a Christian opposition leader out of Romania in 1989, is given considerable weight by its portrait of persecuted Romanian Christians in general. Bambola is Romanian, and her authentic, impassioned voice overcomes a plot leaning heavily on coincidence, seemingly indebted to *The Prisoner of Zenda*.

BAYER, JOHN F. *The Janus Deception.* 2001. Broadman and Holman, paper. 320 pp. ISBN 0-8054-2439-3.
A burned-out medical officer, Jake Madsen, accidentally uncovers a bizarre chemical weapons experiment being conducted on U.S. sailors. Surely, no human being could have authorized it, and as Jake investigates further, he discovers that no human being has.

BUNN, T. DAVIS

Drummer in the Dark. 2001. Doubleday. 432 pp. ISBN 0-385-49616-8.
The governor of Florida exerts political pressure on Wynn Bryant, a rich widower, to assume a congressional vacancy when the old congressman suddenly dies. Wynn soon discovers that his role in Washington is to play stooge for high-rolling interests in international finance. They oppose the Jubilee Amendment, legislation that would reign in currency traders and something of a crusade for Wynn's predecessor. Though Wynn has never been known for his principles, he resents being crudely maneuvered, and joins forces with his new girlfriend to take up the late congressman's fight.

RENDEZVOUS WITH DESTINY
World traveler Bunn chronicles the Cold War in these spy stories, distant cousins of John LeCarre's thrillers.

Rhineland Inheritance. 1993. Bethany, paper. 222 pp. ISBN 1-55661-347-4.
The first novel in the Rendezvous with Destiny series begins in the aftermath of World War II as an American captain, Jake Burnes, and a Resistance fighter, Pierre Servais, go after hidden Nazi treasure and the same beautiful diplomat.

Gibraltar Passage. 1994. Bethany, paper. 191 pp. ISBN 1-55661-380-6.
Jake Burnes, promoted to lieutenant colonel, and Major Pierre Servais attempt the dangerous Gibraltar Passage in search of Pierre's twin brother, a Resistance fighter who had been presumed dead.

Sahara Crosswind. 1994. Bethany, paper. 186 pp. ISBN 1-55661-381-4.
In the sequel to *Gibraltar Passage,* Jake and Pierre have located Pierre's brother, Patrique. But Patrique is weak from imprisonment, and it's difficult to travel with him. Worse, Patrique has uncovered evidence of Nazi collaboration among officials in the Vichy government, and he's a target for mercenaries.

Berlin Encounter. 1995. Bethany, paper. 190 pp. ISBN 1-55661-382-2.
With the war over, Jake undertakes a spy mission into East Germany, trying to help two rocket scientists who want to defect in the fourth Rendezvous with Destiny tale. His new wife, Sally, learns he's in trouble and races to help.

Istanbul Express. 1995. Bethany, paper. 240 pp. ISBN 1-55661-383-0.
In the last of the Rendezvous with Destiny stories, Jake Burnes and his wife, Sally, take the Orient Express to Istanbul, where they learn firsthand of the ravages of war and the treacheries of the Eastern bloc.

TRILOGY
Among Bunn's first efforts at fiction, this trilogy is set in formerly Communist Russia and features displaced KGB agents, Russian mafia, and former Party members bent on survival and intrigue in a confusing political climate.

Florian's Gate. 1992. Bethany, paper. 344 pp. ISBN 1-55661-244-3.
When the Iron Curtain falls, Jeffrey Sinclair, assistant to a British dealer in upscale antiques, journeys with his fiancée, Katya Nichols, to buy art treasures in the old satellite states of the Soviet Union. As he sees firsthand the havoc and sorrow rendered by years under Communism, his journey becomes a spiritual one as well.

The Amber Room. 1992. Bethany, paper. 328 pp. ISBN 1-55661-285-0.
In the second entry of his trilogy set in formerly Communist nations, Jeffrey Sinclair travels to St. Petersburg to trace a clue concerning the Amber Room, a famous czarist artifact supposedly stolen by the Nazis, then destroyed as the war came to an end. Again, Jeffrey's spiritual search in an important part of the story, perhaps too important for readers interested only in the mystery of the Amber Room.

Winter Palace. 1993. Bethany, paper. 344 pp. ISBN 1-55661-324-5.
Jeffrey Sinclair, now married and with enhanced responsibilities for his firm, again travels to St. Petersburg in the conclusion to his trilogy. He's been commissioned to reclaim a nobleman's winter palace, but various Russian heavies get in his way.

FELL, DORIS ELAINE

◀🐟 SEASONS OF INTRIGUE
Using different characters but mostly European settings, Fell devises her melodramatic Cold War intrigues around the fashion industry and international terrorism; art theft and forgery; an American Vietnam War MIA mistakenly branded a traitor; a race to find out if the rumors

Leon Trotsky is alive are true; a mysterious novelist linked to the dark history of Poland under Communist rule; and spies who threaten the running of the Tour de France.

> ***Always in September.*** 1994. Crossway, paper. 256 pp. ISBN 0-89107-760-X.

> ***Before Winter Comes.*** 1994. Crossway, paper. 315 pp. ISBN 0-89107-815-0.

> ***April Is Forever.*** 1995. Crossway, paper. 352 pp. ISBN 0-89107-828-2.

> ***The Twelfth Rose of Spring.*** 1995. Crossway, paper. 350 pp. ISBN 0-89107-861-4.

> ***To Catch the Summer Wind.*** 1996. Crossway, paper. 367 pp. ISBN 0-89107-914-9.

> ***The Race for Autumn's Glory.*** 1997. Crossway, paper. 384 pp. ISBN 0-89107-926-2.

◀❌ ★ GANSKY, ALTON. *Distant Memory*. 2000. WaterBrook, paper. 304 pp. ISBN 1-57856-121-3.

Lisa Keller is a government agent assigned to the Moyer Corporation, a satellite communications company, to investigate its sophisticated snooping and sale of confidential information for dubious uses. But Lisa doesn't know her mission. She awakens in a strange room after a truck runs her off the highway, and she can't even remember her name. A friendly truck driver wants to help, but Lisa isn't sure she can trust him. Despite Gansky's sophisticated style and knack for suspense, the hackneyed amnesia plot would be too much to overcome except for one neat twist: Lisa is saved. Her faith is the one thing she doesn't forget, and eventually it saves her again.

★ HENDERSON, DEE

◀❌ *UNCOMMON HEROES*

YA

> ***True Devotion.*** 2000. Multnomah, paper. 384 pp. ISBN 1-57673-620-2.
> Kelly Jacobs, a lifeguard, is drawn into the sea off southern California to rescue a teenager on a surfboard, causing her to think once more of her husband, Nick, who was brought home dead from a secret Navy SEAL mission. Joe Baker, her husband's commanding officer, rescues Kelly, bringing to his mind what happened on the fateful mission, and forcing his realization that his concern for Kelly is more than devotion to an old friend. Before the two can acknowledge their love, they are drawn into a SEAL mission involving smuggled nuclear arms that reveals at last why Nick died. Henderson's plot is strewn with coincidences, but she has an insider's knowledge of SEAL operations and her action scenes are first-rate.

> ***True Valor.*** 2002. Multnomah, paper. 350 pp. ISBN 1-57673-887-6.
> With her trademark gritty detail, Henderson spins another tale of military valor. Her heroine, a combat pilot named Gracie Yates, goes down behind enemy lines in Iraq. As she struggles to survive, she thinks of Air Force Major Bruce Stanton, the "extractions specialist" assigned to rescue her. The two knew each other stateside, but suppressed their incipient romance because of complications with friends, and because of their separate deployments.

◄●✗ **JONES, SCOTT.** *Heaven's War*. 1998. WaterBrook, paper. 400 pp. ISBN 1-57856-021-7.

British, American, Russian, and Vatican spies are all after the Temple Scroll, a Dead Sea artifact containing prophecy and a sort of map to buried holy treasures. The personal story comes down to a feud between CIA agent Jack Calumet and his nemesis, the Russian Andrei Vartanyan. Jack bested Andrei years ago in the espionage game, but his ruthlessness lost him his girlfriend. The question is whether his character has improved over the years.

◄●✗ **MALONE, L. K.** *Divided Loyalties*. 2001. Kregel, paper. 320 pp. ISBN 0-8254-2796-7.

Giselle Hardy is the daughter of the U.S. Navy's fleet commander for the Mediterranean. Her father is involved in delicate negotiations having to do with peace in the Mideast. A terrorist organization hovers, trying to sabotage the process, and Giselle keeps stumbling into their path, then being rescued by an Israeli-born marine major, Raz Chayill. The plot thickens but never gels; Malone sustains interest through her on-again, off-again romance between Giselle and Raz.

◄●✗ **MCHENRY, PAUL T.** *Code Name: Antidote*. 2000. Broadman and Holman, paper. 318 pp. ISBN 0-8054-2083-5.

A slow-moving, jagged, pedantic, and predictable techno-thriller about a deadly virus that former KGB agents plan to sell to an Islamic terrorist group and the efforts of two stalwart Americans to foil their part. The military scenes are well done.

MILLER, JANICE

◄●✗ *UNTITLED SERIES*

Peter Natale is a CIA operative whose efforts to interdict Mafia drug shipments in Sicily reveal a Moscow connection. The drug assignment escalates to encompass a romance with a born-again fellow agent, Judith Davies, and their attempts together to head off the smuggling of fissionable materials out of Ukraine. In the mix, also, is a nasty Mafia don, Carlo Ricaso, but despite Miller's smooth style, she never manages a convincing portrait of this shadowy world. Peter Natale seems too sensitive for his role, and his love for Judith contrived; the evil they war against is too simplistically arrayed.

> *Final Thunder*. 1994. Moody, paper. pp. ISBN 0-8024-2634-4.
>
> *The Eye of the Octopus*. 1995. Moody, paper. 365 pp. ISBN 0-8024-2729-4.

◄●✗ **NESBIT, JEFF.** *The Capital Conspiracy*. 1996. Nelson, paper. 324 pp. ISBN 0-7852-7812-5.

Nesbit, once Dan Quayle's communications director, shows a sophisticated knowledge of the behind-the-scenes interplay between the White House, Capitol Hill, and the intelligence community during a period of international crisis. Somehow, a huge nuclear reactor has popped up in Algeria. Why was the White House so late in learning of it?

◄●✗ **PARKER, GARY E.** *The Ephesus Fragment*. 1999. Bethany, paper. 352 pp. ISBN 0-76422-256-2.

An ancient parchment that seems to be a message from Mary, mother of Jesus, is unearthed, and a frantic struggle ensues to gain its possession.

SIMON, FRANK

◄E✗ *Veiled Threats.* 1996. Crossway, paper. 352 pp. ISBN 0-89107-880-0.
Biblical archeologists Mars Enderly and Anne McAdams fall in love as they work together to unearth a second great temple in the Old City. Meanwhile, Palestinians attempt to sabotage the Dome of the Rock (and blame it on the Israelis), the Syrians make threatening moves on the Golan Heights, and the Kurds heat up their insurgency against Iraq.

◄E✗ *Walls of Terror.* 1997. Crossway, paper. 368 pp. ISBN 0-89107-952-1.
Newlyweds Mars and Anne Enderly of *Veiled Threats* attempt their honeymoon in London, but Mideast politics exerts powerful pressures, this time with the threat of biological warfare. They discover a wing of Nebuchadnezzar's palace where *mene, mene, tekel, upharsin* is emblazoned on the wall, and biblical prophecies unfold. ■ **Sequel** ■

◄E✗ WINDLE, JEANETTE. *Crossfire.* 2001. Kregel, paper. 617 pp. ISBN 0-8254-4116-1.
Sara Conner, a naive University of Washington coed, is rescued from thugs by a handsome, rich Bolivian, Nicolas Cortez. They are almost immediately married, and Sara is fiercely in love, but even her worship of Nicolas cannot overcome her doubts when she begins to comprehend the status of his family—rich landowners profiting from the cocaine trade. Soon, she is in danger, and must throw herself on the mercies of God and a handsome DEA agent. Windle grew up in South America and worked as a missionary in Bolivia for 15 years. Her story is a bit silly, but her understanding of Bolivian society, and even of the drug trade, is authentic and engrossing.

Legal Thrillers

★ ARVIN, REED. *The Will.* 2000. Scribner. 325 pp. ISBN 0-7432-0148-5.
Henry Mathews is an ambitious young corporate lawyer who is suddenly called home to the windswept, dwindling town of Council Grove, Kansas, to administer the will of the town's only rich man. The will was set up by Henry's dead father, a lawyer who battled for good causes and was always poor. The rich man's son expects to inherit everything, but the rich man has fooled everyone and has left his fortune to the "Birdman," a schizophrenic who spends his days on a park bench talking of divine retribution. Arvin adds to the mix a starry-eyed state environmentalist, Amanda Ashton, who is suspicious the old oil wells are leaking poisons into the aquifer. As Henry investigates, he is soon faced with a dilemma: Will he be like his father, a poor man who battles for justice, or a crooked—but rich—corporate lawyer?

◄E✗ BELL, JAMES SCOTT. *Final Witness.* 1999. Broadman and Holman, paper. 385 pp. ISBN 0-8054-1842-3.

Rachel Ybarra, a Christian Latina, becomes a paralegal for a Los Angeles law firm and is quickly drawn into a case involving deaths within the drug world of the Russian mafia. Another paralegal, and classmate in law school, ridicules Rachel's faith, but she is more than equal to him. Others are impressed with Rachel's clever Christian witness, and a friendly FBI agent provides a tame romance in this predictable, though legally sagacious, thriller.

BUNN, T. DAVIS

◆✕★ *The Great Divide.* 2000. Doubleday/WaterBrook. 391 pp. ISBN 0-385-49615-X.

Meeting with tragedy, attorney Marcus Glenwood spirals downward into divorce, alcoholism, and despair, retreating to his grandmother's home in a black section of a small North Carolina town. There he's presented with an unwinnable case. A young black woman, investigating human rights abuses in Mainland China, has been taken captive as a slave laborer in "Factory 101," which makes designer sports clothing and shoes for an American company, New Horizons. New Horizons has an ugly reputation for its labor practices even in North Carolina, but denies any involvement with the missing woman. On thin evidence Marcus brings suit, and soon there are moves to disbar him, and attempts on his life. As he pursues the case, Marcus attends a black church and comes to terms with his sorrowful past.

◆✕ *The Presence.* 1990. Bethany, paper. 345 pp. ISBN 0-7642-2301-1.

This popular novel, Bunn's first, is a kinder, gentler version of *The Great Divide.* It's about a Republican black lawyer, T. J. Case, from South Carolina whom God summons to Washington, D.C. There ostensibly to work on a program of education reform much like contemporary school voucher initiatives, he instead provides a thunderbolt to the executive branch by way of Bible studies and Christian witness. Soon, much to the discomfort of party hacks, an evangelical fervor cascades from the Oval Office downward.

◆✕ CHITWOOD, CHUCK. *The Trial of Job.* 2000. Victor, paper. 406 pp. ISBN 0-78143-308-8.

Charlie Harrigan wins an important pro bono case for his firm, and there's talk of his becoming a partner, but he finds the ethics of a new case troubling. A rival for partnership turns his Christian scruples against him, forcing him to refuse to go inside a strip club to entertain a client. Charlie angrily denounces all wrongdoing, then in despair hits the sauce. Arriving home late, he learns that his wife has been killed. The life that yesterday seemed so promising has become a nightmare. Can Charlie remain true to his faith despite this sea of troubles?

◆✕ WHITLOW, ROBERT. *The Trial.* 2001. Word, paper. 454 pp. ISBN 0-8499-1642-9.

In profound despair over the death of his wife and two sons, small-town attorney Kent ("Mac") MacClain is about to commit suicide when the phone rings. He's handed a public defendant's role in what is alleged to be the murder of a young woman from a prominent local family. The defendant is a drifter who can't remember what happened, but circumstances clearly point to his guilt. Mac is aided by a pretty out-of-town widow, a Christian psychologist with a son. She quickly goes to work on both Mac's head and his heart in this seamless tale.

Political Thrillers

ALCORN, RANDY

◆✕★ *Deadline.* 1994. Multnomah, paper. 426 pp. ISBN 0-88070-660-0.

When his two oldest friends are killed in a suspicious car accident, Jake Woods, a mushy liberal columnist, is drawn into a murder investigation. The murder may be linked to antiabortion forces or to those advocating the use of a new abortion pill. One of Jake's dead friends was a surgeon who had performed abortions in the past, the other a conservative Christian. Alcorn has Jake look at both sides, not just of the abortion question but of issues ranging from school vouchers to gay rights. Gradually, Jake adopts the point of view of his slain conservative friend.

E✕ *Dominion*. 1996. Multnomah, paper. 603 pp. ISBN 0-88070-939-1.
Jake Woods returns in the didactic sequel to *Deadline*. He works with the protagonist, black columnist and former football player Clarence Abernathy. With Jake's help, Clarence allies himself with a conservative white detective to run down the truth behind a ghetto murder. Gang violence and drug addiction figure prominently, sickening Clarence and dividing him against his Black Muslim brother, Harley. This portion of Alcorn's novel, with its long diatribe against Louis Farrakhan, is passionate and ably presented but may be alienating to some black readers. Clarence, however, is a strong character, as is Jake in a different way, and the two novels have been widely read. ■ **Sequel** ■

E✕ **BURKETT, LARRY.** *The Thor Conspiracy*. 1995. Nelson. 345 pp. ISBN 0-8407-7801-5.
The Communist Chinese have joined forces with the Environmental Protection Agency (EPA) in Burkett's shrill tale. Both want to cripple American industry and deny ordinary citizens access to public land. Would-be whistleblower Dale Crawford discovers that it wasn't fluorocarbons that blew a hole in the ozone layer but secret atmospheric nuclear tests; in fact, the banning of fluorocarbons is but an attempt to deny refrigeration to third world countries that, because of overpopulation, degrade the environment. Burkett's antienvironmental diatribe races to the atomic bombing of Washington, D.C.—at which readers may either cheer or cringe.

E✕ ★ **COLSON, CHARLES, AND ELLEN SANTILLI VAUGHN.** *Gideon's Torch*. 1995. Word. 544 pp. ISBN 0-8499-1146-X.
As Republican president J. Whitney Lowell takes office, a woman walks into a North Dakota abortion clinic and kills a doctor. Lowell cracks down on every antiabortion group nationwide, and a civil liberties debate quickly erupts. Another group steals a National Institute of Health training video containing shots of a brutal third-trimester abortion and manages to up-link the video to the evening news. Still another group stages an Oklahoma City-style bombing on the first of the sinister-seeming Regeneration Centers, which will use fetuses in AIDS research. They botch their escape and are killed, leaving government prosecutors no case except against an alleged accessory, a Maryland preacher named Daniel Seaton. Seaton's courtroom testimony and death in prison are linked to the tribulations of St. Paul and give the novel a certain mournful elegance.

E✕ ★ **HUNT, ANGELA.** *The Justice*. 2002. W Publishing, paper. 400 pp. ISBN 0-8499-1631-3.
Vice President Daryn Austin becomes the first woman president when the sitting president dies. Out of public sympathy and because of her domestic program, her popularity rises, and she looks like a good bet to be re-elected. Then she makes a fatal mistake. She brings in Paul Santana, a Cuban–American, to be White House Counsel, and Paul was her lover long before. The two become lovers again, but Paul is beset with guilt over his betrayal of his sickly wife and college-student daughter. His crisis of conscience reaches the breaking point when Daryn pulls strings to appoint him to the Supreme Court, a post he does not deserve but one that he is determined to discharge ethically. Topical references to the Clinton administration mar this otherwise politically shrewd thriller, but Hunt never lets up on the suspense, and readers of both sexes will enjoy her observations on women in power.

⬛✗ **LARSON, BOB.** *The Senator's Agenda.* **1995. Nelson. 288 pp. ISBN 0-7852-7879-6.**
Wes Bryant, a radio station owner in Denver, becomes embroiled in Colorado's fractious gay rights debate when a sleazy liberal senator runs against a saintly evangelical. Larson stacks the deck: Characters who support gay rights and abortion are lowdown, violent, and in league with Satan by definition.

⬛✗ **MCDOWELL, JOSH, AND ED STEWART.** *Vote of Intolerance.* **1997. Tyndale. 404 pp. ISBN 0-8423-3905-1.**
McDowell and Stewart's paranoid though compelling near-future thriller is set in the two states of California: Southern, where decadence holds sway, and Northern, a conservative Christian enclave. A Los Angeles Christian woman, Stevie Van Horne, is fearful for the fate of her children and heads north, where she works in the campaign for the Christian gubernatorial candidate while fending off her ex-husband, cults, kidnappings, and terrorism. The campaign rapidly focuses on the issue of tolerance or intolerance, depending on how you view it: intolerance for lifestyles that evangelicals think to be deviant, but that their New Age opposition tolerates; intolerance for Christian beliefs, the charge the novel's Christians level against their foes.

⬛✗ ★ **PARKER, GARY E.** *A Capital Offense.* **1998. Nelson, paper. 271 pp ISBN 0-7852-7786-2.**
Connie Brandon is nearly through law school, has good kids, and though her relationship isn't perfect with Jack, her husband, she feels her marriage is solid. The good life is a little compromised lately, however, with attempts by Las Vegas gambling interests to build a casino on the Missouri River a few hundred feet north of Missouri's state capital building in Jefferson City. Jack, a Christian bookstore owner, has been fighting the casino. Then Jack is killed, and Connie must take on dark forces intent on labeling Jack's death a suicide because of bad debts and to cover up an affair. Though Parker's mystery is solid, Connie's faith is really his subject, and she emerges as a fine, courageous woman who, though visited with the trials of Job, remains faithful to her God.   ▪Discussion▪

⬛✗ **QUAYLE, MARILYN TUCKER, AND NANCY TUCKER NORTHCUTT.** *The Campaign.* **1996. HarperCollins/Zondervan. 478 pp. ISBN 0-310-20231-0.**
A black Republican senator with a military background is falsely implicated in the murder of a reporter in this creaky, badly written thriller that remains of interest because of the fame of Quayle.

Chapter 11

The Christian Life

This chapter describes novels and collections that include Christian themes but do not fit easily within the most common genres. Many were published as mainstream fiction or, if not, could have been. G. Roger Corey's *In a Mirror Dimly,* for example, placed in the literary category, is a compelling tale in the old realistic tradition of Conrad and Steinbeck, but it is also the story of one man's search for God.

Some categories, such as "African Americans" and "Humor," draw titles from several genres. They have been grouped here to answer Readers' Advisory questions such as, "Do you have anything funny that's also clean?" and "Do you have any Christian fiction by black writers?"

AFRICAN AMERICANS

Only a few years ago, readers couldn't have found an African American who wrote Christian fiction. That's no longer true.

BENSON, ANGELA. *Awakening Mercy.* **2000. Tyndale, paper. 250 pp. ISBN 0-8423-1939-5.**
CeCe Williams is an unwed mother who has established a career selling Atlanta real estate. She's devoted to—and protective of—her young son, but she's pretty much given up on men. Life hands her a surprise when she's called to court regarding unpaid parking tickets and sentenced to community service at Genesis House, an African American Christian charity. CeCe finds herself counseling teenagers about careers and pregnancy and attracted to Nate Richardson, the charity's assured young director.

BOWEN, MICHELE ANDREA. *Church Folk.* **2001. Warner (Walk Worthy). 368 pp. ISBN 0-446-52799-8.**
Essie Lee Land seems quiet and plain, but she appeals to Theophilus Henry Simmons, a bright young African American pastor in small-town Mississippi. When they marry, reticent Essie is taken aback by the aggressiveness of her husband's "church folk," who descend on her with advice and judgment. But within Essie is a modern woman, after all, and she turns from mousy to flamboyant, all to make a good wife and serve God. The church folk get their comeuppance.

FOSTER, SHARON EWELL

◀E✗★ *Ain't No River.* 2001. Multnomah, paper. 350 pp. ISBN 1-57673-628-8.
Garvin Daniels is a serious, brash, materialistic black lawyer in Washington, D.C. She's handed an impossible case in which she must prove the subtle discrimination of an employer, the plot of her own supervisor to do her in, she thinks. She heads for her North Carolina hometown to chill out and put right another worrisome situation: her elderly grandmother, "Moomaw," seems to have lost her senses over a young fortune hunter, GoGo Walker. Is he a fortune hunter, or is Garvin judging by stereotype, like her employer? Foster, one of the brightest lights of evangelical fiction, turns in a nuanced tale of a contemporary black woman at a moment of crisis who learns to let go, trust God and her wise, colorful grandmother, and love.

◀E✗★ *Passing by Samaria.* 2000. Multnomah, paper. 400 pp. ISBN 1-57673-615-6.
In this widely praised novel a high school girl, Alena, discovers a friend who has been
🅈🄰 lynched and is overcome with such outrage that her parents send her to live with her aunt in Chicago. It is 1918 in Jim Crow Mississippi, and Alena's parents fear that her outspokenness
🄲 will get her in trouble. The world opens up for Alena in Chicago, where she becomes a journalist and meets two men—one who is good for her, one who is not. Eventually, Alena returns home to marry and also to confront the person she thinks to be the killer, the white sheriff, but before she does, he's killed in a "hunting accident." The troubled community begins to heal itself as a young white minister, Alena, the sheriff's family, and aggrieved blacks come together in a series of deeply religious scenes.   ▐ Discussion ▌

◀E✗ *Riding Through Shadows.* 2001. Multnomah, paper. 350 pp. ISBN 1-57673-807-8.
Troubled Shirley Ferris, a bright African American girl, comes of age in the tumultuous 1960s
🅈🄰 in this first of a two-part novel; the second installment is *Passing into Light.* Part of the story is seen through the eyes of Shirley's older self, a single mother coping with poverty and emotional frailty in the 1980s. The younger Shirley suffers from depression and paranoid fantasies, brought on in part because of the antics of her selfish, sometimes hysterical mother. Poor Shirley is at last rescued from her East St. Louis home by "Mother," a black earth mother whose emotional support, uncanny understanding, and spiritual solidity bring Shirley back among the living. Though complicated by elliptical personal references that seem to reflect Foster's own childhood, this is, nonetheless, a compelling and compulsively readable novel.   ▐ Discussion ▌

THOMAS, JACQUELIN. *Singsation.* 2001. Warner (Walk Worthy), paper. 454 pp. ISBN 0-446-52798-X.
Deborah Anne Peterson is a golden-voiced singer in her backwater Georgia church in this mildly salacious romance. Deborah Anne envisions herself in the big-time, and gets her chance when rap star Triage Blue, a hometown boy who made good, returns home and then recommends her as a backup singer for a big rhythm-and-blues act. Deborah Anne is soon a sensation and is even nominated for a Grammy, stretching the reader's credulity. Her Christian values are compromised by life in the fast lane, however, and she wonders whether she can go on. Although there are some wonderful elements in Thomas's novel, such as Deborah's relationship with her parents, much the same story is more believably realized in Reed Arvin's portrait of a young white singer, *The Wind in the Wheat* (p. 227).

ANGELS

The mainstream angel fad has found its reflection in Christian fiction.

ANSAY, A. MANETTE. *River Angel.* **1998. Morrow. 243 pp. ISBN 0-688-15243-0.**

Ansay is an unbeliever who seems desperately to want to believe in her poetic story, based on actual events, of a small, sad boy who drowns and a legendary, protective angel whose domain is a river through Wisconsin farm country.

★ **BUECHNER, FREDERICK.** *On the Road with the Archangel.* **1997. HarperSan-Francisco. 144 pp. ISBN 0-06-061125-1.**

Long ago, when the Jewish people were enslaved, the angel Raphael descended to Earth to answer personally two exceptionally urgent prayers in this wise, enchanting, amusing fable.

◢✗ **BUNN, T. DAVIS.** *The Messenger.* **1995. Bethany. 112 pp. ISBN 1-55661-669-4.**

The angel Ariel is on God's mission to care for an elderly hospital patient but runs into a tough urban scene in Philadelphia, where a pickpocket steals her pass back to Heaven. Ariel does her job and makes it home all right, but the pickpocket finds himself in big trouble, his possession a more extraordinary prize than he could possibly know.

◢✗ **COPELAND, LORI, AND ANGELA HUNT**

HEAVENLY DAZE

Copeland's folksy humor and Hunt's talent for historicals combine in this agreeable series, set on an island off Maine. On his deathbed in 1798, the Frenchman who discovered the beautiful island prayed for deliverance from the miscreants who had taken over. Ever since, seven angels have lived as Earthlings, ensuring that life goes not too badly for the 22 present-day humans who live on the island, in the daze of Heaven, under the guidance of the somewhat befuddled Reverence Winslow Wickam.

> *The Island of Heavenly Daze.* 2001. Word, paper. 270 pp. ISBN 0-8499-4219-5.

> *A Warmth in Winter.* 2002. Word, paper. 270 pp. ISBN 0-8499-4306-X.

◢✗ **TAZEWELL, CHARLES.** *Make Me a Miracle.* **2000. Nelson. 240 pp. ISBN 1-58029-108-2.**

Children's writer Tazewell *(The Littlest Angel,* 1982) offers a sentimental view of Heaven through the eyes of several new arrivals in these six stories written for adults.

◢✗ ★ **WHEELER, JOE, ed.** *The Wings of God.* **2000. WaterBrook. 244 pp. ISBN 1-57856-320-8.**

These tales of angels intervening at crucial times, drawn from magazines such as *Guideposts* and all supposedly true accounts, are beautifully edited, some reading much like folktales.   ■Discussion■

WILLIAMSON, MARTHA, AND OTHERS

◄► *TOUCHED BY AN ANGEL*

These are nonsequential, novelized shows from the television series. Nelson also publishes a children's series based on the show. (See also "Christmas" in this chapter.)

> *It Came Upon a Midnight Clear.* 1999. Nelson, paper. 160 pp. ISBN 0-7852-6947-9.

> *My Dinner with Andrew.* 1998. Nelson, paper. 256 pp. ISBN 0-7852-7130-9.

> *The Spirit of Liberty Moon.* 1999. Nelson, paper. 224 pp. ISBN 0-7852-7132-5.
> See also chapter 12, "Catholic Fiction." the section on Andrew Greeley.

CHRISTMAS

◄► AIKEN, GINNY, KRISTIN BILLERBECK, AND CATHERINE PALMER. *A Victorian Christmas Keepsake.* 2001. Tyndale, paper. 350 pp. ISBN 0-8423-3569-2.

The authors present novellas with a Christmas twist: Aiken's "Memory to Keep," Billerbeck's "Far above Rubies," and Palmer's "Behold the Lamb."

◄► AIKEN, GINNY, CATHERINE PALMER, DEBRA WHITE SMITH, AND PEGGY STOKS. *A Victorian Christmas Quilt.* 1998. Tyndale, paper. 375 pp. ISBN 0-8423-7773-5.

Quilting and Christmas themes in Victorian settings unify these four novellas: Ginny Aiken's "Log Cabin Patch," set in the logging country of Washington State in 1897; Catherine Palmer's "Lone Star," featuring the adventures of a Texas woman in England in 1886; Debra White Smith's "The Wedding Ring," featuring a quilt of rings and set in 1900 Colorado; and Peggy Stoks's "Crosses and Losses," about a quilt's power to address grief, set in 1880 Minnesota.

◄► BALL, KAREN, BARBARA JEAN HICKS, AND LORENA MCCOURTNEY. *Mistletoe.* 1996. Multnomah, paper. 288 pp. ISBN 1-57673-013-1.

A dog unites neighbors in Karen Ball's "An Unlikely Angel"; frazzled Carolyn McAndrews seeks a quiet Christmas in Mexico in "Feliz Navidad," but love makes it noisy; and, in Barbara Jean Hicks's "Tea for Two," Nicolette Weatherspoon, doing a good deed, finds herself the object of endless matchmaking.

◄► BERGREN, LISA TAWN, LAURA KRAUSE, AND SHARI MACDONALD. *Silver Bells.* 1997. Multnomah, paper. 272 pp. ISBN 1-57673-119-7.

Bergren contributes "Wish List," about a woman unwillingly playing the part of a Christmas elf; Krause's "Mystery at Christmas" is about former lovers, brought together again; and MacDonald's "The Best Man," features a whirlwind romance.

BUNN, T. DAVIS

◄► *One Shenandoah Winter.* 1998. Nelson. 128 pp. ISBN 0-7852-7217-8.

In the early 1960s, Dr. Nathan Reynolds sets up practice in the Appalachian community of Hillsboro. His steady skills save lives, but he's a condescending, irreligious man and runs afoul of boosterish Connie Wilkes, Hillsboro's assistant mayor, and her talk of Christianity. Matters come to a head for Connie and Nathan at Christmas, when Connie must swallow her pride and ask the doctor for help.

◆✕ *Tidings of Comfort and Joy.* 1997. Nelson. 233 pp. ISBN 0-7852-7203-8.
Circumstances and duty throw Emily and Marissa, grandmother and granddaughter, together at Christmas. Each approaches the season wearily, but then Emily tells a story of wartime love in England—her story—and Marissa puts her rather shallow life in perspective.

◆✕ **CHUTE, KATHIE, DIANNA CRAWFORD, CATHERINE PALMER, AND PEGGY STOKS.** *Victorian Christmas Tea.* 1997. Tyndale, paper. 212 pp. ISBN 0-8423-7775-1.
Love during the Yuletide, featuring Catherine Palmer's "Angel in the Attic," set in 1880 New Mexico; Dianna Crawford's "A Daddy for Christmas," set near Maine in 1870; Peggy Stoks's "Tea for Marie," set among the immigrant Swede community in Minnesota; and Katherine Chute's "Going Home," set near New Orleans in 1876.

COPELAND, LORI. *Christmas Vows $5.00 Extra.* 2001. Tyndale. 120 pp. ISBN 0-8423-5326-7.
Ben O'Keefe is down on his luck. He's finished a stretch in prison for a holdup and he can't find a job. His wife has died and he has three little kids to feed. On his way to his mother's house for Christmas, the transmission in his car goes out—in the middle of a snowstorm. Enter Henrietta Humblesmith, proprietor of a "marrying parlor" and the angel of Copeland's tearjerker.

◆✕ **COBB, SHARON, AND OTHERS.** *Touched by an Angel: A Christmas Miracle.* 1997. Nelson. 300 pp. ISBN 0-7852-7129-5.
A novelization of one of the TV show's most popular episodes about Wayne Travers, a man who is feeling increasingly constrained by the necessity of caring for his retarded brother, Joey, and a con man whose schemes unwittingly aid angels with their Christmas message.

◆✕ ★ **GRAY, ALICE, ed.** *Christmas Stories for the Heart.* 1997. Multnomah, paper. 126 pp. ISBN 1-57673-809-4.
Gray's collection of extremely short inspirational essays and stories draws from denominational publications, *Reader's Digest,* and books. It features well-known writers from the past, such as Robert Louis Stevenson, Peter Marshall, and Taylor Caldwell, and contemporaries, such as Tim LaHaye, Max Lucado, and Philip Gulley.

GREELEY, ANDREW. *Star Bright!* 1997. Forge. 127 pp. ISBN 0-312-86387-X.
Spellbound by her beauty, a college student brings a young Russian woman, studying at Harvard, home for Christmas to his Irish-Catholic, Chicago family. Odessa's Orthodox ways and uplifting outlook bring good cheer and calm to a fractious home.

KARON, JAN. *The Mitford Snowmen.* 2001. Viking. 32 pp. ISBN 0-670-03019-8.
In this spinoff from her famous Mitford series, Karon's good-hearted citizens drop their work and spontaneously enter into a contest building snowmen. Lavishly illustrated.

◄✠ MAKI, ALAN. *A Choice to Cherish*. 2000. Broadman and Holman. 160 pp. ISBN 0-8054-2338-9.

Alan—seemingly Alan Maki, the author—is a self-centered college student who, at Christmas, is intent on a skiing vacation. Instead, his father calls to direct him to a small town in Montana, where Alan's grandfather is dying. Alan barely knows his grandfather, though he knows that in the past there was family discord. Still, he understands that he's the one the old man wants to see, rather than Alan's father. The two spend an unforgettable Christmas as Alan cuts a tree for them and learns, through the stories associated with the old man's simple, sentimental gifts, the secrets that made his grandfather's life one to be emulated and treasured.

◄✠ ★ MCCUSKER, PAUL. *Epiphany*. 1998. Zondervan. 128 pp. ISBN 0-310-22545-0.

In a pleasing, subtle style, McCusker tells of the recent death of Richard, who "awakens" somewhere not quite in Heaven to discover he still has some work to do as a parent. His grown children have gathered in his house to attend to his affairs. Richard led a contented, productive life and was much valued in his community, but all of his children are troubled in their individual ways. Musing all the while on subjects ranging from pop culture to eternity, Richard invisibly (and wittily) guides them through this crucial juncture in their lives.

◄✠ NORRIS, HELEN. *More Than Seven Watchmen*. 1985. Zondervan. (Out of print.)

Thomas Beckett, the widowed rector of Saint Stephen's, is a good and gentle man who takes comfort in the rituals of the church, having lost contact with their meaning. He dwells in the past with his wife, Katherine, and thinks of the son they never had. But as Christmas nears, a runaway boy breaks up his carefully crafted routines. As he helps the boy and his mother, Thomas passes through a curious crisis of faith: He feels the power and love of God again, but wonders if he's in the right profession.

See also "Pastors," in this chapter.

◄✠ ODELL, JERI, CATHERINE PALMER, DEBRA WHITE SMITH, AND PEGGY STOKS. *A Victorian Christmas Cottage*. 1999. Tyndale, paper. 412 pp. ISBN 0-8423-1905-0.

Four Christmas novellas, set in both Victorian England and America, featuring Palmer's re-telling of the story of Ruth, "Under His Wings" as well as Smith's "Christmas Past," Odell's "A Christmas Hope," and Stoks's "The Beauty of the Season."

◄✠ PALMER, CATHERINE, PEGGY STOKS, AND ELIZABETH WHITE. *Prairie Christmas*. 2000. Tyndale, paper. 284 pp. ISBN 0-8423-3562-5.

Christmas prairie romances, including Palmer's "The Christmas Bride," a spin-off from her A Town Called Hope series (p. 124). Peggy Stoks's "Wishful Thinking," a senior citizen romance, and Elizabeth White's "Reforming Seneca Jones," a romantic tale of the Pony Express, are also included.

◄✠ PARKER, GARY E. *The Last Gift*. 1999. Chariot Victor. 112 pp. ISBN 1-56476-779-5.

Catherine Johnson dies at Christmas without reconciling her bitter troubles with her daughter, Christina. But as Christina discovers during a contemplative stay in her parents' snowbound house, Catherine offers forgiveness from beyond the grave. Christina's faith is rekindled, bringing an acceptance of her unglamorous 40 years to Heaven. She discovers new virtues in the reasonable-but-boring husband she had been about to divorce and considers adopting a child.

POELMAN, ANNE OSBORN. *Secret Santa.* 2000. Shadow Mountain. 128 pp. ISBN 1-57345-792-2.

> The hard times of 1933 have hit the Van Slotens hard, and they reluctantly agree to forego Christmas. The oldest son, Tom, takes his hard-earned college fund and becomes the family's secret Santa.

 TRONSTAD, JANET. *An Angel for Dry Creek.* 1999. Harlequin (Love Inspired), paper. 254 pp. ISBN 0-373-87081-7.

> On the run, police sketch artist Glory Beckett stumbles into cynical Matthew Curtis's life in tiny Dry Creek, Montana. Matthew's twin boys are convinced that Glory is a Christmas angel designated only for them and maybe for their stubborn father, a minister who lost his faith after his wife died. As Glory unites the town with Christmas spirit, Matthew's fears grow that he'll lose her to a hit man.

> See also Calvin Miller's *Snow*, p. 83.

HUMOR

 DAVIS, ANDREW. *God Bless Mr. Devil.* 2000. Moonscape. 253 pp. ISBN 0-9675811-0-9.

> A little before Christmas eight-year-old Katie Hart starts praying for the Devil, thinking that prayer will save him. Cut to Hell, where we meet the jaded old fallen angel himself. He sits in an air-conditioned central chamber, bored with eternity, smoking Cuban cigars and munching popcorn, seldom bothering to get out of his bathrobe. All of a sudden he's overwhelmed with Katie's prayers. He's never had any power against prayer, and now it's directed at him. What's a Devil to do?

 GRIFFIN, WILLIAM, ed. *Carnage at Christhaven.* 1989.

> "Is it possible to make an evangelical laugh?" is one of the concerns of this mystery spoof, the outgrowth of a conference of Christian fiction writers including Walter Wangerin, Stephen Lawhead, Madeleine L'Engle, and Harold Fickett. Writers each wrote their theoretically sequential chapters, with no discernible plot and titles such as "The Shepherd Who Came in from the Cold" and "Mysterious Ways."

★ GULLEY, PHILIP

 ★ *Front Porch Tales: Warm-Hearted Stories of Family, Faith, Laughter, and Love.*
1997. Multnomah, paper. 176 pp. ISBN 1-57673-123-5.

> A blue-collar Hoosier Quaker uses anecdotes about small-town and country folk to draw homespun morals. When a more prosperous local preacher announces his plans to fly to Honduras, he comments, "It was the middle of winter, when God routinely calls us to minister in the tropics." This laconic, seemingly effortless humor is what makes Gulley one of a kind.   **▪ Discussion**

◖✖★ *HARMONY SERIES*

"Gentle" and "nostalgic" describe Quaker minister Sam Gardner's sermons masking as short **YA** stories, though sometimes they have a satirical edge, as in "The World's Shortest Evangelist." Compensating for his shortness, the evangelist comes dressed in camouflage fatigues and preaches of spiritual warfare. Gulley's antecedents are Mark Twain and Ring Lardner; he could happen only in America, and the Midwest at that.   ▮Discussion▮

> *Home to Harmony.* 2000. Multnomah. 200 pp. ISBN 1-57673-613-X.

> *Just Shy of Harmony.* 2002. Harper San Francisco. 256 pp. ISBN 0-06-000632-3.

◖✖ **HICKS, BARBARA JEAN.** *Loves Me, Loves Me Not.* **2000. WaterBrook, paper. 256 pp. ISBN 1-57856-124-8.**

The divorced owner of a gift shop, Bonny Van Hooten, has given up on love. Her mischievous employees characterize her as full of "Denial. Fear. Probably unresolved anger," and run a personals ad for her. Several wildly inappropriate suitors emerge. Meanwhile, reformed and contrite, Bonny's ex- shows up, intent on wooing her. Bonny uses the suitors she has no interest in to make him suffer.

◖✖ **HIGGS, LIZ CURTIS, CAROLYN ZANE, AND KAREN BALL.** *Three Weddings and a Giggle.* **2001. Multnomah, paper. 307 pp. ISBN 1-57673-656-3.**

Three comedies of errors about weddings: Curtis's "Fine Print," about a speech coach and a printing executive with a fear of speaking; Zane's "Sweet Chariot," about two spoiled young people given some lessons by old codgers; and Ball's "Bride on the Run," about a woman who finally rebels against her father's choice of a husband and goes after the man she really wants.

JONES, ANNIE

◖✖ *ROUTE 66*

> *The Double Heart Diner.* 1999. WaterBrook, paper. 225 pp. ISBN 1-57856-133-7.
> Georgia Darling runs afoul of would-be entrepreneur Jett Murphy on Route 66. Georgia wants to save an old diner, and Jett wants to tear it down and get rich selling off the land. Trouble is, even though they want to do opposite things and should be enemies, they're crazy about each other.

> *Cupid's Corner.* 1999. WaterBrook, paper. 256 pp. ISBN 1-57856-134-5.
> Mayor Jenny Fox is trying to set a record for the number of wedding ceremonies performed in a single day in one town, but the paper's new reporter thinks she's full of silly boosterism.

> *Lost Romance Ranch.* 2000. WaterBrook, paper. 234 pp. ISBN 1-57856-135-3.
> The marriage of a couple who starred in a TV show when they were teenagers is on the rocks. But there's talk of remaking the show in this last and least compelling entry in a generally amusing, pleasant trilogy.

MACDONALD, SHARI

◖✖ *SALINGER SISTERS*

Comedies of errors lead to true love for Salinger sisters Cat, Lucy, and Felicia.

> *Love on the Run.* 1998. WaterBrook, paper. 245 pp. ISBN 1-57856-084-5.

A Match Made in Heaven. 1999. WaterBrook, paper. 247 pp. ISBN 1-57856-137-X.

The Perfect Wife. 1999. WaterBrook, paper. 242 pp. ISBN 1-57856-138-8.

PIZZUTI, SUZY

HALO HATTIE'S BOARDING HOUSE
Pizzuti shapes her amusing, lightweight stories around meddlesome Hattie Hopkins and her boarding house.

> *Say Uncle . . . and Aunt.* 1998. WaterBrook, paper. 256 pp. ISBN 1-57856-044-6.
> Hattie prays fervently and matches two career-obsessed people, Sean Flannigan and Julia Evans. Sean is suddenly required to take care of an infant niece and in desperation asks Julia for help. She hasn't a clue, either, but soon both of them are playing mom and dad.

> *Raising Cain . . . and His Sisters.* 1999. WaterBrook, paper. 256 pp. ISBN 1-57856-141-8.
> A lonely widow, Olivia Harmon, doesn't quite know what to pray for. Then a trucker, also a widower but with three children to care for, loses control of his rig and crashes through the side of Hattie's boarding house and into Olivia's life.

★ **RICHARDSON, H. L.** *Split Ticket.* **1996. Word, paper. 313 pp. ISBN 0-8499-3933-X.**

Doug Stewart, a rich Orange County tax lawyer, is placed on the ballot for assemblyman by his fearsome wife, Nadine, while he's fishing down in Baja. With plenty of money to spend and a phalanx of clever consultants, Nadine gets her husband elected, and when Doug returns he finds himself being congratulated for the clever ruthlessness of his campaign. Doug is about to bail out any way he can when Nadine is killed, and he feels forced to go to Sacramento. Partly because of his money and partly because of the reputation his wife established for him, Doug quickly ascends the power ladder, and there's talk of him running for governor or even president. Luckily, he has the sense to take refuge in the mountain country north of Sacramento, where he finds a new love and a cause he can enthusiastically support. Richardson spent more than two decades in the California Senate and his send-up of contemporary politics couldn't be much better.

ROPER, GAYLE. *Enough!* **1997. Multnomah, paper. 202 pp. ISBN 1-57673-185-5.**

Humor for Mom: gentle Molly Gregory is at her wit's end trying to corral her three teenagers. They run her life until the day she cries, not uncle but enough, and goes on strike until they decide to behave like civilized human beings.

SPANGLER, ANN, ed. *She Who Laughs, Lasts.* **2000. Zondervan, paper. 224 pp. ISBN 0-310-22898-0.**

Spangler collects 73 fictional memoirs on subjects such as romance, married life, mothers, Christmas, raising kids, and growing old. It's a collection looking for an Erma Bombeck, offering wholesome, upbeat contemporary wisdom rather than laughter. For ministers, there are some anecdotes and clean jokes that could round out a sermon.

LITERARY

Popular novels that also are of high literary quality are few and far between. More often, the literary novel languishes both in sales and circulation. Jan Karon manages both but probably because of her subject matter: eccentric small-town folk, and a bumbling, lovable minister. (In this volume, Karon is placed under "Nostalgia" later in this chapter.)

And Karon is uplifting, a somewhat uncommon feature of literary fiction. Literary novels in the United States are mostly realistic efforts. There is an active distrust among literary writers of the happy ending as being dishonest or at best outdated. And yet those who work with readers hear again and again the refrain: "I don't want anything that's depressing."

It seems doubtful that any fiction writer begins a novel by announcing, "I want to depress people." Rather, a literary writer seeks the truth. The truth may set the writer—and many readers—free. Others find such explorations depressing precisely because they *are* true. Such readers have encountered all the truth they can take in their workday.

Another sort of reader seeks more, however. She wants to be challenged by language and ideas, and she holds predictable plot lines in contempt. Put another way, novels that challenge the intellect are entertaining for this reader, and what is popularly thought of as entertaining leaves her cold.

Of course, confusing the matter still more, many genre novels are literary efforts as well. Much of the time, genres are assigned to novels simply to market them, and many mysteries and fantasies could also be called "literary." Many biblical novels are written to the highest literary standard. Francine Rivers, basically a romance writer, writes hauntingly and movingly no matter her subject, and John L. Moore's contemporary westerns are high literature. Mary Doria Russell's *The Sparrow* (p. 270) is such an extraordinary piece of work that it ceases to be thought of as science fiction, though clearly that's what it is. The stars (★) in this book are an attempt to point out genre novels that are more literary than their colleagues, but in the end, while it's easy to pinpoint what it is not, "literary" is a fuzzy category.

Certainly, language is a prime concern. One cannot call a novel literary if it is badly written, and many literary writers pride themselves on their style almost to the exclusion of their storytelling. Seeking purity of language and the right voice, literary writers make great efforts to avoid clichés and shopworn concepts; a fine style is nearly synonymous with wisdom.

Plot is less a concern than character. It matters less what happens than the character's feelings and philosophy about it as he or she reacts to the conflict the writer poses.

In a genre romance, the reader can be assured that life will work out for the heroine, that love will find a way. The reader takes her satisfaction from the variations in this ageless story.

Literary novels are seldom so predictable, yet another explanation for why they have difficulty finding readers. Most readers don't want to look at life seriously—or for that matter, comically. They want to escape. But literary writing strives to hold up a mirror to life, even if it is a bent, surrealistic mirror. Literary writing doesn't allow escape—or rather, it may offer the finest escape of all, but it won't do so along predictable trajectories, and always it will comment on life and provoke meditation.

Although it's a stretch to label genre writing as superficial, what you see is often all you're going to get. In literary novels, irony, allusion, and suggestive imagery are often at work, and much goes on beneath the surface.

For many readers, this interplay of language, ideas, and sly shades of meaning is the whole point of reading fiction—these elements are, in fact, the "story." For other readers, the story is simply the plot, and some, perhaps remembering their high school English classes, can actually be angered by the notion of an author's "hidden meaning."

The point is not to insult the reader by trying to dumb down her tastes. But a reader can also be insulted by the advisor's attempt to "improve" upon her tastes. As is always the case, it's good to know what the reader read last.

See also chapter 3, "Christian Classics."

BELD, GORDON. *A Gentle Breeze from Gossamer Wings.* 1999. PREP, paper. 279 pp. ISBN 1-885288-07-7.

Beld dramatizes the story of Ang Lee, a young woman brutalized by Khmer Rouge troops who escaped to Thailand, where she bargained for her passage to the United States by agreeing to marry a family friend. The "novel" is laid out in documentary style, incorporating summaries of the news and an interview with the author. It is a deeply felt, even poetic appreciation of the bravery of Cambodian refugees and the roles churches played in their settlement in the United States. ▟**Discussion**

◄✶ ★ **BENTZ, JOSEPH.** *A Son Comes Home.* 1999. Bethany, paper. 320 pp. ISBN 0-7642-2207-4.

Chris LaRue was never his father's favorite. The favorite son died in a car crash, and somehow Chris carries the blame for it, as if he should have been the one to die. Embittered Chris has made his way as a teacher in Los Angeles and has found a measure of happiness. When he receives the news from Indiana that his father is dying, he's not happy about coming home. But he does, and in some ways assumes the mantle of head of family in this bittersweet, reflective tale.

◄✶ ★ **BRANSFORD, STEPHEN.** *The Last Photograph.* 1995. Nelson. 160 pp. ISBN 0-7852-8011-1.

Two brothers, sons of a grizzled lumberman who becomes an evangelist, have always been rivals. The narrator, Stephen, is the gentler, and follows Christ. But for his brother, Gordon, his experiences in Vietnam are an argument against a merciful or a good God. The rift between the two threatens to deepen, but one day Stephen learns that Gordon has been injured at a remote mountain camp. As Stephen hastens to his brother's side, Bransford tells the family story, which he informs the reader in an afterword is all but literally a true story.

★ **BUECHNER, FREDERICK**

A Presbyterian minister and teacher, a novelist and author of numerous theological treatises, Buechner is a subtle, multifaceted writer with a golden style. If the mentor of many evangelical writers is C. S. Lewis, Buechner's is Paul Tillich, however, and thus he is somewhat too secular for many Christian readers, and somewhat too religious for many secular readers (Buechner 1992). But not once in his long career, beginning in 1950 with *A Long Day's Dying,* has he written anything other than a brilliant book; his "God-haunted" characters are sometimes compared to Graham Greene's.

BEBB SERIES ▟**Discussion**

Lion Country. 1971. Atheneum. (Out of print.)

The nearest Buechner has ever come to bestsellerdom is the satirical Bebb series, featuring Leo Bebb, an ex-con (he exposed himself to a group of children) and con man who runs a mail-order Bible college, the Church of Holy Love, out of his garage in Armadillo, Florida. The narrator, a restless dreamer and failure named Antonio Parr, is intent on revealing this charlatan to the world, but the situation turns out to be far more complex than he'd thought. Bebb knows the Bible backwards and forwards and is not really interested in growing rich. He seems genuinely to want to help the poor, the disabled, the bereaved in spirit, and he often does, including Antonio's own sister. Bebb is a charlatan, but he is also proof that God works in mysterious ways, and many of his rantings and apocalyptic predictions make sense.

Open Heart. 1972. Atheneum. (Out of print.)
In the sequel to *Lion Country,* Bebb takes a great revival to the land.

Love Feast. 1974. Atheneum. (Out of print.)
Buechner's third Bebb book takes place in Princeton, where Bebb goes down in flames at a holy orgy as he attempts to involve the younger generation in his Love Feast movement.

Treasure Hunt. 1977. Atheneum. (Out of print.)
Antonio Parr, introduced in *Lion Country,* reflects on life in the wake of Bebb's death in this last of the Bebb books.

The Final Beast. 1965. Atheneum. (Out of print.)
Irma Reinwasser, a Holocaust survivor who cares for Theodore Nicolet's young daughters after his wife dies, says, "If you got God for a friend, you don't need any enemies." Indeed, it seems so, as Nicolet, a minister, strives mightily to maintain his faith, to rediscover signs of God in the workings of life. The Devil in the form of a small-town newspaperman, a dour, vengeful man who "had learned to be world-weary before he had learned anything very much about the world," makes matters worse for the melancholy, faintly comical minister.

The Storm. 1998. HarperSanFrancisco. 199 pp. ISBN 0-06-061144-8.
Kenzie Maxwell was a bit of a rascal in his youth, but even then he was embarked on a spiritual search. One hazard of his search is his illegitimate daughter, the beautiful and unconventional Bree, whose birth, through a series of complications, exiled Kenzie from New York and drove a wedge between his brother and himself. Now Kenzie's playing out Shakespeare's *The Tempest* on an island off the Florida coast. A tropical storm is about to make landfall. Bree is on her way to join him, and so is his brother. Prospero, Caliban— they're all here in disguise, all decent people who have made mistakes, now at a point of crisis and possibly reconciliation in this lyrical tale steeped in magic and the subtle wisdom accrued over Buechner's long career.

YA *The Wizard's Tide.* 1990. HarperSanFrancisco. 104 pp. ISBN 0-06-061160-X.
Eleven-year-old Teddy Schroeder and his kid sister, Bean, watch the family fortunes fail as the Depression invades a small New Jersey town. Teddy's pretty mother, used to fine things, begins an affair. Teddy's father sinks to alcoholism and eventual suicide (as did Buechner's own father). Yet in Buechner's hands the children's unquestioning love for their parents triumphs, and somehow the children do, too.

COREY, G. ROGER

E *Eden Springs.* 1999. Harvest House, paper. 238 pp. ISBN 0-7369-0105-1.
Reporter Donny Foster tracks down a story of small-town graft even as he deals with the moody behavior of his old friend Tag, an Air Force pilot who has recently returned from the Gulf War.

E ★ *In a Mirror Dimly.* 1998. Harvest, paper. 276 pp. ISBN 1-56507-920-5.
John Brindle is a doctor in a refugee camp about 10 years after the American exodus from Vietnam. Boat people arrive almost daily. Brindle, having lost his family several years before, is a walking dead man, putting himself to sleep with alcohol, indifferent to the love of a young camp worker who senses his pain. Then a young Vietnamese woman, near death, arrives in the camp, and something in her haunted eyes brings him to life again. There are shades of *Lord Jim* here, and Corey captures his milieu—the camp hospital, the desperate but also devious refugees, the corrupt Indonesian hosts—with perfection.

YA ★ **CRAVEN, MARGARET.** *I Heard the Owl Call My Name.* **Originally published in 1973. (Many editions.)**
See discussion in chapter 15, "Young Adult."

E **FISCHER, JOHN.** *Ashes on the Wind.* **1998. Bethany, paper. 256 pp. ISBN 1-55661-678-3.**
A laconic old fellow named Sam Dunn has his wife cremated and her ashes cast to the winds of Florida Bay, much to the chagrin of his righteous daughter-in-law, Bobbi, who never really approved of Sam. There's a mix-up: The ashes are actually those of a traveling evangelist's wife, a plain woman but an indispensable part of the act because she handled snakes. A snakebite killed her, but the evangelist may have planned the death because of his lust for a younger woman. A warrant is issued for the evangelist's arrest even as Sam hunts him for the right ashes and Bobbi follows, all parties converging in Fischer's vivid, hilarious revival service. Somehow, even though the evangelist is a charlatan, faith prospers.

11

GLANCY, DIANE. *Fuller Man.* **1999. Moyer Bell. 190 pp. ISBN 1-55921-271-3.**
Hadley Willigie's coming-of-age is complicated by the harsh fundamentalism of her madly dysfunctional family, though she and her younger sister, Healey, find some success in life: Hadley as a journalist and Healey as a missionary to Africa. Healey is beset with a baffling unease, however, whereas Healey seems serene. Hadley slowly concludes that what she needs is a firm foundation of faith, and she seems to find it at a revival. And yet the entire effect, though sometimes poetic, is undercut with Glancy's elliptical style.

E **HALL, LINDA.** *Sadie's Song.* **2001. Multnomah, paper. 300 pp. ISBN 1-57673-659-8.**
Sadie Thornton is doing the traditional wife-and-mother thing through a long, soulful summer when everyone in her little town is worried over the disappearance of a teenage girl. Not much happens, really, but what does happen grows ever more alarming. Sadie's rule-bound husband, besieged with financial problems, begins to beat her. Her song grows ever more plaintive and desperate, until at last a flood of emotions washes everyone clean.

YA **HUFFEY, RHODA.** *The Hallelujah Side.* **1999. Delphinium Books. 272 pp. ISBN 1-883285-17-8.**
Little happens in this darkly comic tale featuring the family of Assembly of God minister Winston Fish of Ames, Iowa. Young Roxanne Fish, the youngest daughter, is the narrator. Colleen, Roxanne's older sister, shows signs of leaving the faith; the family moves to Pasadena; and Roxanne comes to the Lord with some help from Aretha Franklin. That's all there is to the story, but, much like Marilyn Robinson in the minor classic *Housekeeping* (1980), Huffey can be sidesplittingly funny with her mad, circular dialogues and deft characterizations. Every member of the Fish family feels pursued by demons. They cannot get on with life when the Second Coming could occur at any moment. The Reverend Fish himself is embarked on a project to refute *Das Kapital* with scripture.

YA **IRVING, JOHN.** *A Prayer for Owen Meany.* **1989. Ballantine, paper. 543 pp. ISBN 0-345-41797-6.**
Through the point of view of Johnny Wheelwright, Irving tells the Dickensian, tragicomic tale of young, physically small Owen Meany, convinced he is destined to do God's work and that he will, like Christ, be martyred. Johnny and Owen are forever linked by the foul ball Owen hits that kills Johnny's mother. That is the awful truth of Owen's godly but doomed existence: People around him are hurt, but it is the hurt of life fully lived, and redemption hovers near.

PEARSON, T. R. *Gospel Hour.* **1991. Morrow. (Out of print.)**
With a galloping comic style somewhere between Flannery O'Connor and Harry Crews, Pearson creates good old boy Donnie Huff of the Blue Ridge Mountains. Donnie is miraculously brought back from the dead after a logging accident. He isn't sure of this, but his dour mother-in-law convinces him and takes him to church, where he gives testimony and moves the faithful into near delirium. Shortly, he takes his show on the road and lives the high life of women and booze, a la Erskine Caldwell's Journeyman (in *Journeyman,* 1938). But while Journeyman is vicious and unrepentant, Donnie is good-hearted, and his hypocrisy, even if it was imposed on him by his mother-in-law, begins to bother him. For the first time in his life, he wonders why he's on Earth.

REYNOLDS, SHERI. *The Rapture of Canaan.* **1995. Putnam's. 317 pp. ISBN 0-399-14112-X.**
Fifteen-year-old Ninah Huff takes seriously the warnings of Grandpa Herman, founder of the backwoods South Carolina Church of Fire and Brimstone, that she must walk a narrow path to be prepared for the Rapture. Those who don't are made to endure bizarre, medieval punishments such as dunkings and solitary confinement. But despite the mightiest efforts of Ninah and her prayer partner James, the two at last yield to the delights of the flesh, and Ninah becomes pregnant. Woeful tragedies, miracles, and a feminist liberation of spirit ensue in this widely read coming-of-age story, an Oprah selection showing the influence of Flannery O'Connor, not to mention Erskine Caldwell.

SCHAAP, JAMES CALVIN

◀E► *In the Silence There Are Ghosts.* 1995. Baker, paper. 228 pp. ISBN 0-8010-8381-8.
Emily Doorn led a glamorous life in California as wife to a successful man and as an actress in TV commercials, but now she's divorced and her acting career, such as it was, is over. She needs rest and a good place for her children to grow up, and there's none better than her hometown, Neukirk, Iowa. Using a manner and tone somewhat reminiscent of *The Bridges of Madison County* (1992), Schaap brings Emily together with Norm Visser, a complex man mysteriously linked to Emily's past and the death of her sister.

Paternity. 2001. Quiddity Press. 234 pp. ISBN 0-970-96232-0.
Schaap brings his unique brand of Christian realism to the subject of fatherhood, taking the points of view of fathers, sons, and daughters. Seeking truth, he strips away artifice. All of his characters are on a journey toward grace; they don't always find it.

◀E► *Romey's Place.* 1999. Baker, paper. 288 pp. ISBN 0-8010-6001-X.
Schaap takes readers back to 1950s Wisconsin through the eyes of 14-year-old Lowell Prins, a God-fearing middle-class kid who strikes up a friendship with Romey Guttner, who's from the wrong side of the tracks and has the father to prove it. Romey takes Lowell down a sinful road, though it is not *very* sinful. Labor strife boils over in the little town, with Romey's corrosive father at the center of it. This drives the wedge of class between Lowell and Romey and

gives the novel a nostalgic and regretful feel somewhere between *Stand by Me* and *A Separate Peace*. Unfortunately, the editorial comments of the adult Lowell, trying to come to terms with the actions of his self-righteous father, are intrusive, explaining away much of the novel's narrative drive.

⬛✖★ *The Secrets of Barneveld Calvary*. 1997. Baker, paper. 192 pp. ISBN 0-8010-5755-8.
In a series of polished, linked short stories not unlike those in *Winesburg, Ohio* (1919), Schaap uses a small-town pastor's recollections of the informal testimony of his congregation to frame various characters, each of whom undergoes a spiritual crisis. **Discussion**

⬛✖ SPRINKLE, PATRICIA. *The Remember Box*. 2000. Zondervan, paper. 416 pp. ISBN 0-310-229928.

YA A Presbyterian minister moves with his family to a small church in Job's Corner, South Carolina, where he battles against racial prejudice rather like Atticus Finch in *To Kill a Mockingbird*. His niece, 11-year-old Carley Marshall, also parallels young Scout in Harper Lee's classic, and there are many other similarities, including a black man falsely accused of murder. One difference is that Carley must deal with her father, who appears after being declared dead. Sprinkle knows her Southern community well and effectively evokes the 1950s hysteria surrounding communism and racism. The sullen black servant, Raifa, is brilliantly characterized. But skilled as the novel is, readers will feel they've been here before.

⬛✖ ★ THOENE, BROCK. *The Legend of Storey County*. 1995. Nelson. 256 pp. ISBN 0-7852-8070-7.

YA Thoene's in a whimsical mood in this clever retelling of Mark Twain's *Roughing It* (1872) that also draws upon *The Adventures of Huckleberry Finn* (1885). An old ex-slave named Jim Canfield makes friends with a young riverboat captain named Sam, and, with the imminence of the Civil War and the possibility that Jim will be sold down the river, the two escape to Iowa and then to the Wild West of Nevada's gold camps. **Discussion**

TROBAUGH, AUGUSTA

⬛✖★ *Praise Jerusalem!* 1997. Baker. 288 pp. ISBN 0-8010-1147-7.
William Faulkner and Eudora Welty come to mind with Trobaugh's deeply Southern, stubborn small-town women. Her main character is Georgia, whom poverty forces to sell her house and move to a rundown farm near the town of Jerusalem. Then God brings an illiterate (and funny) hairdresser into her life, but whether to help or annoy her isn't always clear.

⬛✖★ *Resting in the Bosom of the Lamb*. 1999. Baker. 229 pp. ISBN 0-8010-1170-1.
Booklist called Trobaugh's second novel a "contemporary Southern masterpiece," and it may well be the equal of Eudora Welty or Katherine Anne Porter in its brooding lyricism and deceptive simplicity. It's the tale of four aging Georgia matrons as told by Pet, the black servant whose fate is so inextricably woven with that of the white women that she has become a family member. Seeing visions of the past in the person of her long-dead grandmother, Pet pulls the reader ever closer to devastating family secrets that explain why the old women are as they are and that throw light on the long dark journey of race relations in the South.

✦ ★ **TURNER, JAMIE LANGSTON.** *Some Wildflower in My Heart.* **1998. Bethany, paper. 368 pp. ISBN 1-55661-493-4.**

Margaret Tuttle, supervisor of an elementary school cafeteria, bore her grandfather's child 30 years ago and has spent every day since walling off any expression of love, losing herself in her one delight, literature. She's married to a gentle man 20 years older than she with whom she's never slept. Slowly, through the insistence of a new cafeteria worker, Birdie Freeman, Margaret confronts not only the deep sorrow of her life but the mystery of God, who is boundlessly good, she feels, but causes his creatures to suffer. Margaret's story, set in the same region as Dorothy Allison's *Bastard Out of Carolina* (1992), treats the same raw hurts, but Turner is subtler; the slow blooming of the wildflower in Margaret's heart is a thing of transcendent beauty.   **Discussion**

A Garden to Keep. 2001. Bethany, paper. 415 pp. ISBN 0-7642-2154-X.

A Garden to Keep is less a sequel than a companion to *Some Wildflower in My Heart*, although it does feature Margaret Tuttle, who helps the heroine, Elizabeth Landis, to declare herself among the born-again. Elizabeth, like Margaret, is a great reader, and enjoys quoting poetry. Also like Margaret, this aspect of Elizabeth's characterization isn't always believable, though it's the one thing about her that isn't ordinary and drab. Once saved, Elizabeth discovers that her husband is having an affair. She leans on her new faith to save their moribund marriage.   **Sequel**

🅨🅐 ★ **TYLER, ANN.** *Saint Maybe.* **1992. (Originally published in 1991.) Ballantine, paper. 373 pp. ISBN 0804108749.**

Young Ian Bedloe, beginning college, thinks his trusting older brother, Danny, has made a terrible mistake in marrying pretty Lucy, an ingenuous divorcee with two small children from her previous marriage, and one, maybe, from Danny. Ian is convinced Lucy is unfaithful and in a stressful moment blurts this out to Danny. Danny, a little drunk, promptly kills himself in an auto accident, and Lucy dies of sleeping pills not long after. Consumed with guilt, Danny stumbles into the storefront Church of the Second Chance, where the minister counsels him that his own second chance may come but only if he atones for his mistakes by dropping out of college and working to support (and raise) the children, which Danny does in this tragic, comic and affecting small masterpiece.

UPDIKE, JOHN

A Congregationalist, Updike is often identified as a Christian writer in literary and ecumenical circles, but seldom so in evangelical ones, perhaps because of his frank portrayals of sexual relationships. Some sort of religious inquiry informs every Updike novel, however, usually revolving around the difficulty of faith in a secular society.

A Month of Sundays. 1996. (Originally published in 1975.) Fawcett, paper. 271 pp. ISBN 0-449-91220-5.

One of Updike's sexiest tales features the Reverend ("Doubting") Thomas Marshfield, who has been banished to a sanitarium in Arizona to seek a cure for his habit of seducing the women of his church. Not that the women have complained—except for one, an irate ex-organist. Wonderfully satirical of gimmicks introduced into mainline services to attract a jaded public, and at base deeply conservative on matters of faith, the novel is, even so, not for the easily outraged.

In the Beauty of the Lilies. 1996. Knopf. 491 pp. ISBN 0-679-44640-0.

In this family saga loosely based on Abraham, Isaac, and Joseph, Updike tries to capture the flavor of the entire twentieth century. Charles Wilmot, the weakest of patriarchs, is a Presbyterian minister who becomes disenchanted with his faith but cannot succeed at any other endeavor. His son, Teddy, spends his gentle life in confusion. Teddy's daughter, Esther, becomes a movie star, illustrating Updike's sly contention that in an increasingly secular society movies have become religion. But the movies are silly, as Updike's parodic summaries of them gleefully show. Esther neglects her son, Clark, who joins a dangerous cult, reflecting headlines but also returning to Charles Wilmot's failed passions.

Roger's Version. 1986. Knopf. 328 pp. ISBN 0-394-55435-3.
Technological advances have dated this contrivance about Roger Lambert, a professor of divinity and, like Updike, devotee of Karl Barth, and a young computer whiz, Dale Kohler, who seeks Roger's help securing a grant. Roger believes that God's existence can only be taken on faith, whereas Dale thinks that the power of computers is sufficient to demonstrate God's existence scientifically. As usual, Updike enlivens things with sexual escapades: Roger's wife with Dale and Roger with his half-sister's daughter, Verna.

 VAUGHN, ELIZABETH DEWBERRY. *Many Things Have Happened Since He Died and Here Are a Few of the Highlights.* 1990. Doubleday. (Out of print.)
Despite the flippant title and the occasional morbid humor of the narrative, this is not a funny book. Vaughn brilliantly portrays a determined young woman trying to make the rigorous but contradictory morality she's grown up with work in her trailer park society. After her father kills himself, she plunges into marriage with a dental student named Malone. Malone will never make much of a husband, and part of the narrator's maturation is to acknowledge this. Eventually, Malone also kills himself. But the narrator is herself a disturbed personality, ambitious to become a writer but filled with murderous fantasies, and convinced God is in the room when she's having sex. Altogether, she's a convincing, likable, though scary young woman groping blindly to make sense of things; she's also a living, wounded indictment of fundamentalism.

WILSON, A. N. *The Vicar of Sorrows.* 1993. Norton. 391 pp. ISBN 0-393-03610-3.
In this woefully comic tale, Wilson tracks the downturning fortunes of Anglican Father Francis Kreer, a nice fellow who neither believes in God nor loves his wife. Still, he doesn't *dislike* his wife, and turns in a credible job ministering to the needs of his small flock. Then two things happen: Father Kreer's mother dies, and uncomfortable secrets are revealed; and he falls uncontrollably in love with a much younger, disastrously inappropriate woman.

WOIWODE, LARRY
Woiwode was among the brightest lights on the literary scene in the 1970s, the winner of many prizes, and a regular contributor to the *New Yorker.* Toward the end of writing his most widely admired novel, *Beyond the Bedroom Wall* (1975), a worsening marriage and the death of his father brought him to spiritual crisis, and he converted to Presbyterianism.

Though they are always respectfully reviewed, his subsequent novels, memoirs, and religious explorations *(Acts,* 1992) have lost him much of his literary following. He hasn't, on the other hand, caught on among evangelicals, partly because of his high style, more because he does not shy away from profanity and the depiction of explicit sex when he feels his story requires it. Besides Christianity, his other religion is realism (Woiwode 1992).

Born Brothers. 1988. Farrar. (Out of print.)
Born Brothers returns to the family saga of the Neumillers, begun in *Beyond the Bedroom Wall,* with the story of brothers Jerome and Charles. They are dark and light, quiet and outgoing, rootless and spiritual—Esau and Jacob, perhaps. The reader

watches through Woiwode's short, poetic vignettes, from the 1940s through the 1960s, from North Dakota to New York. Initially, they are a perfect match, like halves of the same person. In the end, one brother is damned, the other saved, and they couldn't be further apart.

Indian Affairs. 1992. Macmillan. 290 pp. ISBN 0-689-12155-5.
Indian Affairs is a sequel to Woiwode's highly praised first novel, *What I'm Going to Do, I Think* (1969), about a young couple, Chris and Ellen Van Eenanam, on their honeymoon in Michigan's Upper Peninsula. It is seven years later, and there are some strains in the marriage; there are no children. Chris has come here ostensibly to finish his thesis, and Ellen is resentful, knowing he could finish in a week if he applied himself. But Chris is having an identity crisis over his Native American heritage, exacerbated by the restless, even thuggish Native Americans in the neighborhood. Tragedy must strike before he pulls himself together.

★ *Poppa John.* 1981. Farrar. (Out of print.)
"Poppa John" has grown to fame playing a wise, grandfatherly figure on a TV soap opera. He seems immortal, but then his character is written out of the show, and he must face the truth about himself: He has grown old, he has no job, and, unlike the character he played, he is lost and spiritually bereft. Despairing, he takes to the bottle, but his wife sticks by him, and those Bible verses he spouted to the masses still ring in his head.

WRIGHT, VINITA HAMPTON

◆█✗★ *Grace at Bender Springs.* 1999. Broadman and Holman, paper. 399 pp. ISBN 0-8054-2127-0.
Wright's failing farm and mining town of Bender Springs, Kansas, comes lovingly to life through her familiar, but sharply drawn, characters: the lonely pastor's wife, longing for a more cultural place in life and afflicted with impure thoughts; the seemingly harmless house painter, really an alcoholic and thief; and the sad confirmed bachelor, who falls hopelessly in love. Pain—and grace—await them all.

◆█✗★ *Velma Still Cooks in Leeway.* 2000. Broadman and Holman, paper. 309 pp. ISBN 0-8054-2128-9.
In the loneliness and puzzlement of her old age Velma Brendle, of Leeway, Kansas, has decided to record the histories of some of Leeway's residents. There's the shy girl, date raped by a popular boy; no one believes the girl except Velma, but Velma, like the pastor and the boy's parents, knows the disaster that will result if the girl's story is allowed to be true. There are the stories of the man who suddenly, inexplicably, leaves his wife and family; the honest, widower mechanic who gossips too much; and the loquacious busybody who falls down some stairs and is never "right" again. Characters cross and crisscross, resulting in a novel composed of small sorrows, celebrating faith as a matter of course, quietly triumphant.

MORALITY TALES

Every Christian novel is a morality tale first. Problem romances and the stories of Christians who fall in love with unbelievers clearly favor one course of action to be more moral than another. But in many stories the entertainment value of romances and historicals is submerged in the interest of providing a Christian lesson.

Often written by pastors, the morality tale is an old genre in Christian fiction that throws light on difficult ethical questions and problems of faith. It shows the wages of sin. It deals with the intrusions of the broader, worldly world on Christians trying to lead a godly life. It shows that an overcoming life will be rewarded, and not just in Heaven.

ALCORN, RANDY. *Safely Home.* **2001. Tyndale. 402 pp. ISBN 0-8423-5537-5.**
Alcorn dramatizes the persecution of Christians in Communist China in his tale of Li Quan, a beleaguered Christian, and Ben Fielding, a ruthless corporate executive from Portland. They were roommates in college, and, ironically, Ben Fielding's testimony converted Li Quan. Now, Ben is about to make millions selling microchips to China, and niceties such as the imprisonment and torture of religious minorities don't concern him. That's his attitude, at least, before he learns of Li Quan's predicament.

 ANDERSON, ANN KIEMERL. 1998. *This Is a Story About God.* **Beacon Hill, paper. 96pp. ISBN 0-834-11731-2.**
David Nash believes God will provide him with a liver transplant when he's diagnosed with cirrhosis. At times he's afflicted with doubt that a liver will ever be found and feels he will die. But in the end his faith grows stronger, and his ordeal becomes a spiritual exploration.

 ★ **ARVIN, REED.** *The Wind in the Wheat.* **1994. Nelson. 360 pp. ISBN 0-7852-8146-0.**
YA See discussion in chapter 15, "Young Adult."

BAMBOLA, SYLVIA. *Tears in a Bottle.* **2001. Multnomah, paper. 320 pp. ISBN 1-57673- 802-7.**

Bambola cries out against abortion in her tale of Becky Taylor, a young woman who reluctantly goes along when her parents insist that she have an abortion. As she finishes the procedure, the clinic is raided by a fanatic, and Becky is the only one left alive. In the weeks that come, her guilt and the trauma of the event drive her toward suicide. Then she meets Maggie Singer, a Christian social worker who helps women who have had abortions find forgiveness.

BECHARD, GORMAN. *The Second Greatest Story Ever Told.* **1991. Citadel. 291 pp. ISBN 0-8065-1263-6.**

Christ returns as a teenage girl who spreads her message on talk shows in this bawdy, intermittently funny tale, imitative of Kurt Vonnegut but without his subtlety, that even so points to an exemplary life.

 BENTZ, JOSEPH. *Cradle of Dreams.* **2001. Bethany, paper. 366 pp. ISBN 0-7642-2208-2.**
Laura and Paul have a perfect Christian marriage except they have no children. Because Laura is in her mid-30s, both assume it's her problem, but then Paul reluctantly takes some tests, and they show his sperm count is low. Bentz looks at the problem of infertility in marriage from every conceivable angle, and certainly this marriage seems real enough, but Paul and Laura's desperate protestations wear on the reader, turning obsessive and even a bit strange. None too soon, a solution arrives.

BRADY, JOAN

God on a Harley. 1995. Pocket. 147 pp. ISBN 0-671-53621-4.
Christine Moore, a 37-year-old nurse, returns to her old job in New Jersey and plunges into despair over the fleeting possibility of romantic love. At a bar she meets "Joe," a modern Jesus with a set of commandments for Christine that are fitted especially to her. Following them, she finds happiness and a man finally good enough for her: Jesus himself.

Heaven in High Gear. 1997. Pocket. 212 pp. ISBN 0-671-00772-6.
Though not a sequel to *God on a Harley, Heaven in High Gear* tells almost the same story: this time of Heather Hurley, a Los Angeles stripper who returns to her New Jersey home and falls in love with Jesus.

CALDWELL, TAYLOR

The Listener. 1960. Doubleday. (Out of print.)
Pilgrims bring their agonized stories to a mysterious marble house, where a listener, really Jesus, waits patiently, and hears them out, until they stumble upon the wisdom that in their innermost selves they already knew; all they needed was a listener.   **Discussion**

No One Hears but Him. 1969. Doubleday. (Out of print.)
For some, Caldwell's shrill reactions to social events of the 1960s will mar the stories in *No One Hears but Him*. Otherwise, it follows the same structure as *The Listener*.

CULEA, JOHN

◀️✖ *Light the Night.* 1997. Chariot Victor, paper. 389 pp. ISBN 1-56476-296-4.
The media come in for a drubbing in Culea's uneven *Light the Night,* about a Los Angeles anchorman, Paul Thomas, who spearheads a campaign to clean up neighborhood violence. People turn on their house lights at agreed-upon times, patrol their neighborhoods, and begin talking to one another. So far, so good, but Paul is a quirky character, a mouthpiece for Culea's poltical views, and the result is a periodically interesting harangue.

◀️✖ *Promised Land.* 1998. Chariot Victor, paper. 350 pp. ISBN 1-56476-722-1.
Hoping to escape her boring hometown of Braxton, California, and become a journalist, Shelly Hinson writes a magazine story proclaiming Braxton the best small town in America and somehow gets it published. Both the desperate and the ambitious descend on Braxton seeking the perfect life, and, in no time, the town is struggling with ways to house, educate, and employ the newcomers. Braxton's boosters love the publicity, but then there's an accident at a town event, and the promoters, Shelly included, wonder what they've done. They take a strong look at themselves and grow wiser, perhaps, but it's difficult to know what Culea intended with this muddled novel based on a good premise.

◀️✖ **DEKKER, TED R. *Heaven's Wager.* 2000. Word, paper. 305 pp. ISBN 0-8499-4241-1.**
Software designer Kent Anthony invents the Advanced Funds Processing System for Citibank and thinks he's set for life. He plans an extravagant trip to Paris for his family and picks out a yacht. Then his wife dies, his program is stolen from him, and he's in ruins, on the brink of committing a major crime. It's God's ancient wager with the Devil about Job: see how much a good man can take.

DEMSKY, ANDY. *Dark Refuge.* 1995. Pacific, paper. 240 pp. ISBN 0-8163-1241-9.

YA See discussion in chapter 15, "Young Adult."

DOUGLAS, LLOYD C.

Dr. Hudson's Secret Journal. 1939. (Out of print.)
In *Dr. Hudson's Secret Journal,* written after *Magnificent Obsession* as a prequel, we meet Hudson and find out what those mysterious papers—identified in *Magnificent Obsession*—said.

Magnificent Obsession. 1929. (Out of print.)
Magnificent Obsession enjoyed worldwide popularity because of its prescriptions for living, a sort of Dale Carnegie philosophy crossed with the Sermon on the Mount. Bobby Merrill, the protagonist, is a mediocre, playboy surgeon who turns his life around after causing the death of his renowned fellow surgeon, Wayne Hudson. Deeply moved that his own life has been saved, Bobby peruses the late Hudson's personal papers and decides to become an anonymous philanthropist, on the principle that the good he does will flow back to him in fame and fortune. *Magnificent Obsession* was twice filmed; Rock Hudson played Bobby Merrill in the 1954 version, directed by Douglas Sirk. Sequel

GOUGE, LOUISE. *The Homecoming.* 1998. Crossway, paper. 192 pp. ISBN 0-89107-982-3.

The even yoke of marriage between believers is supposed to guarantee success, but it doesn't always. Janice Griffith, a single mother with a son, is struggling to make ends meet when she gets a call from her ex. He's a professional football player now, and making big money. Better, still, he's turned to God, and wants to get back together. Sounds too good to be true, and it nearly is.

GRAY, AL, AND ALICE GRAY. *Stories for a Man's Heart.* Multnomah, paper. 294 pp. ISBN 1-57673-479-X.

Inspirational stories on subjects such as fatherhood, sports, honoring women, and faith.

GRAY, ALICE

Stories for a Woman's Heart. Multnomah, paper. 289 pp. ISBN 1-57673-474-9.
Subjects include careers, domesticity, married life, children, and growing older.

Stories for a Teen's Heart. Multnomah, paper. 340 pp. ISBN 1-57673-646-6.
YA See discussion in chapter 15, "Young Adult."

HUNT, ANGELA, AND BILL MYERS. *Then Comes Marriage.* 2001. Zondervan. 137 pp. ISBN 0-310-23016-0.

Two of Christian fiction's most admired talents offer marriage counseling by way of a novella: A year after their wedding, Heather and Kurt Stone hate each other. Not really, but they've failed to allow for the differences between men and women. They have yet to surrender to each other, nor have they surrendered their combined wills to God.

◀▣✗ **JENKINS, JERRY B.** *Though None Go with Me.* **2000. Zondervan. 304 pp. ISBN 0-310-21948-5.**

Elizabeth LeRoy is born in January of 1900 and is a sort of "every woman" of the new century, living through many of its great events. She is unremarkable except that, as a teenager, she experiences a profound conversion to Christianity and thereafter resolves that nothing will turn her from the godly path—rather like a devotee of the Christian classic, *In His Steps.* And though her life is full of tragedy, Elizabeth never wavers, never reneges on her promise, even though sometimes she doubts whether there is any earthly reward in serving Jesus.

KINGSBURY, KAREN

◀▣✗ *On Every Side.* 2001. Multnomah, paper. 385 pp. ISBN 1-57673-850-7.

Lawyer Jordan Riley returns to his hometown to challenge in court the presence of a statue of Jesus in the city park. He's opposed by a local newswoman, Faith Moses, who was also his childhood sweetheart. Though based on a real case, Kingsbury's presentation is one-sided, never allowing that Jordan's point of view might have its sober—if politically correct—adherents; instead, she presents Jordan as emotionally damaged by childhood trauma, which he has incorrectly blamed on God. Jordan's love of Faith initiates his remission of sins.

◀▣✗ *Waiting for Morning.* 1999. Multnomah, paper. 366 pp. ISBN 1-57673-415-3.

Blind rage overtakes Hannah Ryan when a drunk driver cuts down her husband and children. She veers from the godly path in her thirst for revenge and cannot comprehend the remorse of the driver. The driver does get punished, but his suffering is only slightly worse than the punishment Hannah inflicts on herself until she finds her spiritual side once more and forgives.

◀▣✗ **MCGUIRE, BARRY, AND LOGAN WHITE.** *In the Midst of Wolves.* **1990. Crossway. (Out of print.)**

YA McGuire, of New Christy Minstrels and "Eve of Destruction" fame, was himself a tough biker in his youth, and his tale of Clint Backer, second in command in a motorcycle gang, rings true. (It's also a collector's item.) Clint wearies of the dissolute life he's leading—the drug use and violence—and comes to Jesus. Then he takes the Christian message to other lost (biker) souls. McGuire's bikers speak in a colorful blue-collar patois; they are often funny, and McGuire is never preachy.

◀▣✗ ★ **MCCUSKER, PAUL.** *The Faded Flower.* **2001. Zondervan. 160 pp. ISBN 0-310-23554-5.**

YA Frank Reynolds loses his job when a conglomerate buys out his little publishing firm. Forced to move back to his Podunk hometown, Frank is further distressed when his son throws out Frank's wishes for him as meaningless and when he discovers that his father, afflicted with the first stages of Alzheimer's, must move into a rest home. But in the rest home—called The Faded Flower—the old man shows that he still has some wisdom to share when it comes both to sons and grandsons. Drawing from events in his own family, McCusker approaches a tough subject without pedantry or sentimentality; as always, his style is a delight.

◀▣✗ **MCWILLIAMS, WARREN.** *Dear Chris: Letters on the Life of Faith.* **1999. Baylor University Press, paper. 186 pp. ISBN 0-918954-70-3.**

A young man, "Chris," drops out of seminary, marries, and takes a job on a newspaper. Old doubts plague him, however, and he writes to his favorite professor at the seminary. The professor answers entertainingly with a series of letters that discuss the uniqueness of Jesus and the nature of Christian life, alluding to sources as disparate as C. S. Lewis and the TV show *Quantum Leap*.

◄✗ MOSER, NANCY. *The Seat Beside Me.* **2001. Multnomah, paper. 450 pp. ISBN 1-57673-884-1.**
Moser tells the tried-and-true story of an air crash and its victims. Some are heroes; others are goats. All are profoundly changed.

RANEY, DEBORAH

◄✗ *In the Still of the Night.* 1997. Bethany, paper. 256 pp. ISBN 1-55661-667-8.
Now that her children are gone, Anna Marquette is intent on a career. Everything looks good until, on a trip to Orlando, she's raped and becomes pregnant. Despite her husband's doubts, she is steadfast in her convictions and refuses to have an abortion. **[Discussion]**

◄✗ *A Vow to Cherish.* 1996. Bethany, paper. 288 pp. ISBN 1-55661-666-X.
Ellen Brighton and her husband Jake have had a tough life and are looking forward to an easier one with the graduation of their youngest child from high school. But Ellen is diagnosed with Alzheimer's, and Jake is in agony, to the point he entertains thoughts of an affair with a younger, comforting woman. **[Discussion]**

RIVERS, FRANCINE

◄✗★ *The Atonement Child.* 1997. Tyndale. 237 pp. ISBN 0-8423-0041-4.
Rivers's antiabortion story, about Dynah Carey, a beautiful college student who is raped and impregnated by an itinerant stranger, gets high marks for its realistic portrayal of Dynah's dilemma and for highlighting the agonizing debate friends and advisors of rape victims go through. Ultimately, Dynah's faith requires that she give birth. Though the tale occasionally becomes a harangue, Rivers's message is powerful: Dynah's child atones for the abortion her mother had years before and, if an innocent baby is a symbol of the infant Jesus, for the sins of humankind. **[Discussion]**

◄✗ *Leota's Garden.* 1999. Tyndale. 350 pp. ISBN 0-8423-3572-2.
Leota Reinhardt is an 84-year-old widow of vast emotional experience who is coming to the end of things full of grief for her indifferently religious daughter, who thrusts her materialism onto Leota's granddaughter, Annie. But Annie has come to Christ on her own. She is much like Leota, making Rivers's point that love is eternal through the generations; if eclipsed for a while, it can be depended on to return. The point is also made when Annie and Corban Solsek, a know-it-all college student who falls in love with Annie, work to restore Leota's grand Victory garden, neglected for years because of the old woman's arthritis.

SMITH, BEVERLY BUSH

◄✗★ *Wings of a Dove.* 1996. Word, paper. 638 pp. ISBN 0-8499-3887-2.
Leslie Harper, Christian mother of two, agonizes over the passage in 1 Peter enjoining wives to be submissive to their husbands. She's married to Charles, who takes her money and ridicules her faith. In the end, when he grows violent, Leslie leaves Charles and is helped through her crisis by a women's group at church. Charles snaps and winds up in prison, where he repents, but Leslie isn't convinced.

 *Evidence of Things Unseen.* 1997. Word, paper. 350 pp. ISBN 0-8499-4040-0.
The loose sequel to *Wings of a Dove* again features the prayer journal of Zoe Lang, this time in intercession for her daughter-in-law, Andrea Lang, married to Zoe's son, Peter. Andrea is a busy professional woman whose daughter, Joy, is kidnapped. Andrea turns to God for help but when there is seemingly no answer, she dabbles in the occult, consulting with white witches.

◄ᴇ❳   **STAHL, HILDA.** *Gently Touch Sheela Jenkins.* **1989. Bethel, paper. 200 pp. ISBN 0-934998-32-9.**
🆈🅰 See discussion in chapter 15, "Young Adult."

TURNBULL, AGNES SLIGH. *Many a Green Isle.* **1968. Houghton Mifflin. (Out of print.)**
A college English teacher, Gavin McAllister, has saved his money for years to take some time off and write his dissertation. As things seem to be turning his way, rich man Loren Scott offers Gavin's college a huge donation for a new library. Gavin speaks out loud and clear that the money is merely a bribe in exchange for a diploma for Scott's playboy son, Lester. When Gavin returns home that evening, he receives the news that Ruth, his daughter, is pregnant by Lester.

TURNER, JAMIE LANGSTON

◄ᴇ❳ *By the Light of a Thousand Stars.* 1999. Bethany, paper. 320 pp. ISBN 0-7642-2153-1.
Catherine Biddle is as repressed a character as Margaret Tuttle in *Some Wildflower in My Heart,* Turner's exemplary novel about sexual abuse (p. 224). But while Margaret has a quirky charm and dignity about her, Catherine is just a fuss-budget. She rails against her unruly neighbors, the Chewnings, who are unquestionably a mess but radiate joy beside Catherine's prissy judgment about what's proper. Of course, that's Turner's point, and Catherine learns her heartfelt lesson. A fine lesson it is, but Catherine remains a chore, and readers may grow impatient with her.

◄ᴇ❳ *The Suncatchers.* 1995. Thomas Nelson, paper. 400 pp. ISBN 0-7852-7911-3.
Perry Warren, a dreamy, impractical writer, is sent on assignment to a small South Carolina town, where's he supposed to portray the backwardness of an evangelical congregation. The tables are predictably turned on Perry, and he becomes a convert, but Turner is often amusing and her minor characters, such as the old woman who clips coupons and chaperones the hapless Perry around supermarkets, are well done.

NOSTALGIA

Although many Christian historicals use elements of nostalgia, some, such as Ann Tatlock's *A Room of My Own* (p. 235), are so imbued with it that other themes seem muted. Typically, the settings are small Midwestern towns in a time thought to be simpler and more moral. Some use standard romance plots, while others have an air of lost love. World War II is a favorite setting. However, many novels evoking nostalgia have contemporary settings; it's just that they bring the golden past into the present.

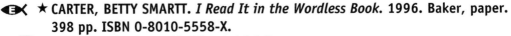   ★ **CARTER, BETTY SMARTT.** *I Read It in the Wordless Book.* **1996. Baker, paper. 398 pp. ISBN 0-8010-5558-X.**
🆈🅰 See discussion in chapter 15, "Young Adult."

★ JENKINS, JERRY B. 2001. *Hometown Legend*. Warner. 303 pp. ISBN 0-446-52902-8.

Jenkins was a sports writer before the Left Behind series, and he returns to his first love in fine form. *Hometown Legend* is about Cal Sawyer, a likable, middle-aged widower trying desperately to raise his daughter, Rachel, properly and to keep his little company, American Leather, in business. American Leather is the last American manufacturer of footballs, and its demise means that the little town of Athens City, Alabama, will probably be doomed as well. The high school is already destined for consolidation, but in its last year Buster Schuler, the school's legendary coach from years gone by, returns. Cal and a young phenom named Elvis Jackson join him for a rousing season that brings hope to Athens City. In the bargain, Cal finds love in this bittersweet, seamless tale.

★ KARON, JAN

★ *THE MITFORD YEARS*

One of the milestones of Christian fiction, Karon's Mitford series started in a small edition and might never have become the phenomenon it is without crossing over to a mainstream publisher, Viking Penguin. In turn, Viking Penguin's editions are among the few mainstream Christian novels to cross back into evangelical circles.

Mitford features the gentle adventures of Father Tim Kavanagh, an Episcopal rector, and the colorful, sometimes eccentric members of his parish. All turns out for the best in Father Tim's universe. But it is a much subtler place than the Mayberry it is often compared with, more like the world of Booth Tarkington's Penrod stories, and there is heartache to be found, even horror. Karon's little town is quaint and nostalgic, but every American recognizes it. It is not so much an unrealistic place as it is a hopeful one and, with Father Tim in charge, blessed.

Jan Karon, who lives in North Carolina near her mythical Mitford, spent many years as an advertising executive before turning to fiction. She brings out a new Mitford story every 18 months (Karon 1999).

See also Jan Karon's Christmas story, *The Mitford Snowmen*, p. 213.

> ***At Home in Mitford.*** 1994. Lion Family, paper. 446 pp. ISBN 0-7459-2629-0.
> In Father Tim's first appearance and Karon's first novel, Father Tim Kavanagh, an Episcopal rector in late middle-age, bumbles his way through several small crises, succeeding by the sheer power of his good intentions. But however naive and clumsy Father Tim is, he's also a wise counselor and a steadfast friend, first to a gigantic stray dog named Barnabas, who responds to Father Tim's admonitory Bible verses; next to his fiercely protective secretary, Emma, whom the parish thrusts upon him as an aid to his chaotic bachelorhood; and perhaps most of all to a small, unloved mountain boy, Dooley, with an unformed, but naturally generous nature. As in every novel of the series, Karon weaves in a number of subplots, here having to do with stolen jewels and cocaine; much happens in little Mitford. But in the end the crux of the story is Father Tim's subtle love affair with his next-door neighbor, the shrewd but zany Cynthia.

> ***A Light in the Window.*** 1995. Viking Penguin. 352 pp. ISBN 0-670-88226-7.
> The comic, though not satirical, sequel to *At Home in Mitford* features two women vying for Father Tim's heart and stomach: Cynthia of the first novel and Edith, a wealthy widow who could add casseroles to her dowry.

These High, Green Hills. 1996. Viking Penguin. 333 pp. ISBN 0-670-86934-1.
Father Tim returns from his honeymoon with Cynthia, and life is joyous, but not without problems. Cynthia's liberated ways initially displease the matrons of the parish. Father Tim is grieved to deal with problems in a tough part of town called the Creek, where poverty, domestic violence, and drug use are common. His faith is tested, but Cynthia's love and pleasure in simple things, not to mention young Dooley's success in school, keeps him going in this multilayered addition to the series, perhaps the best of them all.

Out to Canaan. 1997. Viking Penguin. 342 pp. ISBN 0-670-87485-X.
Change seems to be coming to Mitford in the form of a mayoral candidate's call for development, but the ordinary travails of ordinary people go on. Father Tim continues to help them. With Cynthia, he tries to locate Dooley's scattered brothers and sisters and help them, too. Growing older, the couple wonders if it's not time to retire.

C ***A New Song.*** 1999. Viking Penguin. 400 pp. ISBN 0-670-87810-3.
No sooner have Father Tim and Cynthia retired than they accept a church on Whitecap Island on the Atlantic. It's hard to leave Mitford, but their new parishioners prove to be as colorful as those in Mitford: an eccentric, lonely bachelor; an organist with a past; and a depressed woman whose three-year-old the couple keeps for a while. And there are frequent postings from Mitford, not all of them good news: Dooley spends some time in jail, and the new tenant of the Mitford rectory brings suit.

A Common Life: The Wedding Story. 2001. Viking. 208 pp. ISBN 0-670-89437-0.
Karon fills in the spaces between *A Light in the Window* and *These High, Green Hills* in this flashback—in other words, between Father Tim's proposal to Cynthia Coppersmith and the beginning of their happy marriage. All the familiar characters are here, variously stunned and delighted by the news.

★ **MARSHALL, CATHERINE.** *Christy.* **1967. (Many editions.)**
See discussion in chapter 15, "Young Adult."

★ **MARSHALL, CATHERINE.** *Julie.* **1984. (Many editions.)**
See discussion in chapter 15, "Young Adult."

SHANDS, LINDA. *A Time to Embrace.* **1995. InterVarsity, paper. 232 pp. ISBN 0-8308-1932-0.**
Celia Freeman wistfully chronicles doings on the WWII home front as her husband fights in the Pacific. Earthy and simple, Celia plants a victory garden, cries with friends over letters of condolence from commanding officers, and sits in with young mothers giving birth to babies who may never see their fathers.

STOKES, PENELOPE

YA ★ ***The Blue Bottle Club.*** 1999. Word. 352 pp. ISBN 0-8499-1573-2.
See discussion in chapter 1. 　　　　　　　　　　　　　　　　　　■Discussion■

FAITH ON THE HOME FRONT

Home Fires Burning. 1996. Tyndale, paper. 345 pp. ISBN 0-8423-0851-2.
In Eden, Mississippi in 1943, new soldiers Link Winsom and Owen Slaughter strike up romances with Libba and Willie Coltrain, respectively, and then are shipped off to the front. Both men are patriotic, heroic, and their private behavior is beyond reproach; both women are faithful and pure.

Till We Meet Again. 1997. Tyndale, paper. 327 pp. ISBN 0-8423-0852-0.
Link has returned home after it was feared he'd been killed. But he's paralyzed, and thus must fight a new battle, to put his faith in God and Libba, and walk again.

Remembering You. 1997. Tyndale, paper. 363 pp. ISBN 0-8423-0857-1.
In the last volume of Stokes's trilogy, Owen Slaughter has returned home, but combat traumas have robbed him of his memories, even those of his true love, Willie.

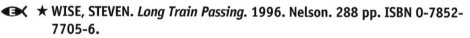 ★ **TATLOCK, ANN.** *A Room of My Own.* **1998. Bethany, paper. 400 pp. ISBN 0-7642-2023-3.**
See discussion in chapter 15, "Young Adult."

TURNBULL, AGNES SLIGH. *The Richlands.* **1974. Houghton Mifflin. (Out of print.)**
Jim Ryall so loves the family farm in nineteenth century western Pennsylvania that he turns down a chance to attend college to run it in this tale that was old-fashioned even in its own time. Jim's two brothers are less enamored and run afoul of him as he grows more fierce and tyrannical. Two women, the normal tragedies of life, and a growing sense that the land is not his, but God's, mellow him.

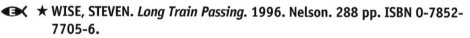 ★ **WISE, STEVEN.** *Long Train Passing.* **1996. Nelson. 288 pp. ISBN 0-7852-7705-6.**
Two people with disabilities, a gravedigger and a schoolteacher, are drawn together because both wish to befriend a youngster named Jewel. Jewel is a sensitive boy with the potential to become a fine scholar, but he's saddled with a brutal, alcoholic, and yet, as the owner of a pool hall and bar, influential father. Set during WWII in a small Missouri town, Wise evokes a kinder and gentler time, symbolized as a long train passing.

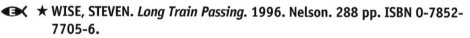 **WUBBELS, LANCE**

The Bridge Over Flatwillow Creek. 1998. Bethany, paper. 320 pp. ISBN 0-7642-2046-2.
Only answers from God can guide Annie Harding, a rich girl intent on marrying a rich man in Bradford, Minnesota in 1901. She finds herself in love with the man who has saved her life, Stuart Gray. Stuart, who is poor, has always meant to become a minister, but Annie tempts him to pursue the more lucrative career of medicine.

GENTLE HILLS
Wubbels tone is so sweet that for some it will seem cloying, but the series is a sincere portrait of a time and the details of farming ring true.

Far from the Dream. 1995. Bethany, paper. 464 pp. ISBN 1-55661-631-7.
When the Japanese attack Pearl Harbor, Jerry Macmillan, a Minnesota farmboy, marries his sweetheart Marjie and then joins the Navy. The heady times, a baby, and Jerry's near demise on an aircraft carrier bring the couple to God.

Whispers in the Valley. 1995. Bethany, paper. 303 pp. ISBN 1-55661-419-5.
When Jerry Macmillan comes home after the sinking of his aircraft carrier, he's a hero. But there are troubles on the home front in this sequel to *Far from the Dream*. Jerry's father is in ill health, and Jerry must consider a hardship discharge from the Navy to tend the farm.

Keeper of the Harvest. 1995. Bethany, paper. 288 pp. ISBN 1-55661-420-9.
Jerry and Marjie tend their Minnesota farm in this sequel to *Whispers in the Valley.* The appearance of a missionary to Borneo and his tales of the Japanese rekindle their faith. But nature deals some hard blows, and the war drags on in Europe with loved ones at risk.

Some Things Last Forever. 1996. Bethany, paper. 272 pp. ISBN 1-55661-421-7.
The Allies prepare for D-Day and Jerry's brothers are on active service, but domestic concerns dominate the last volume of Gentle Hills. Friends prepare for a missionary calling, and there's infighting at the church. Marjie is pregnant again.

In the Shadow of a Secret. 1999. Bethany, paper. 320 pp. ISBN 0-7642-2183-3.
Revisiting the territory of his Gentle Hills series, Wubbels spins a Depression-era romance between Andrew Regan, a new minister in a small Minnesota town, Liberty Center, and Christina Ellington, a portrait artist who has reluctantly returned from Chicago because of her mother's illness. The two fall in love, but their future together is complicated by secrets in Christina's family history and Andrew's problems with the snippy members of his congregation.

See also chapter 5, "Historical Christian Fiction."

PASTORS

The influence of Charles Sheldon's *In His Steps* remains vital in stories featuring pastors. Characters drawn in the tradition of Sheldon follow—or should follow—the tolerant, forgiving, and yet evangelizing example of Jesus. The unspoken assumption of such stories, each in its way a spiritual search, is that if a character chooses the moral path, he or she will be rewarded.

◄ⓔ✗ ★ ARTHUR, RANDALL. *Betrayal.* 1999. Word, paper. 416 pp. ISBN 0-8499-3738-8.
This cautionary, wages-of-sin tale portrays Clay McCain, a fundamentalist missionary to Sweden who falls for a woman who is both beautiful and rich. Clay is overwhelmed, throwing over his family and—admittedly difficult—ministry. He journeys the world with his dissolute girlfriend, and when he awakens to his folly, it's too late. He tries to redeem himself before dying a horrid death from AIDS, but of more interest may be Clay's betrayed, blameless wife, Rachel, who can find no comfort in her legalistic church. In fact, the fathers of the church regard her as an embarrassment and blame her for Clay's sins. Through them, Arthur indicts rule-bound faiths as worse than the disease.

◄ⓔ✗ ★ FICKETT, HAROLD. *The Holy Fool.* 1983. Crossway, paper. 284 pp. ISBN 0-89107-227-6.
Things aren't going well for Ted March, pastor of a failing Baptist church in a middle-class suburb of Los Angeles. Ted is wracked with doubts, and his sermons are all but incoherent. The congregation is restive, and, most instructive of all, Ted's own wife refuses to come to services, of the opinion that her husband's calling is nonsense and that he should get a real job. Desperate, Ted calls on an old friend from seminary days who has become a great success leading nationwide revivals, and the results are both comic and surprising in this delightful tale that, unlike many evangelical novels, is unafraid to satirize either the ministry or the unwashed masses.

GOLDSMITH, OLIVER. *The Vicar of Wakefield.* **1766.**
See discussion in chapter 3, "Christian Classics," p. 19.

HAMLIN, RICK

◆✕ *Mixed Blessings.* 2000. Bethany, paper. 299 pp. ISBN 0-7642-2326-7.
Lurlene Scott had a rough young womanhood and has never believed the stuff her boss, Pastor Bob, preaches, though she's a wonderful secretary, propping him up more reliably than his feisty wife. Lurlene has one great delight in life, her unmarried son, and when a letter comes in to the pastorate from a likely young woman, requesting prayer for the perfect mate, she plays matchmaker. Surprisingly, the match takes, and in the process Lurlene's faith quickens in this gentle, sometimes amusing portrait of the ordinary doings of a contemporary church.

◆✕ *Hidden Gifts.* 2001. Bethany, paper, 304p. ISBN 0-7642-2327-5.
Pastor Bob and Lurlene return in this likable sequel to *Mixed Blessings,* in which a burned-out Christian musician, Roger Kimmelman, finds renewed inspiration in a Christmas program and in the company of Lurlene. ■ Sequel ■

HINTON, LYNNE. *Friendship Cake.* 2000. HarperSanFrancisco. 212 pp. ISBN 0-688-17147-8.
United Church of Christ minister Hinton's loosely organized novel concerns five Southern church women who serve on a committee to a create a cookbook of members' recipes. One woman is a sad widow; another, a closet lesbian for 40 years; still another, the only African American. Their stories, punctuated with recipes, emerge to portray Hope Springs, North Carolina—at least, if one were to compare it with Flannery O'Connor's Georgia or Eudora Welty's Mississippi—as a rather cosmopolitan place.

◆✕ **KAUFFMAN, CHRISTMAS CAROL.** *Light from Heaven.* **2000. (Originally published in 1948.) Christian Light, paper. 458 pp. ISBN 0-87813-963-X.**
Kauffman's biographical novel of the evangelist Joseph Armstrong originally appeared as a serial in a Christian magazine and was so popular it was all but forced into book form. Though a galvanizing speaker, deep down Armstrong has so little self-confidence that the merest setback sends him into depression. Such problems could be traced to his overbearing father, not an evil man but a perfectionist and petty tyrant. Armstrong at last triumphs because of the unrelenting prayers of his mother and, of course, his surrender to God's will.

◆✕ **MOELLER, ROBERT.** *The Stirring.* **1994. Zondervan, paper. 208 pp. ISBN 0-310-47931-2.**
The minister of a troubled church, troubled himself, takes a vacation. In his absence a powerful revival sets in, threatening to send the minister himself packing if he doesn't join in what shortly becomes, a la *In His Steps,* a sweeping national movement.

◆✕ **MORRIS, DEBORAH, AND GARRETT W. SHELDON.** *What Would Jesus Do?* **1998. Broadman and Holman, paper. 186 pp. ISBN 0-8054-0189-X.**
The retelling of Charles Sheldon's classic *In His Steps* for a contemporary audience; Garrett Sheldon is the great grandson of Charles.

◀✦ MYERS, BILL. *When the Last Leaf Falls.* **2001. Zondervan. 144 pp. ISBN 0-310-23091-8.**

Reverend Paul Newcombe is faced with the possibility that his daughter, Ally, may die of bone cancer. It's hard for him to comprehend how God could allow this, and he argues with his father, who pastored Paul's church before him. His father tells him what Paul already knew: that the matter is beyond his understanding or control; that to serve God fully he must present him with a "broken" spirit. Meanwhile, Ally also battles with her faith, glumly looking out the window at a tree and saying that when its last leaf falls, she will die.   **█ Discussion**

✦ PALMER, CATHERINE. *The Happy Room.* **2002. Tyndale, paper. 350 pp. ISBN 0-8423- 5421-2.**

Peter and Julia Mossman converge on a hospital room in southern Missouri when news arrives that their younger sister, Debbie, appears to be dying from anorexia. The siblings' parents, retired missionaries, can't linger at their sick daughter's bedside, because they have duties in a nearby town running a vacation Bible school. But it was always that way, the children reflect. Instead of attending to their children's needs, the elder Mossmans would send them to the "happy room." Palmer is herself the child of missionaries, and her scenes in Kenya are richly detailed and provocative. She frames the issue: How does a life of service to God conflict with parental duties?

◀✦ SAMSON, LISA E. *The Church Ladies.* **2001. Multnomah, paper. 264 pp. ISBN 1-57673-748-9.**

Poppy Fraser has always been a Christian, but when her husband announces he wants to bow out of his lucrative career to become a minister, she doesn't know what to think. Their marriage, after 20 years, is showing some strains, and the church her husband is called to is like a mini-corporation, in hot competition with all the others. Then Poppy meets Mildred McClure, wife of a former minister, and the two form a support group of ministers' wives.

★ SHEPARD, ROY. *The Latest Epistle of Jim.* **1996. MidList, paper. 192 pp. ISBN 0-922811-26-1.**

Shepard builds great suspense when his hero, a small-town liberal minister named Jack Andrews, receives a letter that will tell him whether or not he'll be hired as pastor of a big urban church, but delays opening it. We learn what a wonderful, but vulnerable and sad, man Jack is as he goes through his day, preaching a funeral and musing on how disappointed his parents were in his choice of a career, and how the small-town life has constricted his wife's opportunities.

SLAUGHTER, FRANK G. *Gospel Fever.* **1980. Doubleday.**

Slaughter portrays a TV evangelist, Brother Tim Douglas, who seems much like Jim Baker in the days before his fall.

SLEEM, PATTY. *Back in Time.* **1997. PREP, paper. 164 pp. ISBN 1-885288-03-4.**

In this bizarre but irresistible tale, Sleem conjures a nutty graduate from Yale's divinity school, Maggie Dillitz. Dillitz is ditsy. She has a knack for offending people and is always in trouble. When she finally lands a church, she preaches a fiery sermon based on the book of Amos. The church ladies are offended, and to sidestep a hearing on her dismissal Maggie heads off for hurricane-ravaged Jamaica. There a colleague makes a pass at Maggie in her cocktail dress. Maggie longs to cry sexual harassment, but then her colleague is found dead. What next?

11

⬤✕ SPROUL, R. C. *Johnny Come Home.* **1984. (Out of print.)**

Sproul relates the coming-of-age of Dr. Richard "Scooter" Evans, a working-class kid who goes to college and seminary. The story is also about Johnny Kramer, Scooter's high school buddy and lifelong friend who does not fare well in life, losing a great deal of money in bad investments and cheating on his wife. But Johnny's role is quite minor in the end, and Scooter's efforts to help him are minimal. Rather, this is the engaging but undramatic tale of a theologian's rise, not dissimilar from Sproul's own biography. It was reprinted in 1988 under the title *Thy Brother's Keeper.*

★ TURNBULL, AGNES SLIGH. *The Bishop's Mantle.* **1948. Macmillan. (Out of print.)**

This fine story, a believable and affecting portrait of a pastor at work set a few months before World War II, features Hilary Laurens, who has his hands full taking over a Pennsylvanian Episcopal parish when the old priest, Hilary's grandfather, dies. Hilary can't persuade his will-o'-the-wisp girlfriend, Lexa, to marry him; his superior proves troublesome; and he has hardly begun work when he begins to receive anonymous letters characterizing him as a tool of the complacent capitalists constituting his parish. But Hilary soon proves his mettle counseling a bereaved family after a suicide and continues to meet every challenge nimbly and compassionately.

⬤✕ TURNER, CHARLES. *Sometimes It Causes Me to Tremble.* **1998. Lion, paper. 256 pp. ISBN 0-74593-867-1.**

To his infinite surprise, one person in Pastor Georg McKenna's congregation takes his sermon on following biblical admonitions seriously. A widow, Rose Templeton, invites a homeless man into her house. When she's murdered and her guest turns up missing as well, Pastor McKenna turns sleuth in pursuit of the homeless man.

WILBUR, SANFORD R. *If God Is God.* **1996. Symbios, paper. 383 pp. ISBN 0-9651263-0-7.**

Talky but entertaining tale of a minister who tries to use the "What Would Jesus Do?" precept of *In His Steps* on a modern congregation; he is soon overwhelmed with the smoldering sins and dilemmas of nearly everyone he knows.

See also chapter 12, "Catholic Fiction," the section "Nuns and Priests as Sleuths"; chapter 10, "Mysteries and Thrillers," the section "Pastors as Sleuths"; and Jan Karon's Mitford series, under "Nostalgia" in this chapter.

POPULAR

Popular novels draw their characters and lessons broadly, are heavily plotted, and generally end happily.

⬤✕ ALEXANDER, HANNAH

THE HEALING TOUCH

Hannah Alexander is the pseudonym for a husband-and-wife team, one of whom is an emergency room physician. The series consistently avoids preachiness and soap opera, focusing instead on the real issues facing doctors and patients.

Sacred Trust. 1999. Bethany, paper. 352 pp. ISBN 0-7642-2242-2.

Lukas Bower is an emergency room physician with a checkered past—checkered because he has never been able to go with the flow. He is rigidly ethical, and that's gotten him in trouble in big city environments. He takes a job in southern Missouri, deep in the Bible Belt, hoping his values will fit in. They do, but he's a bit much—running in a respected physician for a minor mistake and going after a child abuser who's also a powerful man in the community. What saves Lucas is his saintly vulnerability. He's untactful, naive in some respects, and shy. Readers will begin to like him even as they are impressed with Alexander's command of medical detail.

Solemn Oath. 1999. Bethany, paper. 351 pp. ISBN 0-7642-2348-8.

Despite his shyness Lucas falls in love in the sequel to *Sacred Trust,* as his overbooked schedule places him beside another emergency room physician, Mercy Richmond. Otherwise, his take-no-prisoners principles have paid off because now he's interim director of Knolls Community Hospital. Perhaps that's a dubious distinction because, rightly or wrongly, the hospital is under investigation, and an arson epidemic has the emergency room reeling with burn patients.

Silent Pledge. 2001. Bethany, paper. 352 pp. ISBN 0-7642-2444-1.

Lukas moves to a temporary position in a rural clinic several hours away from his hospital. He attempts to clean up corruption and complaisance while dealing with an endless variety of patients, all of whom are convincingly portrayed. The separation is hard on his relationship with Mercy, but she has her own problems to work out before the two can consider tackling the world together.

FISCHER, JOHN

◆✖★ ***Saint Ben.*** 1993. Bethany, paper. 286 pp. ISBN 1-55661-259-1.

In the charming, bestselling *Saint Ben*, readers are introduced to the friendship of two boys, 🆈🅰 Ben Beamering and Jonathan Lieberman. Jonathan tells the story of his nine-year-old friend, a new kid in town and a preacher's kid. Ben at first appears to be incorrigible, but slowly the reader understands that he is unfailingly honest—as if born that way—and that his funny escapades result merely from trying to live according to the example of Jesus. There is charm, too, in Fischer's gentle humor, and the nostalgia for youth forever lost.

◆✖ ***The Saints' and Angels' Song.*** 1995. Bethany, paper. 320 pp. ISBN 1-55661-474-8.

In the sequel to *Saint Ben,* Jonathan is now a teenager, plagued with the usual problems but 🆈🅰 also still troubled by Ben's death. Ben, an angel, gives Jonathan advice on how to help Donna, an unhappy girl on the verge of becoming a champion skater.   ■ Sequel ■

◆✖ **HUNT, ANGELA ELWELL.** *The Proposal.* **1996. Tyndale, paper. 317 pp. ISBN 0-8423-4950-2.**

Hapless writer Theodora Russell is mistaken for the famous but reclusive novelist Theodore Russell in Hunt's wry tale. A high-powered editor offers Theodora half a million for what is really Theodore's proposal for a novel, and Theodora, like the editor unaware that the novelist has been kidnapped, pursues the idea as nonfiction, bending the ethics of the situation somewhat, but not actually stealing Theodore's idea. She likes the subject: the high risk of breast cancer for women who have had abortions and never borne children. Why shouldn't she have her 15 minutes of fame?

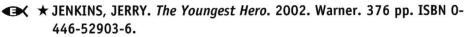

⬛✕ ★ JENKINS, JERRY. *The Youngest Hero.* 2002. Warner. 376 pp. ISBN 0-446-52903-6.

🅨 See discussion in chapter 15, "Young Adult."

⬛✕ KELLY, VICTOR J. *Macintosh Mountain.* 1983. Zondervan. (Out of print.)

🄶🄼 A new pastor and his family, Jerome and Jael Springer and their daughter, Tammi, come to the farming country of Vermont's Green Mountains. But their marriage is troubled, and Tammi is troubled. A farm couple, who themselves reeled from family strife long before, offers their friendship and counsel.

MORRIS, GILBERT

⬛✕★ *All That Glitters.* 1999. Crossway. 384 pp. ISBN 1-58134-107-5.

🅨 Though it has not enjoyed the popularity of Morris's other novels, *All That Glitters* may be his most original. It's about an aging film director, Kyle Patton, who is down in Kentucky shooting a family picture. He's trying both to recoup and redeem his long career, which has fallen into decline. Into the mix comes Kyle's born-again daughter, Afton Burns, who has grown up with Kyle's ex in Scotland. All of Afton's relatives (except Kyle) work with the Salvation Army. When her mother dies and Afton comes to Kentucky, both father and daughter are in for some surprises.

⬛✕ *Through a Glass Darkly.* 1999. Bethany, paper. 288 pp. ISBN 1-55661-145-5.

Through a Glass Darkly tells the workmanlike tale of "Adam," recovering slowly from burns and memory loss. As he remembers, he falls in love, so it would be inconvenient if he turned out to be married. He was a heroic chaplain in the Gulf War, he finally recalls. And single.

⬛✕ ★ PALMER, CATHERINE. *A Dangerous Silence.* 2001. Tyndale, paper. 300 pp. ISBN 0-8423-3617-6.

A crusty old farmer, Big Ed Morgan, steals the show in this romance with a realistic edge. Big Ed's daughter, a St. Louis physician named Marah, gets a call that her father has been injured in a farm accident. Returning to Kansas is a step back in time for Marah, who liked farming well enough but could never get along with her authoritarian father. Father and daughter remain deeply estranged, and once the harvest is in, Marah wants to park Big Ed in a rest home. Big Ed, though bound to a wheelchair, doesn't think so. Their struggle is so appealing that the rest of the story, concerning a mysterious archaeological crew that is unearthing Native American skeletons on the farm, and a new farmhand Marah finds herself attracted to, almost gets in the way.

⬛✕ PETERSON, TRACIE. *A Slender Thread.* 2000. Bethany, paper. 320 pp. ISBN 0-7642-2251-1.

🅨 Ashley, Brook, Connie, Deirdre, and Erica gather at the funeral of their mother, Rachelle Barrister, a film actress. Rachelle left home early, gave birth to twins, but her marriage was a bad one, and she turned over raising the kids to her Godfearing mother, Mattie. She did the same with the other girls, providing for them financially but not emotionally as her fame spread, so that if the sisters feel anything for her, it's bitterness and resentment. They have each gone on to their more or less successful lives. Reunited, they compare notes, realize how fortunate they were to be raised by Mattie, and bond in their shared faith to help each through life's difficulties, most of which revolve around men.

◐✕ ★ VERWEERD, JOHANNA. *The Winter Garden.* **2001. Tr. by Helen Richardson-Hewitt. Bethany, paper. 269 pp. ISBN 0-7642-2523-5.**

When Ika Boerema, a landscape designer, receives a letter from her sister, Nelly, that their
YA mother is dying and Ika must come home, Ika is thrown into a quandary. Nelly was always the
favored one, whereas Ika was an illegitimate daughter and grew up a near outcast. Nelly's return
home is a spiritual search and a search for identity as well because her mother has never revealed
the name of Ika's father. Ika is herself a winter garden, but as she comes to terms with her
past, she struggles to become a whole woman and to blossom. Verweerd is a Dutch writer;
this was her first novel.

◐✕ VITTI, JAMES ALAN. *A Little Piece of Paradise.* **1996. Nelson. 336 pp. ISBN 0-7852-7780-3.**

Carole Augustine, an aged movie actress, owns valuable property on the unspoiled Channel
Islands. There's an argument among her son Dex, a financier; her son, Gabe, a missionary;
and her daughter Edie, a U.S. representative, about what to do with their mother's legacy.
Each of Carole's offspring has some sort of spiritual malady that Gabe's ministry will eventually
address, all brought to climax when Edie introduces a bill to sell off all of the Channel Islands
and use the proceeds to reduce federal deficits.

SENTIMENTAL

These novels are best read with a box of Kleenex nearby. *Sentimental* is a pejorative term
literarily, but what makes one reader ill is noble and fine to another. (See also "Nostalgia" in this chapter.)

◐✕ BEDFORD, DEBORAH. *A Rose by the Door.* **2001. Warner, paper. 352 pp. ISBN 0-446-67789-2.**

Bedford tells the sad story of Gemma, a young woman so desperate that readers may be driven
YA to laughter, and her little daughter, who's given to pronouncements so cute that readers may
want to swear off children forever. Gemma and the adorable kid arrive on the doorstep of Bea
Bartling days after Bea has learned of the death of her estranged son, Nathan. Destitute
Gemma says she was Nathan's wife. Bea can't believe Gemma's wild story, and rejects her. Gemma
takes a job as a waitress and soon all the town loves her. When Bea sees the light, her life is
worth living again, and once more she takes pride in the roses by her doorstep.

◐✕ BLACKSTOCK, TERRI. *Seaside.* **2001. Zondervan. 208 pp. ISBN 0-310-23318-6.**

Maggie Downing is a hard-charging nature photographer with a knack for turning "beauty
into bucks." Mysteriously, she draws her two daughters, Sarah and Corinne, together at an
exclusive Florida Beach. Sarah and Corinne, as driven as their mother, are mildly irritated at
the interruption in their busy lives and have a hard time getting their own problems out of
their heads. Then Maggie discloses that she's dying of cancer.

BUNN, T. DAVIS

◐✕ *The Gift.* 1994. Bethany. 160 pp. ISBN 1-55661-527-2.

A short tale in gift book format about two quite different women, one middle-aged and devout,
the other young and independent. They share a hospital room, become friends, and grow together
spiritually.

EX *The Music Box.* 1996. Bethany, paper. 176 pp. ISBN 1-55661-900-6.
A widowed music teacher, Angie Picard, befriends a lonely little girl, Chrissy.
YA Chrissy has great natural musical ability but seems unable to make progress. Love is
kindled between Angie and Chrissy's father as Angie tries to help, and with Angie's
steadfast faith and the homespun counsel of Angie's mother, Chrissy's talents flower.

EX CLAIRMONT, PATSY. *Stardust on My Pillow.* 2000. WaterBrook. 208 pp.
ISBN 1-57856-369-0.
These 13 stories, some contemporary, some set in America's rural past, all place
their protagonists in quiet crises of faith resulting from such traumas as loss of a
loved one or a mastectomy. Faith is restored through semimiraculous demonstra-
tions of God's grace.

EX HOFF, B. J. *The Penny Whistle.* 1996. Bethany. 192 pp. ISBN 1-55661-
877-8.
In the late 1800s, a beloved teacher faces rapidly declining health in a coal-mining
YA town in eastern Kentucky. His health is mystically linked to the theft of his silver
flute, which, when he plays it, somehow sustains him. Two naive schoolgirls devise
a childish but sincere plan to save their kind teacher.

EX LAHAYE, BEVERLY, AND TERRI BLACKSTOCK

YA *Seasons Under Heaven.* 1999. Zondervan. 384 pp. ISBN 0-310-22137-4.
Four families who live around an upper-middle-class cul-de-sac come together
when one boy, eight-year-old Joseph Dodd, needs a heart transplant.

YA *Showers in Season.* 2000. Zondervan. 384 pp. ISBN 0-310-22138-2.
In the sequel to *Seasons Under Heaven,* the cul-de-sac buzzes over Tory Sullivan's
pregnancy because the baby will have Down Syndrome.   ■ Sequel ■

YA *Times and Seasons.* 2001. Zondervan. 336 pp. ISBN 0-310-23319-4.
Single mom Cathy Flaherty's son, Mark, is placed in juvenile detention for drug
dealing, testing Cathy's relationship not only with her son but also with her fiancé.
The women of the Cedar Circle cul-de-sac rally to support Cathy.

EX OKE, JANETTE

YA *Nana's Gift.* 1996. Bethany. 144 pp. ISBN 1-55661-898-0.
Lizzie's (Nana's) husband, Duncan, is a poor farmer, but he loves her so much he
saves for 30 years to buy her a pearl necklace. As the pearls are handed down they grow
to become a perfect symbol of married love, especially to Lizzie's great-granddaughter,
Beth, who is all but paralyzed in an accident days before her wedding but whose
fiancé stands nobly by her.

YA *The Red Geranium.* 1995. Bethany, paper. 72 pp. ISBN 1-55661-662-7.
Life seems to be running down for Gran Thomas, a recent stroke victim consigned to
a nursing home, but her heart swells at the gift of her grandson, a geranium he dug
from Gran's own garden.

◄Ӿ OKE, JANETTE, AND T. DAVIS BUNN

YA *Return to Harmony.* 1996. Bethany, paper. 223 pp. ISBN 1-55661-878-6.
The famous team writes of two childhood friends, Jodie and Bethan, in the small town of Harmony, North Carolina, around 1915. Bethan is a simple Christian girl who marries a local pastor. Jodie is a child prodigy who wants to enter the brand-new field of biochemistry. When Jodie's mother dies a cruel death, Jodie replaces God with science as her faith, and the friends fall out.

YA *Another Homecoming.* 1997. Bethany, paper. 251 pp. ISBN 1-55661-934-0.
The well-known team relies on false reports of death, babies switched at birth, and over-wrought hospital scenes for its emotional effects in its tale of Kyle Adams, given up for adoption when her mother learns that her husband has died in North Africa in WWII. Kyle grows up rich but lonely, and unfortunately she's forsworn to a nasty rich boy by her wicked stepmother. Meanwhile, her angelic brother grows up unappreciated by Kyle's real mother and father (he didn't die, after all).

YA *Tomorrow's Dream.* 1998. Bethany, paper. 224 pp. ISBN 0-76422-054-3.
In the sequel to *Another Homecoming,* after Kyle has found her biological parents, become acquainted with her brother, and gotten married, Kyle loses her young son and turns her back on God, though only briefly. The series is neither writer's finest hour.   ■ Sequel ▮

◄Ӿ PEART, JANE. *The Heart's Lonely Secret.* 1994. Revell, paper. 312 pp. ISBN 0-8007-5542-1.
Woebegone Ivy Austin, an orphan, is adopted by the circus and becomes an act. Then she's injured and cast upon the cruel world again, but a wealthy family adopts her, and she learns to cast off her background and embrace Christian values.

◄Ӿ YATES, CYNTHIA. *Brenda's Gift.* 2000. Broadman and Holman, paper. 320 pp. ISBN 0-8034-2147-5.
A gentle young woman, Brenda Martin, gives a copy of Psalms to a troubled boy who is dyslexic. At first it helps him learn to read, and then it solaces him through the Vietnam War. But the book also makes its way through other lives, all under the invisible supervision of a guardian angel named Bashar.

SHORT STORIES

Outside the romance genre, short story collections are a rarity in Christian publishing.

◄Ӿ BALL, KAREN, ed. *The Storyteller's Collection: Tales from Home.* 2001. Multnomah, paper. 320 pp. ISBN 1-57673-738-1.
Tales from home, as opposed to "faraway places," seems a logical sequel to Melody Carlson assemblage (discussed next), and Ball's collection is entertaining throughout. But somehow the special quality of the first book is lost, perhaps because so many Christian writers have had missionary experience and so have a unique perspective on faraway places.

EX **CARLSON, MELODY, ed.** *The Storytellers' Collection: Tales of Faraway Places.*
2000. Multnomah. 320 pp. ISBN 1-57673-738-1.

ChiLibris, a writers' group, sent Carlson 40 short stories with exotic settings for this
YA collection dedicated to overseas missionary work. Gathered are writers such as
Angela Elwell Hunt, Randy Alcorn, Dave Jackson, Jerry Jenkins, Terri Blackstock,
Lauraine Snelling, and Gayle Roper. Most stories have contemporary settings, such
as Athol Dickson's moving tale, "Hannah's Home," of an adopted Mexican Ameri-
can girl, an unhappy misfit who returns to rural Mexico to search out her birth
mother; and Sharon Ewell Foster's "A Trip to Senegal," about an African American
woman's trip to Senegal and discovery of faith while getting her hair done. But
Sigmund Brouwer drops back in time with a grim historical tale of Christian martyrdom,
"At the Village Gate."   **Discussion**

CURTIS, C. MICHAEL, ed. *God: Stories.* **1998. Houghton Mifflin. 400 pp. ISBN 0-395-**
92677-7.

Though *Atlantic* editor Curtis includes stories from J. F. Powers and Flannery
O'Connor, his emphasis is mostly Protestant in this collection of 25 stories that
range from a pure questioning of faith to its celebration. Included also are John
Updike's "Made in Heaven," James Baldwin's "Exodus," and Elizabeth Spencer's
"A Christian Education."

See also chapter 8, "Romance," the section "Short Stories."

Chapter 12

Catholic Fiction

Catholic fiction has a distinguished history, but it is a relatively short one. It was born with the Catholic Literary Revival of nineteenth century England, partly in reaction to a strain of anti-Catholicism running through the Anglican Church. Cardinal John Henry Newman, the Anglican who became a Catholic and who is usually thought of as the leading exponent of the Oxford Movement, published *Callista* in 1855 (p. 21) in a kind of fictional rebuttal of Charles Kingsley's anti-Catholic *Westward Ho*, and one might mark the beginning of the Literary Revival, and Catholic fiction, here. Yet the most accomplished writer the Literary Revival produced was not a novelist but the Jesuit (reformed Anglican) poet Gerard Manley Hopkins.

There is no towering early figure in Catholic fiction, in other words, like a Bunyan or even a MacDonald. Compton MacKenzie was widely popular both in England and the United States at the turn of the twentieth century, but at the turn of the twenty-first, his novels are all out of print and difficult even to find.

The first writer of significance who is still widely read is G. K. Chesterton, not for his theological insights so much as the brand he put on the mystery, which has blended with the prototypes of Poe and Conan Doyle to form the modern mystery. If you've watched an episode of *Columbo,* you've seen the influence of Chesterton (Calvert 1935).

After Chesterton, there are many writers still widely read: Evelyn Waugh, Graham Greene, and Flannery O'Connor, to name only a few. A distinction that grew among them was high literary intent, carried forward in the next generation by Brian Moore, Mary Gordon, and Walker Percy, again naming only the most widely known. Such writers became fodder for college literature courses and are thought of first as literary presences, second as Catholic writers.

They are generally published in the mainstream press. So, too, are a host of Catholic mystery writers: William Kienzle, Ralph McInerny, Margaret Coel, Veronica Black, and Andrew Greeley, among others. Most Catholic fiction is mainstream fiction, and the extremely large Catholic press, much of it the expression of individual orders, is mainly devoted to liturgical or scholarly matters, as well as religious self-help. A vital exception is Ignatius Press, which regularly publishes Catholic fiction of high quality:

IGNATIOUS
Div. of Guadalupe Assoc.
2525 McAllister St.
San Francisco, CA 94118
415-387-2324
info@ignatius.com

CLASSICS

BARRETT, WILLIAM E. *The Lilies of the Field*. 1962. (Many editions.)

Homer Smith, a black ex-soldier, helps a group of nuns from East Germany build a chapel in the desert—arguing all the while with the formidable Mother Maria Marthe—in this short, feel-good classic about race relations. Sydney Poitier won an Academy Award for his portrait of Homer in the 1963 film of the same title; it also starred Lilia Skala, as Mother Maria. The director was Ralph Nelson.

BERNANOS, GEORGES

A fervent French nationalist, the highly philosophical Bernanos had an international audience through the 1950s, though now is little read. He felt that the religious and the political were inseparable, but ultimately his political philosophy was unique and somewhat imponderable, causing him, at times, to be a hero both to the left and the right. His fiction advocates a pure and innocent faith put into action by saintly figures such as Joan of Arc.

★ *The Diary of a Country Priest*. 1984. (Originally published in 1937.) Carroll & Graf; paper. 304 pp. ISBN 0-88184-013-0.

Bernanos's most famous novel, first published in 1937, charts the course of a naive, soulful young priest assigned to a monastery in northern France. No amount of prayer, hard work, self-denial, or agonizing remonstration changes the ugly little town, Ambricourt, into anything remotely resembling the rather extreme Christianity he preaches. He tries to help the poor, who think him a crackpot; merchants cheat him; industrialists rudely dismiss him. His own superiors, in long rants, urge him to accept the world as it is. Truth is, he has no charisma, nothing to offer but the love of Christ. "Therein lies my whole strength," he writes. "The strength of children and weaklings." It is not enough. The reader begins to sense that he is ill, and in due course cancer takes him, a poor fool, innocent as Christ, his life given for the corrupt and ungrateful. His last words are, "Does it matter? Grace is everywhere . . ."

The Imposter. 1999. Tr. By J. C. Whitehouse. University of Nebraska, paper. 250 pp. ISBN 0-8032-6153-5.

First published in 1927, this highly philosophical, ironic novel features an eminent priest and scholar who follows his flawless logic to the point where he no longer believes. Realizing his folly, he consults with a shy priest whom he once befriended, an innocent trusted by the poor and powerless. Their dialogues illustrate 1st Corinthians 1:27: "But God hath chosen the foolish things of the world to confound the wise."

YA   ★ CATHER, WILLA. *Death Comes for the Archbishop*. 1927. (Many editions.)

Written during a period when Cather was herself puzzling out her spiritual dimensions, *Death Comes for the Archbishop* is a biographical novel about the first Bishop of Santa Fe, Frenchman Jean Lamy. Sent to New Mexico in the late 1840s, Father Lamy was a cultured man, the perfect vehicle for Cather to explore her frequently visited themes of the Old World versus the New; sensitivity and restraint versus bawdy abandon; and the spirituality she and other writers have ascribed to expansive western landscapes. Father Lamy is a hero, a knight-errant not unlike other western "good guys": at one point he pulls a gun and rescues a damsel in distress. More important, he works tirelessly to weed out dissolute priests from his diocese and to improve the living standards of the Hopi. The novel is episodic but it doesn't matter, for Cather weaves together her appreciation of New Mexican landscapes, Native American lore, and Father Lamy's adventures seamlessly, all in service of a quiet, enormously appealing spiritual search. Many feel this is Cather's finest novel.

CHESTERTON, G. K.

★ *The Father Brown Omnibus.* 1951. Dodd, Mead. (Out of print.)
Father Brown—the reader never learns his first name—is the quiet, frumpy priest who seems a bumbler, seems, in fact, not even to be involved in the case, but who knows more about crime than either the criminals or the police, and solves the mystery no matter how fiendishly clever. Chesterton's dry wit is never far removed.

Without Father Brown, there would be none of the priestly sleuths to follow (see "Nuns and Priests as Sleuths" in this chapter), or at least they would take a much different form. This volume collects all the Father Brown stories from five books published between 1911 and 1935, but other editions are available.

★ *The Man Who Was Thursday.* 1990. (Originally published in 1908.) Penguin, paper. 184 pp. ISBN 0-14-018388-4.
Feckless Gabriel Syme is hired by the London police to track down bombing plots among anarchists. Through a stroke of luck Gabriel manages to be elected to the Council of Seven, as Thursday. Monday, Tuesday, Wednesday, and so forth, each a parody of certain revolutionary or intellectual stances, are represented as dangerously evil until Syme comes to the understanding that they are all disguised policemen, on the same mission that he is. Only Sunday, a menacing, mischievous figure whom Chesterton likens to Pan, is a true anarchist, or is he? Is he the Devil? Is he God? As the novel progresses it grows ever more surreal, culminating with the policemen being chased across France by the legions of Hell, except that they aren't really from Hell, and Armageddon is a mock Armageddon.

★ **CRONIN, A. J.** *Keys of the Kingdom.* **1984. (Originally published in 1941.) Little, Brown, paper. 344 pp. ISBN 0-316-16184-5.**
The simple faith of Scottish priest Francis Chisholm, of humble submission to Christ, tolerance, and honesty, didn't make him a good village priest, at least in the eyes of his arrogant, intolerant, and dishonest supervisor, Bishop Mealey. But as a missionary to China, all but banished to one its remotest districts, Father Chisholm's tenacity, unwavering devotion, and even heroism eventually triumph. Made into what became a classic Catholic movie of the same title (1941), starring Gregory Peck.

HULME, KATHRYN. *The Nun's Story.* 1956. Atlantic Monthly Press. (Out of print.)
Sister Luke (Gabrielle Van der Mal) is a dedicated nurse serving in the Congo—a heroic nurse, laboring under adverse conditions—with the difference that her life is wholly given over to God. Even so, she struggles with her feelings for the amazing Dr. Fortunati, as well as with the professional conflict inherent in being both a full-time nurse and a full-time nun. Hulme based her story on a real nun, a lifelong friend; she captures the details of living as a nun perfectly, and her Sister Luke is, though human, completely sympathetic. Audrey Hepburn played her in the 1959 film, also starring Peter Finch as Dr. Fortunati; the director was Fred Zinnemann.

JANNEY, RUSSELL. *The Miracle of the Bells.* 1946. Prentice-Hall. (Out of print.)
Olga Trocki, the neglected daughter of a drunk, became Olga Treskovna, famous stage actress. Now, having finished her one and only film, she's being brought home for burial to the little coal-mining town of her birth. Bill Dunnigan, her Hollywood friend, relays Olga's request that the church bells of the town ring for three days to mark her passing—or possibly, the ringing of the bells is merely a publicity stunt to get the studio to release Olga's movie. In any case, the results are surprising. The

popular film, made in 1948, starred Fred McMurray as Bill Dunnigan and Frank Sinatra as Father Paul; it was directed by Irving Pichel.

JOYCE, JAMES

The reputation for difficulty of *Ulysses* (1922) and *Finnegan's Wake* (1939) obscures the fact *Portrait of the Artist as a Young Man* and *Dubliners,* while not simple books, are perfectly accessible. For those readers who have heard that *Ulysses* is the greatest novel of the twentieth century, but then find themselves completely lost, perhaps Joyce's early works are alternatives, appetizers to the feast.

Dubliners. 1914. (Many editions.)

Each of the 15 stories in *Dubliners* is a classic all by itself. Sharpening his talents for the monumental task of *Ulysses,* Joyce ranged among priests and alcoholic clerks, reckless young men and corrupt political operatives, desperate young women and terrified boys, portraying lost souls in Dublin a little before WWI. The stories are dense, ironic, multilayered, sad but not hopeless.

A Portrait of the Artist As a Young Man. 1916. (Many editions.)

Joyce brings music to language: "Once upon a time and a very good time it was there was a moocow coming down along the road and this moocow that was coming down along the road met a nicens little boy named baby tuckoo" in an evocation of the world as seen by the child Stephen Dedalus, who grows up in a strict Catholic family in the late nineteenth century. Other periods in his life take on the appropriate language in what are really periods in Joyce's own life. As Stephen comes of age he has the problems of many another young man, in discovering his sexuality (which he cannot seem to suppress despite his religious training) and rebelling against the politics of his father. A conflict arises in him between his deeply religious view of the world and his fiery desire to become an artist; art sets him free, to fly like Dedalus free of his captors.

MAURIAC, FRANCOIS. *Vipers' Tangle.* 1933. Tr. by Warre B. Wells. Sheed & Ward. 288 pp. (Out of print.)

As an old man lies dying he turns over in his mind his miserly, often evil life and wonders at the estrangement of his family and the barrenness of his soul. Through reasoning, and then with a leap of faith, he finds a measure of redemption and yields up his soul to Christ, though he cannot completely effect reconciliation with those he has harmed.

ROLPHE, FREDERICK (pseudonym Baron Corvo). *Hadrian the Seventh.* 2001. (Originally published in 1904.) New York Review of Books, paper. 416 pp. ISBN 0-940322-62-5.

This quirky tale concerns a mentally unstable, latently homosexual priest, Arthur Rose, who is suddenly asked to become Pope. When he leaves his drab little apartment, he is swept away into a surrealist Vatican, impossibly grand, filled with splendid medieval tapestries of God sitting in judgment on Hadrian's enemies, and a throne that is truly ethereal, as if the Pope were constantly in touch with the farthest planets of the cosmos.

SILONE, IGNAZIO. *Bread and Wine.* 1988. (Originally published in 1936.) Tr. by Eric Mosbacher. Signet, paper. 272 pp. ISBN 0-451-52500-0.

Silone surprised the world with his insider's look at Italian fascism under Mussolini. His somewhat autobiographical protagonist, the Communist organizer, Pietro Spina, must flee from the fascists, or die. Pietro returns to a remote Italian village disguised as a priest, Don Paulo, and the sweet irony of Silone's story is that Don Paulo, as he begins once more to spread the words of Marx, becomes more and more the emissary of Christ.

★ **WAUGH, EVELYN.** *Brideshead Revisited.* **1944. (Many editions.)**
The novel many regard as Waugh's finest is the long recollection of Charles Ryder, a bone-weary, cynical soldier speaking near the end of WWII. Ryder recalls his love for the charmingly gay or perhaps bisexual Sebastian Flyte during carefree days at Oxford. Sebastian introduces him to the decadent high society of the supposedly Catholic Marchmains, whose estate is called Brideshead. Ryder falls in love with the elusive Julia Marchmain, Sebastian's sister, who may or may not love him in turn. But at any rate the old estate is doomed, as are the days of British hegemony in the world. As tragedy engulfs them—particularly old Lord Marchmain, and ultimately Sebastian—the Brideshead residents tentatively embrace their faith again, and Ryder, too, discovers religion. One of the more famous PBS series starring Jeremy Irons as Ryder and Lawrence Olivier as Lord Marchmain (1982).

HISTORICALS

Fourth Century

 DE WOHL, LOUIS. *The Restless Flame: A Novel About Saint Augustine.* **1997. (Originally published in 1951.) Ignatius, paper. 303 pp. ISBN 0-89870-603-3.**
Drawing from Augustine's own *Confessions,* De Wohl portrays the saint from young manhood, when he was already a precocious scholar, but also vain, impious and contemptuous of women.

WAUGH, EVELYN. *Helena.* **1950. Little, Brown. 247 pp.**
Written at the height of Waugh's Catholic period, *Helena* is the almost wholly imagined story of St. Helena, who was credited with finding a remnant of the Cross and whose whole existence depends on it; otherwise, she is an ordinary young woman: unassuming, joyous, witty. She is much like any young Englishwoman of Waugh's own time, in fact. Through Helena's efforts new churches are built in Bethlehem and the gospel becomes the true religion of her son, Constantine, who was to repudiate the old gods and make Christianity the religion of the Roman Empire.

Sixth Century

★ **BUECHNER, FREDERICK.** *Brendan.* **2000. (Originally published in 1987.) Harper-SanFrancisco, paper. 256 pp. ISBN 0-06-061178-2.**
The magical world of St. Brendan, following St. Patrick's evangelization of Ireland a generation before, is seen through the eyes of Finn, his long time companion. Finn describes Brendan's own efforts to supplant druidism with Christianity as he founds a number of monasteries and sometimes practices magic. But Brendan's voyages in search of the Terrestrial Paradise, taking him to the Canary Islands and possibly even to America, are the most astonishing feature of Buechner's novel; they border on magical realism.

DE WOHL, LOUIS. *Citadel of God.* **1994. Ignatius, paper. 345 pp. ISBN 0-89870- 404-9.**
De Wohl tells the quiet story of St. Benedict, who turned away from a sinful world to seek Christ through prayer and solitude and to form the "rules" of monasticism.

Twelfth Century

BUECHNER, FREDERICK. *Godric.* **1983. HarperSanFrancisco. 192 pp. ISBN 0-06-061162-6.**
Godric was a hermit under the influence of another hermit, St. Cuthbert, which does not sound like promising material for a novel. But the always amazing Buechner captures the flavor of language—poetic and earthy at the same time—of St. Godric's England and manages to show the nobility in what at times is his weak fight to conquer pride and lust. Here is Godric, warts and all, in a vivid medieval tableau.

Thirteenth Century

YA **DE WOHL, LOUIS.** *The Quiet Light: A Novel About Thomas Aquinas.* **1996. (Originally published in 1950.) Ignatius, paper. 377 pp. ISBN 0-89870-595-9.**
Thomas Aquinas defies his family's wishes by taking a vow of poverty and joining the Dominicans. As De Wohl says, he effected a "happy synthesis between Aristotelian and Christian wisdom."

KAZANTZAKIS, NIKOS. *Saint Francis.* **1962. Tr. by P.A. Bien. Simon & Schuster. (Out of print.)**
St. Francis of Assisi's story is narrated by his traveling companion, Brother Leo, and like Zorba, Leo is earthy, pithy, and fond of the simple joys of the peasants to whom St. Francis preaches. But though Leo's narrative is worldly, it is also rich, multilayered, and reverent. Kazantzakis was deeply moved by St. Francis: his vow of poverty that still informs the Franciscans and, most of all, his divine attempt to overcome the temptations of the flesh to "transubstantiate the matter which God entrusted to us, and turn it into spirit."

Fourteenth Century

YA **DE WOHL, LOUIS.** *Lay Siege to Heaven: A Novel About Saint Catherine of Siena.* **1991. Ignatius, paper. 346 pp. ISBN 0-89870-381-6.**
"Fire is my nature," St. Catherine says of herself, and she's fiery even as a young girl, rebelling against the makeup her mother wants her to wear so that she can attract a man. Already she knows she wants to serve God. A powerful historical figure, Catherine persuaded the Pope, living in France, to return to Rome and negotiated peace among Italy's warring city-states.

Fifteenth Century

YA **DE WOHL, LOUIS.** *Set All Afire: A Novel About Saint Francis Xavier.* **1991. Ignatius, paper. 280 pp. ISBN 0-89870-351-4.**
One of the first Jesuits, Francis Xavier took the gospel to countries in the Far East—India, Malaysia, Japan—and to an island off the coast of China, where he died. The son of a French noble, young Francis seems an idle though virtuous boy. Studying in Paris, he comes under the influence of St. Ignatius, and is "set afire." (See also Shusaku Endo's *Silence,* discussed later.)

MARCANTEL, PAMELA. *An Army of Angels.* **1997. St. Martin's. 578 pp. ISBN 0-312-15030-X.**
Marcantel presents a workmanlike, conscientious biography of Joan of Arc.

Sixteenth Century

★ **ENDO, SHUSAKU.** *Silence.* **1969. Tr. by William Johnston. Tuttle. (Out of print.)**
Endo was among the most preeminent of post-war Japanese novelists and was translated into many languages. His other novels, such as *Volcano* and *When I Whistle,* easily fall under the rubric of Catholic fiction, and are well worth reading. But *Silence,* with its meditations on the gulf between East and West and vivid portrait of early Japan, is extraordinary. Drawing from the letters to Portugal of Jesuit Father Sebastian Rodrigues, Endo constructs a sort of diary, chronicling the adventures and trials of Rodrigues and his two fellow priests as they make the perilous missionary journey to what, for them, was the end of the world. They encounter imprisonment and unspeakable tortures and ultimately their efforts fail, despite thousands of converts. And yet, they are also successful, for a remnant of their flock remains in Japan even today.

YANOW, MORTON LEONARD. *The Nolan.* **1998. Crossroad, paper. 330 pp. ISBN 0-8245-1743-1.**
A biographical novel of Giordano Bruno, or "the Nolan," who was executed in 1600 for refusing to recant his belief in an infinite universe with numerous inhabited worlds. Yanow tells the Nolan's story through Pietro Guidotti, a shrewd peasant who serves the scholarly priest, Robert Bellarmine. Bellarmine is enjoined by forces of the Inquisition to argue the Nolan's heresy and in 1597 sends Guidotti on a kind of spy mission to discover the truth about the Nolan.

Seventeenth Century

★ **MOORE, BRIAN.** *The Black Robe.* **1985. (Out of print.)**
Moore tells the first part of the story of the heroic seventeenth century Jesuit Father Pierre-Jean DeSmet, who explored much of the Canadian wilderness and became one of the few figures to be trusted by American, Canadian, and Native American leaders alike. Here, the young Jesuit and his even younger companion are sent into the wilderness at the onset of winter to join two priests at a remote monastery—if the priests are still alive.

Every missionary venture has thus far failed in the land of the Algonquin, who are portrayed as earthy, libidinous, clever, and profane innocents who abandon Father DeSmet, the Black Robe, to the wilderness and almost certain death. But through undaunting faith, incredible perseverance, and his passionate acceptance of his possible martyrdom, Black Robe survives and brings the word of God to the new land. Made into a beautiful film, directed by Bruce Beresford, in 1991.

Nineteenth Century

WERFEL, FRANZ. *The Song of Bernadette.* **1989. (Originally published in1942.) St. Martin's, paper. 576 pp. ISBN 0-312-03429-6.**
Fleeing from the Nazis, Werfel took a brief refuge in Lourdes, where he was so moved by the shrine to Bernadette that he vowed to write a novel about her. Bernadette, a poor peasant girl, remained true to her vision of the Virgin Mary in 1858, even though at first no one believed her. Made into what was to become a classic film, starring Jennifer Jones and directed by Henry King (1943).

Twentieth Century

★ **MCCULLOUGH, COLLEEN.** *The Thorn Birds.* **1977. (Many editions.)**
What distinguishes this famous generational saga, often rightly compared to *Gone with the Wind,* is its deeply authentic portrait of the New South Wales Outback—the fires, the drought, the flies, the sheep—and its equally fine appreciation of pioneer Queensland and bustling, historic Sydney. A real nation emerges here from an astonishing number of vistas: Cockney, aristocratic, and priestly. But with all its breadth and passion, in the end the tale comes down to the mostly unrequited love affair between Father Ralph de Bricassart and Maggie Cleary. Father Ralph rises to become a cardinal powerful in Vatican politics, and Maggie becomes matriarch of a great Australian sheep station. Ralph takes his vows seriously, though Maggie tempts him, and he falls. Maggie tries to love other men, but only Ralph will do. Their continuing passion gave us what may be the greatest soap opera ever written. (See also chapter 6, "Sagas.")

LITERARY

CALIA, CHARLES LAIRD. *The Unspeakable.* **1998. Morrow. 214 pp. ISBN 0-688-15119-1.**
This fine first novel is told from the point of view of Father Peter Whitmore, an "administrator" for the Archdiocese of St. Paul whose bishop sends him on a troublesome mission to ferret out the truth of reports that a friend of Whitmore's from long before, Father Jim Marbury, has become a faith healer. Marbury came to the priesthood after a reckless young manhood, plagued with tragedy and bad luck and his own culpability, and as a priest has tried to atone for all of humankind's maladies: running a shelter for the homeless, ministering to a near-forgotten parish of deaf people. He restores hearing to the deaf, cures neurological diseases, even brings the dead back to life—or does he? At the least, he may be able to heal Whitmore, who at last confesses to his friend the horror of his own sad youth over a death he might have prevented.

★ **COSSÉ, LAURENCE.** *A Corner of the Veil.* **1999. Tr. from the French by Linda Asher. Scribner. 272 pp. ISBN 0-684-84667-5.**
Cossé's mock thriller portrays French Casuists—Jesuits—trying to cope when irrefutable proof of the existence of God emerges. The Jesuit hierarchy considers suppressing the news, the French government fights for its control, and the Vatican is thrown into panic at the international implications of such certainty. Because this God appears to be Christian, how will Muslims and Hindus react? Cossé's tale is amusing and nimble, satirical yet affectionate, a *Morte D'Urban* by way of *The Mouse That Roared.*

DAY, MARELE. *Lambs of God.* **1998. Penguin Putnam. 330 pp. ISBN 1-57322-079-5.**
Sisters Iphigenia, Margarita, and Carla have lived in a rundown monastery on a remote island for years, tending their sheep, worshipping God in their ritual, almost pagan way. Their lonely, oddly satisfying life is disrupted when a priest visits, intent on turning the island into a kind of church-run resort. The nuns work to defeat the priest's purpose despite their instinctive attraction to him and the awakening of long-dormant sexual feelings.

GORDON, MARY

The Company of Women. 1980. Random. 291 pp. ISBN 0-3994-50508-5.
Felicitas Maria Taylor is the fond hope of five women, all of whom virtually worship a dynamic priest, Father Cyprian. Felicitas is a prodigy, a spoiled brat, and an independent spirit. She breaks away from her spiritual enclave and the mentorship of Father Cyprian, heading for

Columbia University and the company of men. Soon she's caught up in the experimental 1960s, but as Isabel did in *Final Payments* (discussed next), Felicitas must redress her rebellion and come to terms with her innate spirituality.

 ★ *Final Payments.* 1978. Random. 297 pp. ISBN 0-394-42793-9.
Women especially find Gordon's novel a real landmark in their emotional and intellectual development. It's the story of Isabel Moore, a good Catholic girl who has cared for her invalid father for 11 years, denying herself male companionship or any sort of worldly pleasure. Her father dies, and she finds herself entering life at age 30 with naiveté, exhilaration, and an overwhelming sense of liberation, but there are lessons to learn, and final payments to her cloistered past.

★ GREENE, GRAHAM

On anyone's list of the finest writers of the twentieth century, Greene for a time was also thought of by many as the finest Catholic writer, primarily because of his so-called Catholic trilogy, *Brighton Rock, The Power and the Glory,* and *The Heart of the Matter.* Greene was a converted Catholic and faithful at least to the point that he attended Mass every week, but the attraction of the Church was for him to be found in its rituals and traditions that he could use as props. Readers wrote to Greene because of his profound—and always entertaining—examinations of the faith. But his priests were fallen priests or at most ineffectual, and he was far more interested in sin than in virtue. Suffering, sin, and guilt are in endless supply in Greene's fiction; redemption and joy are virtually absent (Shelden 1994).

Brighton Rock. 1993. (Originally published in 1938.) Knopf. 299 pp. ISBN 0-619-42034-7.
Greene's notorious "Pinkie" rises out of his violent Catholic boyhood in Brighton to commit violent crimes, one of which proves his undoing. Pinkie does not triumph over evil or regret his life; he rushes headlong toward Hell. His girlfriend is the hapless Rose, a waitress drawn to the energy and vigor of his criminal life. The efforts of a priest and an amateur sleuth, both of whom befriend Rose, to make sense of Pinkie's life fail: He is evil incarnate.

A Burnt-Out Case. 1992. (Originally published in 1961.) Viking Penguin, paper. 200 pp. ISBN 0-14-018539-9.
A burnt-out case is cured of leprosy but bears its awful scars, which Greene uses as the metaphor for his famous architect, Quarry, the acclaimed designer of Catholic churches who feels he is a fraud because he does not believe in God. In large measure, Greene rewrites *Heart of Darkness,* with Quarry as Kurtz. Quarry exiles himself to a Belgian Congo leper colony run by the Catholic Church in a last attempt to find meaning in life, but as always Greene does not take the easy path, and the answers he contrives for Quarry to find are full of ironies and contradictions.

The End of the Affair. 2000. (Originally published in 1951.) Viking Penguin, paper. 192 pp. ISBN 0-14-029709-1.
Based on Greene's own affair with a rich married woman named Catherine Walston who wrote to Greene about the Catholic faith, *The End of the Affair* is a detailed, even clinical look at the rise and dissolution of a love affair, set upon the background of wartime and post-war England. Maurice, a novelist, eventually loses his love, Sarah, to God—and then to death—but amid his theological considerations he allows that his is not a love story but a chronicle of hate. The 1999 film starred Ralph Fiennes and was directed by Neil Jordan.

The Heart of the Matter. 1991. (Originally published in 1948.) Viking Penguin, paper. 272 pp. ISBN 0-14-018496-1.

Greene considers the unforgivable sin of suicide in his portrait of Scobie, a British official in a bleak Sierra Leone town who no longer loves his wife. Scobie is nominally Catholic. He feels that God reveals himself through suffering. He undertakes an affair with a younger woman not out of lust so much as boredom and a desire to make an intolerable situation worse.

Monsignor Quixote. 1982. Simon & Schuster. 221 pp. ISBN 0-671-45818-3.

In this comic and, for Greene, gentle story, humble Spanish Father Quixote, newly promoted to monsignor, heads out to do good works and explore the contradictions of modern life in his old car Rocinante, accompanied by the ex-mayor of his town, a communist named Sancho Zancas.

The Power and the Glory. 1940. (Many editions.)

An alcoholic priest wanders the wasteland of backwater Mexico, the last priest in a revolutionary regime that has outlawed the Church. The priest faces every sort of temptation, and yields; he is unable to provide solace to the most elemental, traditional needs of grieving peasants. However, when at last he is killed, he does seem to have achieved a perverse saintliness. Many feel this to be Greene's greatest novel.

YA **HANSEN, RON.** *Mariette in Ecstasy.* **1991. HarperCollins. 179 pp. ISBN 0-06-018214-8.**

In spare, sensual, reverential prose, Hansen tells of a beautiful 17-year-old, Mariette Baptiste, a postulant at a convent in upstate New York. Mariette is devout, studious, though overeager. But the nuns are grateful for her presence until, in her sleep, she begins to assume the stigmata. When she wakes, her wounds disappear, and she recollects that she has spoken with Christ. This throws the convent into an uproar, not to mention the surrounding community and Mariette's father, a practical, almost disbelieving man. Are Mariette's experiences genuine? If not, why do the stigmata appear?

HASSLER, JON. *Grand Opening.* **1987. Morrow. 309 pp. ISBN 0-688-06649-6.**

Young Brendan Foster watches the anguish of his parents, Hank and Catherine, when they leave Minneapolis for the remote village of Plum, throwing their hopes and all their savings into a Ma and Pa grocery. The grocery is in disarray, despite what their good Catholic friends told them; the townspeople are clannish and eccentric; and there is a sharp religious divide between Catholics and Lutherans. Stranger still, an odd, possibly criminal, and extremely lonely young man attaches himself to Brendan. Brendan is himself lonely, but he isn't sure how friendly to be.

HASSLER, JON. *North of Hope.* **1990. Ballantine. 518 pp. ISBN 0-345-36910-6.**

Respecting his dying mother's wishes, Frank Healy decides to become a priest at age 11. In high school he meets the love of his life, Libby Girard, but he has made a vow he intends to honor. Twenty years later, a weary man indeed, Father Healy comes home to Minnesota to take up a parish among the Ojibway in Minnesota's lake country. And there is Libby, in Frank's eyes as beautiful as ever and as profoundly disappointed in life as he.

KAZANTZAKIS, NIKOS. *The Greek Passion.* **1999. (Originally published in 1953.) Tr. by Jonathan Griffin. Transaction Publishers. 680 pp. ISBN 1-56000-453-3.**

A huge cast populates this ironic, sometimes horrifying tale set during one of the periods of Turkish occupation of Greece. The Turks stand in for the Roman authority, Orthodox priests for the Sanhedrin, as Greek and Turk peasants mount a passion play. All goes well until Manolios, the young shepherd chosen to portray Jesus, sees a vision of Jesus and is convinced that he must speak out against the religious authorities of his village.

MACLAVERTY, BERNARD. *Lamb.* 1980. George Braziller. 152 pp. ISBN 0-8076-0990-0.

The lamb—the sacrificial lamb—is a young boy, Owen, consigned to a bleak Irish reformatory run under Catholic auspices. The lamb is also a sad young priest, Michael Lamb, known in the "school" as Brother Sebastian. When his father dies and leaves him a small inheritance, Michael takes the boy away in hopes that he can save one soul in a miserable world, manage one act of unassailable purity. Michael and the boy become like father and son, but Michael's cure is ultimately worse than the disease, dramatizing the difficulty of virtue in an overwhelmingly sinful world and of trying to build right actions on wrong premises. *Lamb* was filmed in 1986, with Liam Neeson as Brother Sebastian.

MCINERNY, RALPH. *The Priest.* 1973. Harper & Row. (Out of print.)

Set in 1968, McInerny's third novel offers an enduring snapshot of the Church poised between its traditions and the reforms of Vatican II. Father Frank Ascue, fresh from his studies in Rome, expects an academic assignment stateside but instead is assigned to an old parish presided over by an old, conservative priest. He likes parish work, but the atmosphere is baffling: priests and nuns renouncing their vows, traditionalists arguing with liberals, priests claiming the Church has lost its relevance. He wonders if he should enter into a relationship with a woman he's attracted to. Meanwhile, the larger tumult of the 1960s pounds at everyone's preconceptions.

MOORE, BRIAN

Moore, who died in 1999, was always more popular in Canada and England than in the United States, where he lived much of his life. An Irish-Catholic literary writer from Belfast, he was an indifferent practitioner. But the effects of faith, particularly on those who have lost or never professed it, fascinated him, and many of his novels are seen as religious inquiries in the dark tradition of Graham Greene. His popularity appears to be growing, still, and his books remain available. (See also *The Black Robe*, discussed previously under "Historical," subsection "Seventeenth Century.")

Catholics. 1972. Holt, Rinehart, & Winston. 107 pp. ISBN 0-030-06957-3.
Any Catholic who lived through the effects of Vatican II will love this short novel about a monastery on a cold island off the coast of Ireland, where the monks refuse to abandon their ancient rituals of Latin mass and private confession. The media descend; more significantly, a modern priest is dispatched from the Vatican to bring the priests in line.

Cold Heaven. 1983. Holt, Rinehart, & Winston. 265 pp. ISBN 0-030-63257-9.
Marie Davenport is about to leave her cold fish of a husband, with whom she is vacationing in France, for another man. Then her husband is accidentally killed and, irony upon irony, he disappears from the morgue, as do his identification papers at the hotel. In the midst of this nightmare, Marie begins having religious visions. She screams that she is the wrong person, too sinful for visions, but they terrifyingly persist.

The Color of Blood. 1987. Dutton. 182 pp. ISBN 0-525-24539-1.
Moore draws from the heady days of the breakup of Eastern European communism for his political thriller featuring Cardinal Stephan Bem. The cardinal is a good man doing his best in a terrible situation. For years, to keep his church alive, he has walked a fine line between the communist state and the militancy of the church leaders he directs. Suddenly, his life is threatened and he must flee underground, though it is

unclear why. The cardinal's groping for understanding as he moves among the poor he has grown so remote from amounts to a spiritual renewal for him, but the country's politics, and his own fate, have spun out of control.

No Other Life. 1993. Doubleday. 223 pp. ISBN 0-385-41515-X.
One of Moore's most unsettling novels is set on a fictional Caribbean island much like Haiti. Through the eyes of the Canadian priest Father Paul Michel, Moore charts the rise of an orphan boy, Jean-Pierre Cantave, first to the priesthood and then to political power. The charismatic Jean-Pierre seems almost Christ-like and is a great hero to the poor. But as his power grows his liberation theology worries Church officials, and they expel him. No matter, for when the island's brutal dictator dies, Jean-Pierre quickly becomes the new leader, only to surround himself with thugs and strongmen and, at least at first, to seem no better than his sadistic, repressive predecessor.

★ **O'CONNOR, FLANNERY.** *Flannery O'Connor: Collected Works: Wise Blood/A Good Man Is Hard to Find/The Violent Bear It Away/Everything that Rises Must Converge/Essays & Letters.* **Ed. by Sally Fitzgerald. 1988. Library of America. 1,281 pp. ISBN 0-940450-37-2.**

Everything O'Connor wrote can be collected in one volume, but it's no measure of her influence. Her polished, funny, convoluted short stories are among the best of all time, and she had only found her stride when she died at age 39, from the painful, paralyzing effects of lupus.

For the casual reader, however, she is not easily conquered. O'Connor's odd, unforgettable characters wrestle to deny their faith or seem to mock God. The violence in her stories is so vividly rendered that she seems almost to advocate it. Evil often seems to triumph. But O'Connor's Catholic faith informs her writing every step of the way, and she is always working toward a substantiation of grace (Wyatt 1992).

In *Wise Blood* (1952), O'Connor's short first novel, Hazel Motes's faith in God seems to be innate, but he fights against it. He joins with a charlatan named Asa Hawks and his grotesque daughter in various blasphemous or at least grotesque acts, trying to comfort his tortured soul in the delights of the physical world or in false prophets such as the "New Jesus." But in the end he can only find grace through the quaint faith of his youth. John Huston made a fine film from *Wise Blood* in 1979.

The Violent Bear It Away (1960) tells somewhat the same story as *Wise Blood,* though it is not as well-known. Young Francis Marion Tarwater had the misfortune to be raised by his grand-uncle Mason, a religious tyrant. "Not only the world, but the Lord Himself had failed to hear the prophet's message," O'Connor writes, and when the mean old man dies, Francis is grateful enough to be taken under the wing of his uncle, George Rayber. George is a rational, educated man who sees old Mason's beliefs as the worst sort of fanaticism, but George is as intolerant in his way. Francis weaves from extreme to dark extreme as good and evil war for his soul. And then he has a vision.

★ **PERCY, WALKER**
Walker Percy's story is well-known: Trained as a physician, he contracted tuberculosis at the age of 26, and the several years he spent in a sanitarium proved the most important of his life. He read voraciously, turning himself into a philosopher.

Percy wrote novels of ideas, rather than family stories or chronicles of maturation. At heart a conservative Catholic, he saw himself as a propagandist for his faith, a prophet bemoaning the watering down of Christianity that, among other causes, he felt resulted from the split between the arts and sciences. The split has given rise to "scientism," or false sciences, such as astrology, that take the place of actual science and become popular religion. Much influenced by French thinkers such as Derrida, Sartre, and Camus, Percy might also be called an existential Christian. This mix of scientific detachment, traditional Catholicism, and postmodernist thought is what distinguished Percy from all other writers (Montgomery 1993).

Percy was only incidentally a Southern writer, despite his strong ties to Louisiana and his keen appreciation of Southern traditions. His novels remain popular as much for their scathing wit and entertaining narratives as their Christian content, which is so subtly argued and so steeped in philosophy that some readers fail to recognize it. Percy died in 1990.

Lancelot. 1999. (Originally published in 1977.) St. Martin's, paper. 272 pp. ISBN 0-312-24307-3.
We meet Lancelot Andrewes Larmar through his old friend Percival, a priest who visits him at the insane asylum. He confesses his sins to Percival: murdering his wife and lover and trying to take his own life. And then he confesses why: the rot of American society, every idea of corruption and miscommunication and damnation that Percy has entertained. Lancelot will be released, it seems. A grandiose knight-errant, he wants to found a holy order where women will be pure and men strong. Percival has another message, the simple gospel, and Lancelot, cured of his madness, may be ready to receive it.

The Last Gentleman. 1998. (Originally published in 1966.) Random. 560 pp. ISBN 0-679-60272-0.
In his much-admired second novel Percy created a sort of wayfaring stranger, Will Barrett, a displaced Southerner who, as the story opens, is living restlessly in New York, a "humidification" engineer at Macy's. Haunted by his father's suicide, an emotional wreck, and a little unhinged, Will returns to Louisiana to reason out what exactly his father, a sort of latter-day Stoic, stood for. In touch with his roots, Will is ready to receive the good news of the gospel.

Love in the Ruins. 1999. (Originally published in 1971.) St. Martin's, paper. 384 pp. ISBN 0-312-24311-1.
In a tale set in the near future, physician/psychiatrist Tom More takes his invention, the Ontological Lapsometer, round the country in "his adventures of a bad Catholic at a time near the end of the world." It's a bad time. The automobile culture has broken down. Manhattan is sprouting weeds. There's an interminable war in Ecuador. The Catholic Church is fragmented and no one believes in anything, or beliefs are polarizing. Dr. More can diagnose the problem, any spiritual malady, but can he provide a cure? Enter a stranger, a drug salesman with an invitation to a journey, and an answer to Dr. More's question. But it may be Faust's answer.

The Moviegoer. 1961. Knopf. 241 pp. ISBN 0-394-43703-9.
Percy's witty first novel remains his best known and has never gone out of print. It's about the lukewarm Catholic Binx Bolling, a young New Orleans stockbroker and ladies' man who is crippled by his keen intelligence. Seeing nothing but death of the spirit in the lives he intersects, he seeks some kind of spiritual path and embarks on a number of philosophical inquiries. But only the movies have meaning for him, the characters signifying reality while reality itself remains elusive. Through movies Binx connects with people, one woman in particular, and he decides to marry. And yet the reader will not be perfectly convinced that he has found in her the meaning he seeks. Winner of the National Book Award.

The Second Coming. 1999. (Originally published in 1971.) St. Martin's. 368 pp. ISBN 0-312-24324-3.

Will Barrett, the wanderer of *The Last Gentleman,* has become convinced that the return of Christ is imminent, and seeks everywhere for signs and portents. As is often the case in Percy's novels, Will may be deluded. But even at the end, when he is "cured," he still wonders how and if Christ will manifest Himself.

The Thanatos Syndrome. 1987. Farrar. 372 pp. ISBN 0-374-27354-5.

Ironic as ever, Dr. Tom More (of *Love in the Ruins*) returns in Percy's last novel. Tom has been released from Angola Prison and is practicing psychiatry again. There is something decidedly wrong with his patients, who have taken on a kind of childlike clarity, as if part of them has been lobotomized. The condition, or syndrome, leads them into bizarre sexual behavior, somehow connected with the mysterious Belle-Ame, the "school" where Tom's estranged wife is sending his children. Or maybe it's in the water, entirely a chemical condition. With his cousin Lucy Lipscomb, an epidemiologist, Tom investigates, all the while absorbing the rants of Father Simon Smith, whose prophecies Percy camouflages as madness.

POWERS, J. F.

★ ***Morte D'Urban.*** 2000. (Originally published in 1962.) New York Review of Books. 336 pp. ISBN 0-940322-23-4.

Father Urban, as his name suggests, is urbane, gifted at finding new sources of funding for the church, and in demand nationally for his unthreatening religious speeches. Unfortunately, he belongs to the Order of Clementines, who were, in Powers's typically comic phrase, "unique in that they were noted for nothing at all." Father Urban has marked out a good life for himself in Chicago, but then he's assigned to an obscure, impoverished monastery in Minnesota, peopled with incompetent though endearing priests who give Powers plenty of opportunity for satire. Father Urban succeeds even here, organizing a golf tournament and taking fishing trips with the influential, but in his triumph are the seeds of his ruin. And yet the ruin heralds spiritual breakthrough in this sly masterpiece. Winner of the National Book Award.

Wheat That Springeth Green. 2000. (Originally published in 1988.) New York Review of Books. 327 pp. ISBN 0-940322-24-2.

Powers's only other novel charts the unsteady course toward holiness of Joe Hackett, a worldly priest somewhat like Father Urban, but in the beginning with ambitions toward helping the poor. Taken under the wing of a well-known, influential priest, Father Joe settles into the mundane (though funny) realities of the Church under Vatican II: He becomes an expert in supervising building programs. When he gets his own parish, all his time is taken up in Rotary-like, small-town activities, such as backyard barbecues and posing with cheerleaders at the mall. He's middle-aged, overweight, and obsessed with church finances. Then he's given a young assistant whose humility and earnestness undermine his own arrogance and futile reliance on the props of the Church and return him to his first calling, helping the poor.

MORALITY TALES

BREMER, FRANCES WINFIELD. *Running to Paradise.* **2000. Prospect Press, paper. 124 pp. ISBN 1-892668-24-6.**

Nothing much happens to Father Frank, a likable, earnest young priest who decides to run in the New York City marathon and keeps a combined running and prayer journal. Running becomes a metaphor both for the discipline of serving God and for life's race. Father Frank's difficulties in running a modern parish are symbolized by the marathon, which he finishes but does not excel at. The process is never done, the race never won. All a humble priest can do is help ordinary people in their eternal struggle for goodness.

CALDWELL, TAYLOR. *Dialogues with the Devil.* 1967. Doubleday. (Out of print.)

Caldwell's rendition of the Fall mixes the lore of ancient Atlantis with the biblical tale of Lucifer, here engaged in correspondence with the Archangel Michael. Lucifer points out that Man himself is fallen and has an essentially sinful nature, whereas Michael defends Man as God's perfectable creation. Because it was his political views that precipitated his ouster from Heaven, Lucifer is an almost attractive figure. His analysis of humankind is shrewd, if self-serving. Though the theology is more or less Catholic, *Dialogues* is otherwise quite similar to *Screwtape Letters* (p. 24).

GIRZONE, JOSEPH

JOSHUA SERIES

Joseph Girzone is a retired priest who began writing in 1981. All of his Joshua books remain in print in hardcover, paper, large print, and audio editions. Because the novels are simply written and their message is universal, they are appropriate for all libraries. They are nonsequential, though Girzone's own spiritual growth is discernible.

Simply put, Joshua is Jesus placed in modern times, and the stories echo the Gospels. Some find them simplistic. Others find them uplifting and quietly reassuring, and for such readers Girzone's are favorite books, to be returned to again and again.

Joshua. 1983. Richelieu Court. 310 pp. ISBN 0-911519-03-3.
The gentle, almost childlike Joshua shows up in a small town riven with denominational strife and quietly demonstrates a simple, unifying gospel of love.

Joshua and the Children.1989. Macmillan. 224 pp. ISBN 0-02-543945-6.
The sequel to *Joshua* is much the same: Pursuing Girzone's overarching theme of Christian unity, Joshua heals violent rifts among the adults of another ordinary, even nondescript town through his loving admonitions to children.

The Shepherd. 1990. Macmillan. 246 pp. ISBN 0-02-543947-2.
Girzone's most ambitious effort fictionally features David Campbell, a seemingly hidebound bishop who, through Joshua's counsel, transforms his ministry into a call to break down sectarian barriers and return to a gospel of love.

Joshua in the Holy Land. 1992. Macmillan. 205 pp. ISBN 0-02-543445-4.
The fourth entry in the Joshua series parallels the original story of Jesus in some ways, as Joshua, returned to his beloved profession of woodcarving in contemporary Israel, once more takes up the cause of peace among religious— Christian and Jewish—sects.

Joshua and the City. 1995. Doubleday. 242 pp. ISBN 0-385-47420-2.
Joshua works miracles with a poor black family in a city much like New York.

Joshua, the Homecoming. 1999. Doubleday. 259 pp. ISBN 0-385-49509-9.
There's hardly a story to be found in Girzone's latter-day attempt to deal with widespread fears of apocalypse.

The Parables of Joshua. 2001. Doubleday. 176 pp. ISBN 0-385-49511-0.
The Parables of Joshua tells no story but feebly attempts to construct modern-day parables in the spirit of the originals; at best, Girzone's parables may inspire readers to get out their New Testaments.

KEADY, WALTER. *Mary McGreevy.* **1998. MacMurray & Beck. 261 pp. ISBN 1-878448-83-8.**
In this wry, agreeably predictable, distinctly Irish tale, an unhappy nun leaps at the chance to leave her convent when she inherits the family farm. She soon turns out to be a rebel in more ways than one, attracting all the men in her little village. Mary wants a child but regards marriage as a bondage worse than the Church. This runs her afoul of the parish priest, a gentle and forgiving soul named Father Mulroe. He falls desperately though chastely in love with Mary, and she with him.

VETERE, RICHARD. *The Third Miracle.* **1997. Carroll & Graf. 232 pp. ISBN 0-7867-0413-6.**
Father Frank Moore is appointed devil's advocate to explore accounts of miracles associated with a statue of the Virgin Mary that seems to cry tears of blood. Pilgrims flock to the scene, the church of St. Stanislaus. Father Moore is a weary, jaded priest, exactly right to explore Vetere's theme whether miracles are real, or imagined out of deep psychological need.

NUNS AND PRIESTS AS SLEUTHS

BLACK, VERONICA

SISTER JOAN
Sister Joan of the Order of the Daughters of Compassion is a naturally curious—or nosy—woman who, in the first entries, is engagingly troubled by how to balance her spiritual life with the intrusive but terribly interesting larger world. The conflict deepens when she finds herself attracted to Detective Sergeant Mill, a cynical, unhappily married man, and her partner in crime solving. In later entries, although the mysteries remain entertaining, there is less spiritual artifice.

> *A Vow of Silence.* 1990. St. Martin's. 207 pp. ISBN 0-312-04441-0.
>
> *A Vow of Chastity.* 1991. St. Martin's. 191 pp. ISBN 0-312-07112-4.
>
> *A Vow of Sanctity.* 1993. St. Martin's. 192 pp. ISBN 0-312-09408-6.
>
> *A Vow of Obedience.* 1994. St. Martin's. 190 pp. ISBN 0-312-10573-8.
>
> *A Vow of Penance.* 1994. St. Martin's. 208 pp. ISBN 0-312-11092-8.
>
> *A Vow of Devotion.* 1995. St. Martin's. 186 pp. ISBN 0-312-13206-9.
>
> *A Vow of Fidelity.* 1995. St. Martin's. 174 pp. ISBN 0-312-14064-9.
>
> *A Vow of Poverty.* 1996. St. Martin's. 173 pp. ISBN 0-312-14756-2.
>
> *A Vow of Adoration.* 1996. St. Martin's. 190 pp. ISBN 0-312-18205-8.
>
> *A Vow of Compassion.* 1998. St. Martin's. 208 pp. ISBN 0-312-19354-8.

COEL, MARGARET

FATHER JOHN O'MALLEY
Coel works hard to break free of the inevitable comparisons with Tony Hillerman in this mystery series set on Wyoming's Wind River Arapaho Reservation and featuring the combined sleuthing talents of Jesuit Father John O'Malley, mission priest, and divorced Arapaho lawyer Vicky Holden. In formulaic terms, she fails; as in Hillerman, some aspect of Native American culture

is wrapped around a murder. She succeeds, however, in her articulate and passionate interweaving of contemporary Native American issues; her knowledge of the historical West gained from nonfiction work; and in her subtle, ongoing portrait of both the priest, battling alcoholism and loneliness, and the lawyer, battling the conflicting values of her upbringing and her education.

The Eagle Catcher. 1995. University Press of Colorado. 186 pp. ISBN 0-87081-367-6.
The unlikely duo track who killed a tribal chairman before a crucial powwow and form their unusual relationship.

The Ghost Walker. 1996. Berkley. 243 pp. ISBN 0-425-15468-8.
In the sequel to *The Eagle Catcher,* Father O'Malley stumbles upon a dead body, and then it promptly disappears, a "ghost walker."

The Dream Stalker. 1997. Berkley. 244 pp. ISBN 0-425-15967-1.
The tendency for using reservations as landfills (for nuclear waste, in this case) provides the subtext of *The Dream Stalker,* in which Vicky, recovering from encounters with drugs and dubious male companions in *The Ghost Walker,* emerges into a full, compelling character.

The Story Teller. 1998. Berkley. 256 pp. ISBN 0-425-16538-8.
By this fourth entry of the series Father O'Malley and Vicki seem inseparably linked, and there's even a suggestion of romance in the air, which confuses them both. Otherwise, the two search for a missing Arapaho scholar, and are drawn into tribal history.

The Lost Bird. 1999. Berkley. 304 p. ISBN 0-425-17059-4.
Father O'Malley takes over the investigative chores in the series's fifth entry. The murder of his assistant seems to be linked to the appearance on the reservation of a young Hollywood actress.

The Spirit Woman. 2000. Berkley. 272 pp. ISBN 0-425-17597-9.
Father O'Malley and Vicki investigate the death of a scholar, which in turn leads them to a historical mystery surrounding Sacajawea.

The Thunder Keeper. 2001. Berkley. 288 pp. ISBN 0-425-18188-X.
The delicate tension between Father O'Malley and Vicky Holden—not quite love, but more than friendship—may be the best part of the seventh entry in Coel's series. The story this time around is about a vision quest undertaken by an unhappy young seeker named Duncan Grover. His quest becomes a suicide, but Vicky and the padre suspect murder. Fair enough, but Coel leans on too many stock elements in framing the case: dumb cops, for instance, and unscrupulous developers taking advantage of the poor Indians.

KIENZLE, WILLIAM X.

FATHER KOESLER

Likable Father Robert Koesler, a parish priest, mystery reader, and editor of a small Catholic newspaper, has enjoyed a long run of popularity following *The Rosary Murders,* in which he helps police find who's been killing priests and nuns in the Detroit Archdiocese. Kienzle was himself a parish priest; thus, there is authenticity to his formula of crime plus Catholic issues plus genial priest. Over the years Kienzle has formed mysteries around all of Catholicism's hot-button issues, from euthanasia to marriage for priests and nuns, though never with the panache of Andrew Greeley.

As the 1990s ended, Kienzle alienated fans more interested in mystery than religion by writing stories in which Father Koesler was only marginally present and in which the effects of Vatican II dominated, rather than simply formed the milieu.

Hardcover editions of Father Koesler mysteries, originally from Andrews & McMeel, have mostly gone out of print; Ballantine paper editions appear periodically. Except for Father Koesler's aging, the series is not rigorously sequential.

The Rosary Murders. 1979.

Death Wears a Red Hat. 1980.

Mind Over Murder. 1981.

Assault with Intent. 1982.

Shadow of Death. 1983.

Kill and Tell. 1984.

Sudden Death. 1985.

Deathbed. 1986.

Deadline for a Critic. 1987.

Marked for Murder. 1988.

Eminence. 1989.

Masquerade. 1990.

Chameleon. 1991.

Body Count. 1992.

Dead Wrong. 1993.

Bishop As Pawn. 1994.

Call No Man Father. 1995.

Requiem for Moses. 1996.

The Man Who Loved God. 1997.

No Greater Love. 1999.

Till Death. 2000.

The Sacrifice. 2001.

MANUEL, DAVID

BROTHER BARTHOLEMEW

A Matter of Roses. 1999. Paraclete. 355 pp. ISBN 1-55725-234-3.
Andrew Doane, now Brother Bartholemew of Faith Abbey, loved Laurel Winslow years ago. As she comes back into his life, causing him to question his vows, his attentions are diverted by the murder of a local real estate tycoon by a Vietnam veteran, Maurice, who grows roses. He's married to an old friend whom the dead man was once in love with.

But Maurice is disabled and found unconscious in his garden. How could he be the murderer? Bartholemew joins with a local detective to track down just who did murder Maurice in this engaging though rather crowded first entry.

A Matter of Diamonds. 2000. Paraclete. 289 pp. ISBN 1-55725-258-0.
The sequel to *A Matter of Roses* is much more streamlined. Bartholemew meets with darkest evil when he solves the sad puzzle of Dorothy Hansen, an amateur diamond smuggler for the boss she's in love with, and who doesn't love her.

MCINERNY, RALPH

FATHER DOWLING

A long-time philosophy professor at Notre Dame and authority on St. Thomas Aquinas, Ralph McInerny is best known for his mysteries. His long-running Father Dowling series features a cool, detached, and yet compassionate prelate; crisp prose; and ironic running commentary on human folly. To contrast McInerny with Father Greeley, McInerny is subtle, even elegant, whereas Greeley is direct and visceral. Father Dowling was transformed into an ABC series, starring Tom Bosley, that ran from 1989 to 1991.

Both McInerny's Father Dowling series and his Sister Mary Theresa series (discussed later) are in and out of print in paper, and many individual titles can be found in large print format.

Her Death of Cold. 1977. Vanguard.

The Seventh Station. 1977. Vanguard.

Bishop As Pawn. 1978. Vanguard.

Lying Three. 1979. Vanguard.

Second Vespers. 1980. Vanguard.

Thicker Than Water. 1981. Vanguard.

A Loss of Patients. 1982. Vanguard.

The Grass Widow. 1983. Vanguard.

Getting a Way with Murder. 1984. Vanguard.

Rest in Pieces. 1985. Vanguard.

The Basket Case. 1987. St. Martin's.

Four on the Floor (short stories). 1989. St. Martin's.

Abracadaver. 1989. St. Martin's.

Slight of Body. St. Martin's.

Judas Priest. 1991. St. Martin's.

Desert Sinner. 1992. St. Martin's.

Seed of Doubt. 1993. St. Martin's.

A Cardinal Offense. 1994. St. Martin's.

The Tears of Things. 1996. St. Martin's.

Grave Undertakings. 2000. St. Martin's. 252 pp. ISBN 0-312-20309-8.

SISTER MARY THERESA

McInerny's Sister Mary Theresa series, written under the pseudonym Monica Quill, is set in the Chicago environs of the Order of Martha and Mary, a body even less vital than J. F. Powers's Clementines of *Morte D'Urban.* Seemingly modeled on Nero Wolfe, Mary Theresa is an elderly, overweight sleuth who frequently lends her logical skills to Chicago Police Department's Captain Moriarity; two other nuns, Sisters Kim and Joyce, assist her. The series is mostly out of print.

> *Not a Blessed Thing.* 1981. Vanguard.
>
> *Let Us Prey.* 1982. Vanguard.
>
> *And Then There Was Nun.* 1984. Vanguard.
>
> *Nun of the Above.* 1985. Vanguard.
>
> *Sine Qua Nun.* 1986. Vanguard.
>
> *Veil of Ignorance.* 1988. St. Martin's.
>
> *Sister Hood.* 1991. St. Martin's.
>
> *Nun Plussed.* 1993. St. Martin's.

REYNOLDS, FATHER BRAD, S. J.

FATHER MARK TOWNSEND

> *The Story Knife.* 1996. Avon, paper. 256 pp. ISBN 0-380-78400-9.
> Seattle-based Father Mark Townsend, a coolly logical Jesuit, begins his sleuthing career tracking down a murder in an Eskimo village where he once served as priest.
>
> *A Ritual Death.* 1997. Avon, paper. 242 pp. ISBN 0-380-78401-7.
> Father Townsend visits some of the same territory of David Guterson's *Snow Falling on Cedars* with a murder apparently linked to the Swonomish Indians out on Puget Sound.
>
> *Cruel Sanctuary.* 1999. Avon, paper. 341 pp. ISBN 0-380-79843-3.
> Father Townsend's attempt to befriend a homeless Eskimo youth gets him incriminated in the boy's murder in the series' third entry.
>
> *Deadly Harvest.* 1999. Avon, paper. 291 pp. ISBN 0-380-79844-1.
> A touch of apocalypse informs the fourth entry of Reynolds's series, featuring Father Townsend on a trip to the Yakima Valley to investigate the strange doings of a professed prophet called Brother Gabriel.
>
> See also chapter 10, "Mysteries and Thrillers," the section "Pastors As Sleuths."

Historical Mysteries

★ **ECO, UMBERTO.** *The Name of the Rose.* **1980. Tr. By William Weaver. Harcourt. 502 pp. ISBN 0-15-144647-4.**
Though Sean Connery's performance in the 1986 film of the same title was riveting, and the setting (1327) a visual feast, Eco's famous novel has rather more to it. It's a murder mystery solved by the Sherlock Holmes-like Brother William of Baskerville. But Brother William has been sent to ferret out heresy, and the truth behind the grisly deaths of seven monks over a period of

seven days will reveal that heresy. Both the ignorance and the learning the Church stood for in medieval Europe—and the Inquisition with all its horrors—are intricately, convincingly rendered in learned asides and speculations. They account for the novel's continuing popularity at least as much as its compelling mystery.

FRAZER, MARGARET

SISTER PREVISSE MEDIEVAL MYSTERIES

Set in fifteenth century England with great attention to period detail, not to mention a reverence for Chaucer, there is little of religious inquiry to Frazer's series, though her likable and compassionate sleuth, Benedictine Sister "Dame" Previsse, professes a deep piety. The mysteries themselves, featuring Dame Previsse's Sherlock Holmes-like deductions, are first-rate and have twice been nominated for Edgars.

> **The Novice's Tale.** 1992. Berkley, paper. 240 pp. ISBN 0-425-14321-X.
>
> **The Servant's Tale.** 1993. Berkeley, paper. 234 pp. ISBN 0-425-14389-9.
>
> **The Bishop's Tale.** 1994. Berkley, paper, p 208p. ISBN 0-425-14492-5.
>
> **The Outlaw's Tale.** 1995. (Originally published in 1994.) Berkley, paper. 224 pp. ISBN 0-425-15119-0.
>
> **The Boy's Tale.** 1995. Berkley, paper. 240 pp. ISBN 0-425-14899-8.
>
> **The Murderer's Tale.** 1996. Berkley, paper. 240 pp. ISBN 0-425-15406-8.
>
> **The Prioress' Tale.** 1997. Berkley, paper. 256 pp. ISBN 0-425-15944-2.
>
> **The Maiden's Tale.** 1998. Berkley, paper. 245 pp. ISBN 0-425-16407-1.
>
> **The Reeve's Tale.** 1999. Berkley, paper. 288 pp. ISBN 0-425-17667-3.
>
> **The Squire's Tale.** 2000. Berkley. 288 pp. ISBN 0-425-17678-9.

12

PETERS, ELLIS

CHRONICLES OF BROTHER CADFAEL

Peters is the pseudonym of Englishwoman Edith Pargeter, the writer of many mysteries besides Brother Cadfael's adventures. Brother Cadfael is a Benedictine monk in twelfth century England, a gentle, older man who sowed some wild oats in his youth, during which he went on a Crusade and fathered a son. Nowadays, the contemplative life—and celibacy—suits him fine, and he takes great satisfaction from his herb garden. But the contentment he gains from gardening is always being breached with murder, and, reluctantly but wittily and on the whole cheerfully, he brings his sleuthing skills to bear. Peters's series is pleasant, diverting; her settings and sense of history are beautifully realized. Novels from the series have periodically been adapted for the BBC and have appeared on PBS outlets in the United States; most of the earlier entries are out of print in cloth but are often reissued in paper and large print. Note: *A Rare Benedictine,* published in 1989, contains three nonsequential novellas.

> **A Morbid Taste for Bones.** 1977.
>
> **One Corpse Too Many.** 1979.
>
> **Monk's Hood.** 1980.

St. Peter's Fair. 1981.

The Leper of Saint Giles. 1982.

The Virgin in the Ice. 1982.

The Sanctuary Sparrow. 1983.

The Devil's Novice. 1983.

Dead Man's Ransom. 1984.

The Pilgrim of Hate. 1984.

An Excellent Mystery. 1985.

The Raven in the Foregate. 1986.

The Rose Rent. 1986.

The Hermit of Eyton Forest. 1988.

The Confession of Brother Haluin. 1988.

Heretic's Apprentice. 1990.

The Potter's Field. 1990.

The Summer of the Danes. 1991.

The Holy Thief. 1992.

Brother Cadfael's Penance. 1994.

APOCALYPSE

FOLSOM, ALLAN. *Day of Confession.* **1998. Little, Brown. 566 pp. ISBN 0-316-28755-5.**
Los Angeles lawyer Harry Addison rushes to Italy to claim the body of his dead brother, a priest, but his brother may not be dead and may in fact have murdered a prominent cardinal. At the root of all this confusion is a dark, conspire-with-the-Devil plot to set up a new Holy Roman Empire in, of all places, China.

MACFARLANE, BUD. *Pierced by a Sword.* **1995. Saint Jude Media, paper. 568 pp. ISBN 0-9646316-0-1.**
An anti-pope arises, and a World Union. Militias grow in strength in reaction to the growing intrusiveness of the United Nations. Still, a handful of traditional Catholics survive these years as the Marian Apparitions—or appearances of the Virgin Mary—herald an apocalypse. Finally, the old and true pope surfaces and begins a series of broadcasts on shortwave radio, joining the great battle of the end times.

MARTIN, MALACHI. *Windswept House.* **1996. Doubleday. 640 pp. ISBN 0-385-48408-9.**
Martin's "Slavic" pope is a traditionalist, but global politics have blunted his message of belief and redemption. Global religion is on the rise, Europe is united, and the reign of the Antichrist is imminent.

O'BRIEN, MICHAEL

★ *CHILDREN OF THE LAST DAYS*

Children of the Last Days is a thematic series, loosely related, and one entry is not apocalyptic but provides context for the other novels. Though O'Brien's passion occasionally turns shrill and punishing, each of these novels is compelling, and all have been popular. They make for an interesting alternative to the Left Behind series.

Father Elijah. 1996. Ignatius, paper. 597 pp. ISBN 0-89870-580-0.
The Church has been deeply compromised by the fulfillment of biblical prophecies. The pope is convinced that these are the Last Days and commands Father Elijah, a converted Jew, Holocaust survivor, and prophet, to look for the Antichrist. Though this is a long, complex novel, it's fast paced and full of surprises.

Strangers and Sojourners. 1997. Ignatius, paper. 571 pp. ISBN 0-89870-609-2.
O'Brien tells the offbeat, tender love story of Anna Ashton, a nurse, and an Irish expatriate, Stephen Delaney in this unrelated sequel to *Father Elijah.* Anna's sweet soul has been wounded by WWI experiences with wounded soldiers, and she immigrates to the backcountry of Canada to reinvent her life. She marries Stephen, bears their children, and pursues her career, running an experimental school. But it takes a lifetime for the marriage to work because of religious differences and Stephen's reticent ways.

Eclipse of the Sun. 1998. Ignatius, paper. 857 pp. ISBN 0-89870-687-4.
"Practically overnight" Canada becomes a police state. With a heavy hand, O'Brien suggests why in his portrait of a hippie colony in British Columbia that has, over time, devolved into a petty dictatorship. An old priest, Father Andrei, steals upon the colony to rescue a child who may hold the key to the resurgence of civil liberties taken away by those liberals who, in O'Brien's eyes, are Nazis in their newest manifestation.

Plague Journal. 1999. Ignatius, paper. 275 pp. ISBN 0-89870-610-6.
Plague Journal, the conclusion to O'Brien's Children of the Last Days series, is a good recommendation for readers of Frank Peretti's *This Present Darkness.* It's about Nathaniel Delaney, the editor of a small-town newspaper who speaks out when an increasingly authoritarian government begins to abrogate personal freedoms.

SHAPIRO, DAVID. *The Promise of God.* 2000. Simcha Press, paper. 335 pp. ISBN 1-55874-744-3.

Cardinal Isaac Cortes is renowned because of his scholarship and also his courageous crusade against South American drug cartels and is the likely successor to the ailing Pope. But as he ascends to the papacy, it becomes clear that he is the Jewish Messiah, not, like Christ, divine, but a holy man chosen by God to unite his far-flung people.

See also chapter 3, "Christian Classics," the sections on George MacDonald and the Inklings; chapter 9, "Fantasy and Science Fiction," the section on apocalypse; and "West, Morris," in this chapter.

SCIENCE FICTION

BLISH, JAMES. *A Case of Conscience.* 1958. Walker. (Out of print.)

Readers of *The Sparrow* (discussed later), Mary Doria Russell's widely praised novel, will be struck with its similarities to this earlier novel. Like Emilio Sandoz of that novel, Ramon Ruiz-Sanchez is Hispanic, a Jesuit, and an accomplished linguist—the first to crack the complicated language of the reptilian race of Lithia. His task is to learn enough of Lithian culture to assign their place in the divine order, but it seems, sophisticated as the Lithians are, that they have never known God. The more Father Ramon learns, the more his faith is shaken.

MILLER, WALTER M., JR.

YA ★ *A Canticle for Leibowitz.* 1997. (Originally published in 1960.) Bantam, paper. 368 pp. ISBN 0-553-37926-7.

This hilarious, bleak, almost unbearably ironic classic tells of the attempt of monks in a Utah cloister to keep learning alive about 600 years after nuclear annihilation. Accidentally, they discover a holy artifact that they are barely able to read, let alone make sense of. It's the memo of an engineer: "Pound pastrami, can kraut, six bagels—bring home for Emma." Deeply steeped in the lore of the Church, Miller's novel comments savagely on the cyclical nature both of secular and religious history.

Saint Leibowitz and the Wild Horse Woman. (Completed by Terry Bisson.) 2000. Bantam, paper. 448 pp. ISBN 0-553-38079-6.

The discursive sequel to *A Canticle for Leibowitz,* completed after Miller's death, is mostly for Miller's loyal fans. It's about a fallen member of the Leibowitz order, Brother Blacktooth St. George, who comes under the influence of Cardinal Brownpony, a Machiavellan sort trying to bring order and governance to decimated, far-flung, perhaps irredeemable humankind.

★ RUSSELL, MARY DORIA

YA *The Sparrow.* 1996. Random (Villard). 405 pp. ISBN 0-679-45150-1.

When the Arecibo radio telescope hears "singers" from the planet Rakhat in Alpha Centauri, Emilio Sandoz, a linguist and Jesuit priest who has pulled himself up from poverty, pushes hard to lead a mission there. The tale is told through direct accounts of the mission and from afterward, when we meet a broken Emilio, bedeviled with cruel, mad dreams, who may have lost his faith in God. What Emilio and his crew find on Rakhat are two races reminiscent of those H. G. Wells portrayed in *The Time Machine*: an inferior, gentle people, the Runa, and a "superior" race, the Jana'ata, who raise the Runa like cattle and eat them. As the crew begins to understand the planet's sociology, they realize that their scientific dispassion and religious intent are regarded as comical and primitive. All die but Sofia, a married scientist whom Emilio might be in love with were he not a priest, and Emilio himself, who is sold into slavery. As he gives himself up to the will of God, he is brutally raped and nearly goes mad. Winner of the James Tiptree, Jr. Award.   `Discussion`

YA *Children of God.* 1998. Random (Villard). 436 pp. ISBN 0-679-45635-X.

In the sequel to *The Sparrow,* Emilio quits the Jesuits and marries. But he is shanghaied onto the second Jesuit mission to Rakhat, where the Runa, spurred on by Sofia, are fomenting a revolution against the Jana'ata. Emilio and Sofia at last allow their love to flourish, perhaps the strongest aspect of the story; but it is in every way a worthy sequel, full of fascinating minor characters and a complex anthropology that recalls Ursula Le Guin's *Left Hand of Darkness.*   `Discussion`

THRILLERS

See also chapter 10, "Mysteries and Thrillers," p. 185.

BARNHARDT, WILTON. *Gospel.* 1993. St. Martin's, paper. 788 pp. ISBN 0-312-11924-0.

Theological student Lucy Dantan and a former Jesuit priest, Patrick O'Hanrahan, follow trails from Ireland to Africa to Italy in pursuit of a lost gospel, the finding and authentication of which they feel sure will shake up modern Christianity. Patrick has seen better days and is prone to alcoholism, but his knowledge of the ancient world is bottomless; Lucy is a timid neophyte but comes into her own. Barnhardt's sprawling, footnoted scholarship, peppering the narrative throughout, will be too much of a good thing for some, but the plot is otherwise a roller coaster, with even the CIA getting into the act. *Gospel* is ponderous at times, but even so, it's a good next novel for those who enjoyed *The Name of the Rose* (p. 266).

GOLD, ALAN. *The Lost Testament.* 1994. HarperCollins, paper. 581 pp. ISBN 0-06-100892-3.

Dead Sea Scroll scholars, clerics, and journalists descend on Israel when an Arab boy discovers the ancient testament of Jesus.

HEWLETT, MARTINEZ. *Divine Blood.* 1994. Ballantine, paper. 286 pp. ISBN 0-449-00292-6.

Josh Francis, an Arizona academic researching cancer treatments, is thrust into international intrigue over the discovery by French priests of the Shroud of Hautecombe, purportedly the wrapping cloth of Christ in the tomb. When Josh authenticates the age of the shroud and teases out a DNA sample, a televangelist, the National Institute of Health, and the Vatican vie for control, heralding events leading to a crisis for Josh.

MONTALBANO, WILLIAM. *Basilica.* 1998. Putnam. 296 pp. ISBN 0-399-14418-8.

Veteran journalist Montalbano, who covered the Vatican for many years, mixes the apparent murder of a priest at St. Peter's Basilica with church intrigue in a tale featuring an ambitious new pope and Brother Paul, a Miami ex-cop turned priest, brought in to ferret out the murderer.

PEREZ-REVERTE, ARTURO. *The Seville Communion.* 1995. Tr. by Sonia Soto. Harcourt. 375 pp. ISBN 0-15-100283-5.

Father Lorenzo Quart, a troubleshooter for the Vatican, is dispatched to Seville when Vatican computer security is breached with a message from "Vespers" about saving Our Lady of the Tears, an ancient church slated for demolition by developers. Father Quart is an expert in maneuvering Vatican politics as well as that of high-powered financiers, but the situation grows more complicated when he must deal with the alluring Macarena Gavira, wife of a dishonest young banker, and with two murders on church grounds.

VATICAN

DE ROSA, PETER. *Pope Patrick.* 1995. Doubleday. 349 pp. ISBN 0-385-48548-4.

Around 2010, as a new world order emerges comprising the decadent West, a third world sinking from starvation, and a fierce fundamentalist Muslim federation in the Mideast, a new pope is elected, the seemingly bland, none-too-bright Brian O'Flynn. But O'Flynn—or Pope Patrick—undergoes a catharsis and proceeds to enact sweeping reforms, such as the approval of contraception and marriage for priests. Unwittingly, Patrick may actually have played into the hands of the Muslims, who take the role of invading barbarians in De Rosa's broad satire. De Rosa's provocative ideas are diluted through his cartoonish style, but his setpieces—the dying Pope John Paul II inveighing against contraception in dozens of languages—are often brilliant.

★ FARRELL, MICHAEL J. *Papabile: The Man Who Would Be Pope.* 1998. Crossroad, paper. 191 pp. ISBN 0-8425-1730-X.

In the days when the communists wielded power in Eastern Europe they still had to reckon with the Church. Idealistic young Hugo Ovath, a fervent communist, is given the assignment to infiltrate the Church, which he does zealously, becoming a priest and then a cardinal. He must undertake important negotiations on behalf of the Church with a new communist government, but a change has come over him. He no longer believes in the Party, and when he is asked to leave the Church, he doesn't want to. He wonders, now that he has ambitions to become pope, whether he believes in God, and whether any belief is profounder than dazzling ambition.

MCINERNY, RALPH. *The Red Hat.* 1998. Ignatius. 600 pp. ISBN 0-89870-681-5.

In his mind's eye, Julian O'Keefe is still a priest, but he was tossed out of seminary long ago. He plots revenge and even becomes a murderer as he seeks a way to expose the sexual past of Thomas Lannan, an archbishop newly appointed a cardinal. Some sort of scandal is about to surface, but then the old pope dies and a Tanzanian takes his place, dividing the Church between the traditionalist third world and the decadent West. And there's more, still, in McInerny's wild plot, all of it punctuated with wry scholarly asides and doctrinal discussions that some, used to McInerny's mysteries, will find off-putting.

SZULC, TAD. *To Kill the Pope.* 2000. Scribner. 317 pp. ISBN 0-684-83781-1.

Szulc's thriller is based on the attempted assassination of Pope John Paul II in 1981, which Szulc knows a great deal about because of his research for a biography of John Paul and his years of covering the Vatican as a reporter (*Library Journal* 2000). In the novel, his John Paul is called Gregory XVII and is a Frenchman rather than a Pole, and Szulc makes other changes to protect his sources—high in the Vatican, he claims. But the assassin remains Turkish, and the novel seems so close to the truth in most respects that readers may find Szulc's employment of a sleuth, the stereotypical Father Ted Savage, Jesuit, Vietnam veteran, and former CIA operative, confusing. When Savage begins an affair with a nun, many readers will quit the book, convinced that Szulc, if he can trade upon such a tired device, has no idea what's he writing.

WEST, MORRIS

Though not all of his 25 novels concern Catholics, West, who is from Australia, has had a long career writing Catholic suspense novels. These begin with *The Devil's Advocate* in 1959 and are as recent as *Eminence* (1998). A lifelong Catholic, West spent 10 years in a monastery but never took his vows; for a time he covered the Vatican for the *London Daily Mail*.

The Devil's Advocate. 1959. (Many editions.)
A stoical English priest, Monsignor Blaise Meredith learns that he has only a few months to live and sinks into depression from the uselessness of the life he has lived. Then he is sent to play devil's advocate in the case for canonization of a rural Italian hero, and as he nears death finds a full life through his discoveries.

Eminence. 1998. Harcourt. 352 pp. ISBN 0-15100439-0.
As a young priest Cardinal Luca Rossini was brutally tortured by the Argentinian military with the tacit consent of the Church. In exchange for his silence, Rossini has lived a privileged exile in Rome under the protection of the pope and is a highly respected figure. When the pope dies and Rossini becomes a candidate to replace him, his anguished memories, including a brief romance with a brave Argentinian woman, haunt him anew.

TRILOGY

★ ***The Shoes of the Fisherman.*** 1963. (Many editions.)
A Ukrainian peasant-priest becomes pope in West's most famous novel, the first in a loose trilogy about the papacy that was made into a movie of the same title, starring Anthony Quinn, in 1968. We are introduced to the pope as Father Kiril Lakota, a cardinal negotiating with the Soviets and Americans to head off World War III; in one of the novel's most affecting scenes, he must negotiate with the man who tortured him during his long years in prison camps. Although the politics are dated, the charm and authenticity of Father Lakota remain fresh.

The Clowns of God. 1981. (Out of print.)
West's second papal novel features Pope Gregory XVII, who wants to make public his private revelation of the Second Coming. The College of Cardinals concludes this to be evidence of Gregory's attempt to bring messianic glory upon himself and forces him to abdicate. As Gregory plunges into ill health and a lonely spiritual search, the Soviet Union and the United States once again edge toward irreversible confrontation and apocalypse.

Lazarus. 1990. (Out of print.)
With the passing of the Soviet threat, West turns to Mideast turbulence and the rise of Islamic fundamentalism for the political background in the conclusion of his papal trilogy. But the principal story is the more contemplative one of Ludovico Gadda, who rises to the papacy through endless scheming and proves to be a hidebound, unlikable pope. Then he nearly dies from heart disease and is reborn in compassion.

ANDREW GREELEY

Chicagoan Father Greeley's talents sprawl so prolifically and with such abandon that he is a category all his own. Greeley has written almost 30 novels in 20 years, enough short stories to form a collection, a syndicated column, a number of articles, and two autobiographies. (Greeley wrote nonfiction from the late 1950s; he turned to fiction in the late 1970s.) The rapid-fire delivery—many of his novels began as dictations, written as he made his appointed international rounds—shows up in his style, which is fast paced and easy to read but also repetitive and shallow. But Greeley has never pretended to be James Joyce.

The controversy he inspired derived from the sexual content of his novels, the early ones, such as *The Cardinal Sins,* in particular. Published in 1981 and surely among Greeley's best efforts, it lingered on the bestseller list for a year and established his novelistic career.

The novel lays out many of the themes that Greeley returns to repeatedly. It begins in the resort community north of Chicago in the 1940s with the rivalries and loves of two novice Irish-American priests, Patrick Donahue and Kevin Brennan. Kevin is the narrator, though Greeley frequently jumps into the point of view of Donahue as well to portray his battles with lust, which he always loses in sometimes rather brutal sex.

Both priests rise rapidly in Chicago's Catholic hierarchy, but Kevin is the moral one, even bailing Patrick out of trouble from time to time as his sexual escapades threaten to overwhelm his career. Kevin himself is tempted by the flesh, specifically by an old girlfriend with whom he stays friends through the years and aids from time to time. That theme, the lost love that sometimes symbolizes lost faith, appears repeatedly in Greeley's world.

Like Greeley, Kevin is a political priest who believes in liberalizing the Church's stand against contraception and in marriage for priests and nuns. He is frequently at odds with the church hierarchy, which he believes is composed of doddering old men, both incompetent and out of touch. The Kevin Brennan character appears in one form or another in every Greeley novel.

In other novels, Greeley explores such issues as homosexuality among priests, marital fidelity, celibacy, pedophilia, the relationship of love and sex and the extent to which sexuality is an expression of God's love. In Greeley's peculiar ethos, the search for love and its sexual expression are a search for God. Mary is the ideal woman, and she is sexual; sexual fulfillment can itself be redeeming, a stop on the road to grace. The search for love often takes a wrong turn, however, and results in sin. And the sin needs to be demonstrated as clearly as the grace that sometimes follows it.

The Catholic—and indeed the popular—press almost uniformly condemned Greeley, however, as an author not far removed from Harold Robbins, pandering to the worst appetites of readers for sex and pyrotechnics. Some thought that Greeley should be defrocked. Greeley countered that he reached millions of disaffected, non-churchgoing laity, mostly women, with a message not merely of sin but of redemption (Greeley 1999).

As the 1990s began, serious discourse about Greeley had waned in Church circles. Although he still proclaimed his faith, he was seen as peripheral to the Church and its ongoing doctrinal dialogues. And by the mid-1990s, Greeley's popular impact was scarcely religious: He had become a reliably entertaining mystery writer.

Greeley's stand-alone novels precede discussion of his series. Many of the older novels remain available in paper or large print.

Death in April. 1980. McGraw-Hill. (Out of print.)
Many of the themes Greeley returns to repeatedly are already present in this early novel: the lost love that one at last finds (likened to lost faith); the mystical resort country of one's childhood; the corrupt world that inflicts its wounds and forces a retreat; and the opportunity for grace, or redemption. James O'Neill is a famous novelist at a point of disillusionment; Lynnie Slattery is his lost love, and she's still at the resort. James must come to her defense when a Chicago public prosecutor wages a vendetta against her.

The Cardinal Sins. 1981. Warner. (Out of print.)
See above discussion.

Patience of a Saint. 1987. Warner Books. (Out of print.)
Red Kane, a jaded newspaper columnist with a mistress, has a moment of divine revelation and falls in love again with his deeply estranged wife. At the same time, his attempt to solve a brutal murder puts his own life in peril.

All About Women. 1989. Tor. (Out of print.)
Greeley collects 23 short stories most of which were published in the early 1980s and all of which are titled after the women of the stories. Each woman seeks or is offered grace; some accept it.

The Cardinal Virtues. 1990. Warner Books. (Out of print.)
Not a sequel to *The Cardinal Sins, The Cardinal Virtues* portrays the priesthood as it could be, centering on Father Laurence O'Toole, a weary, bored suburban priest whose life in Christ is rejuvenated when a new priest is assigned to him. The young man is full of idealism, joy, and also naiveté. O'Toole wonders if the church hierarchy will be his undoing.

The Search for Maggie Ward. 1991. Warner Books. (Out of print.)
Though masking as realism, *The Search for Maggie Ward* is almost purely a sexual fantasy. It's set in a post-war, highly nostalgic Chicago and Arizona and features Navy hero Jerry Keenan. He falls in love with Maggie Ward, who may be imaginary but certainly seemed real until she disappeared during the couple's idyll in a ghost town. Note: Maggie also makes an appearance in *The Cardinal Virtues*.

An Occasion of Sin. 1991. Putnam. (Out of print.)
Returning to the themes of *Virgin and Martyr* (discussed later), Greeley casts a priest, Laurence McAuliffe, in the role of devil's advocate to investigate the possible canonization of a cardinal slain in Nicaragua. No one questions the cardinal's good works, but the presence of Marbeth Quinlan, his longtime companion and possibly his lover, complicates matters.

Wages of Sin. 1992. Putnam. (Out of print.)
Greeley recycles the themes of previous novels in this tale of rich man Lorcan Flynn, who, through the help of a psychiatrist, revisits his idyllic childhood and finds a long-lost love.

Fall from Grace. 1993. Putnam. (Out of print.)
The closet homosexuality of her husband, a senatorial candidate, threatens to wreck the marriage of Kathleen Donahue; meanwhile, her brother, a bishop, must deal with a young parishioner who wants to confront publicly an eminent priest's pedophilia.

Star Bright! 1997. Forge. 127 pp. ISBN 0-312-86387-X.
See discussion in chapter 11, "The Christian Life," in the "Christmas" section.

Summer at the Lake. 1997. Forge. 412 pp. ISBN 0-312-86082-X.
Many of the elements of *Cardinal Sins* reappear in this story of childhood left behind at a summertime resort, the reunion of friends, and an unhappy priest on the verge of forsaking his vows for love of a woman.

PASSOVER TRILOGY

Thy Brother's Wife. 1982. Warner Books. (Out of print.)
Two Irish Catholic brothers, one a priest and one with aspirations to the presidency, are in love with the same woman.

Ascent Into Hell. 1983. Warner Books. (Out of print.)
A novice priest takes his vows, though he is tempted by one extraordinary woman. Then, disillusioned with parish workings, he leaves the priesthood to marry her.

Lord of the Dance. 1984. Warner Books. (Out of print.)
The Farrell clan, a successful Chicago Irish family whose sons include a priest, a professor, and a lost pilot, has a secret to hide.

FATHER BLACKIE RYAN

Arguably, Greeley's best work can be found in the Blackie Ryan series; at the least, mystery fans think so. That may be because Blackie is clearly a descendant of G. K. Chesterton's Father Brown, the nondescript priest who nonetheless knows more about crime than the criminals.

The Blackie Ryan series has seen several publishers, and some entries have appeared as original paperbacks; thus, they present a somewhat confusing publishing profile. In addition, some are also part of Greeley's Time Between the Stars series.

Virgin and Martyr. 1985. Warner. 438 pp. ISBN 0-446-51287-7.
Blackie is introduced and plays a pivotal role in unraveling the story of what happened to Cathy Collins, a nun who is raped and killed in the prototypical Latin American country of Costaguana. In fact, she is the focus rather than Blackie, and the story is actually a dramatization of Greeley's opposition to Liberation Theology.

Happy Are the Meek. 1985. Warner, paper. 264 pp. ISBN 0-446-32706-9.
Blackie comes fully into his own in the sequel to *Virgin and Martyr,* when he unravels a murder linked with a Satanic cult. *Happy Are the Meek* is also the first to take its title from the Beatitudes. Such titles tip off a more or less traditional mystery featuring Blackie, but eventually Greeley ran out of Beatitudes and used Blackie's new rank of bishop in his titles.

Happy Are Those Who Thirst for Justice. 1987. Mysterious. 302 pp. ISBN 0-892-96180-5.
Blackie moves among Chicago's decadent rich, coming to the aid of sexy young Fionna Downs, accused of killing her grandmother.

Rite of Spring. 1987. Warner. 436 pp. ISBN 0-446-51295-8.
Once more Blackie takes a minor role in advising his cousin, Brendan Ryan, a lawyer undergoing a midlife crisis who is accused of murder. Brendan is the major character, in love with a woman who disappears and yet holds the key to his innocence, not to mention his happiness.

Happy Are the Clean of Heart. 1988. Warner, paper. 268 pp. ISBN 0-446-32708-5.
Lisa Malone, famous singer and actress and an old friend of Blackie's, is struck down, and Blackie searches for her assailant.

Love Song. 1989. Warner Books.
A minor character, Blackie counsels a fierce female prosecutor, the Irish beauty Diana Lyons, who falls in love with her chief opponent.

St. Valentine's Night. 1989. Warner. 435 pp. ISBN 0-446-51475-6.
Neil Connor, a jaded TV reporter, returns to his old neighborhood and meets his old girlfriend but in the process finds himself battling Chicago's violent drug culture. Blackie is a minor character.

Happy Are the Merciful. 1992. Jove. 240 pp. ISBN 0-515-10726-3.
Greeley is stage center again in *Happy Are the Merciful.* A prosecutor whose arguments send a woman to prison for killing her adoptive parents becomes convinced of her innocence and turns to Blackie for what results in a dangerous corroboration.

Happy Are the Peacemakers. 1993. Jove, paper. 300 pp. ISBN 0-515-11075-2.
A seductive widow may have killed her third husband. Blackie resists her charms.

Happy Are the Poor in Spirit. 1994. Jove, paper. 295 pp. ISBN 0-515-11502-9.
Blackie becomes an exorcist, winnowing out the secret of a murderous "ghost."

Happy Are Those Who Mourn. 1995. Jove, paper. 288 pp. ISBN 0-515-11761-7.
A dead priest seems to haunt a suburban Chicago parish, but Blackie looks for a rational explanation.

Happy Are the Oppressed. 1996. Jove, paper. 307 pp. ISBN 0-515-11921-0.
Blackie must solve a 100-year-old murder in a prominent Chicago family to prevent the murder of a beautiful woman who has married into the present-day family.

White Smoke: A Novel About the Next Papal Conclave. 1996. Forge. 384 pp. ISBN 0-312-85814-0.
While retaining Blackie in his sleuthing role, Greeley dramatizes one of his grievances against the Church: the manner of papal elections. The old pope dies, and Blackie accompanies Chicago's Cardinal Cronin to the Vatican, where Blackie's counsel repairs a marriage. But there are rumors of a banking scandal that will rock the Church, and someone with a gun seems to be awaiting the first appearance of the new pope; Blackie, therefore, is only a minor character.

The Bishop at Sea. 1997. Berkeley, paper. 304 pp. ISBN 0-425-16080-7.
Sans Beatitudes, Blackie returns as the major character, solving murders aboard an aircraft carrier.

The Bishop and the Three Kings. 1998. Berkley, paper. 298 pp. ISBN 0-425-16617-1.
Blackie is in Germany, tracking down a stolen Catholic relic and doing his best to stay alive.

The Bishop and the Missing L Train. 2000. Forge. 288 pp. ISBN 0-312-86875-8.
Blackie returns to Chicago, where his boss the archbishop calls upon him to find a missing L car and the universally despised bishop who has disappeared with it.

NUALA ANNE MCGRAIL MYSTERIES
There are priests in the background of this romantic mystery series, but in the main it's a secular series in a Catholic milieu, told from the point of view of a young Chicagoan, Dermot Coyne.

Irish Gold. 1994. Forge. 334 pp. ISBN 0-312-85813-2.
Tracing his ancestry, which Dermot suspects is linked to the great Irish hero Michael Collins, Dermot falls hopelessly in love with Nuala McGrail, a woman beautiful as a Celtic goddess who helps him in his quest through her inexplicable psychic powers.

Irish Lace. 1996. Forge. 303 pp. ISBN 0-312-86234-2.
Dermot and Nuala have moved to Chicago, where Nuala's psychic powers solve a great mystery of the Civil War.

Irish Whiskey. 1998. Forge. 317 pp. ISBN 0-312-85596-6.
Greeley draws out Dermot's courtship still longer, while Nuala solves a mystery from Prohibition-era Chicago.

Irish Mist. 1999. Forge. 319 pp. ISBN 0-312-86569-4.
Newlyweds Dermot and Nuala return to Ireland to solve the mystery of who killed Michael Collins's successor, Kevin O'Higgins.

Irish Eyes. 2000. Forge. 320 pp. ISBN 0-312-86570-8.
The Coynes have an infant daughter who has apparently inherited some of her mother's ESP talents because it is she who first senses the shipwreck—with its attendant mystery—beneath Lake Michigan's cold waters.

O'MALLEY FAMILY

A Midwinter's Tale. 1998. Forge. 383 pp. ISBN 0-312-86571-6.
Greeley tries his hand at nostalgia, conjuring enlisted man Charles O'Malley of the Chicago O'Malleys, who looks for love in post-war Germany.

Younger Than Springtime. 1999. Forge. 348 pp. ISBN 0-312-86572-4.
Charles "Chucky" O'Malley leaves the military to begin study at Notre Dame, where he does battle with a dour priest/hall monitor and chases women.

SCIENCE FICTION

Greeley gives a Catholic spin to the literary angel fad of the late twentieth century in several of these novels, creating contemporary, female, voluptuous angels who chastely intervene in the lives of troubled souls. He ventures into cyberspace with *God Game*, a less-than-convincing tale, and reads a bit like Orson Scott Card in *The Final Planet,* about a ship of Christian pilgrims—a Catholic order—bound for the mysterious planet Zylong.

Angels of September. 1985. Warner Books. (Out of print.)

God Game. 1986. Warner Books. (Out of print.)

The Final Planet. 1987. Warner Books. (Out of print.)

Angel Fire. 1988. Warner Books. (Out of print.)

Angel Light. 1995. Forge. 352 pp. ISBN 0-312-86080-3.

Contract with an Angel. 1998. Forge. 304 pp. ISBN 0-312-86081-1.
See also Greeley's Christmas novel, *Star Bright!,* p. 213.

Chapter 13

Amish, Mennonite, and Quaker Fiction

Most distinctly Amish fiction comes from Herald Press[*] in Scottdale, Pennsylvania (www.mph .org/hp.htm). Herald Press publishes both Carrie Bender and Mary Borntrager (see chapter 15, "Young Adults," for coverage), writers in the Old Order Amish tradition who have a large appeal outside their denominational audience. Ironically, the best-known Amish fiction currently on the market is from Bethany House—Beverly Lewis's novels described later in this chapter. Lewis takes great care to describe the Amish lifestyle and beliefs correctly, but hers is not an insider's view.

One of the things Amish and Mennonite fiction shows is that the romantic notions the broad public has about the Amish lifestyle are mostly poppycock. The Amish life doesn't seem much simpler than any other, for instance. Still, the deeply held attachment to animals and the land, the pacifism, the strong family values, are all there, and it's easy to admire these people.

AMISH AND MENNONITE

◄📧 BENDER, CARRIE

🆈🅰 DORA'S DIBARY
A spinoff from Bender's popular Miriam's Journal series (discussed next), featuring the adopted daughter of Miriam's family, Dora Kauffman. After kicking up her heels a bit in the sheer joy of youth, Dora leaves Pennsylvania to teach in a Minnesota Amish community, then works as a hired girl and begins to date.

Birch Hollow Schoolmarm. 1999. Herald, paper. 192 pp. ISBN 0-8361-9095-5.

Lilac Blossom Time. 2001. Herald, paper. 160 pp. ISBN 0-8361-9137-4.

---

[*]Do not confuse with Herald Press of Charlotte, North Carolina, or Herald House, the publishing arm of the Reorganized Mormon Church headquartered in Independence, Missouri, neither of which is active with fiction.

YA ★ *MIRIAM'S JOURNAL*
A soulful series of short novels, all cast as a journal, about Miriam, an Old Order farmer's wife and mother whose concerns are her ailing husband, Nate, her children, those who move in and out of the community, and even those who consider leaving it permanently. The considerable charm of Bender's series lies in its intimate portrait of Amish life, completely free of the romantic gloss the mainstream culture attempts to assign it. Bender, herself an Old Order Amishwoman, tell us that life is sweet among the Amish but no less perilous than any other life. The series is also available in one volume.

> *A Fruitful Vine.* 1993. Herald, paper. 191 pp. ISBN 0-8361-3613-6.
>
> *A Winding Path.* 1994. Herald, paper. 157 pp. ISBN 0-8361-3656-X.
>
> *A Joyous Heart.* 1994. Herald, paper. 160 pp. ISBN 0-8361-3668-3.
>
> *A Treasured Friendship.* 1996. Herald, paper. 157 pp. ISBN 0-8361-9033-5.
>
> *A Golden Sunbeam.* 1996. Herald, paper. 192 pp. ISBN 0-8361-9055-6.

YA ★ **BLOCK, KEVIN JAMES.** *Without Shedding Blood.* **1994. Wildflower Communications, paper. 183 pp. ISBN 1-895308-17-8.**
Samuel Beamer, a young Mennonite coming of age on the Canadian side of Niagara Falls, wants to fight for the British during the War of 1812. Because war is wrong, all sides are wrong, church leaders tell him, but Samuel joins the militia anyhow. After the loss of his home, the death of his daughter, and irrevocable damage to his marriage, young Samuel comes to understand the wisdom of his church.

EX **BORNTRAGER, MARY CHRISTNER**

ELLIE'S PEOPLE
See chapter 15, "Young Adults."

YA **KAUFFMAN, CHRISTMAS CAROL**

Escape from Kyburg Castle. 1954. (Out of print.)
Kauffman, a Mennonite, takes the reader back to Switzerland in 1525, when the state, with its official Catholicism, persecuted Anabaptists because of their refusal to baptize infants. The internment of Anabaptists in Kyburg Castle is seen through the eyes of young Regina Strahm, who does her best to resist falling in love with Peter Reimann, seemingly one of the persecutors.

Hidden Rainbow. 1957. (Out of print.)
John and Anna Olesh, Yugoslavian Catholics in the early twentieth century, are ostracized and then persecuted when they accept the teachings of a Mennonite missionary.

EX **LEWIS, BEVERLY**

YA *HERITAGE OF LANCASTER COUNTY*

> ★ *The Shunning.* 1997. Bethany, paper. 283 pp. ISBN 1-55661-866-2.
> *The Shunning* introduces young Katie Lapp, who is uncomfortable with her strict Amish upbringing, longing to wear fancy "English" dresses and play the guitar. She pines for her true love, Daniel Fisher, supposedly drowned. But Katie is resigned to marry a widower

and become a good Amish wife until she discovers a baby dress in her parents' attic, and further, that she was adopted. Now, though she agonizes over the decision, she cannot fully embrace Amish ways and is shunned as she heads forth into the English world in search of her birth mother.

The Confession. 1997. Bethany, paper. 286 pp. ISBN 1-55661-867-0.
The sequel to *The Shunning* follows Katie, now with the last name of Mayfield, as she experiences the English world of her birth mother, whom she locates after much travail. Her mother is dying, but it looks as though there will be an inheritance. Another plot line follows Daniel Fisher, the sweetheart of Katie's childhood, who has returned to the Amish country looking for her.

The Reckoning. 1998. Bethany, paper. 283 pp. ISBN 1-55661-868-9.
With her mother's death, Katie finds herself moderately wealthy, the owner of Mayfield Manor in this final installment of the Heritage of Lancaster County series. A new suitor presents himself; meanwhile, Daniel searches on for his lost love. Katie, pining for her Amish upbringing, finds some spiritual solace in the more liberal *ordnung* of the Mennonites, which allows her to play her guitar in services.

The Postcard. 1999. Bethany, paper. 314 pp. ISBN 0-76422-211-2.
New Order Amishwoman Rachel Yoder, from Lancaster, Pennsylvania, loses her husband and son in a buggy accident. She takes a job at a bed-and-breakfast where she meets a high-powered journalist, Philip Bradley, in Lancaster to do a story on the Amish. Their fate is linked when they pursue the mystery behind an old postcard.

The Crossroad. 1999. Bethany, paper. 312 pp. ISBN 0-76422-239-2.
Philip finds he can't get Rachel out of his mind and returns to Lancaster in the sequel to *The Postcard.* Both Rachel and he wonder if the gulf between them represented by Rachel's religion is too wide to cross.

YA **The Redemption of Sarah Cain.** 2000. Bethany. 320 pp. ISBN 0-310-21892-6.
Lewis again uses family tragedy to thrust an English character into the Amish world, in this case realtor Sarah Cain, a cold woman taking comfort in her material successes. Sarah's Amish sister, a widow struggling to maintain her farm in Lancaster County, dies and inexplicably names Sarah as guardian of her five surviving children. The eldest, 17-year-old Lydia, is the true head of the family and runs afoul of her worldly aunt over courtship issues, but her younger sister, who has emotional problems, awakens maternal instincts in Sarah and kindles her dormant faith. Sarah is never believable, nor is her long-suffering boyfriend and his miraculous conversion, but as usual Lewis has done her research, so her portrait of Amish life is convincing and even irresistible.

LEWIS, BEVERLY, AND DAVID LEWIS. *Sanctuary.* 2001. Bethany, paper. 336 pp. ISBN 0-7642-2510-3.

Melissa James flees to Pennsylvania and a previous identity, leaving her husband, Ryan, in bafflement. As he searches for her, Melissa relates her troubled history to her sympathetic Amish landlord.

PLETT, DELBERT F. *Sarah's Prairie.* 1995. Windflower, paper. 349 pp. ISBN 1-895308-20-8.

A generational saga of Mennonites in Manitoba, spanning almost 150 years from their emigration from Russia to present-day difficulties the sect faces in keeping their young people on the farm.

ROPER, GAYLE

✺ *AMISH SERIES*

The Key. 1998. Multnomah, paper. 256 pp. ISBN 1-57673-223-1.
Weary of the fast lane, Kristie Matthews rents some rooms on the farm of an Amish family, the Zooks, near Lancaster, Pennsylvania. Some of the Zooks observe the old order, and some have left the ways of the "Plain People" behind.

As Kristie moves in, a German shepherd bites her and a family friend of the Zooks, Jon Griffin, rushes her to the emergency room. It's love at first bite, but their future is complicated by a key an old man gives Kristie at the hospital. Though he's quite mysterious about it, Kristie agrees to keep the key for him, and its mystery puts her at peril.

The Document. 1998. Multnomah, paper. 274 pp. ISBN 1-57673-295-9.
In the sequel, romance writer Cara Bentley, an adoptee searching for her biological parents, takes over Kristie's rooms and employs Kristie's ex-boyfriend, not Jon but the attorney Todd Reasoner, to help her. Cara gets along better with Todd than Kristie did, and they overcome the obstacles to the truth about Cara. Romance loyalists will enjoy the heroine's asides defending her craft: "A romance doesn't have to be shallow, you know."

The Decision. 1999. Multnomah, paper. 360 pp. ISBN 1-57673-406-4.
The final installment of Roper's Amish series begins dramatically as Rose Martin, a nurse specializing in care for the critically injured, watches helplessly as a car bomb kills one of her patients. As she struggles both with her grief and the mystery, she finds solace in the humility and sensitivity of a character introduced in *The Key,* Jake Zook, who is bound to a wheelchair. Zook bears the cross of his handicap nobly but struggles with the spiritual meaning of his Amish heritage and doesn't feel he's worthy of Rose. She disagrees.

✺ ★ **WOJTASIK, TED.** *No Strange Fire.* **1996. Herald, paper. 400 pp. ISBN 0-8361-9041-6.**
See discussion in chapter 15, "Young Adults."

✺ ★ **YODER, JAMES D.** *Black Spider over Tiegenhof.* **1995. Herald Press, paper. 232 pp. ISBN 0-8361-9012-2.**
See discussion in chapter 15, "Young Adults."

QUAKER

The best-known Quaker publisher is Friends United Press, 101 Quaker Hill Drive, Richmond, IN 47374-1980.

GULLEY, PHILIP
See chapter 11, "The Christian Life," the "Humor" section.

MCCRACKEN, SUSAN

FRIENDS TRILOGY
Fans of Janette Oke will enjoy these prairie romances portraying Friends settlements in nineteenth century Iowa.

For the Love of a Friend. 1994. Friends United Press, paper. 168 pp. ISBN 0-944350-29-1.

Set in the 1840s, *For the Love of a Friend* features 16-year-old Rebecca Wilson of relatively civilized Indiana, who is not happy when her family takes up farming in eastern Iowa.

For the Gift of a Friend. 1995. Friends United Press, paper. 193 pp. ISBN 0-944350-35-6.

By 1853 Rebecca is a grown woman with a full complement of life's woes to deal with. She marries her childhood sweetheart but quickly finds herself a widow.

For the Call of a Friend. 1997. Friends United Press, paper. 313 pp. ISBN 0-944350-41-0.

Set in 1879, the concluding entry of McCracken's trilogy is the story of Rebecca's daughter, Julia, also 16 and headed for boarding school. Notably, *For the Call of a Friend* offers a portrait of historical personage Elizabeth Comstock, the Quaker activist who, as secretary of the Kansas Freedman's Relief Association, fought valiantly for the welfare of former slaves settling in Kansas.

NEWMAN, DAISY

KENDALL SERIES

Newman told pleasant, nostalgic stories set in Kendall, Rhode Island, an idyllic place where men and women fall in love and are hopelessly devoted to each other. The Friends United Press editions are reprints of mainstream editions published from the 1950s through the 1970s.

The novels are not quite sequential; several characters come to prominence and then recede. The first tale is of Diligence "Dilly" Bliss, a 52-year-old widow whose Friends' meetings and involvement in the community give her a contented life. But on holiday in New York City, visiting her cousin, she meets Durand Smith, a gentle man with whom she has a delightful time, though she's not quite willing to call it love. She goes home trying to convince herself she's too old for such nonsense. Then she learns Durand has had an accident, and she realizes her feelings are too strong to resist.

The Autumn's Brightness. 1991. Friends United Press, paper. 251 pp. ISBN 0-944350-18-6.

Indian Summer of the Heart. 1997. Friends United Press, paper. 376 pp. ISBN 0-944350-15-1.

I Take Thee, Serenity. 1994. Friends United Press, paper. 314 pp. ISBN 0-944350-09-7.

Diligence in Love. 1992. Friends United Press, paper. 253 pp. ISBN 0-944350-22-4.

 ★ **WEST, JESSAMYN.** *Friendly Persuasion.* **1991. Harcourt, paper. 214 pp. ISBN 0-15- 633606-5.**

Originally published in 1940, these warm, funny short stories of Jess and Eliza Birdwell have something in common with Jan Karon's work, though their milieu is much different: the Civil War. Eliza is a Quaker minister and assertive woman, whereas Jess is a bit of a bumbler and minor sinner, though he is clever as well, and a superb nurseryman. "Music on the Muscatatuck" is typical: Jess, who yearns for the kind of music he once heard at a Methodist service, is talked into buying an organ by a slick salesman. Eliza is mortified but allows it to be kept in the attic. The stories also have their somber side, as both man and wife help to smuggle slaves to freedom. In 1956, the stories were made into a popular, now classic film, directed by William Wyler, starring Gary Cooper as Jess, Dorothy McGuire as Eliza, and a youthful Anthony Perkins as Josh, their son. **Discussion**

WISEHART, RANDALL

See discussion in chapter 15, "Young Adults."

Chapter 14

Mormon Fiction

Mormons and evangelicals are far apart on most things, but contemporary Mormon fiction parallels its evangelical counterpart in that it began to grow more popular in the 1980s. One writer, Orson Scott Card, enjoys international popularity—primarily with his science fiction, though he also has written several overtly Mormon titles (discussed in this chapter). Card's influence is so wide that many of his readers don't realize he's Mormon.

After Card, Mormon fiction, though of high quality, is a phenomenon restricted to the influence of the Church. There are Mormon bookstores in Utah, and, of course, the Mormon Church is large and has international influence. But outside of Utah, Mormon fiction is seldom reviewed in library or mainstream media and, consequently, seldom found in libraries. The librarian wishing to stock it will need to make a special effort.

A number of publishers issue Mormon titles, but three are especially active:

SIGNATURE BOOKS
564 W. 400 N.
Salt Lake City, UT 84116-3411
801-531-1483
http://www.signaturebooks.com

Signature is the most literary of Mormon publishers, and its titles are often highly critical of the Church.

COVENANT COMMUNICATIONS
920 E. State Rd.
American Fork, UT 84003
801-756-9966
www.covenant-lds.com

Covenant Communications, the Bethany House of Mormon publishers, publishes science fiction, mysteries, and romances comparable in quality to the best evangelical efforts, but with a clear Mormon content.

DESERET BOOK COMPANY
40 E. South Temple
Salt Lake City, UT 84111
801-517-3328
http://www.deseretbook.com

Deseret fiction is always of high literary quality. It presents the orthodox view of Mormonism. Deseret operates bookstores throughout Utah and in some other states as well, such as Arizona, California, and Colorado.

Those readers drawn to the fascinating study of early Mormon literature might wish to consult the Mormon classic, *A Believing People: Literature of the Latter-day Saints,* edited by Richard H. Cracroft and Neal E. Lambert (Brigham Young University Press, 1974).

HISTORICALS

CARD, ORSON SCOTT. *Saints.* 1988. Tor, paper. 713 pp. ISBN 0-812535219.

Card tackles Mormonism's polygamous history with his portrait of Dinah Kirkham, an English convert who makes her way to Nauvoo, where Joseph Smith approaches her to be his second wife. Then Smith is killed, and Dinah follows the Saints to Utah. Polygamy, and Joseph Smith, are presented warts and all, and Dinah is not a mere contrivance: She's a conflicted, deeply spiritual woman involved in a strange but altogether real new world.

LUND, GERALD N.

WORK AND THE GLORY

The Work and the Glory is a massive historical series fictionalizing the history of the Mormom Church from its beginnings in upstate New York.

Pillar of Light. 1990. Bookcraft Publications. 437 pp. ISBN 0-88494-770-X.

Like a Fire Is Burning. 1991. Bookcraft Publications. 515 pp. ISBN 0-88494-801-3.

Truth Will Prevail. 1991. Bookcraft Publications. 541 pp. ISBN 0-88494-853-6.

Thy Gold to Refine. 1993. Bookcraft Publications. 605 pp. ISBN 0-88494-893-5.

A Season of Joy. 1994. Bookcraft Publications. 575 pp. ISBN 0-88494-960-5.

Praise to the Man. 1994. Bookcraft Publications. 732 pp. ISBN 0-88494-999-0.

No Unhallowed Hand. 1996. Bookcraft Publications. 634 pp. ISBN 1-57008-277-4.

So Great a Cause. 1997. Bookcraft Publications. 511 pp. ISBN 1-57008-358-4.

NOBLE, DIANE. *The Veil.* 1998. WaterBrook, paper. 400 pp. ISBN 1-57856-014-4.

See discussion, p. 71.

★ SORENSEN, MICHELE. *Broken Lance.* 1997. Deseret, paper. 285 pp. ISBN 1-57345-270-X. *[Historical]*

New converts Angus and Callie McCraken cross the Atlantic and head for Utah, but it's 1857 and the trek is perilous. Angus is killed in an attack by Cheyennes, leaving Callie to fend for herself and her three children. Unlikely aid comes from a wounded Cheyenne called Three Elk. At first, accepting his kindness seems like making a bargain with the Devil, but in the end Callie must admit to herself that her Christian beliefs will not allow such hatred.

SORENSEN, VIRGINIA. *The Evening and the Morning.* **1999. Signature, paper. 356 pp. ISBN 1-56085-124-4.**

> Californian Kate Alexander, a social worker in her 50s, who for her day seems a liberated woman, returns to her small hometown in Utah to fill out the papers for a pension. Estranged from her faith though not an apostate, her visit with family, friends, and an old love kindles bittersweet memories in this moving evocation of Mormon life through three generations, from the days before the Manifesto, when polygamy was legal, through the first decades of the twentieth century.

 WELLS, MARIAN. *The Starlight Trilogy: The Wishing Star, Star Light, Star Bright, Morning Star.* **2001. Inspirational Press, paper. 736 pp. ISBN 0-88486-238-0.**

> This evangelical trilogy has been reissued periodically; it was first published in the mid-1980s. Through the eyes of a young convert, Jenny Cartwright, it tells the story of Mormonism and of Joseph Smith from the early days in upstate New York through Smith's assassination in an Illinois jail. While not virulently anti-Mormon, Wells does see the faith as a cult with dark and objectionable doctrines. Readers wanting a friendly account of Mormonism's early days might try Orson Scott Card's much better-written *Saints* (discussed previously); those wanting objectivity should probably steer clear of fiction altogether.

WHIPPLE, MAURINE. *Giant Joshua.* **1982. (Originally published in 1941.) Western Epics. 637 pp. ISBN 0-914740-17-2.**

> Whipple's novel tells of the founding of St. George in southern Utah from the point of view of an appealing heroine, Clorinda McIntyre. Polygamy is treated with sensitivity. Because of that, and because the setting is essentially the same, *Giant Joshua* is an interesting alternative to *Riders of the Purple Sage,* Zane Grey's classic western that looks at Mormonism rather critically.

 14

WOOLLEY, DAVID G. *Pillar of Fire.* **2000. Covenant Communications. 544 pp. ISBN 1-57734-722-6.**

> This first in a projected seven volumes retelling the *Book of Mormon* occurs in 601 B.C. and centers around the efforts of a brusque, unsavory character from 1 Nephi, Laban. After the war with Babylon, Laban has risen to Captain of the Guard, with ambitions to become King of Israel. Much of his claim to authority derives from his possession of certain brass plates containing Hebrew sacred texts and of a sacred sword symbolizing the Jewish lineage. Lehi and Uriah, leaders of a sect representing Israel's true lineage and future, rise in opposition. Woolley interweaves biblical, Mormon, and fictional characters in this sprawling tale, but it's unlikely to appeal to any but Mormon readers.

YORGASON, BLAINE M. *Massacre at Salt Creek.* **1979. Doubleday. 183 pp. ISBN 0-385-15200-0.**

> Yorgason takes what few facts are known of the Salt Creek Canyon Massacre of 1858, in which renegade Utes killed a small party of Mormon pilgrims bound for Sanpete Valley, and imagines the dramatic flight of the party's two survivors, a young woman and her infant. The anonymous woman, an embittered second wife, draws near to God in her desperate flight from the crazed Ute and delivers her child to safety.

YOUNG, MARGARET BLAIR, AND DARIUS ALDEN GRAY

STANDING ON THE PROMISES TRILOGY

★ *One More River to Cross.* 2000. Deseret. 350 pp. ISBN 157345-629-2.
With imaginative but carefully researched narratives, the first entry in Young and Gray's groundbreaking trilogy tells the story of sanctuary that a number of freed slaves found in Joseph Smith's new church. Elijah Abel, for instance, proclaims his new faith with enthusiasm and rises in the hierarchy of the church, even as some of his colleagues continue to hold slaves. Both a pioneer narrative and a striking piece of African American history, *One More River to Cross* mines overlooked Americana and puts it in contemporary, universal perspective.

CONTEMPORARY

YA **BENNION, JOHN.** *Falling Toward Heaven.* 2000. Signature, paper. 316 pp. ISBN 1-56085-140-6.
Elder Howard Rockwood, barely 20, is staggering through the last celibate days of his two-year missionary stint in Texas when he falls head over heels in love with Allison Warren. She's the "man-eating pagan" his grandfather warned him about. Fighting it as much as Howard, she, too, falls in love, and preys upon him to accompany her to Alaska, where she's been offered a lucrative job as a computer programmer. Howard gives up the girl back home in Utah, his church, and a solid if predictable future to follow her, and the two embark on a roller-coaster life together that in the end brings them both into a deep consciousness of God, but without any answers for the tragedies He inflicts.

YA **CARD, ORSON SCOTT.** *Lost Boys.* 1992. HarperCollins, paper. 544p. ISBN 0-06-109131-6.
Step Fletcher and wife DeAnne, devout Mormons, move their family to North Carolina when Step's fortunes as a computer programmer go south. They like their new church except that a do-gooder there gives unwanted advice. Step's job is a minefield, DeAnne's pregnant again, and the house is infested with insects. But the real crisis is with their eight-year-old son, Stevie, an introverted boy who becomes addicted to computer games he plays with his imaginary playmates. Eerily, those playmates have the same names as several missing boys that, the suspicion is, were victims of a serial killer. Card's first mainstream novel touchingly portrays a fine family in crisis, though Card's Gentile characterizations are thin and his tone is more preachy than in his science fiction.

YA **FILLERUP, MICHAEL.** *Beyond the River.* 1995. Signature, paper. 256 pp. ISBN 1-56085-068-X.
Facing a tough midlife crisis, Jon Reeves returns home to small-town Utah, where he tries to come to terms with a ghost from his youth. In high school, he had an intense love affair with a mixed-up girl who, when Jon went off to college, quickly married, bore a child, and killed herself. Though uneven, Fillerup's story is sincere and moving, much enriched by the amusing account of Jon's year of obligatory missionary work in Mexico.

★ **PETERSON, LEVI S.** *The Backslider.* 1990. Signature, paper. 368 pp. ISBN 1-56085-015-9.

> The readers of John L. Moore will respond to this earthy tale of a young Mormon cowboy, Frank Windham, who prays for guidance to the "Cowboy Jesus" but gives in to his sexual desires, repenting, backsliding, and ultimately seeking grace of the Mormon sort with sincerity. Peterson has a knack with minor characters, whether Mormon or Protestant, and a feel for rural, often scatological humor. Sometimes, Mark Twain comes to mind. The novel pushed Peterson into the forefront of Mormon literary figures and earned him something of a national following.

SILLITOE, LINDA. *Sideways to the Sun.* Signature. 255 pp. ISBN 0-94121-456-7.

> A woman pregnant with her fifth child wakes up to find that her husband is gone. She does the best she can to support her family and eventually discovers her husband has been having an affair with a young Navajo woman. What's more, the girl is pregnant.

SMITH, MARION. *Riptide.* 1999. Signature, paper. 200 pp. ISBN 1-56085-131-7.

> The desire for revenge wars with the necessity for forgiveness in the mind of Laurel Greer, a 62-year-old grandmother confronted with child abuse in her own family. As Laurel drives through Utah, everything tumbles at once through her mind in a narrative that is nearly stream-of-consciousness. Laurel is sorrowful, angry, and violated, not the victim but still victimized.

VAN WAGONER, ROBERT HODGSON. *Dancing Naked.* 1999. Signature. 372 pp. ISBN 1-56085-130-9.

> In this bold, brooding story, Terry Walker seems to have life on the run. He has a secure job teaching math and a quiet suburban life outside of Salt Lake City. Then his son, Blake, kills himself, unable to face the shame of his homosexuality and the reprobation of his father, a homophobe. Terry tries to come to terms with his guilt-filled, empty life.

MYSTERIES

ARNOLD, MARILYN

> *Desert Song.* 1998. Covenant Communications. 180 pp. ISBN 1-57734-254-2.
> *Desert Song* is a likable, seemingly autobiographical first novel about English professor Delia McGrath, a moderately feminist, even somewhat apostatized, young woman at a crucial point in her life. She's undergoing her first review for tenure; a friend in a troubled marriage is shot by her husband; another friend must undergo chemotherapy; and her father dies. Delia's woes make her ponder her childhood faith, which she views as preposterous but at the same time grand and necessary. Her discovery of a set of tablets in a desert canyon also gives rise to religious speculations. The tablets are mysteriously stolen, and in seeking their recovery Delia meets, at last, someone to love.

> *Song of Hope.* 1999. Covenant Communications, paper. 199 pp. ISBN 1-57734-429-4.
> More fast pacing, including a car jacking, accompany Delia's return, and her chances for romance increase.

Sky Full of Ribbons. 2000. Covenant Communications, paper. 220 pp. ISBN 1-57734-605-X. Delia's mother, Polly, is featured, while Delia attempts to unravel the mystery of a robbery.

IRVINE, ROBERT

MORONI TRAVELER

Irvine's tough, Marlowe-like private eye is named after the Mormon prophet Moroni, but he no longer can bring himself to believe. He sometimes does work for Mormons, but the story of *Called Home* is more typical: An entire town refuses him information because of his lack of faith. Though the series grows older, and individual titles are out of print, it's worth retaining for its uniqueness and its unvarnished look at Utah and Mormonism.

Baptism for the Dead. 1988.

The Angel's Share. 1989.

Gone to Glory. 1990.

Called Home. 1992.

The Spoken Word. 1992.

The Great Reminder. 1993.

The Hosanna Shout. 1994.

Pillar of Fire. 1995.

ROMANCE

BELL, MICHELE ASHMAN

Yesterday's Love. 2000. Covenant Communications. paper. 342 pp. ISBN 1-57734-602-5. Widow Miranda Kensington, who learns of her husband's philandering after his death, slowly puts her life together with the help of her childhood sweetheart, Garrett Erickson. Garrett is so godly and kind that the reader keeps waiting for the other shoe to fall, but it never does. Still, Miranda's ongoing problems—centered mainly around her teenaged son, who hasn't dealt well with his father's death and is taking drugs—have the ring of truth, and non-Mormons will find the frank, though positive look at Mormon life to be enlightening.

An Unexpected Love. 1998. Covenant Communications, paper. 246 pp. ISBN 1-57734-243-7. Fitness instructor Alex McCarty hasn't been in touch with her sister, Jamie, for some years. That's because of Jamie's Mormonism, which Alex blames for their father's death. Jamie's difficult pregnancy sends Alex to Idaho to help, but on the way she runs her car off the road in a snowstorm. She's immediately attracted to her rescuer, Rich Greenwood, but he turns out to be Mormon—and the business partner of Alex's holier-than-thou brother-in-law.

An Enduring Love. 1998. Covenant Communications, paper. 332 pp. ISBN 1-57734-333-6. In the sequel to *An Unexpected Love,* Rich and Alex are an item, but business opportunities take them each in opposite directions. Alex has an opportunity to work in Europe and wonders why Rich doesn't put up a stronger opposition. The separation becomes a test for their love and also for Alex's newfound faith. ■ Sequel ■

HANSEN, JENNIE. *The River Path.* 2000. Covenant Communications, paper. 240 pp. ISBN 1-57734-620-3.

> Matt Bingham's job keeps him away from home a good deal, so when he discovers bruises on his infant son, he has no explanation for how they got there. They persist, and worsen. Slowly, he begins to suspect his wife, Dana, and his accusations wreak havoc on their marriage.

JOLLEY, JOANN. *Secrets of the Heart.* 1998. Covenant Communications, paper. 299 pp. ISBN 1-57734-331-X.

> Paula Donroe is an immensely successful advertising executive, and she has the trinkets to prove it: expensive clothing, jewelry, and a new Jaguar. She has two young sons who seem to be doing well despite seeing little of their mother. Her neglect of them does nag at her, and something else does as well: Years ago, in poverty, she gave up a baby for adoption. So when her younger son, TJ, dies, she's primed to fall to pieces.

JONES, ANNA. *Haven.* 2000. Covenant Communications, paper. 202 pp. ISBN 1-57734-603-3.

> Allison Melton's husband, Ken, has lost his job, and the marriage was already rocky. She books a room at Haven, a bed-and-breakfast in North Wales run by Mormon Gwen Evans. Other guests, also troubled, arrive, and Gwen ministers to them all, as well as fending off the attentions of an itinerant Australian. Meanwhile, things look up for Allison and Ken.

STANSFIELD, ANITA

> *The Gable Faces East.* 1999. Covenant Communications, paper. 499 pp. ISBN 1-57734-525-8.
>
> There's a lot of heavy breathing is these historical romances set in nineteenth century Australia, but no real salaciousness. In the first, a bitter feud arises between Jess Davies and the Byrnehouse clan, specifically the villainous Chad Byrnehouse. Jess is threatened with ruin until young Anita Byrnehouse comes to work for him and they raise some champion horses.

> *Gables Against the Sky.* 2000. Covenant Communications, paper. 567 pp. ISBN 1-57734-607-6.
>
> The sequel to *The Gable Faces East* features Jess and Anita's twins, Emma and Tyson, who are brought up in the great wealth Jess and Anita have acquired. ▮ Sequel ▮

SCIENCE FICTION

Though Orson Scott Card dominates the scene, there is a quantity of Mormon science fiction beyond his work. Those readers interested might want to check out Marny K. Parkin's "Bibliography of Mormon Speculative Fiction" at http://home.earthlink.net/~marnyparkin. For Card's work that is less demonstrably Mormon, see the section on hard science fiction, chapter 9, "Fantasy and Science Fiction."

CARD, ORSON SCOTT

The Folk of the Fringe. 1989. Phantasia Press. 238 pp. ISBN 0-932096-49-2.
In these interconnected short stories, Card frames an apocalyptic Utah: The few Mormons who survive the end of civilization slowly gather in a new kingdom in the Rocky Mountains, reenacting the historic Mormon Trek as they do so.

THE HOMECOMING SAGA

The Memory of Earth. 1992. Tor, paper. 336 pp. ISBN 0-81253-259-7.
With many allusions to the Book of Mormon, Genesis, and a certain kinship as well to Frank Herbert's *Dune,* Card's grand series begins with the tale of Nafai (after Nephi) and his family of the city of Basilica on the planet Harmony. Eons ago, Harmony was settled by colonists from a decimated Earth, who to avoid any violence in their future submitted to rule by a sentient computer, the Oversoul. But now the Oversoul is deteriorating and must direct its charges back to Earth, from which it may be renewed by the "Keeper of Earth." The Oversoul proceeds to teach the people of Harmony the nature of space flight by providing the seeress Lady Rasa with visions that are both spiritual and instructive.

The Call of Earth. 1993. Tor, paper. 352 pp. ISBN 0-81253-261-9.
Nafai and his people rally in the cause of the Oversoul and Lady Rasa, and a warrior, General Moozh, takes his errant battle against Basilica.

The Ships of Earth. 1994. Tor, paper. 384 pp. ISBN 0-81253-263-5.
The prophet Nafai and his band flee across the Harmonian desert after Moozh's victory and prepare for their journey to Earth.

Earthfall. 1995. Tor, paper. 352 pp. ISBN 0-81253-296-1.
The Oversoul's chosen people flee toward their ancient home in the wake of Moozh's destruction of Basilica. Nafai is master of the starship on its 100-year journey, but must deal with the rebellion of his stern older brother, Elemak. The starfarers find an Earth dissimilar even to their own legends of it, "peopled" by sentient rats and bats, and with no Keeper of Earth to be found.

Earthborn. 1996. Tor, paper. 378 pp. ISBN 0-81253-298-8.
The search continues for the Keeper of Earth as the lost earthlings divide into factions, feuding over territory and means of government.

YA ★ THE TALES OF ALVIN MAKER

Alvin Miller is the seventh son of a seventh son and destined for great and magical things. He comes of age in one of the most original alternative universes ever imagined: frontier America, but one where the visions of Indians come true and where hexes and folk cures actually work. Alvin Miller is a Maker, a healer and future leader who will help form the new country's destiny. He is a magical version of Joseph Smith, and his followers, the people of Vigor Church, are allegorical Mormons who will eventually found Crystal City.

The series will conclude with *Crystal City* and *Master Alvin.*

Seventh Son. 1988. Tor, paper. 241 pp. ISBN 0-8125-3305-4.
The mischievous young Alvin runs afoul of a literal-minded Presbyterian preacher, who may be an agent of the mysterious Unmaker, or the antithesis of the good forces the powerful omen of Alvin's birth represents. But Alvin is guided by an angel and by the Taleswapper, who tells tall tales and introduces Card's delightful folkloric tone.

Red Prophet. 1988. Tor, paper. 320 pp. ISBN 0-8125-2426-8.
Troubles with the Indian nation west of the Mizzipy threaten to boil over from the plotting of an exiled Napoleon and the dreams of glory of William Henry Harrison, a brutal personage who sells "likker" to the Indians. One Indian, Lolla-Wossiky, escapes to become the "dream-beast" of Alvin, that magical child, and shows him how to resist the corruption of his powers by the Unmaker. As war erupts among several factions, Lolla-Wossiky becomes a peaceful prophet to his people.

Prentice Alvin. 1989. Tor, paper. 320 pp. ISBN 0-8125-0212-4.
Alvin learns the trade of a blacksmith west of the Hio River and falls in love with his future wife, Peggy, who has a certain ability to foretell the future.

Alvin Journeyman. 1995. Tor, paper. 416 pp. ISBN 0-8125-0923-4.
Alvin develops followers farther west, in the town of Vigor Church high on the Wobbish River, near the site of the Battle of Tippy-Canoe. But before Alvin and his followers can build their Crystal City—a sort of hybrid of Oz and Salt Lake City—Alvin must stand trial, a politicized, sham trial like the one given to Joseph Smith at Nauvoo. It is all the working of the Unmaker.

Heartfire. 1998. Tor, paper. 336 pp. ISBN 0-8125-0924-2.
The dream of Crystal City is much nearer fruition. Alvin visits the province of New England to study the nature of cities, where he protests the persecution of witches and finds himself in jail, but Mike Fink and John Adams come to his aid. Meanwhile, Alvin's pregnant wife, Peggy, heads to one of the kingdoms of the South, where she preaches against slavery to an exiled King Arthur in his quaint "kingdom" of Camelot.

HEIMERDINGER, CHRIS

YA *TENNIS SHOES ADVENTURE SERIES*
The reader who enjoys Orson Scott Card's Alvin Maker series will also like Heimerdinger's popular time-travel series, which introduces the Book of Mormon in imaginative ways. In the first adventure, 13-year-old Jim Hawkins and his pal, Garth Plimpton, find themselves in ancient Israel among the warring Nephites and Lamanites.

Jim is an unhappy camper when it comes to the Church, whereas Garth can't get enough of religion. Readers revisit with the friends, now in college at Brigham Young University, in the sequel, in which they are pursued by robbers from the old times; before the dust has settled, they are in ancient Mexico.

Subsequent volumes occur some years later, when Jim is a widower raising two teenage daughters, Melody and Stephanie, and a son who is a chip off the old block, 10-year-old Harry. The family returns to ancient Israel at about the time of the Crucifixion. Several years later, son Harry tries to find his way back to the same time but reaches A.D. 70 instead, when Christianity seems to have gone seriously awry, and there are Antichrists as well as believers to be found. Harry is swept up in pursuit of a sacred scroll that holds the secrets of the universe.

Tennis Shoes Among the Nephites. 1991. Covenant Communications. 228 pp. ISBN 1-57734-467-7.

Gadiantons and the Silver Sword. 1992. Covenant Communications. 320 pp. ISBN 1-57734-612-2.

The Feathered Serpent, Part One. 1995. Covenant Communications. 329 pp. ISBN 1-57734-489-8.

The Feathered Serpent, Part Two. 1996. Covenant Communications. 337 pp. ISBN 1-55503-916-2.

Tennis Shoes and the Seven Churches. Covenant Communications. 329 pp. ISBN 1-57734-217-8.

The Lost Scrolls. 1999. Covenant Communications. 279 pp. ISBN 1-57734-418-9.

The Golden Crown. 2000. Covenant Communications, paper. 338 pp. ISBN 1-57734-498-7.

SHORT STORIES

BARBER, PHYLLIS. *Parting the Veil: Stories from a Mormon Imagination.* 1999. Signature, paper. 124 pp. ISBN 1-56085-120-1.

> Barber carefully documents her sources for these well-crafted tales of miracles and premonitions that often have the quality of folklore.

CARD, ORSON SCOTT, AND DAVID DOLLAHITE, eds. *Turning Hearts: Short Stories on Family Life.* 1994. Bookcraft, paper. 307 pp. ISBN 0-884949-48-6.

> For the most part these are positive stories about families that turn on some sort of spiritual or ethical issue. Some are specifically Mormon, but most take up topics of general interest such as divorce, children, and aging parents.

RALEIGH, ROBERT, ed. 1998. *In Our Lovely Deseret.* Signature, paper. 300 pp. ISBN 1-56085-119-8.

> Realistic short stories by such craftsmen as Levi Peterson and Robert Hodgson Van Wagoner, depicting a Utah and a Mormonism that fail as much as they succeed: At issue are homosexuality, adultery, and hypocritical church figures.

Chapter 15

Young Adults

Two periodicals, *Christian Library Journal* and *Voya* (see coverage in chapter 2), conscientiously cover Christian young adult novels, and the selector or Readers' Advisory librarian actively seeking a Christian alternative in the juvenile collection should follow these journals.

There are several caveats. First, although Christian young adult novels are published in abundance, they are often moralistic, so much so that many teens will react by being bored or with the feeling they are being talked down to (Maifair 1998). Thus, although a librarian can stock her shelves with materials Christian parents will approve of, she may find that Christian teenagers pass them by.

Second, Christian young adult novels tend to be aimed at the younger of the young adult audience—really, middle school. Mid- or late-teen novels are harder to come by.

Such novels are more often published as adult novels: the stories of Janette Oke, for example. Although Oke's novels are clearly addressed to an adult audience, her protagonists are predominantly young women, her style is simple, and there's a strong emphasis on the story line. Thus, Oke's and many other adult Christian novels are often a better choice for young adults than those novels expressly aimed at them. (Adult titles particularly suited to teens are marked **YA** in previous chapters.)

The Readers' Advisory librarian seeking a wholesale solution for young adult collections might consider the offerings of Bethany House, with its inexpensive, generally reliable titles. Judy Baer's two series—Live at Brentwood High and Cedar River Daydreams, which, through 1999, had run to 28 entries—are typical. They work hard to deal with social issues, such as racism, unwed pregnancy, and disabilities, though it must be said that they are less subtle concerning more personal matters, such as loneliness, peer pressure, and, of course, faith. All in all, however, Baer's titles don't differ markedly in quality from mainstream series such as Sweet Valley High, and parents can be assured there will be no issues of explicit sex or profanity.

Another dependable Bethany performer is Patricia H. Rushford, whose long-running Jennie McGrady series features a young sleuth reminiscent of Nancy Drew—a Nancy Drew who stops frequently to whisper a prayer.

Though aimed at the junior high level, Bethany's Trailblazer series about Christian heroes will appeal to some young adults and is a terrific choice for Christian schools and home schools. A typical entry is Dave and Neta Jackson's *Forty-Acre Swindle* (ISBN 0-7642-2264-3), about George Washington Carver and Tuskegee Institute.

Robin Jones Gunn's Christy Miller series went through 12 installments before graduating to the Christy and Todd series in *Until Tomorrow* (1999, Bethany, 2000, 320 pp. ISBN 0-7642-2272-4), reflecting Christy's 12-year (in publishing terms) journey through high school and into college. Christy is highly emotional, and her constant talk of Jesus may be tiresome to some, but she finds herself in a number of scrapes and adventures that will be recognizable to teenage girls, and the series has been Bethany's most popular. By late 1999, Gunn had also published 12 installments of the companion Sierra Jensen series (the heroines sometimes cross paths), also about a high school girl, and also published by Bethany. The Christy series ended in 2001 with *I Promise* (Bethany, paper, 288 pp., ISBN 0-7642-2274-0), the story of Christy and Todd finishing college and getting married.

Fewer Christian series focus on boys. Though it grows older, one good one is Sigmund Brouwer's ice hockey series, Lightning on Ice, published by Word. Brouwer also writes a young adult sports mystery series and a Tom Swiftian science fiction spoof series, Dr. Drabble. He's one of the best stylists in the field, and his religious presentation is subtle.

Another series aimed at boys—or perhaps, boys and girls—is Gilbert Morris's Bonnets and Bugles series from Moody (discussed later).

HISTORICALS

Biblical

SHOTT, JAMES R.

◀Ε✕★ *PEOPLE OF THE PROMISE*
Presbyterian minister Shott's understated, highly readable series concerns Old Testament figures in their youth. Shott stays as near to Scripture as he can and tells powerful, unvarnished stories with immense appeal to adults and teens alike.

> *Leah.* 1990. Herald Press, paper. 160 pp. ISBN 0-8361-3526-1.

> *Joseph.* 1992. Herald Press, paper. 144 pp. ISBN 0-8361-3576-8.

> *Hagar.* 1992. Herald Press, paper. 168 pp. ISBN 0-8361-3590-3.

> *Esau.* 1993. Herald Press, paper. 216 pp. ISBN 0-8361-3601-2.

> *Deborah.* 1993. Herald Press, paper. 168 pp. ISBN 0-8361-3643-8.

> *Othniel.* 1994. Herald Press, paper. 168 pp. ISBN 0-8361-3661-6.

> *Abigail.* 1996. Herald Press, paper. 144 pp. ISBN 0-8361-9030-0.

> *Bathsheba.* 1996. Herald Press, paper. 149 pp. ISBN 0-8361-9039-4.

Nineteenth Century United States

◀Ε✕ ★JACKSON, DAVE. *Lost River Conspiracy.* 1995. Good Books, paper. 220 pp. ISBN 1-56148-183-1. *[Historical]*
In this sturdy western, a young Mennonite is cast upon the winds when he loses his Illinois farm. He drifts to Oregon, where he becomes embroiled in the treacheries of the Modoc Indian War of 1872.

★ **RIVERS, FRANCINE.** *The Last Sin Eater.* **1998. Tyndale. 336 pp. ISBN 0-842-33570-6.**
See discussion in chapter 5, "Historical Christian Fiction," p. 53.

WISEHART, RANDALL

Luke's Summer Secret. 1991. Friends United Press, paper. 165 pp. ISBN 0-944350-17-8. Luke Thomas, 13, leaves his home in Cincinnati to join Hoosier Quaker Levi Coffin, an actual historical figure, in his efforts to shelter slaves running away from Kentucky plantations.

A Winding Road to Freedom. 1999. Friends United Press, paper. 183 pp. ISBN 0-944350-47-X.
In the sequel to *Luke's Summer Secret,* the escaped slave Cassie comes to prominence when Luke helps her rescue her infant son.   ████ **Sequel** ████

Civil War

MORRIS, GILBERT

BONNETS AND BUGLES
Morris's Civil War series illustrates history through the lives of two friends from the border state of Kentucky: Jeff Majors, who becomes a drummer boy for the Confederates, and Jeff Carter, who becomes a sutler in the Union Army.

> *Drummer Boy at Bull Run.* 1995. Moody, paper. 182 pp. ISBN 0-8024-0911-3.
>
> *Yankee Belles in Dixie.* 1995. Moody, paper. 164 pp. ISBN 0-8024-0912-1.
>
> *The Secret of Richmond Manor.* 1995. Moody, paper. 154 pp. ISBN 0-8024-0913-X.
>
> *The Soldier Boy's Discovery.* 1996. Moody, paper. 169 pp. ISBN 0-8024-0914-8.
>
> *Blockade Runner.* 1996. Moody, paper. 151 pp. ISBN 0-8024-0915-6.
>
> *The Gallant Boys of Gettysburg.* 1996. Moody, paper. 168 pp. ISBN 0-8024-0916-4.
>
> *The Battle of Lookout Mountain.* 1996. Moody, paper. 165 pp. ISBN 0-8024-0917-2.
>
> *Encounter at Cold Harbor.* 1997. Moody, paper. 154 pp. ISBN 0-8024-0918-0.
>
> *Fire Over Atlanta.* 1997. Moody, paper. 168 pp. ISBN 0-8024-0919-9.
>
> *Bring the Boys Home.* 1997. Moody, paper. 128 pp. ISBN 0-8024-0920-2.

RODDY, LEE

BETWEEN TWO FLAGS
Between Two Flags is a Civil War series featuring young adults forced by the war to make difficult decisions.

> *Cry of Courage.* 1998. Bethany, paper. 160 pp. ISBN 0-76422-025-X.
>
> *When Bugles Call.* 1998. Bethany, paper. 160 pp. ISBN 0-76422-026-8.

Burden of Honor. 1999. Bethany, paper. 144 pp. ISBN 0-76422-027-6.

Road to Freedom. 1999. Bethany, paper. 144 pp. ISBN 0-76422-028-4.

Uprising at Dawn. 2000. Bethany, paper. 159 pp. ISBN 0-76422-029-2.

Twentieth Century

England

✦ THOENE, JAKE, AND LUKE THOENE
Jake and Luke are the sons of Christian fiction's best-known writing team, Brock and Bodie Thoene. They have also written an adult series, Portraits of Destiny (p. 101).

BAKER STREET MYSTERIES
Sherlock Holmes calls on several boys, the Baker Street Brigade, to solve mysteries.

The Mystery of the Yellow Hands. 1995. Moorings, paper. 149 pp. ISBN 0-345-39561-1.

The Giant Rat of Sumatra. 1995. Moorings, paper. 145 pp. ISBN 0-345-39560-3.

The Jewelled Peacock of Persia. 1996. Moorings, paper. 152 pp. ISBN 0-345-39559-X.

The Thundering Underground. 1998. Nelson, paper. 132 pp. ISBN 0-7852-7081-7.

United States

★ MARSHALL, CATHERINE
Daughter of a minister, Marshall always wanted to be a writer, and before her death in 1983 had written about 20 books. Most were spiritual guides, though her *A Man Called Peter* (1951), a perennial bestseller, told of her marriage to Peter Marshall, a chaplain of the U.S. Senate in the 1940s who died an early death in 1949. Her most influential books, however, are the two novels described below, both young adult classics.

Christy. 1967. (Many editions.)
In 1912 Christy Huddleston, a 19-year-old middle-class city girl, takes a job teaching in a remote area of the Smoky Mountains. Energetic, inventive, and boundlessly optimistic, she draws inspiration from a wise Quaker missionary and is courted by two men, an idealistic minister and a cynical (until Christy works on him) doctor. A one-woman crusader against ignorance and poverty, Christy's warmth and what might be called her realistic optimism was and remains an inspiration for young Christian women, and Marshall's semiautobiographical (that is, she based the novel on her mother's experiences) model for the Christian novel has been much imitated. *Christy* was a popular TV series in 1994, directed by Michael Ray Rhodes with Kellie Martin as Christy.

Julie. 1984. (Many editions.)
Julie Wallace, who in many ways is a young Catherine Marshall, moves with her family to Pennsylvania in 1934. It's the middle of the Depression, and Julie's family has had a hard time. Her father lost his post as a minister because of his stand on racial issues, and is recovering from a mental breakdown. In Pennsylvania he pursues his other passion, running a newspaper. The vivacious, endearing, and sometimes slightly devious Julie wants to be a writer and throws herself into helping out, even as an older man, a suave Britisher, chases after her, competing with two other beaus. Julie crusades against the callous social policies of a local steel mill and

reports on a dam upcountry that looks to be unsafe. Sure enough, it breaks. Marshall's description of the ensuing flood is magnificent; the ensuing crisis draws out the best in Julie, who in turn draws out the best in everyone around her.

⊂✗ WISE, STEVEN. *Long Train Passing.* **1996. Nelson, paper. 288 pp. ISBN 0-7852-7705-6.**
See discussion in chapter 11, "The Christian Life," p. 209.

Europe—World War II

⊂✗ HORTON, DAVID

★ *A Legion of Honor.* 1995. Victor, paper. 324 pp. ISBN 1-56476-540-7.
A Legion of Honor is a subtle, intelligent story of derring-do among the French Resistance featuring young Marcel Boussant, who wants to be in action but instead is assigned to what he thinks is the boring job of smuggling Jews out of Vichy France. Then he falls in love with beautiful Isabelle Karmazin, a Jew, is nearly killed getting her to Switzerland, and suddenly his work is more interesting.

The Sign of the Cross. 1997. Chariot Victor, paper. 350 pp. ISBN 56476-611-X.
Though Isabelle and her child reach Switzerland, trouble remains for them. The Swiss are overwhelmed with Jewish refugees, the United States does not want them, and despite the kindness of her Christian hosts Isabelle faces a tenuous, even grim future. Meanwhile, Marcel is imprisoned by the Nazis and tortured by the infamous Klaus Barbie, ably characterized by Horton as a scary but not quite inhuman figure. Marcel makes a daring escape with the help of his Resistance friends and heads for Switzerland, only to find that other obstacles have arisen to his love for Isabelle. ▪ Sequel ▪

⊂✗ ★ YODER, JAMES D. *Black Spider over Tiegenhof.* **1995. Herald, paper. 232 pp. ISBN 0-83619-012-2.**
A peaceful Mennonite family tries to hide a teenaged Jewish girl, Ruth, from the Nazis, but a German girl turns informer. Ruth is interned and nearly dies. The brutality done to Ruth is almost unbearably moving, and the agony of the Mennonite family, forced to send two of their sons into battle, is hardly less. The sobering question Yoder poses is this: How do you stand passively against absolute evil, when absolute evil will simply snuff you out?

MYSTERIES

★ **PERETTI, FRANK.** *The Veritas Project: Hangman's Curse.* **2001. Nelson. 288 pp. ISBN 0-8499-7616-2.**
The sleuthing Springfield family—Nate and Sarah, father and mother of teenage twins, Elisha and Elijah—go undercover to investigate devilish events at a high school in Washington State in the well-known Peretti's direct bid for a young adult audience. The Springfields uncover an evil network that includes witchcraft, the ghost of a sad boy who hanged himself, and a strange malady that sends star athletes into comas. The surprising passion of Peretti's tale, with its strong allusions to Columbine High School, will appeal to readers who enjoyed Orson Scott Card's *Lost Boys* (p. 288).

EX ★ **SHAW, LOU.** *Honor Thy Son.* **1994. Abingdon, paper. 240 pp. ISBN 0-68709-982-X.**

Lawyer Jack Ingraham's ex-wife seeks him out to inform him that their son, who has Down Syndrome, has been charged with murder. This brings to the surface 20 years of guilt because the reason Jack fled from the marriage was that he couldn't bear to deal with a Down Syndrome baby, while his wife couldn't bear to give her baby up. Jack gets to know his son in a series of hair-raising and amusing scenes; Jack's attempt to teach his son to drive in various stolen cars is hilarious. Shaw, who has a daughter with Down Syndrome and who created the TV series *Quincy,* turns in a routine mystery, but the father and son stuff is a knockout.

EX ★ **WOJTASIK, TED.** *No Strange Fire.* **1996. Herald, paper. 400 pp. ISBN 0-8361-9041-6.**

Wojtasik's mystery, set among the "Nebraska" Amish of Pennsylvania, speculates on the causes of barn fires that nearly destroyed the community in 1992. The chief suspect is disaffected Jacob Hostetler, who, nearing baptism, the rite of passage for the Amish, strikes out into the world of the "Englisch," where he smokes, drinks, drives cars, and finds a girlfriend—but still can't seem to fit in. The Amish are wonderfully observed as an admirable, though imperfect people; the agony of Amish farmers as their livestock die in fires leaps from the page.   **Discussion**

SCIENCE FICTION AND FANTASY

EDWARDS, GENE

EX *CHRONICLES OF THE DOOR*

Quite popular in the mid-1990s, Edwards's spiritual warfare series tells the entire Christian story. As directed by God, the angels Michael and Gabriel venture through the door to Heaven, sealed up by fallen Lucifer, to aid in God's plan of redemption for humankind. Behind the scenes of the human story, they do battle with Lucifer and his agents at crucial points and otherwise bear witness to biblical history and prophecy.

The Beginning. 1992. Tyndale, paper. 192 pp. ISBN 0-8423-1084-3.
The Genesis account of Creation is dramatized.

The Escape. 1993. Tyndale, paper. 164 pp. ISBN 0-8423-1255-2.
The flight from Egypt.

The Birth. 1991. Tyndale, paper. 134 pp. ISBN 0-8423-0158-5.
The Nativity.

The Triumph. 1995. Tyndale, paper. 186 pp. ISBN 0-8423-6978-3.
The Resurrection.

The Return. 1996. Tyndale, paper. 161 pp. ISBN 0-8423-5601-0.
The Second Coming.

EX **HAND, BILL.** *The OnePrince.* **1999. (Originally published in 1992.) Xlibis, paper. 640 pp. ISBN 0-7388-0479-7.**

Five hundred years ago, the elusive OnePrince made the spell that gave Pentatutinus, king of Redaemus, his long life and gave power to the symbol of his authority, the Ruby Scion. But now Pentatutinus has died, the Ruby Scion has lost its power, and young King Quad, a reluctant, bookish ruler, must seek out the OnePrince before his kingdom is overwhelmed by evil Lord Demio of the far north. Talking rats and badgers "people" Hand's kingdom, and like Harry Harrison, Hand writes in a kind of slapstick, though of course he's not scatological. *The OnePrince* is a good recommendation for teenage boys; this edition also contains Hand's sequel, *The Hidden City.*

LAHAYE, TIM, AND JERRY JENKINS

LEFT BEHIND: THE KIDS

The spin-off from the historically popular adult series tells the story of four high-school kids who didn't think Jesus was cool and who thought their pastor's warnings of the Rapture were silly. Boy, were they wrong, but this series, theoretically aimed at young teens, should be looked upon with caution: For evangelicals, it may prove too adult; for liberal Christians or secular readers, too inflammatory. Impressionable kids may be greatly distressed, in other words.

The Vanishings. 1998. Tyndale, paper. 160 pp. ISBN 0-84232-193-4.

Second Chance. 1998. Tyndale, paper. 160 pp. ISBN 0-8423-2194-2.

Through the Flames. 1998. Tyndale, paper. 160 pp. ISBN 0-8423-2195-0.

Facing the Future. 1998. Tyndale, paper. 160 pp. ISBN 0-8423-2196-9.

Nicolae High. 1999. Tyndale, paper. 144 pp. ISBN 0-8423-4325-3.

The Underground. 1999. Tyndale, paper. 128 pp. ISBN 0-8423-4326-1.

Busted! 2000. Tyndale, paper. 114 pp. ISBN 0-8423-4327-X.

Death Strike. 2000. Tyndale, paper. 126 pp. ISBN 0-8423-4328-8.

The Search. 2000. Tyndale, paper. 176 pp. ISBN 0-8423-4329-6.

On the Run. 2000. Tyndale, paper. 176 pp. ISBN 0-8423- 4330-X.

Into the Storm. 2000. Tyndale, paper. 149 pp. ISBN 0-8423- 4331-8.

Earthquake! 2000. Tyndale, paper. 138 pp. ISBN 0-8423- 4332-6.

The Showdown. 2001. Tyndale, paper. 132 pp. ISBN 0-8423-4294-X.

Judgement Day. 2001. Tyndale, paper. 130 pp. ISBN 0-8423-4295-8.

Battling the Commander. 2001. Tyndale, paper. 140 pp. ISBN 0-8423-4296-6.

Fire from Heaven. 2001. Tyndale, paper. 142 pp. ISBN 0-8423-4297-4.

Terror in the Stadium. 2001. Tyndale, paper. 176 pp. ISBN 0-8423-4299-0.

Darkening Skies. 2001. Tyndale, paper. 176 pp. ISBN 0-8423-4312-1.

Attack of Apollyon. 2002. Tyndale, paper. 140 pp. ISBN 0-8423-4313-X.

A Dangerous Plan. 2002. Tyndale, paper. 140 pp. ISBN 0-8423-4314-8.

LAWHEAD, STEPHEN

◆✕★ *DRAGON KING TRILOGY*

This series was Lawhead's first big success, and also his most overtly Christian.

In the Hall of the Dragon King. 1996. (Originally published in 1982.) Zondervan, paper. 367 pp. ISBN 0-310-20502-6.

Young Quentin is a humble servant in Ariel's temple. He comes to prominence when a wounded knight dispatches him with an urgent message for the queen of Mensander. Nimrood the Necromancer is on a rampage of evil, with only the weak forces of the good king Eskevar to stand against him. En route, Quentin has many worthy adventures and becomes aware that Ariel is a false god. There is only one god, the Most High, and serving him will save Mensander from Nimrood. Quentin's heroics restore the kingdom to Eskevar.

The Warlords of Nin. 1996. (Originally published in 1983.) Zondervan, paper. 368 pp. ISBN 0-310-20503-4.

Eskevar is dying, even as Nin gathers his forces for a great invasion. Fulfilling prophecy, Quentin seeks the sword called Zhaligkeer, that mighty symbol of the Most High, and himself becomes Dragon King.

The Sword and the Flame. 1996. (Originally published in 1984.) Zondervan, paper. 320 pp. ISBN 0-310-20504-2.

Quintin is tested yet again, undergoing trial after trial as Nin surfaces a final time, kidnapping Quintin's son, young Gerin, and murdering his most faithful servant, the hermit Durwin. The Dragon King's weapons, all of the comforts of his kingdom, are torn from him. Only his strength as a warrior and his faith in the Most High can help.

★ L'ENGLE, MADELEINE

L'Engle is one of those few writers who draw the adjective "beloved." All of her books are fine choices for young people and for the young at heart. In 1998 she received The Margaret Edwards Award (Lifetime Achievement Award for Writing in the Field of Young Adult Literature) from the American Library Association.

L'Engle's fiction observes her fictional concept of Chronos (chronological time) and Kairos (cosmic time): yes, each novel was published in a particular year, but the body of work is about time, a slippery concept, indeed. Thus, although there is an attempt in this chapter to place L'Engle's novels into series chronologically, a character in one series often pops up in another, and L'Engle did not write in sequence.

But the reader coming to her work for the first time would certainly want to begin with *A Wrinkle in Time*, the novel that made L'Engle's reputation. After experiencing the adventures of the Murry family, the reader might want to move into the parallel universes of the Austin and O'Keefe families. An absolute chronology will never emerge, however.

One other note: Madeleine L'Engle reads much like C. S. Lewis in his Narnia stories. The children have the same matter-of-fact, almost comic calm in the face of astounding events as they "tesser" their way through wrinkles—wormholes—in time. L'Engle is an original, but more clearly than any other writer she is Lewis's heir (Gonzales 1991).

AUSTIN FAMILY

This science fiction/fantasy series features Vicky Austin, wife of scientist Wallace Austin, and they live with their children in a rambling country house much like the house of the Murry family (discussed later). But Vicky makes appearances as a child and as a young woman with telepathic abilities; other characters, such as young Maggy Hamilton, a ward of the Austin family, also are featured.

> ***Meet the Austins.*** 1960. (Out of print.)
>
> ***The Moon by Night.*** 1963. (Out of print.)
>
> ***The Young Unicorns.*** 1968. (Out of print.)
>
> ***A Ring of Endless Light.*** 1980. (Out of print.)
>
> ***Troubling a Star.*** 1994. (Out of print.)

O'KEEFE FAMILY

Also a time-travel series (into Earth's distant past), the O'Keefe family features Calvin, his wife, Meg (from *A Wrinkle in Time*), and several children. Daughter Polly is the chief adventurer.

> ***The Arm of the Starfish.*** 1965. (Out of print.)
>
> ***Dragons in the Waters.*** 1976. (Out of print.)
>
> ***A House Like a Lotus.*** 1984. (Out of print.)

> ***An Acceptable Time.*** 1989. (Out of print.) (*Note:* Could also be thought of as Murry family.)

TIME QUINTET (Murry family)

This best known of L'Engle's series features the Murry family of two scientists, Kate and Alex Murry, and their children: Meg, the twins Sandy and Dennys, and Charles Wallace. Meg's friend Calvin O'Keefe is also featured; Meg marries him by the time *of A Swiftly Tilting Planet,* and both show up in the O'Keefe family series.

Like the Narnia series, *A Wrinkle in Time* is the story of the triumph of good over evil. Meg Murry, a high school girl, is transported with Charles Wallace and her long-in-the-future husband, Calvin, to rescue her father on a faraway planet called Camazotz. A charming, daffy angel, Mrs. Whatsit, guides the children. They discover that Dr. Murry is being held captive by an evil force called the Dark Thing, which Charles Wallace tries to battle using the sheer power of intelligence. But something more than intelligence is needed, and Charles Wallace is turned into a sort of robot. Speaking the words of the Dark Thing, Charles Wallace guides Meg and Calvin to Dr. Murry. The three manage to escape to another planet, Ixchel, where they find respite. But Charles Wallace is still a prisoner on Camazotz, and, with the help of Mrs. Whatsit, Meg undertakes to return there and rescue him, armed with the one weapon the Dark Thing cannot defeat: love.

> ***A Wrinkle in Time.*** 1962. (Many editions.) Winner of the Newbery Award.
>
> ***A Wind in the Door.*** 1973. Yearling Books, paper. 211 pp. ISBN 0-4404-8761-7.
>
> ***Many Waters.*** 1987. Yearling Books, paper. 310 pp. ISBN 0-4404-0548-3.
>
> ***A Swiftly Tilting Planet.*** 1981. (Originally published in 1978.) Yearling Books, paper. 278 pp. ISBN 0-4404-0158-5. Winner of the American Book Award.
>
> ***An Acceptable Time.*** 1989. Laurel Leaf, paper. 343 pp. ISBN 0-4402-0814-9. (*Note:* Could also be thought of as O'Keefe family.)

◄❑✕ ★ **MADDOUX, MARLIN.** *The Seal of Gaia.* **1998. Word, paper. 480 pp. ISBN 0-8499-3715-9.**

See discussion in chapter 9, "Fantasy and Science Fiction," p. 159.

MORRIS, GILBERT

❑✕ *SEVEN SLEEPERS*

Rather like the children of the Narnia series, Morris's teenagers (most of them 14 or 15) find themselves in the mystic land of NuWorld, much of which is underwater and draws upon the mythology of lost Atlantis. They fight the Dark Lord and his lust for world dominion, and are always able, even unto the last great battle, to call upon the good lord "Goel"—the symbol of their faith. As in the Hardy Boys series, the dialogue is wooden, the characterizations thin, but Morris does devise excellent otherworldly creatures, and boys will read the series.

> *Flight of Eagles.* 1994. Moody, paper. 182 pp. ISBN 0-8024-3681-1.

> *The Gates of Neptune.* 1994. Moody, paper. 150 pp. ISBN 0-8024-3682-X.

> *The Sword of Camelot.* 1995. Moody, paper. 172 pp. ISBN 0-8024-3683-8.

> *The Caves that Time Forgot.* 1995. Moody, paper. 144 pp. ISBN 0-8024-3684-6.

> *Winged Raiders of the Desert.* 1995. Moody, paper, 135p. ISBN 0-8024-3685-4.

> *Empress of the Underworld.* 1996. Moody, paper. 153 pp. ISBN 0-8024-3686-2.

> *Voyage of the Dolphin.* 1996. Moody, paper. 160 pp. ISBN 0-8024-3687-0.

> *Attack of the Amazons.* 1996. Moody, paper. 165 pp. ISBN 0-8024-3691-9.

> *Escape with the Dream Maker.* 1997. Moody, paper. 166 pp. ISBN 0-8024-3692-7.

> *The Final Kingdom.* 1997. Moody, paper. 166 pp. ISBN 0-8024-3693-5.

◄❑✕ **MURRAY, KATHERINE.** *Jake.* **1995. Nelson, paper. 186 pp. ISBN 0-7852-8095-2.**

Jake is an affecting allegory about a young English girl, Jeannie, who finds herself drawn—in no way romantically—to a gentle man who lives by the sea. For some time a gang of hoodlums has terrorized Jeannie's village. One day Jake stands up to the thugs and is killed. His sacrifice causes the villagers to rally against the evil gang and pushes the sadder but wiser Jeannie into adulthood.

◄❑✕ **PERETTI, FRANK E.** *This Present Darkness.* **1989. Crossway, paper. 375 pp. ISBN 0-89107-390-6.**

See discussion in chapter 9, "Fantasy and Science Fiction," p. 159. Though clearly intended for adults, all of Peretti's novels are favorites with boys because of their Stephen King-like qualities.

◄❑✕ **SIEGEL, ROBERT.** *Alpha Centauri.* **1980. Cornerstone. (Out of print.)**

An American girl, daughter of a visiting history professor, enters a dark wood and finds herself in ancient England among a band of benevolent centaurs. They are at war with men and may soon be overwhelmed. Somehow, Becky holds the key to their salvation in this likable fantasy with much of the quality of a Madeleine L'Engle tale.

WHITE, JOHN

 THE ARCHIVES OF ANTHOPOS
Canadian teenagers Wesley, Kurt, and Lisa are magically transported into the kingdom of Anthropos, where they do battle with the evil Mirmah in this Chronicles of Narnia readalike.

> *The Sword Bearer.* 1986. InterVarsity. (Out of print.)

> *Gaal the Conqueror.* 1989. InterVarsity. (Out of print.)

> *The Tower of Geburah.* 1978. InterVarsity. (Out of print.)

> *The Iron Sceptre.* 1981. InterVarsity. (Out of print.)

> *Quest for the King.* 1995. InterVarsity. (Out of print.)

 ★ WILLIS, PAUL J. *No Clock in the Forest.* **1991. Crossway. (Out of print.)**
Strong ecological concerns inform Willis's sly, witty fantasy of young William, rather vain about his mountain-climbing skills, and Grace, a spoiled suburbanite teenager whose parents have signed her up for a wilderness trek in Washington State. The two become separated from their separate parties, then become reluctant heroes in a battle of the forest primeval between a good queen and a bad (the mountains surrounding them are called the Three Queens), while a third, "lost" queen provides them with the magic to defeat the bad queen's master, the Lava Beast. The novel's texture is considerably enriched by Willis's knowledge of wilderness flora and his allusions to classical myths.

TEEN LIFE

These stories deal with the passage through adolescence from a contemporary teenager's point of view. Most are coming-of-age stories, though some, like Melody Carson's Diary of a Teenage Girl series, offer snapshots of daily life and possibly moral guidance, rather than a defining denouement that leaves childhood behind.

 ALCORN, RANDY, ANGELA ALCORN, AND KARINA ALCORN. *The Ishbane Conspiracy.* **Multnomah, paper. 300 pp. ISBN 1-57673-817-5.** Sequel
See discussion, p. 160.

 ★ ARVIN, REED. *The Wind in the Wheat.* **1994. Nelson, paper. 360 pp. ISBN 0-7852-8146-0.**
Kansas farm boy Andrew Miracle has an extraordinary gift for writing and singing music. He's discovered by an agent from Nashville, who signs Andrew with a gospel producer, Dove Records, but also, unknown to Andrew, engineers a deal with a huge pop company. Andrew's most heartfelt song, "Lost Without You," meant as a contemporary hymn to Jesus, takes a strange odyssey into a rock song with heavily sexual overtones, and for a time Andrew is at a loss to fight back. Then, with his Christian girlfriend, he does, in this universal coming-of-age story that authentically shows the power of faith and of love.

BORNTRAGER, MARY CHRISTNER

⬤✖ *ELLIE'S PEOPLE*

The descendants of Ellie Maust, all seen as young adults who become full-fledged Amish men and women, are featured in this likable series from Mennonite Borntrager. Though broader themes, such as the difficulties of marriage and the Amish relation to the outside, or "English," world, are present, these clearly are meant as instructional stories for Amish youth. Amish growing-up problems turn out to be much the same as everyone else's, however, as in *Andy,* the story of an angry teenager with a weight problem who runs off (briefly) to become a hobo.

> *Ellie.* 1988. Herald Press, paper. 168 pp. ISBN 0-8361-3468-0.
>
> *Rebecca.* 1989. Herald Press, paper. 176 pp. ISBN 0-8361-3500-8.
>
> *Rachel.* 1990. Herald Press, paper. 158 pp. ISBN 0-8361-3539-3.
>
> *Daniel.* 1991. Herald Press, paper. 160 pp. ISBN 0-8361-3548-2.
>
> *Reuben.* 1992. Herald Press, paper. 160 pp. ISBN 0-8361-3593-8.
>
> *Andy.* 1993. Herald Press, paper. 142 pp. ISBN 0-8361-3633-0.
>
> *Polly.* 1994. Herald Press, paper. 144 pp. ISBN 0-8361-3670-5.
>
> *Sarah.* 1994. Herald Press, paper. 144 pp. ISBN 0-8361-9019-X.
>
> *Mandy.* 1996. Herald Press, paper. 142 pp. ISBN 0-8361-9046-7.
>
> *Annie.* 1997. Herald Press, paper. 144 pp. ISBN 0-8361-9070-X.

BRINKERHOFF, SHIRLEY

⬤✖ *NIKKI SHERIDAN*

Nikki Sheridan is a series popular with teenage girls in middle school or early high school. In the first entry, Nikki becomes pregnant and must decide whether to abort the fetus or give her baby up for adoption; not least in all of this is facing her parents. She becomes a Christian as the series moves forward, but life is still tough—drug use among friends and a father having an affair. By the time of *Second Choices* Nikki is 20 years old.

> *Choice Summer.* 1996. Bethany, paper. 182 pp. ISBN 1-56179-484-8.
>
> *Mysterious Love.* 1996. Bethany, paper. 184 pp. ISBN 1-56179-485-6.
>
> *Narrow Walk.* 1997. Bethany, paper. 195 pp. ISBN 1-56179-539-9.
>
> *Balancing Act.* 1998. Bethany, paper. 160 pp. ISBN 1-56179-559-3.
>
> *Tangled Web.* 2000. Bethany, paper. 166 pp. ISBN 1-56179-737-5.
>
> *Second Choices.* 2000. Bethany, paper. 160 pp. ISBN 1-56179-880-0.

CARLSON, MELODY

⬤✖ *DIARY OF A TEENAGE GIRL*

> *Diary of a Teenage Girl.* 2000. Multnomah, paper. 300 pp. ISBN 1-57673-735-7.
> Boy-crazy Caitlin O'Conner, 16, has tiffs with her best friend, wonders what career to pursue at one moment and who she'll go to the Valentine's Day dance with the next and,

most important of all, undergoes a crisis in faith as she weighs the compromises involved in being popular against the demands of walking the straight and narrow.

It's My Life. 2001. Multnomah, paper. 300 pp. ISBN 1-57673-772-1.
In the sequel to *Diary of a Teenage Girl,* Caitlin begins a full life as an almost-adult believer, balancing a mission trip to Mexico with her church group and how to help her friend Beanie, who's pregnant. Though Carlson's moral instruction weighs heavily, her series skillfully portrays the ambivalence toward life, and the outright fear, that teens feel.

Who I Am. 2002. Multnomah, paper. 252 pp. ISBN 1-57673-890-6.
Zealous Christian Caitlin becomes even more interested in missionary work after her trip to Mexico. But her parents pressure her to attend college, and her boyfriend, Josh, seems to be getting serious. Racial issues arise at school when Caitlin's friend Beanie begins dating an African American.

CARTER, BETTY SMARTT. *I Read It in the Wordless Book.* **1996. Baker, paper. 398 pp. ISBN 0-8010-5558-X.**
Carrie Grietkirk, who is 12, lives with her grandmother in Dutch Falls, Virginia, while her father serves out his chaplaincy tour in Vietnam. A bright, vivacious girl, Carrie's spirits go into high gear upon the arrival of Ginger Jordan, a former Broadway actress, still glamorous and sophisticated, who takes over Carrie's Vacation Bible School class. The world is a great big wonderful place, Ginger tells her, and you belong in it. But Carrie also belongs in the complicated world of her father, who brings home a Vietnamese wife, a sensitively drawn character named Phuong. Carrie grows up longing for the worldly world and yet bound to serve Jesus in this lyrical, likable novel with appealing minor characters, much like those of Jan Karon's stories.

COLSON, CONSTANCE. *Chase the Dream.* **1996. Multnomah, paper. 448 pp. ISBN 0-88070-928-6.**
A feel for the contemporary West and the life of rodeo performers informs this tale of Forrest Jackson, who watches as his father is gored to death by a bull but still pursues his rodeo dreams. Forrest has a partner, Tom, and they fall in love with two young women who are friends. The foursome rallies around Forrest's great potential, putting their trust in God.

CRAVEN, MARGARET. *I Heard the Owl Call My Name.* **(Originally published in 1973.) (Many editions.)**
A young Anglican priest, Mark Brian, is sent as vicar to a seaside community of Kwakiutl Indians in remote British Columbia. Mark does not know that he is dying. But the Indians know that the owl has called his name and minister to him as much as he does to them, teaching him to live fully in the little time that remains.

DEMSKY, ANDY. *Dark Refuge.* **1995. Pacific, paper. 240 pp. ISBN 0-8163-1241-9.**
A brilliant but unhappy teenage girl breaks away from her emotionally abusive mother to strike out on her own, only to come under the influence of a compelling preacher and his cult.

◄█✕ **GRAY, ALICE.** *Stories for a Teen's Heart.* **Multnomah, paper. 340 pp. ISBN 1-57673-646-6.**

A group of teens helped Alice Gray select entries for this collection of short stories and inspirational pieces focusing on school, friendship, self-confidence, and success.

◄█✕ ★ **JENKINS, JERRY.** *The Youngest Hero.* **2002. Warner. 376 pp. ISBN 0-446-52903-6.**

Elgin Woodell is an obsessed young baseball player who makes it all the way to the majors at age 14. Elgin has spent hour after hour practicing on his fther's old hitting machine in the basement of his mother's apartment building. He's obsessed with his father and baseball, and part of the story's appeal is Elgin's reconciliation with his father, a one-time major league prospect whose boozing brought him down. Jenkins, coauthor of the Left Behind series, packs his story with baseball lore, affectionately rendering a hapless major league enterprise Cubs fans will recognize. *The Youngest Hero* is a rewrite of Jenkins's 1991 novel *The Rookie.*

◄█✕ **MCCOURTNEY, LORENA.** *Canyon.* **1998. Multnomah, paper. 256 pp. ISBN 1-57673-287-8.**

See discussion in chapter 8, "Romance," p. 133.

◄█✕ **OKE, JANETTE.** *The Tender Years.* **1997. Bethany. 270 pp. ISBN 1-556-61952-9.**

All of Janette Oke's novels are good young adult selections for girls. See discussion in chapter 7, "Romancing the West," p. 103.

◄█✕ **OKE, JANETTE, AND LAUREL OKE LOGAN.** *Dana's Valley.* **2001. Bethany, paper. 310 pp. ISBN 0-76422514-6.**

For a long time, nothing seems to happen in this story of Dana Walsh told by her younger sister, Erin. The Walshes are almost militantly ordinary. Then it becomes clear that Dana, sick throughout the novel, is dying of cancer, and all the pages the authors used describing Erin's silly adventures suddenly have a point. This is a good family and Erin is a good girl, and Dana's death will devastate them as surely as it would if they were less blameless.

◄█✕ **STAHL, HILDA.** *Gently Touch Sheela Jenkins.* **1989. Bethel, paper. 200 pp. ISBN 0-934998-32-9.**

At 24, Sheela is making her way in the world, but projects a cold reserve and won't allow anyone to touch her. Her mother, Bobby, abused her relentlessly, and coming to terms with the abuse, even forgiving it, proves a difficult journey.

◄█✕ ★ **TATLOCK, ANN.** *A Room of My Own.* **1998. Bethany, paper. 368 pp. ISBN 0-7642-2023-3.**

Tatlock's first novel is a coming-of-age tale set in 1932, when the Depression arrives in earnest in Ginny Eide's little Minnesota town. Ginny's father is a physician who patiently attends to the poor down in "Soo City," a Hooverville that has sprung suddenly to life. About the same time, Ginny's uncle loses his job and must move his family into the Eide house, causing Ginny to lose her room. And yet Ginny learns that in a world of universal hardship, the noblest thing is to be of service. In fact, service may be more important than having a room of one's own.

References

CHAPTER 1

Arvin, Reed. 2000. *The Will.* New York: Scribner.

Baker, John F. 1997. More Than Half Now Buy Their Books in Chains—PW survey. *Publishers Weekly,* 12 June, 13.

Duffy, Martha, and Andrea Sachs. 1995. The Almighty to the Rescue. *Time,* 13 November, 103.

Johnson, Carol. 2000. Interview with author, June 2000; and "Christian Fiction in the General Market," a speech given at the Book Expo Conference, June 2000, Chicago.

Rabey, Steve. 1999. Apocalyptic Sales Out of This World. *Christianity Today,* 1 March, 19.

Schaap, James Calvin. 1997. On Truth, Fiction, and Being a Christian Writer. *Christian Century,* 17 December, 1,138.

Stokes, Penelope. 1998. *The Complete Guide to Writing and Selling the Christian Novel.* Cincinnati, OH: Writer's Digest Books.

Stokes, Penelope. 1999. *The Blue Bottle Club.* Dallas, TX: Word.

CHAPTER 3

Carpenter, Humphrey. 1978. *The Inklings: C. S. Lewis, J. R. R. Tolkien, Charles Williams, and Their Friends.* Boston: Houghton Mifflin.

Eliot, T. S. 1948. Introduction to *All Hallows' Eve,* by Charles Williams. New York: Pellegrini & Cudahy.

Fairweather, Eugene Rathbone. 1964. *The Oxford Movement.* Oxford, UK: Oxford University Press.

Ferré, John P. 1988. *A Social Gospel for Millions: The Religious Bestsellers of Charles Sheldon, Charles Gordon, and Harold Bell Wright.* Bowling Green, WI: Bowling Green University Popular Press.

Hedrick, Joan D. 1994. *Harriet Beecher Stowe: A Life.* Oxford, UK: Oxford University Press.

Karr, Jean. 1948. *Grace Livingston Hill: Her Story and Her Writings.* New York: Greenberg.

Phillips, Michael. 1987. *George MacDonald: Scotland's Beloved Storyteller.* Minneapolis: Bethany House.

Rhodes, Royal. 1995. *The Lion and the Cross: Early Christianity in Victorian Novels.* Columbus, OH: Ohio State University Press.

CHAPTER 5

Funderburk, Robert. 1996. Dedication of *The Fires of Autumn,* by Robert Funderburk. Minneapolis: Bethany House.

CHAPTER 9

Fisher, G. Richard. 1996. From High Places to Heresy: Evaluating the Writings of Hannah Hurnard. *Personal Freedom Outreach* Web site. Available: http://www.pfo.org.

CHAPTER 11

Buechner, Frederick. 1992. On Spiritual Autobiography: An Interview with Frederick Buechner. Interview conducted by Stephen Kendrick. *Christian Century,* 14 October, 900–905.

Karon, Jan. 1999. A Conversation with Jan Karon. *JB online: Author interviews.* Available: http://www.josephbeth.com.

Woiwode, Larry. 1992. The Reforming of a Novelist. Interview conducted by Timothy Jones. *Christianity Today,* 26 October, 86–88.

CHAPTER 12

Calvert, Alexander. 1935. *The Catholic Literary Revival.* Milwaukee: Bruce Publishing Company.

Greeley, Andrew M. 1999. *Memoirs of a Parish Priest.* New York: Forge.

Montgomery, Marion. 1993. Walker Percy and the Christian Scandal. *First Things,* 32: 38–44.

Shelden, Michael. 1994. *Graham Greene: The Enemy Within.* New York: Random House.

Szulc, Tad. 2000. Review: *To Kill the Pope. Library Journal,* 125: 206.

Wyatt, Bryan N. 1992. The Domestic Dynamics of Flannery O'Connor. *Twentieth Century Literature,* 39: 66–89.

CHAPTER 15

Gonzales, Doreen. 1991. *Madeleine L'Engle: Author of* A Wrinkle in Time. New York: Dillon Press.

Maifair, Linda Lee. 1998. Writing Juvenile Fiction for the Christian Market. *The Writer,* 111: 12, 16–20.

Suggested Readings

Armstrong, Karen. 2000. *The Battle for God.* New York: Knopf.
> One of the most respected contemporary authorities on religion—and among the few who are widely popular—takes fundamentalism as her subject: Jewish, Muslim, and, of course, Protestant. She sees its rise as a reaction to the profound changes modern society has imposed on everyone, and there is little in it that she likes.

Bauer, Susan Wise. 1997. *Seven Words You Can't Say in the CBA.* Available: http://www.susanwisebauer .com/essaysonline.html.
> Bauer discusses the stance against profanity and sexual explicitness imposed by evangelical publishers, which often results in handicapping the ability of fiction writers to produce realistic work.

Bennion, John. 1997–1998. Popular and Literary Mormon Novels: Can Weyland and Whipple Dance Together in the House of Fiction? *BYU Studies,* 37: 159–182.
> Bennion is the authority on Mormon literary efforts, and this essay sums up the scene in Utah admirably.

Carpenter, Humphrey. 1977. *Tolkien: The Authorized Biography.* Boston: Houghton Mifflin.
> There are many books about Tolkien, but Carpenter's authorized biography is a good place to begin in the study of this complex, private man.

Gottcent, John H. 1986. *The Bible: A Literary Study.* Boston: Twayne Publishers.
> Like other Twayne studies, *The Bible* is a survey, grounding the reader in the salient points of discussion when the Bible is regarded literarily, rather than historically or as the indisputable word of God. Thus, Gottcent emphasizes sweeping narratives with mythological dimensions, such as the story of the Flood and the flight from Egypt; larger-than-life personages who can be seen as heroes (Moses and Samson); the epitome of suffering (Job); or those who vivify the complexity of interpersonal relationships (Ruth). Gottcent spends more time with the Old Testament than the New Testament, but he also ponders the parables as literary artifacts, as well as the character Paul as portrayed in the Acts of the Apostles.

Hadfield, Alice Mary. 1983. *Charles Williams: An Exploration of His Life and Work.* Oxford, UK: Oxford University Press.
> One can read Charles Williams's work, or about him, and grow steadily more puzzled, but Hadfield's explication is as clear as any.

Hein, Rolland. 1998. *Christian Mythmakers: Lewis, L'Engle, Tolkien & Others.* Chicago: Cornerstone Press.
> Hein's book is a fine first stop for the reader curious about where Christian fiction, particularly the fiction of allegory and myth, came from. He discusses John Bunyan, George McDonald, G. K. Chesterton, Charles Williams, J.R.R. Tolkien, C. S. Lewis, and the contemporaries Madeleine L'Engle, Walter Wangerin, and Hannah Hurnard.

Impastato, David. 1999. Culture of Doom. *Christianity and the Arts,* 6: 6–11.
> Impastato meditates on apocalypse and literature.

Kurian, George Thomas, editor. 2001. *Nelson's New Christian Dictionary.* Nashville, TN: Nelson.
Consulting *Nelson's New Christian Dictionary* is a quick way to orient yourself on topical Christian matters such as the career of a missionary, the location of a monastery, or the significance of a great thinker such as Soren Kierkegaard. Myriad black-and-white photographs add to understanding.

Lewis, C. S. 2001. *Mere Christianity.* San Francisco: HarperSanFrancisco.
Lewis's essays grew from a series of radio broadcasts he delivered to a war-weary Britain in 1942 and thus are conversational and informal, though as finely reasoned as anything Lewis wrote. The "mere" of his title is, of course, not dismissive: Lewis tried to describe the bedrock of his faith when denominational considerations were stripped away, and almost inadvertently produced a classic statement of faith.

Logan, Laurel Oke. 1993. *Janette Oke: A Heart for the Prairie.* Minneapolis: Bethany House.
There is, naturally enough, nothing critical of Oke in this biography by her daughter, but one learns where Oke came from and what it was like to grow up in her household.

Metzger, Bruce M., and Michael D. Coogan. 1993. *The Oxford Companion to the Bible.* Oxford, UK: Oxford University Press.
Poised somewhere between a Bible dictionary and a commentary, Metzger and Coogan's work is an invaluable guide for putting biblical characters and events in context.

Rivers, Francine. 1995. Hooked on Romance. *Today's Christian Woman,* 17: 38–39.
Rivers's succinct statement clearly expresses the esthetics of most evangelical writers.

Thompson, James. 1994. Walker Percy's Guide for the Perplexed. *World & I,* 9: 408–436.
Thompson's examination of the complicated message of Walker Percy makes a fine introduction to his work.

Winston, Kimberly. 1999. The Good News on Fiction. *Publishers Weekly,* 246: 32–34.
Winston discusses Christian fiction as a publishing phenomenon.

Wood, Ralph C. 1995. The Baptized Imagination: C. S. Lewis's Fictional Apologetics. *Christian Century,* 112: 812–816.
Why C. S. Lewis is so important to evangelical fiction.

Index